CW01262837

ANTI-SEMITISM AND THE LEFT

ANTI-SEMITISM AND THE LEFT

Ian Hernon

AMBERLEY

For Reuben, Freya and Theo

First published 2020

Amberley Publishing
The Hill, Stroud
Gloucestershire, GL5 4EP

www.amberley-books.com

Copyright © Ian Hernon, 2020

The right of Ian Hernon to be identified as the Author of this work has been asserted in accordance with the Copyrights, Designs and Patents Act 1988.

All rights reserved. No part of this book may be reprinted or reproduced or utilised in any form or by any electronic, mechanical or other means, now known or hereafter invented, including photocopying and recording, or in any information storage or retrieval system, without the permission in writing from the Publishers.

British Library Cataloguing in Publication Data.
A catalogue record for this book is available from the British Library.

ISBN 978 1 3981 0223 1 (hardback)
ISBN 978 1 3981 0224 8 (ebook)

Typeset in 11pt on 14pt Sabon.
Typesetting by Aura Technology and Software Services, India.
Printed in the UK.

'For anti-Semitism betokens a retarded culture...'
Friedrich Engels, 1890

Contents

Acknowledgements	9
Introduction	10
1 Bad Marx	12
2 Shylock, Fagin and the Children of the Ghetto	28
3 When Two Tribes Go to War	41
4 Between the Wars	66
5 George Orwell and the Fight against Fascism	86
6 Post-war Palpitations	109
7 Oh! Jeremy Corbyn	126
8 Labour Pains	155
9 Post-natal Blues	197
10 The End?	221
Afterword	249
Notes	257
Bibliography	268
Index	278

Acknowledgements

Given this book's subject, I'm expecting a tsunami of online abuse from keyboard Corbynistas. My message to them is: don't bother because I don't do social media. Researching the subject I have already had some less than supportive emails, including: 'Just what the world needs – another pile of steaming shite about alleged anti-Semitism in the Labour Party.' And that was from a comrade who remains a friend.

For the record, I am a lifelong socialist and supporter of the Labour Party and will continue to be so despite misgivings over the Leadership. I was raised a Roman Catholic but have been an atheist since my teens. I have been a journalist for fifty years, the last forty-one of them based in the House of Commons. And – *mea culpa* – I've enjoyed the convivial company of some Tories in Westminster bars, although Liberal Democrats have been more problematic. All of which may be a reason that Momentum have never come knocking at my door.

My biggest thanks go to my family, as always. Followed by the team at Amberley Publishing who have had confidence in my writing and supported my efforts.

At Westminster my special thanks go to Louise Ellman, James Floyd, Gerry Sutcliffe, Ronnie Campbell, Carol Porteous, Rebecca Harris, Lord (John) Reid, David Healy, Jon Smith, Peter Willoughby, Colin and Mandy Brown, George Osgerby, Mike Parker, Frank Field and Bob Stewart, and Richard Pengelly, Anthony Cree and Will Conway in the House of Commons' Strangers' Bar.

Very special 'credit' must also go to Jeremy Corbyn who has, albeit unwittingly, provided so much material for this book.

Introduction

'What is the worldly religion of the Jew? Huckstering. What is his worldly God? Money.' Jews are 'the real invaders from the East... the oriental parasite'. The Jew 'has no bowels of compassion'. The Jews were an 'imperialist' cabal that promoted war for their own ends. The Jews were 'pushing to the front of the queue'. And 'a little Liverpool Jew, a thorough guttersnipe' had a face like 'some low-down carrion bird'.

You might be forgiven for thinking that such quotes emerged from the fervent racism of Nazi propaganda chief Josef Goebbels in the run-up to the Holocaust. You might think that such phrases were daubed on synagogues or desecrated headstones, or broadcast by Lord Haw-Haw. But you would be wrong. They were said or written by, in order, socialist icons Karl Marx, George Bernard Shaw, John Burns, Keir Hardie, Ernest Bevin and George Orwell.

Only someone stranded on a desert island – or maybe Sheppey – in recent years would not recognise that it was Jeremy Corbyn who castigated British Jews for their lack of 'English irony' while sharing platforms with his 'friends' in Hamas and other murderous racist terrorist organisations. The antisemitism row within the Labour Party, along with the Brexit paralysis of Parliament, has dominated headlines for several years, but it is the strand of anti-Semitism that has existed on the left since the birth of socialism as an effective movement which is hard to fathom. Especially as Jews played an integral part in the creation of both the British trade union movement and the Labour Party. Especially as no-one with a single brain cell can doubt the persecution and death camps of the twentieth century.

Introduction

And especially as Zionism – opposition to which is now used as a dodgy excuse for anti-Semitism – was for decades embraced by the left as a template for a socialist paradise.

With the benefit of hindsight, there are many ironies to be drawn. To modern 'woke' sensibilities it is uncomfortable to discover that many Suffragettes – having fought for and won the vote – were drawn to Oswald Mosley and his Blackshirts in part because of a hatred of Jewry. Or that the 'science' of eugenics which aimed to weed out 'weaker' species of humanity was also embraced by such social reformers as Marie Stopes. The past has always been a strange country for those who delve into it.

Institutionalised anti-Semitism certainly played a part in the December 2019 general election, although to what extent has yet to be fully analysed. How could it be that Labour, a party based on ideas of freedom, justice, fairness, equality and anti-racism could inspire such fear within the Jewish community that almost half of those polled have considered emigrating and a leading rabbi considered that Corbyn's push for power constituted 'a danger for Jewish life as we know it'? Comparisons with Tsarist pogroms, Nazi genocide and ISIS massacres are, of course, over-exaggerated, but the fear is there all the same. How could it be that Jewish MPs, most notably Louise Ellman, who have devoted a lifetime of service to creating a fairer society, have been hounded out of Labour by incessant abuse, intimidation and, in some cases, death threats?

I used to believe that the catalyst in the late 1960s/early 1970s was the Israeli occupation of Palestinian territories and some of the atrocities permitted or instigated by the only democratic state in the Middle East as part of an often over-the-top defence mechanism. In fact, the roots of anti-Semitism go far deeper and this book aims to understand, but certainly not condone, the reasons for that.

Something that will be repeated several times throughout this book is the certainty that the most virulent anti-Semitism has over the last century or so come from the Far Right, the British Establishment, the aristocracy and home-grown bigots of all classes. But that does not excuse the left for its, in some instances, overlapping racism due to populist pursuit of power, bigotry, ignorance or a twisted understanding of history and socialist ideals.

Ian Hernon, December 2019

1

Bad Marx

'This alien monster...'

Herschel Marx was the first in his family to receive a secular education in Trier, then within the border of Prussia's Lower Rhine province. His mother's father was a Dutch rabbi, while his paternal Jewish line had supplied the town's rabbis since 1723. He took to the law and lived a prosperous life, funded by his legal practice and family vineyards. In 1818 King Frederick William III reneged on promises to liberalise laws curbing the freedoms and rights of Jews and banned them from all academic and official positions in the Rhineland. Herschel was among those summarily dismissed because of their faith and he pragmatically converted to the Evangelical Church of Prussia, taking the German forename Heinrich.[1] He was a man of the Enlightenment, paying mere lip service to religion and influenced by the ideas of Voltaire and Immanuel Kant. He joined protests against the Prussian monarchy and in 1819 moved his family to a ten-room property near the Porta Nigra.[2] His wife, Henriette, belonged to a Jewish family that later founded Philips Electronics, and her sister married into a family whose wealth was based on tobacco and heavy industry.

Their son Karl was born on 5 May 1818, the third of nine children. His older brother died when he was an infant and Karl and his surviving siblings were baptised into the Lutheran Church when he was six.[3] Aged seventeen, Marx travelled to the University of Bonn hoping to study philosophy and literature, but his father insisted on law. He was excused military duty due to a 'weak chest',[4] joined the radical police-monitored Poets' Club, became a co-president of a drinking society, and fought a duel. His post-university life was not so flamboyant. With Friedrich Engels he produced *The Communist Manifesto* and during exile in England he relied heavily on his Dutch / Jewish family for financial support.

Although Marx described capitalists as vampires sucking workers' blood, he wrote that drawing profit is 'by no means an injustice'. The problem is the 'cancerous cell' of capital, relations between workers and owners, and the economic system in general. He stressed that capitalism was essentially unstable, prone to periodic crises, and that over time capitalists would invest more in new technologies and less in labour.[5] In section one of *The Communist Manifesto*, Marx described feudalism, capitalism and the role internal social contradictions play in the historical process: 'We see then: the means of production and of exchange, on whose foundation the bourgeoisie built itself up, were generated in feudal society. At a certain stage in the development of these means of production and of exchange, the conditions under which feudal society produced and exchanged ... the feudal relations of property became no longer compatible with the already developed productive forces; they became so many fetters. They had to be burst asunder... Into their place stepped free competition, accompanied by a social and political constitution adapted in it, and the economic and political sway of the bourgeois class. A similar movement is going on before our own eyes ...'

Marx believed that those structural contradictions within capitalism necessitated its end, giving way to a communist society: 'The development of Modern Industry, therefore, cuts from under its feet the very foundation on which the bourgeoisie produces and appropriates products. What the bourgeoisie, therefore, produces, above all, are its own grave-diggers. Its fall and the victory of the proletariat are equally inevitable.'[6]

Marx was one of the most influential figures in history and *Das Kapital*, written in London, cemented his fame and his legacy. Much, but not all, of his analysis remains true today and although some of his forecasts proved faulty, no-one can doubt the impact of his ideas on the following century and a half. However, of the millions of words Marx wrote, some on the left justify anti-Semitism from a two-part essay – *On the Jewish Question* – he wrote in 1843. It was first published in Paris the following year under the German title *Zur Judenfrage* in the *Deutsch-Franzosische Jahrbucher*, a journal which only lasted one issue. A French translation appeared in

1850 in Paris, while an English translation had to wait until 1926 in a Soviet-published collection of Marx essays. But in continental political and philosophical circles it swiftly gained notoriety. The essay criticised two studies by Marx's fellow embryonic socialist Bruno Bauer who argued, in the context of the Jewish struggle for human rights in Prussia, that true political emancipation requires the abolition of religion. Marx delivered his own analysis of liberal rights, arguing that Bauer was mistaken in his assumption that in a 'secular state' religion would not play a prominent role in social life. He gave as a prime example the widespread and pervasive religious belief in the US, which, unlike Prussia, had no state religion.

So far, pretty uncontroversial. But in the second part of the essay, Marx disputed Bauer's analysis that the renouncing of religion would be especially difficult for Jews, because Judaism was at a 'primitive' stage in the development of Christianity. He wrote: 'What is the worldly religion of the Jew? Huckstering. What is his worldly God? Money .... Money is the jealous god of Israel, in face of which no other god may exist. Money degrades all the gods of man – and turns them into commodities.... The bill of exchange is the real god of the Jew. His god is only an illusory bill of exchange.... The chimerical nationality of the Jew is the nationality of the merchant, of the man of money in general.' He argued: 'In the final analysis, the emancipation of the Jews is the emancipation of mankind from Judaism.' He wrote: 'Let us look at the real Jew of our time; not the Jew of the Sabbath ... but the Jew of everyday life. What is the Jew's foundation in our world? Material necessity, private advantage. What is the object of the Jew's worship in this world? Usury ... What was the essential foundation of the Jewish religion? Practical needs, egotism. Money is the zealous one God of Israel, beside which no other God may stand. Money degrades all the gods of mankind and turns them into commodities. Money is the universal and self-constituted value set upon all things. It has therefore robbed the whole world, of both nature and man, of its original value. Money is the essence of man's life and work, which have become alienated from him. This alien monster rules him and he worships it.'

He went on: 'An organisation of society which would abolish the preconditions for huckstering, and therefore the possibility of huckstering, would make the Jew impossible. His religious consciousness would be dissipated like a thin haze in the real, vital air of society. On the other hand, if the Jew recognises that this practical nature of his is futile and works to abolish it, he extricates himself from his previous development and works for human emancipation as such and turns against the supreme practical expression of human self-estrangement. We recognise in Judaism, therefore, a general anti-social element of the present time, an element which through historical development – to which in this harmful respect the Jews have zealously contributed – has been brought to its present high level, at which it must necessarily begin to disintegrate.

'The Jew has already emancipated himself in a Jewish way. The Jew, who in Vienna, for example, is only tolerated, determines the fate of the whole Empire by his financial power. The Jew, who may have no rights in the smallest German state, decides the fate of Europe. While corporations and guilds refuse to admit Jews or have not yet adopted a favourable attitude towards them, the audacity of industry mocks at the obstinacy of the material institutions.' This is no isolated fact. The Jew has emancipated himself in a Jewish manner, not only because he has acquired financial power, but also because, through him and also apart from him, money has become a world power and the practical Jewish spirit has become the practical spirit of the Christian nations.'

In the century and more that followed, the essay fuelled a massive debate over whether it showed Marx to be indelibly anti-Semitic. According to Hyam Maccoby, Marx argued in the essay that the modern commercialised world is the triumph of Judaism, a pseudo-religion whose god is money. Maccoby has suggested that Marx was embarrassed by his Jewish background and used the Jews as a 'yardstick of evil'.[7] Robert Wistrich, a notable expert on anti-Semitism, stated 'the net result of Marx's essay is to reinforce a traditional anti-Jewish stereotype – the identification of the Jews with money-making – in the sharpest possible manner.'[8]

Scholar Larry Ray wrote: 'Marx's position is essentially an assimilationist one in which there is no room within emancipated humanity for Jews as a separate ethnic or cultural identity.' Fellow academic Dennis Fischman wrote: 'Jews, Marx seems to be saying, can only become free when, as Jews, they no longer exist.'[9] And Stephen Greenblatt accused Marx of possessing a 'sharp, even hysterical, denial of his religious background'.[10] Amira Isenberg blogged: 'Karl Marx is referring to the stereotype of Jews being greedy and loving money more than anything else. Basically, Marx seemed to believe that Jews are dirty money-grabbers and that type of people could not exist in his idea of a perfect world, so he hated them. There are scholars who say that he isn't anti-Semitic, but if I listed them this would go on forever, as it is an ongoing debate whether he was truly a hater of Jews or not.'[11] The debate did indeed rage but in 1964, Shlomo Avineri, a leading commentator on Marx, wrote: 'That Karl Marx was an inveterate anti-Semite is today considered a commonplace which is hardly ever questioned.'[12]

That was not always so, however. In the 1930s Franz Mehring wrote:

> What Marx achieved with this treatise was a twofold gain. He went to the very roots of the connection between society and the State. The State was not, as Hegel imagined, the reality of the moral idea, absolute reason and the absolute aim itself, and it had to content itself with the incomparably more modest task of presiding over the anarchy of bourgeois society which had enrolled it as watchman. This anarchy was the general struggle of man against man, of individual against individual, the universal war of all individuals, separated from each other only by their individuality, the general and unhindered movement of all the elementary forces released from their feudal fetters. It was actual slavery, although the individual seemed free and independent to himself, mistaking the unhindered movement of his alienated elements such as property, industry and religion for his own freedom, whereas in reality it represented his complete enslavement and alienation from humanity.
>
>   And then Marx recognised that the religious questions of the day had no more than a social significance. He showed the development of Judaism not in religious theory, but in industrial and commercial practice which found a fantastic reflection in the Jewish religion. Practical Judaism is nothing but the fully developed Christian world. As bourgeois society is of a completely commercial Jewish character the Jew necessarily belongs to it and can claim political emancipation just as he can claim the general rights of man. However, the emancipation of humanity is a new organisation of the social forces, which will make man the master of those sources which give him life. Thus, in shadowy contours, we observe an outline of socialist society beginning to form.[13]

The political-scientist Professor Iain Hampsher-Monk wrote: 'This work has been cited as evidence for Marx's supposed anti-Semitism, but only the most superficial reading of it could sustain such an interpretation.'[14] Francis Wheen wrote: 'Those critics, who see this as a foretaste of "Mein Kampf", overlook one essential point: in spite of the clumsy phraseology and crude stereotyping, the essay was actually written as a defence of the Jews. It was a retort to Bruno Bauer, who had argued that Jews should not be granted full civic rights and freedoms unless they were baptised as Christians.' Although he claimed to be an atheist, Bruno Bauer viewed Judaism as an inferior civilisation.[15]

Sociologist Robert Fine believed that Bauer's essay 'echoed the generally prejudicial representation of the Jew as "merchant" and "moneyman"', whereas 'Marx's aim was to defend the right of Jews to full civil and political emancipation (that is, to equal civil and political rights) alongside all other German citizens.' Fine argued that the 'line of attack Marx adopts is not to contrast Bauer's crude stereotype of the Jews to the actual situation of Jews in Germany', but 'to reveal that Bauer has no inkling of the nature of modern democracy'. Fellow sociologist Larry Ray agreed that Marx's essay was an ironic defence of Jewish emancipation, but pointed out that Marx saw 'no room within emancipated humanity for Jews as a separate ethnic or cultural identity', and advocated 'a society where both cultural as well as economic difference is eliminated'. Ray sees Marx in a 'strand of left thinking that has been unable to address forms of oppression not directly linked to class'.[16]

Other scholars and apologists have also strived to deny Marx's antisemitism, claiming that critics misinterpret or mythologise the essay, or do not understand his 'ironic' style of writing. The trouble with that is that Marx repeated anti-Semitic motifs and stereotypes both in his writings and in private correspondence. In an 1856 article published in New York, Marx wrote: 'Thus we find every tyrant backed by a Jew, as is every pope by a Jesuit. In truth, the cravings of oppressors would be hopeless, and the practicability of war out of the question, if there were not an army of Jesuits to smother thought and a handful of Jews to ransack pockets ... the real work is done by the Jews, and can only be done by them, as they monopolise the machinery of the loanmongering mysteries by concentrating their energies upon the barter trade in securities... Here and there and everywhere that a little capital courts investment, there is ever one of these little Jews ready to make a little suggestion or place a little bit of a loan. The smartest highwayman in the Abruzzi is not better posted up about the locale of the hard cash in a traveller's valise or pocket than those Jews about any loose capital in the hands of a trader... The language spoken smells strongly of Babel, and the perfume which otherwise pervades the place is by no means of a choice kind. ... Thus do these loans, which are a curse to the people, a ruin to the holders, and a danger to the governments, become a blessing to the houses of the children of Judah. This Jew organisation of loanmongers is as dangerous to the people as the aristocratic organisation of landowners... The fortunes amassed by these loanmongers are immense, but the wrongs and sufferings thus entailed on the people and the encouragement thus afforded to their oppressors still remain to be told.... The fact that 1,855 years ago Christ drove the Jewish moneychangers out of the temple, and that the moneychangers of our age enlisted on the side of tyranny happen again chiefly to be Jews, is perhaps no more than a historical coincidence. The loanmongering Jews of Europe do only on a larger and more obnoxious scale what many others do on one smaller and less significant. But it is only because the Jews are so strong that it is timely and expedient to expose and stigmatise their organisation.'[17]

Marx's correspondence also makes deeply uncomfortable reading. Michael Ezra pointed out that while Marx happily took loans from the rich Bamberger family to see himself through difficult patches, he referred to the father and son as 'Jew Bamberger' or 'little Jew Bamberger'. A man called Spielmann, whose name appears frequently in correspondence between Marx and Engels, was referred to as 'Jew Spielmann'. In a postscript to a letter from Marx to Arnold Ruge he said: 'I have just been visited by the chief of the Jewish community here, who has asked me for a petition for the Jews to the Provincial Assembly, and I am willing to do it. However much I dislike the Jewish faith, Bauer's view seems to me too abstract. The thing is to make as many breaches as possible in the Christian state and to smuggle in as much as we can of what is rational. At least, it must be attempted – and the embitterment grows with every petition that is rejected with protestations.'[18] When on holiday in Ramsgate in 1879, Marx reported to Engels that the resort contained 'many Jews and fleas'.[19] In an earlier letter to Engels, Marx referred to Ferdinand Lassalle as a 'Jewish nigger'. In a 1942 Soviet English language publication of *Karl Marx and Frederick Engels: Selected Correspondence, 1846-1895*, a note was included: 'With reference to the use of the word "nigger" which occurs in this book: Marx used the word while living in England, in the last century. The word does not have the same connotation as it has now in the US and should be read as "Negro" whenever it occurs in the text.' Marx was referring to his many financial difficulties. He wrote: 'The Jewish nigger Lassalle, who fortunately leaves at the end of this week, has happily again lost 5,000 Thaler in a fraudulent speculation. The fellow would rather throw money in the dirt than make a loan to a "friend" even if interest and capital are guaranteed. He acts on the view that he must live like a Jewish baron...'[20] In 1960 the World Socialist Party of the US, when the letter was drawn to their attention, responded: 'That Marx was in a black mood when he wrote these words is obvious. That the mood was brought on by illness and concern over debts would be quite clear to anyone familiar with his life and works. That it is proof of anti-Semitism is ridiculous.'[21] Ezra wrote: 'The excuse seems to be along the lines of: "Yes, a racist term is used, but pretend that a non-racist term was used instead." It is a simply ludicrous excuse and it exposes the depths to which apologists of Marx will sink.'[22]

In 1959 the Ukrainian-American philosopher Dagobert D. Runes, a friend of Albert Einstein, published an English translation of Marx's *On the Jewish Question* under the title *A World without Jews*. Runes wrote an introduction that was antagonistic to extreme Marxism and included a glossary of anti-Semitic Marx quotes, including the notorious Lassalle letter referred to above and the reference to fleas in Ramsgate. Others included: 'It is the circumvention of law that makes the religious Jew a religious Jew.'[23] And 'the Jews of Poland are the smeariest of all races.'[24]

Far-left groupings on both sides of the Atlantic were incensed. The World Socialist Party of the US, later renamed the Workers' Socialist Party, responded: 'Marx lived and carried on his work barely half a century from the French revolution, at a time when Europe seethed in revolutionary ferment. His works were published under difficulty, sometimes interfered with by the authorities. He was exiled from his homeland. The greater part of his life was spent in poverty. He was subjected to a steady campaign of slander and misrepresentation. How many under similar conditions could have exercised the objectivity, patience and, clarity of thought that stand out so prominently in the great mass of his work? Certainly not Runes. He lives, it is reasonable to assume, under conditions quite remote from the kind that harassed Marx. Yet, far from being able to use his favoured circumstances to quietly examine, assess and discuss the mighty legacy of this nineteenth-century thinker, he succeeds in finding nothing in Marx but a rabid, vicious, malevolent, debased and sick-minded Jew-baiter. Marx was opposed to Judaism. He was also opposed to Christianity and to religion, generally. To Marx religious organisations were preserved chiefly for their usefulness in helping to protect the dominant position of the ruling class. And he opposed all such agencies, both religious and nonreligious. But opposition to Judaism is not necessarily the same as anti-Semitism.' It added: 'Enough, we think, has been said to show that Rune's chief concern is to bury Marx beneath a thick coating of mud. His efforts should be comforting to the owning class.'[25]

In a letter to the party's periodical, Runes wrote: 'It has been quite some time since I could still be shocked at a refusal of organisations, groups or individuals to place facts and reason above personal prejudices and personal involvement. The World Socialist Party is deeply involved in Marxism and will therefore attempt, through its spokesmen – or penmen – to refute any charge against Karl Marx, regardless of fact or fancy... I have collected 108 statements by Karl Marx from his correspondence, his books, his conversations with contemporaries – and all of them, my dear comrade, are viciously, malevolently anti-Semitic. If you have the courage to let your readers read what I am writing now, let them judge how little or how much difference there is between the profundity of Adolf Hitler and the debasement of Karl Marx. Needless to emphasise that in the Soviet Union, especially in the Ukraine, attacks against the Jews of today run surprisingly close to the tracks of Karl Marx.'[26] There would be no end to such uncomradely rows.

Modern-day 'Marxists' find it uncomfortable to accept that Marx dabbled in 'yellow' journalism through dire necessity and the journalistic 'horses for courses' ethos has been used as an excuse for his anti-Semitic tropes. That does not stand scrutiny. In his early years in London, his immediate family endured extreme poverty whenever handouts from his sister's family and Engels' father dried up. He had also got used to addressing the working classes directly in Germany as editor of his own newspaper. In London, without finances to run a newspaper themselves, he and Engels turned to international journalism. At one stage they were being published by six newspapers from England, the United States, Prussia, Austria and South Africa. Marx's principal earnings came from his work as European correspondent, from 1852 to 1862, for the *New-York Daily Tribune*.

The *New-York Daily Tribune* had been founded in April 1841 by Horace Greeley, an abolitionist, and had wide working-class appeal as at two cents, it was inexpensive. With about 50,000 copies per issue, its circulation was the widest in the US. Marx's first article for the paper, on the British parliamentary elections, was published in 1852. Recession in the US economy in 1852 gave Marx and Engels grounds for optimism for revolutionary activity, yet when the 'Panic of 1857' spread globally, it broke all economic theory models.[27] But once again, at least in part, Jews were made scapegoats amongst the 'enlightened' elite which shed many tears about African slavery, a trend which would last into the twenty-first century. Historian Iver Bernstein wrote: 'Greeley was an eclectic and unsystematic thinker, a one-man switch-board for the international cause of "Reform". He committed himself, all at once, to utopian and artisan socialism, to land, sexual, and dietary reform, and, of course, to anti-slavery. Indeed, Greeley's great significance in the culture and politics of Civil War-era America stemmed from his attempt to accommodate intellectually the contradictions inherent in the many diverse reform movements of the time.'[28] During the period that Marx wrote for him, Greeley promoted various conflicting causes, switching to and from every issue which he deemed would sell the most newspapers while not disturbing his own conscience. He opposed slavery, liquor, tobacco, gambling, prostitution, and capital punishment, urged free common-school education for all, promoted Western expansion and championed producers' cooperatives. But he opposed women's suffrage and Abraham Lincoln's presidential re-nomination, and signed the bail bond of former Confederate president Jefferson Davis in 1867. He died in an institution. But such were the contradictions and vagaries of the newspaper world at the time. And since.

Friedrich Engels, co-author of *The Communist Manifesto*, appears to have given Marx some leeway regarding anti-Semitism. The son of a textiles magnate, his father sent him to the Engels factory in Manchester to 'cure' him of his radical ideas. Engels was appalled by the city's slums and took notes of its horrors, notably child labour, the despoiled environment, and overworked and impoverished labourers.[29] He later collected these articles for his influential first book, *The Conditions of the Working Class in England* (1845), in which he described the 'grim future of capitalism and the industrial age'.[30] He used his family money to support Marx during the writing of *Das Kapital*. After Marx's death in 1883, Engels edited the second and third volumes of *Das Kapital*, organised Marx's notes to produce a 'fourth volume', and published *The Origin of the Family, Private Property and the State* on the basis of Marx's ethnographic research.

He was well aware of the charges of anti-Semitism that were already surfacing posthumously against his comrade and in 1890 wrote *On Anti-Semitism*, an article extraordinary for its acknowledgement that anti-Semitism was indeed something to be fought against, although his claim that it was limited to continental cadres does not bear scrutiny. That said, it is worth quoting at some length to provide a contrast with Marx's earlier journalism:

> ... For anti-Semitism betokens a retarded culture, which is why it is found only in Prussia and Austria, and in Russia too. Anyone dabbling in anti-Semitism, either in England or in America, would simply be ridiculed... In Prussia it is the lesser nobility, the Junkers with an income of 10,000 marks and outgoings of 20,000, and hence subject to usury, who indulge in anti-Semitism, while both in Prussia and Austria a vociferous chorus is provided by those whom competition from big capital has ruined – the petty bourgeoisie, skilled craftsmen and small shop-keepers. But in as much as capital, whether Semitic or Aryan, circumcised or baptised, is destroying these classes of society which are reactionary through and through, it is only doing what pertains to its office, and doing it well; it is helping to impel the retarded Prussians and Austrians forward until they eventually attain the present-day level at which all the old social distinctions resolve themselves in the one great antithesis – capitalists and wage-labourers. Only in places where this has not yet happened, where there is no strong capitalist class and hence no strong class of wage-labourers, where capital is not yet strong enough to gain control of national production as a whole, so that its activities are mainly confined to the Stock Exchange – in other words, where production is still in the hands of the farmers, landowners, craftsmen and suchlike classes surviving from the Middle Ages – there, and there alone, is capital mainly Jewish, and there alone is anti-Semitism rife.
>
> In North America not a single Jew is to be found among the millionaires whose wealth can, in some cases, scarcely be expressed in terms of our paltry marks, gulden or francs and, by comparison with these Americans, the Rothschilds are veritable paupers. And even in England, Rothschild is a man of modest means when set,

for example, against the Duke of Westminster. Even in our own Rhineland from which, with the help of the French, we drove the aristocracy ninety-five years ago and where we have established modern industry, one may look in vain for Jews. Hence anti-Semitism is merely the reaction of declining medieval social strata against a modern society consisting essentially of capitalists and wage-labourers, so that all it serves are reactionary ends under a purportedly socialist cloak; it is a degenerate form of feudal socialism and we can have nothing to do with that. The very fact of its existence in a region is proof that there is not yet enough capital there. Capital and wage-labour are today indivisible. The stronger capital and hence the wage-earning class becomes, the closer will be the demise of capitalist domination. So what I would wish for us Germans, amongst whom I also count the Viennese, is that the capitalist economy should develop at a truly spanking pace rather than slowly decline into stagnation.

In addition, the anti-Semite presents the facts in an entirely false light. He doesn't even know the Jews he decries, otherwise he would be aware that, thanks to anti-Semitism in eastern Europe, and to the Spanish Inquisition in Turkey, there are here in England and in America thousands upon thousands of Jewish proletarians; and it is precisely these Jewish workers who are the worst exploited and the most poverty-stricken. In England during the past twelve months we have had three strikes by Jewish workers. Are we then expected to engage in anti-Semitism in our struggle against capital? Furthermore, we are far too deeply indebted to the Jews. Leaving aside Heine and Börne, Marx was a full-blooded Jew; Lassalle was a Jew. Many of our best people are Jews. My friend Victor Adler, who is now atoning in a Viennese prison for his devotion to the cause of the proletariat, Eduard Bernstein, editor of the London Sozialdemokrat, Paul Singer, one of our best men in the Reichstag – people whom I am proud to call my friends, and all of them Jewish! After all, I myself was dubbed a Jew by the Gartenlaube and, indeed, if given the choice, I'd as lief be a Jew as a 'Herr von'![31]

Engels encouraged his supporters to work among the East European Jews living in London and spoke highly of the work of the Jewish socialists.

In the years following Engels' death, the Czech-Austrian philosopher and journalist Karl Kautsky (1854-1938) was the leading orthodox Marxist theoretician as executor of Marx's literary estate, editor of *Die Neue Zeit*, and a prolific author of popular Marxist tracts. Jack Jacobs wrote: 'It is scarcely an exaggeration to say that an entire generation of socialists around the world were taught Marx through Kautsky.'[32] Edmund Silberner asserted that Kautsky had a 'contempt for Judaism' differing in intensity, but not differing in essence, from that of Marx.[33] George Mosse claimed that 'for both Marx and Kautsky the Jews' supposed lack of humanity was of crucial concern.'[34] However, Jacobs wrote: 'While there is reason to accept the view that Marx held anti-Semitic attitudes to some extent, the evidence put forth by those who make this claim about Kautsky does not withstand a close examination... Kautsky did not want Marxism to be associated with anti-Semitism, and, above all, did not want his own work to be associated in any way with an anti-Jewish perspective. However, Kautsky was also unwilling to criticise Marx openly unless absolutely necessary. For Kautsky saw his role as interpreter and defender of the Marxist tradition and was eager to avoid giving ammunition to the opponents of Marxism by himself attacking Marx.'[35]

Jacobs pointed out that Kautsky never mentioned Marx's notorious article *On the Jewish Problem*, although its widespread republications meant he must have known about it. 'Thus, Kautsky sidestepped his problem by writing works on the Jewish question wholly different in tone from Marx's *Zur Judenfrage*, but written in Marxist terminology and using a Marxist mode of analysis. In so doing, Kautsky probably comforted himself with the knowledge that Engels and Bernstein – the two men from whom he had learned the most about Marxism – had also broken with the tone of Marx's *Zur Judenfrage* in their writings on the Jewish question.'[36]

In his own writings before and after Marx's death he showed an awareness of, and contempt for, anti-Semitism. In October 1882 he wrote: 'It is a characteristic sign that Jew-baiting breaks out precisely in those lands where "divine right" rules uncontestedly.'[37] There could be no doubt that the Austrian government was ultimately responsible for the attacks on the Jews which occurred in the Austro-Hungarian Empire. In explaining why the people had participated in anti-Jewish actions, Kautsky noted that in those places where the people are absolutely without rights, they tend to strike where they are least likely to encounter resistance. Thus, in Austria-Hungary Jews were likely victims precisely because they were weak. 'A thing like this,' Kautsky concluded, 'would not be possible in a free land.' The following year Kautsky wrote a manifesto to the workers of Austria in which he stressed the reactionary character of anti-Semitism: 'Not the birth cries of a new society, but the death spasms of an old one manifest themselves in Hungarian Jew-baiting.' In an 1884 letter to Engels, Kautsky wrote: 'The anti-Semites are now our most dangerous opponents, more dangerous than in Germany, because they pose as oppositional and democratic, thus comply with the instincts of the workers.'[38] He later added: 'What appears to us as the unbridgeable racial opposition between the "Aryan" and the "Semite" is, in truth, only the opposition between the peasant and the city dweller driven to the extreme by special circumstances.' Kautsky believed that such divisions would slowly disappear over time. In that he was to be proved wrong.

The debate continued to rage well into the twenty-first century. After Labour Shadow Chancellor John McDonnell praised *Das Kapital*, Conservative MP Bob Seeley wrote:

> Karl Marx's conspiratorial view of the world is at the rotten root of both hard left and Right. Marx helped provide the intellectual base for both the Holocaust of the Jews and the Holodomor – mass starvation – of the Ukrainians. Between them these acts claimed the lives of more than ten million people. In his 1843 essay, Marx, whose father converted from Judaism to Protestantism, equated emancipation from capitalism and Judaism as being one and the same. He jumbled together hostility to private property and capitalism, and his personal hatred of Jews as self-interested, rootless and enablers of secret control, updating miserable medieval tropes for the modern world. In denouncing Judaism and capitalism, Marx helped lay the intellectual foundations for the ethnically-based genocide of the National Socialists in Germany and the economically-based genocide in the USSR, although it should be said that the Soviets conducted ethnic genocides too. As well as the organised famine of the Ukrainians – arguably both economic and ethnic – this includes the mass expulsions of ethnic groups ranging from Lithuanians to Chechens in the 1940s. A second holocaust of the Jews, this time in the Soviet Union in the 1950s, was scrapped only with Stalin's death. Occasionally, left writers admit structural problems with anti-Semitism (the hard Right has long since embraced it) but mask it with pious mitigations over the left's campaigning record on 'good causes'.

Anti-Semitism and the Left

— That's true, but only up to a point. The British intelligentsia has a dreadful record. It was co-opted by Stalin's Popular Front in the 1930s, despite the mass murders taking place at the time. Left intellectuals such as the Fabians' founders, Sidney and Beatrice Webb, helped suppress knowledge of the killings. Since then, many on the hard-left have embraced any two-bit revolutionary anti-capitalist thug. The final, malign achievement of Marx was to update medieval anti-Semitism concepts for the modern era. In Europe from the late nineteenth century through to the mid-twentieth century, anti-Semitism and anti-capitalism swirled in unholy alliance. Marx wasn't the only one responsible, but his rancid writings help explain why the hard-left and the hard-right swim in the same moral and intellectual cesspit.

— Today, Trump flirts with the fringes of white identity police and economic nationalism while tweeting headlines from a site accused of plugging anti-Semitic stories. Does he recognise his debt to Marx? I suspect not. In Britain, anti-Israeli campaigning has become a cover for hatred of US 'imperialism' and a casual anti-Semitism... John McDonnell has said, 'there's a lot to learn from Capital.' If he's such a fan, McDonnell should read his idol's words more carefully.[39]

Like all historical figures, it is legitimate to argue that Marx was a man of his time and in thrall to the prejudices of that time, and that modern interpretations of morality and social acceptability should not be imposed on the past. UK Chief Rabbi Jonathan Sacks said that the term 'anti-Semitism' to Marx is an anachronism because when Marx wrote *On the Jewish Question*, most major philosophers had expressed similar views, and the word 'anti-Semitism' had not yet been coined, and little awareness existed of the depths of European prejudice against Jews. Marx simply expressed the commonplace thinking of his era.[40]

But the problem is that Marx, a well-educated man whose father was sacked because of his Jewishness, could hardly have been unaware of legally imposed anti-Semitism during his formative years in the Rhineland of Prussia. The order of Teutonic Knights, who ruled East Prussia from the thirteenth century, in 1309 expressly prohibited Jews from entering their territory. When Jews were eventually re-admitted for pragmatic commercial and economic reasons, the regimes imposed on them were harsh. Under Frederick the Great, Jews were excluded from almost all professions and expressly prohibited from brewing, innkeeping, and farming. Trade in livestock, wool, leather, and most local produce was prohibited; the permitted occupations were moneylending and dealing in luxury wares and old clothes. Yet during his wars of expansion and conquest, his armies were provisioned by Jewish military contractors and in periods of peace he encouraged the small number of very wealthy Jews to invest their capital in industry and manufacture. In 1769 he ordered every Jew to purchase and export a certain quantity of expensive, inferior porcelain produced by the royal factory whenever he needed to boost the royal coffers. By the time of Marx's childhood, Jews were in turn repressed and exploited. Reforms were hotly contested, introduced and then scrapped, and dominated regional political debate. Marx, as a student and then as a struggling hack, must have been enmeshed in the arguments.

If, however, that debate somehow passed him by, his subsequent London-based decades should have made him more aware, as we shall see in the next chapter.

2

Shylock, Fagin and the Children of the Ghetto

'the only gentleman in the play, and the most ill-used.'

In 1879, as an impoverished Marx was struggling with the second volume of *Das Kapital* and worrying about his daughter Eleanor's ambition to become an actress, London was agog over a groundbreaking performance of *The Merchant of Venice* by renowned actor-manager Henry Irving in partnership with stage star Ellen Terry. His sympathetic depiction of the vengeful Jewish merchant Shylock as a man of principle and courage was a break with traditional interpretations. Irving and Terry were the superstars of their day and Marx could not have been unaware of the production at the Lyceum Theatre close to his temporary accommodation.

Henry Irving – a working-class Dorset lad who had reached the top of his profession – had spotted a Jewish merchant while on a Mediterranean cruise. 'Picturesque ... old, but erect,' he seemed the perfect model for Shakespeare's Jew. Aged 40 and having played over 500 parts, Irving was regarded as the most unconventional actor of his generation.[1] The character of Shylock had for centuries reflected Western attitudes to Jews.

They had arrived in England following William the Conqueror's 1066 invasion – which they helped to finance – but from King Stephen's reign (1135–54) they had suffered periodic religious discrimination. The blood libel which accused Jews of ritual murder originated in England in the twelfth century. The York massacre of 1190 saw 150 killed. And exactly a century later the Edict of Expulsion saw all Jews officially expelled. Some, however, stayed living an underground life of public denial. Jews were readmitted to the UK by Oliver Cromwell in 1655, and for a time

Jewish contribution to the economy and their philanthropic contributions saw an easing of tensions. But from the Normans onwards, the work they could do was severely limited. As usury was a practice banned for Christians, moneylending was one of the few occupations permitted to them. As was gold- and silversmithing. Both occupations, welcome when the Crown needed such services, became anathema for the lower classes during periods of recession. Most Christian kings forbade Jews to own land for farming or to serve in the government, and craft guilds usually refused to admit Jews as artisans. The stereotype of the greedy, grasping Jew was born.

Historian Ian Buruma put that in its historical context:

> Before 1789, Jews formed a separate community within Christian (or indeed Muslim) societies, with its own religious and cultural traditions. Jews were cursed for killing Jesus Christ and tainted with the blood libel. The Church also condemned Jewish usury. But since Jews were prevented from exercising political power, they could be tolerated as a distinct and highly visible minority. This changed when Jews were given equal rights after the Revolution. Emancipation allowed them to blend in, even assimilate. They lost their special status. And political power was now within their reach. With the collapse of the *ancien régime*, the onset in the nineteenth century of a self-regulating market economy and the rise of a newly empowered urban bourgeoisie, various groups felt victimised. In Catholic countries, the Church and aristocracy were deeply resentful of losing their traditional privileges. The guilds and corporations, which no longer had a role to play in the capitalist economy, were equally bitter. And the peasant class, no longer protected by traditional patronage, felt excluded in the new economy that privileged liberal urban elites, such as bankers, financiers and businessmen.
>
> The winners in the new society of secular republicanism and economic liberalism, in France at least, were often the very people who had been disadvantaged before. They included Protestants, of course; but behind the Protestants, in the view of anti-Revolutionaries, stood the power-hungry Jews. Old theological attacks on usury were redirected at Jewish bankers and financiers. The Jews were no longer a despised but more or less tolerated outside group; now they were the enemy within, conspiring to destroy every last vestige of the traditional order and, through capitalist manipulation, to dominate the Christian world. Hence,

the formation of an anti-capitalist, anti-Semitic coalition of Church, nobility, guilds, unions, Christian socialists and reactionary monarchists, who blamed the Jews for everything they had lost.[2]

German academic Reinhard Rurup wrote:

> Old and new augmented and intensified one another in the anti-Semitic movements of the late nineteenth and early twentieth centuries. In many countries, and the case studies make this very clear, political Catholicism drew on the old anti-Jewish resentments just as much as the new anti-Semitic tendencies in its struggle against liberalism, capitalism and secularisation. Protestantism, mostly closely tied to political and social conservatism, took quite a similar course in those countries where it represented the majority. Wherever anti-Semitism emerged as a reasonably distinct factor in politics, it represented the first non-conservative protest movement against modern society, or the modernisation tendencies in a society in transition. The prevailing social-political mood underpinning and sustaining anti-Semitic agitation was anti-liberal in every respect, and the supporting strata almost always belonged to those who felt threatened by the economic and social changes triggered by the technological-industrial revolution and capitalism's rapidly advancing penetration of all economic relations. In countries where the government and its agencies were politically liberal or at least welcomed modernisation, anti-Semitic protest was able to also focus on state institutions. This also proved to be the case when conservative governments called in the military to protect Jewish communities in an effort to reassert public peace in the wake of anti-Jewish disturbances and riots.[3]

Returning to Shakespeare, Jews were often presented on the Elizabethan stage in hideous caricature, with hooked noses and bright red wigs. They were depicted as avaricious usurers – Christopher Marlowe's play *The Jew of Malta* featured a comically wicked Jewish villain called Barabas, as evil, deceptive, and greedy. Shakespeare's play reflected the anti-Semitic tradition. The title page of the *Quarto* indicates that the play was sometimes known as *The Jew of Venice*, echoing Marlowe's script. One interpretation of the play's structure is that Shakespeare meant to contrast the mercy of the main Christian characters with the vengeful Shylock. Similarly, it is possible that Shakespeare meant

Shylock's enforced conversion to Christianity to be a 'happy ending' for the character, as it 'redeems' Shylock. Anti-Semites have used the play to support their views throughout its history. The 1619 edition has a subtitle of 'With the Extreme Cruelty of Shylock the Jew ...' The Nazis used it as a cultural template in the 1930s.

However, many modern readers and audiences have read the play as a plea for tolerance, with Shylock as a sympathetic character. Shylock's 'trial' at the end of the play is a mockery of justice, with Portia acting as a judge when she has no real right to do so. The same people who berated Shylock for being dishonest resorted to trickery in order to win. Shakespeare gives Shylock one of his most eloquent speeches: 'Hath not a Jew eyes? Hath not a Jew hands, organs, dimensions, senses, affections, passions; fed with the same food, hurt with the same weapons, subject to the same diseases, heal'd by the same means, warm'd and cool'd by the same winter and summer as a Christian is? If you prick us, do we not bleed? If you tickle us, do we not laugh? If you poison us, do we not die? And if you wrong us, shall we not revenge? If we are like you in the rest, we will resemble you in that. If a Jew wrong a Christian, what is his humility? Revenge. If a Christian wrong a Jew, what should his sufferance be by Christian example? Why, revenge. The villainy you teach me, I will execute, and it shall go hard but I will better the instruction."[4] Shylock's fatal flaw is to depend on the law, but 'would he not walk out of that courtroom head erect, the very apotheosis of defiant hatred and scorn'?[5]

That was reflected in Irving's performance, although he was not the first to tone down the traditional racist interpretation. Edmund Keen took a sympathetic line in sharp contrast to the tradition of the role being 'by a comedian as a repulsive clown or, alternatively, as a monster of unrelieved evil'. Edwin Booth, later the assassin of Abraham Lincoln, played him as a villain, pure and simple. Keen's Shylock established his reputation as an actor.[6] Henry Irving set his version in a romanticised Venice using chiaroscuro effects to spell out the impossibility of discerning good from evil. With a Jewish prime minister, Benjamin Disraeli, in power, Irving decided to make his interpretation more politically relevant to his times – he saw Shylock as 'the type of a persecuted race; almost the only gentleman in the play, and the most ill-used'.

The production was never going to please everybody. Henry James, who a few years earlier had reviewed George Eliot's proto-Zionist novel *Daniel Deronda* in an anti-Semitic skit, wrote of Irving: 'He looks the part to a charm, or rather we should say, to a repulsion ... he has endeavoured to give us a sympathetic and, above all, a pathetic Shylock... Mr Irving's Shylock is neither excited nor exciting, and many of the admirable speeches, on his lips, lack much of their incision.' As for Terry, he found her 'too free, too familiar, too osculatory'. But the *Saturday Review*'s critic was won over by a Shylock with 'the horrible stillness and fascination of the rattlesnake. There is something appalling in his aspect... He is still in his despair, but it is the stillness of one suffering.' *The Spectator*'s critic described 'a moment when, as he stood with folded arms and bent head, the very image of exhaustion, a victim, entirely convinced of the justice of his cause, he looked like a Spanish painter's Ecce Homo'.[7]

Alexander Granach, who played Shylock in Germany in the 1920s, wrote: 'How does it happen that Shylock's defence becomes an accusation? ... The answer must be a perfectly simple one. God and Shakespeare did not create beings of paper, they gave them flesh and blood! Even if the poet did not know Shylock and did not like him, the justice of his genius took the part of his black obstacle [Shylock, the obstacle to the plans of the young lovers] and, out of its prodigal and endless wealth, gave Shylock human greatness and spiritual strength and a great loneliness – things that turn Antonio's gay, singing, sponging, money-borrowing, girl-stealing, marriage-contriving circle into petty idlers and sneak thieves.'[8]

The depiction of Jews in the literature of England and other English-speaking countries was indelibly influenced by the Shylock character and similar stereotypes. With slight variations much of English literature up until the 20th century depicts the Jew as 'a monied, cruel, lecherous, avaricious outsider tolerated only because of his golden hoard'. That depiction influenced Marx's writings, but that cannot be justified by his own dire straits and his daily workload in the British Library.

When Marx settled in London in 1850, Charles Dickens had established himself as the premier man of letters of the Victorian age together with his reputation as a campaigning journalist, parliamentary sketch-writer and editor. The *Pickwick Papers*, *A Christmas Carol*, *Nicholas Nickleby*, *The Old Curiosity Shop*, *Barnaby Rudge* and *Martin Chuzzlewit* had been devoured by an eager public, mainly in serial form, due to a surge in literacy among the working classes. Marx himself was an avid reader of the novels, and a great fan of Dickens. For the next twenty years, until Dickens' death in 1870, they were London contemporaries and, albeit in very different styles, they shared many interests, particularly the plight of the poor.

Stephen Hand blogged: 'Both Dickens and Marx observed the aches and pains, the groaning and suffering of an industrialising Europe – of the dissonance between the Scrooges and the Tiny Tims of this world. Both could see that capitalism without a conscience was a cultural dead-end that would lead the masses into alienation from each other and the world around. The one did so as an artist, with his finger-to-the-wind, sensing and feeling the direction of his moment, mid-nineteenth century England; the other did so as a political philosopher, with his brilliant mind at work on the social and economic reasons for the cracks in the capitalist dream that led to such alienation.' He went on: 'Dickens was not the first novelist to draw attention of the reading public to the deprivation of the lower classes in England, but he was much more successful than his predecessors in exposing the ills of the industrial society including class division, poverty, bad sanitation, privilege and meritocracy and the experience of the metropolis. In common with many nineteenth-century authors, Dickens used the novel as a repository of social conscience. However, as Louis James argues: "Dickens is at once central and untypical in the 'social novel'. A novelist universally associated with social issues, he was attacked for allowing his imagination to come between his writing and his subject, and his underlying attitudes can be evasive. In his fiction, most characters have a job, but Dickens rarely shows them at work. His novels are centrally about social relationships, yet his model for this would seem, as Cazamian noted, a perpetual Christmas of warm feelings, and the benevolent paternalism of Fezziwig in *A Christmas Carol* (1843). Even his explicit working-out of class and industrial issues in *Hard Times* (1854), based on a hasty visit to a factory strike in Preston, identified the factory problem not with economics but with the Utilitarian denial of human imagination, and juxtaposed the factories of Coketown against the bizarre world of Sleary's travelling circus."'[9]

Dickens used fiction effectively to criticise economic, social, and moral abuses in the Victorian era. He felt real empathy with the vulnerable and disadvantaged, derived from his traumatic childhood experiences when his father was imprisoned in the Marshalsea Debtors' Prison. Aged 12 he worked in a shoe-blacking factory (it has been claimed that Dickens took the name Fagin from a factory co-worker) and developed a strong social conscience. In a September 1858 letter to his friend Wilkie Collins, Dickens wrote: 'Everything that happens shows beyond mistake that you can't shut out the world;

that you are in it, to be of it; that you get yourself into a false position the moment you try to sever yourself from it; that you must mingle with it, and make the best of it, and make the best of yourself into the bargain.'[10] His deeply felt social commentaries helped raise the collective awareness of the reading public as literacy mushroomed. Indirectly, he contributed to a series of legal reforms, including the abolition of imprisonment for debts, reform of the magistrates' courts, more humane prison management, and fewer crimes that warranted capital punishment.

A passage from *The Pickwick Papers* illustrates Dickens's lifelong concern with the effects of industrialisation, a preoccupation he shared with Marx:

> It was quite dark when Mr Pickwick roused himself sufficiently to look out of the window. The straggling cottages by the roadside, the dingy hue of every object visible, the murky atmosphere, the paths of cinders and brick-dust, the deep-red glow of furnace fires in the distance, the volumes of dense smoke issuing heavily forth from high toppling chimneys, blackening and obscuring everything around; the glare of distant lights, the ponderous wagons which toiled along the road, laden with clashing rods of iron, or piled with heavy goods – all betokened their rapid approach to the great working town of Birmingham. As they rattled through the narrow thoroughfares leading to the heart of the turmoil, the sights and sounds of earnest occupation struck more forcibly on the senses. The streets were thronged with working people. The hum of labour resounded from every house; lights gleamed from the long casement windows in the attic storeys, and the whirl of wheels and noise of machinery shook the trembling walls. The fires, whose lurid, sullen light had been visible for miles, blazed fiercely up, in the great works and factories of the town. The din of hammers, the rushing of steam, and the heavy clanking of engines was the harsh music which arose from every quarter.[11]

All of which put Dickens firmly on what would now be called the left of the political spectrum, but Marx was aware that at least one of his early novels, *Oliver Twist*, serialised between 1837-39, was controversial in his lifetime for its portrayal of a Jewish villain. Dickens's aim was to explore the abuses of the new Poor Law system, the evils of the criminal world in London and the victimisation of children. He gave the most uncompromising critique of the Victorian workhouse, which was run according to a regime of prolonged hunger, physical punishment, humiliation and hypocrisy. Dickens challenged the Victorian idea of charity for the so-called 'deserving poor', which failed to solve the scourge of poverty and unwanted children. But the problem was his characterisation of Fagin.

Fagin, described as a 'receiver of stolen goods', teaches children the art of pickpocketing, beats them when they fail to bring back sufficient stolen goods, and with lies causes the death of a young woman. The novel refers to Fagin by his racial and religious origin 257 times as opposed to 42 uses of 'Fagin' or 'the old man'. Fagin's character could be based on the notorious criminal Ikey Solomon, a fence and London underworld 'kidsman' who would recruit children and exchange food and shelter for stolen goods. In the public mind at least, Fagin was an 'archetypical Jewish villain'.[12] Novelist Norman Lebrecht wrote: 'A more vicious stigmatisation of an ethnic community could hardly be imagined and it was not by any means unintended.'[13] Dickens, who had extensive knowledge of London street life, wrote that he had made Fagin Jewish because: 'It unfortunately was true, of the time to which the story refers, that the class of criminal almost invariably was a Jew.'[14] Dickens also claimed that by calling Fagin 'the Jew' he had meant no imputation against the Jewish people, adding: 'I have no feeling towards the Jews but a friendly one. I always speak well of them, whether in public or private, and bear my testimony (as I ought to do) to their perfect good faith in such transactions as I have ever had with them ...'[15]

The criticism certainly stung Dickens as in later editions he excised over 180 instances of 'Jew' from the text. Yet when he sold his London home in 1860 to a Jewish banker, James Davis, who objected to the emphasis on Fagin's Jewishness in the novel, Dickens allegedly told a friend: 'The purchaser of Tavistock House will be a Jew Money-Lender,' before later saying: 'I must say that in all things the purchaser has behaved thoroughly well, and that I cannot call to mind any occasion when I have had money dealings with anyone that has been so satisfactory, considerate and trusting.'[16] Dickens became friendly with Davis's wife Eliza who told him in an 1863 letter that Jews regarded his portrayal of Fagin a 'great wrong' to their people. Dickens then started to revise *Oliver Twist*, removing all mention of 'the Jew' from the last 15 chapters. He wrote in reply to Eliza: 'There is nothing but good will left between me and a people for whom I have a real regard and to whom I would not wilfully have given an offence.' In one of his final public readings in 1869, a year before his death, Dickens cleansed Fagin of all stereotypical caricature. A contemporary report observed: 'There is no nasal intonation; a bent back but no shoulder-shrug: the conventional attributes are omitted.'[17] In *Our Mutual Friend* (1865) Dickens created a number of Jewish characters, the most important being Mr Riah, an elderly Jew who finds jobs for downcast young women in Jewish-owned factories. One of the two heroines, Lizzie Hexam, defends her Jewish employers: 'The gentleman certainly is a Jew, and the lady, his wife, is a Jewess, and I was brought to their notice by a Jew. But I think there cannot be kinder people in the world.'[18] Dickens had shown contrition, going against the social mores of his time. There is less evidence that Marx regretted the offence he had caused before his death in 1883.

Marx had approved of Dickens's gradual shift from the examination of individual social ills to that of society as a whole, particularly its laws, education, industrial relations and the terrible conditions of the poor. The social consequences of industrialisation and urbanisation are perhaps most persuasively depicted in *Hard Times* (1854) which deals with infant trade unionism, education and class division. David Lodge wrote: 'On every page *Hard Times* manifests its identity as a polemical work, a critique of mid-Victorian industrial society dominated by materialism, acquisitiveness, and ruthlessly competitive capitalist economics.' Dickens was concerned with the conditions of the urban labourers and the excesses of laissez-faire capitalism. He exposed the exploitation of the working class by unfeeling industrialists and the damaging consequences of propagating statistics at the expense of feeling and imagination but 'was better equipped to examine the symptoms of the disease than to suggest a possible cure'.[19]

In the 1960s and 1970s, Dickens was considered well-meaning but naive; his 'programme' was thought to be poorly worked out and inconsistent – not Marxist enough. After Marxism went out of fashion, Dickens's amorphous social critique came to seem more universally true because it was based on feelings of generosity and brotherhood.[20]

Throughout their time in London, Marx and Engels were engaged in disputes with the leaders of the anarchist movement which emerged from the dissolution of the Young Hegelians in the 1840s during the revolutionary upheavals that swept across Europe. Mikhail Bakunin, a Russian aristocrat and archetypal revolutionary firebrand, is the most famous and important of nineteenth-century anarchists and knew Engels well. He regarded the state as the representative of evil.

He wrote: 'A popular insurrection, by its very nature, is instinctive, chaotic, and destructive, and always entails great personal sacrifice ... The masses are always ready to sacrifice themselves; and this is what turns them into a brutal and savage horde, capable of performing heroic and apparently impossible exploits.'[21] In 1871, with Paris surrounded by Prussian troops after France had capitulated, the workers of Paris rose up and seized power. The International Workingmen's Association actively participated through its Parisian section. The Commune was eventually overthrown by a reactionary army and workers were slaughtered. During the last decades of the nineteenth century the socialist movement, including Marxism, progressed while anarchism became marginalised and was generally reduced to terrorism and sabotage.

However, Jewish anarchists came to public prominence towards the end of Marx's life. During the thirty-odd years that Marx was based in London, Jewish immigration surged due to the exodus from Russian pogroms. Many settled in the East End, which became the hub of Britain's Jewish community, and fuelled the working class's growing awareness of their power within a capitalist economy. Jewish workers and activists were at the forefront of public dissatisfaction with poor working conditions and poverty-level wages. In sweat shops clothing workers slaved for up to 18 hours a day, six days a week. The first effective action took place in 1889, when the Great Dock Strike brought the East End to a standstill with the active help of thousands of recent Jewish immigrants under the leadership of Rudolf Rocker, the German-Jewish editor of a radical Yiddish newspaper, *The Workers' Friend*. The son of a Catholic lithographer, Rocker joined a group of Jewish anarchists, and although neither a Jew by birth nor by belief, he ended up frequenting the group's meetings. Rocker became convinced that the source of political institutions is an irrational belief in a higher authority, as Bakunin claimed in *God and the State*. In London he worked as the librarian of the Communist Workers' Educational Union and was appalled by the poverty he witnessed in the predominantly Jewish East End. He joined the Jewish anarchist *Arbeter Fraint* group. There, he met his lifelong companion Milly Witkop, a Ukrainian-born Jew who had fled to London in 1894.[22]

The secretary of the Tailors' Strike Committee was Woolf Wess, better known as William. Wess, a Lithuanian-born Anglo-Jewish anarchist and a factory machinist, joined the Socialist League located in the East End, becoming the overseer of its printing office In 1888, he was the first witness called at the inquest into the death of Elizabeth Stride, a victim of Jack the Ripper.[23] Wess became heavily involved in the local labour movement and during the 1889 action ensured that the strikers and their families were fed and clothed from philanthropists and other trade unions, including £100 from the dockers' union. The strike committee's chairman was Lewis Lyons, the son of German Jewish immigrants. In 1885, he joined the Social Democratic Federation, and while attending one of its meetings he was arrested for obstructing the police. Because he was Jewish, he was given a harsh sentence of two months' imprisonment with hard labour, and a fine of 40 shillings. William Morris attended the court hearing, and got the sentence overturned.[24] Wess and Lyons built links with local non-Jewish campaigners in the area through William Morris's Socialist League. Solidarity from Irish Catholic dockers, who replenished the strike fund when it was nearly exhausted, saw the bosses cave in, agreeing to a 12-hour working day with meal breaks. It was a significant victory, and newspaper coverage of the bitter dispute put a spotlight on the appalling living and working conditions of the East End's Jewish community.

Israel Zangwill, previously a teacher at the Jews' Free School working with the children of newcomers, was the first to offer an insider's perspective on immigrant lives in London with his 1892 novel *Children of the Ghetto*. Zangwill had lived most of his childhood in Spitalfields and he was used to dealing with youngsters who spoke no English when they entered school. As a graduate of London University who had moved to Bloomsbury and renounced religious practice, he also observed the Spitalfields Jews with a sympathetic gaze, albeit at arm's length. His novel was intended to give voices to the voiceless and it was an instant best-seller.

The novel focuses on close family ties among people who had been forced to live in isolation for centuries and the schisms that can ensue when family members seek to break away. Its colourful cast list includes rabbis, schoolteachers and philanthropists, garment workshop bosses and machinists, socialist organisers and poets, immigrant parents and English-born children.

There was considerable pressure on Israel Zangwill to produce an uplifting account of Jewish Spitalfields, and he deliberately left out of the novel the endemic gang violence, the prostitution, and gambling clubs. But he took a bold stand against a number of contemporary stereotypes. Petticoat Lane market, for example, at the heart of the immigrant area, was invariably associated with danger and dodgy dealing, Zangwill describes it as a place where Jews of all social classes congregate to experience the smells and tastes that remind them of their roots. 'The Lane was always the great market-place,' he wrote, 'and every insalubrious street and alley abutting on it was covered with the overflowings of its commerce and its mud ... The famous Sunday Fair was an event of metropolitan importance, and thither came buyers of every sect ... A babel of sound, audible for several streets around, denoted Market Day in Petticoat Lane, and the pavements were blocked by serried crowds going both ways at once.' The distinctive dynamism of immigrant culture, for him, was precisely what was valuable about it. Unusually for a Victorian novelist, he regarded London's multiculturalism as an asset to be prized.

Zangwill also broke new ground in depicting the diversity of contemporary Jewish life. Although it would have been easier to represent Jewish immigrants as a cohesive community with shared needs and aspirations, he instead drew the novel's dramatic scenes from the conflicts of class, religion and generation that fissured it. He intended, he wrote, 'to exhibit clearly that the Jew, like the Englishman, cannot be summed up in any single, or indeed in any score, of types'. *Children of the Ghetto* explored divisions among Jews who are wealthy and poor, orthodox and secular, immigrant and English-born, men and women, parents and children.

Children of the Ghetto, although now largely forgotten, was reprinted for several decades. Nadia Valman wrote: 'Victorian readers found more than novelty in its pages: they also encountered the story of a daughter rebelling against her father's authority, a father striving to understand his son's lack of interest in his family's traditions, a woman longing for the warmth and security of her childhood home. Readers discovered that the struggles of Jewish immigrants in Victorian London were not so different from their own.'[25]

Zangwill's novel was published in a general election year in which immigration was a hot political topic. Initially there had been widespread sympathy for the plight of Jews escaping pogroms but by the early 1890s there were concerns about the social impact of immigration. 'My first impression on going among them,' wrote a Mrs Brewer in the *Sunday Magazine* in 1892, 'was that I must be in some far-off country whose people and language I knew not. The names over the shops were foreign, the wares were advertised in an unknown tongue, of which I did not even know the letters, the people in the streets were not of our type, and when I addressed them in English the majority of them shook their heads.' The anti-immigration campaigner Arnold White declared that, unlike Christian refugees to England, Jews formed 'a community proudly separate, racially distinct, and existing preferentially aloof ... A danger menacing to national life has begun in our midst,' he warned, 'and must be abated if sinister consequences are to be avoided.'[26]

Conservative backbenchers put pressure on the government to control immigration. They formed the British Brothers League and a mass rally in January 1902, held at the People's Palace, Mile End Road, was advertised as a 'great public demonstration in favour of restricting the further immigration of destitute foreigners into this country'. They succeeded in pushing through Parliament the first immigration restriction act for a century, the Aliens Act of 1905. The Act, while retaining the right to asylum on political or religious grounds, gave government inspectors power to 'prevent the landing of undesirable immigrants', including 'invalids' and 'paupers' – those who could not show that they were capable of supporting themselves – and thus excluded not only the sick and elderly but also those who arrived destitute, often having been conned or robbed of their assets on the journey.

Nadia Valman wrote: 'Popular anti-immigrant feeling helped to channel and defuse East End anger at their chronic poverty and insecurity. Jews were accused of lowering the standard of living with "sweatshops" – small workshops characterised by poor working conditions, long hours, low pay and seasonal fluctuation, and of causing the housing shortage that had led to extreme overcrowding. Yet both problems were rife in the East End long before the Jews' arrival. Hostility to immigrants came from pervasive lack of understanding about the real economic causes of local unemployment, such as trade depressions, mechanisation, and competition from manufacturers in the provinces.'[27]

Jewish first- and second-generation immigrants had taken a lead in the trade union movement and they would again be at the forefront of the struggle which created the Labour Party.

3

When Two Tribes Go to War

'the Socialism of Fools'

After the success of the docks and garment strikes (*see previous chapter*), the trades unions mounted another series of stoppages for better working conditions and gave birth to Britain's Labour Party. From its start, Labour was widely supported by Jewish members and drew some of its most active leaders from the Jewish community. That, however, was not always appreciated by the leaders of the new national political movement. It is difficult for the modern left to acknowledge that some of the icons of their early predecessors – Keir Hardie, H.M. Hyndman, John Burns, J.A. Hobson and Edward Carpenter – shared prejudices common at the turn of the century and exacerbated by anti-war sentiments which still apply.

The Second Boer War (1899–1902) was the first major military conflict of the twentieth century and produced a long butcher's bill in terms of lives lost and ruined while damaging the reputation of the British Empire abroad. In Europe, particularly Germany, the Netherlands and France, it provoked outrage, while on the home front the nation was divided between jingoism and pro-Boer, anti-imperial sentiment, mainly from the Liberal and embryonic Labour camps.[1] During the 1870s premiership of the Jewish-born Benjamin Disraeli anti-Semitism had appeared to be in retreat. The war brought it back with a vengeance.[2]

Anti-Semitic agitation deliberately set 'Jewish capitalist interests' against those of the British nation in what was dubbed a 'Jews' war'. There were already widespread concerns over the entry of some 144,000 Jewish migrants escaping Russia and Eastern Europe. Such concerns would eventually lead to the passage of the

1905 Aliens Act, the first modern law designed to monitor and control immigration.[3] They also resulted in the portrait of the Jew as eternal alien, relegated to 'the status of a hermit in the nation's no-man's-land'.[4] Correspondents, many on the left, highlighted alleged Jewish involvement in capitalist war profiteering.

Labour figures opposed to the war asserted that Jewish gold mining operators and financial backers had orchestrated the conflict for their own ends. The now-sainted Keir Hardie insisted that Jews were part of a secretive 'imperialist' cabal that promoted war.[5] In February 1900 he accused 'half a dozen financial houses, many of them Jewish, to whom politics is a counter in the game of buying and selling securities' of leading the UK to war.[6] Hardie (1856-1915), a Lanarkshire miner from the age of 10, a strike leader and the founder in 1893 of the Independent Labour Party, remains perhaps the most iconic leader of the movement which grew out of the trade unions. In his youth he had honed his oratory skills as an evangelical preacher and platform performer at union and Temperance meetings. In 1900 he helped to found the Labour Representation Committee, later renamed the Labour Party. His biographer, Kenneth Morgan, sketched Hardie's personality: 'I found him a man who was not only an idealistic crusader, but a pragmatist, anxious to work with radical Liberals whose ideology he largely shared, subtle in building up the Labour alliance with the trade unions and the other socialist bodies, and supremely flexible in his political philosophy, a very generalised socialism based on a secularised Christianity rather than Marxism. "Socialists," he proclaimed, "made war on a system not a class ..." He was no economist and was ill-informed on many issues, but he had uniquely the charisma and vision that any radical movement needs.'[7] Maybe his anti-Semitic conspiracy rant was an aberration, or simply tailored to his audience.

Much of the early Labour Party antipathy towards the Jews was a result of its anti-capitalist worldview. With Jewish people seemingly occupying a disproportionately high number of prominent positions within global political and financial institutions, they were readily associated with the suppression of the workers. The Social Democratic Federation stormed: 'Jew moneylenders now control every Foreign Office in Europe.'[8] Hardie's ILP and the Trade Union Congress (TUC) blamed 'Jewish capitalists' as 'being behind the war and imperialism in general'.[9] The 1900 TUC passed a resolution arguing the war was being fought 'to secure the gold fields of South Africa for cosmopolitan Jews, most of whom had no patriotism and no country'.

Dave Rich wrote: 'Back when (the newspaper) *Labour Leader* was writing about the Rothschilds, German Social Democrats had a name for fellow socialists, who mixed opposition to capitalism with anti-Semitic conspiracy theories about Jewish bankers. They called it the Socialism of Fools, because it looked like a progressive, emancipatory politics that sought to free the working masses from the exploitation of global finance, but in fact was just a socialist version of Europe's oldest and most adaptable prejudice. The British left has never been immune to this Socialism of Fools.'[10]

Even before the war broke out, the social democratic weekly *Justice* and its editor H. M. Hyndman focused on the alleged part played by rich Jews in fostering the conflict. Henry Mayers Hyndman (1842–1921), the son of a wealthy businessman, was originally a conservative but was converted to socialism by *The Communist Manifesto*. He launched Britain's first left-wing political party, the Democratic Federation, later known as the Social Democratic Federation, in 1881. He was the first author to popularise Marx's works in English. But his authoritarian manner caused a schism and key SDF members, including William Morris and Eleanor Marx, left to form the Socialist League. Anti-Semitism was also an issue. Eleanor Marx wrote privately that 'Mr Hyndman whenever he could do with impunity has endeavoured to set English workmen against foreigners.' Hyndman had previously attacked Eleanor in anti-Semitic terms, noting that she had 'inherited in her nose and mouth the Jewish type from Marx himself'.[11] Hyndman took part in unemployment demonstrations 1887 and was put on trial for his share in the West End Riots of 1886 but was acquitted. He was chairman at the 1896 International Socialist Congress held in London.[12]

In June 1899 Hyndman identified financial Jews and their money interests as the driving force behind the 'campaign against Kruger and the Transvaal Boers'. Hyndman sarcastically referred to those culpable as 'such true-born Britons as Beit, Eckstein, Rothschild, Joel, Adler, Goldberg, Israel, Isaac and Co'.[13] The better-known individuals out of this group were either naturalised British subjects or Englishmen. The Berlin-based academic Susanne Terwey wrote: 'Hence, the exclusion of Jews was driven by two forces, first, a conflict between self-seeking pursuits by individuals at the expense of the majority, a pattern of behaviour that was identified as "Jewish", which was set against a selfless caring for the nation as well as the furthering of the common good; second, by a redefinition of Britishness and national belonging. Contrasting "Englishmen" with "true born Britons", Hyndman suggested a concept of Britishness based on culture which excluded Jews as immigrants and citizens with an immigrant background.'[14]

Hyndman charged 'Beit, Barnato and their fellow-Jews' with aiming to create 'an Anglo-Hebraic Empire in Africa stretching from Egypt to Cape Colony'.[15] Hyndman believed Jews were central to 'a sinister "gold international" opposed to the "red international" of socialism'. Hyndman had supported the anti-Semitic Viennese riots of 1885, arguing that they represented a blow against Jewish finance capital. Hyndman committed to anti-Jewish conspiracies, remarking that 'unless you said that they [Jews] were the most capable and brilliant people of the earth, you had the whole of their international agencies against you.'[16]

On the eve of the war, Hyndman raised another common trope that has lasted to the present day – that Jews have a disproportionate influence on government and the levers of power. He expressed 'detestation for those aliens' who, 'under the guise of patriotism' were bullying the British government into 'a criminal war of aggression'. The Jews were, according to Hyndman, hell-bent on a war for the interests of the few, not the many. He took the argument further a few days later when, after a well-publicised meeting between Lord Rothschild and Arthur Balfour, he wrote that 'questions of war and peace' depended largely on decisions of the Jews and the Rothschild Bank.[17] British ministers had become 'willing agents' of the 'Jew financier'. That was incendiary stuff, but another contemporary commentator was even more direct.

The journalist and theorist of imperialism, John Atkinson Hobson (1858–1940), the son of a prosperous newspaper proprietor, taught classics and English literature but turned to economics as England was caught in a major economic depression. Establishment economists could not explain vicious boom-and-bust business cycles, and Hobson was drawn to the Social Democrats, the Fabians and the Christian Socialists. In the 1890s he argued that large-scale Jewish immigration from the Russian Empire to the UK harmed the interests of native workers. Hobson was recruited by the *Manchester Guardian* as its South African correspondent.[18] In February 1900 he published *The War in South Africa – Its Causes and Effects* based on a series of articles he had written in autumn 1899. He claimed the British were fighting for the interests of Jews only. For the purposes of this book, it is worth including the most-quoted chapter at length:

> It is difficult to state the truth about our doings in South Africa without seeming to appeal to the ignominious passion of

Judenhetze (Jew-baiting). Nevertheless, a plain account of the personal and economic forces operative in the Transvaal is essential to an understanding of the issue, and must not be shirked. A few of the financial pioneers in South Africa have been Englishmen, like Messrs. Rhodes and Rudd; but recent developments of Transvaal gold-mining have thrown the economic resources of the country more and more into the hands of a small group of international financiers, chiefly German in origin and Jewish in race. By superior ability, enterprise, and organisation these men, out-competing the slower-witted Briton, have attained a practical supremacy which no one who has visited Johannesburg is likely to question.

Although their strength does not really consist in numbers, the size of the Hebrew population is very considerable. Public statistics are most deceptive in this matter; many of these persons rank as British subjects by virtue of a brief temporary sojourn in some English-speaking land, and as for names, Smith, Newman, Phillips, Gordon, Bruce are just as good as Marks or Cohen, and are often preferred. So the census of Johannesburg, taken in July 1896, only recognises 6,253 Jews. But while the total population of Johannesburg has probably not increased since that date, it is generally agreed that the Jewish population is very much larger. A well-informed Jew, drawing his conclusion from synagogic and other private sources, told me there must be at least 15,000 Jews in Johannesburg and the district. The evidence of the directory, borne out by the casual testimony of the streets, would lead me to believe this an under, rather than an over, estimate. The great majority are undoubtedly Russian, Polish, and German Jews (commonly classed under the generic title of "Peruvian"), who ply the business of small shopkeepers, market salesmen, pedlars, liquor dealers, and a few rude handicrafts. These are everywhere to be seen, actively occupied in small dealings, a rude and ignorant people, mostly fled from despotic European rule, and contrasting sharply with their highly intelligent, showy, prosperous brethren, who form the upper crust of Johannesburg society. It is with the latter we are directly concerned if we would understand the economic and political import of the present movements.

It is not too much to say that this little ring of international financiers already controls the most valuable economic resources of the Transvaal. The first and incomparably the most important industry, the goldmines of the Rand, are almost entirely in their hands. The following brief enumeration of the leading companies, which represent the recent consolidation of many mining interests, will serve to show the extent of their power. First comes Wemher, Beit & Co., more commonly known by the name of the managing director as the "Eckstein Group". This comprises twenty-nine mines and three other financial businesses. The nominal capital is £18,384,567, but the market value at the beginning of August 1899 was over £76,000,000. This Eckstein Group is the leading member of a larger, effective combination, which includes, for most practical purposes, the Consolidated Goldfields, S. Neumann & Co., G. Farrar and A. Bailey. Of these, the largest is the Goldfields (virtually Beit, Rudd, and Rhodes), with nineteen mines, and a nominal capital of £18,120,000. Next in size comes Neumann, with a capital of £8,806,500. In more separate working, but virtually under the same ulti- mate control, are two other important groups of mines, largely repositories of German capital, Goetz & Co. and Albu & Co. The financial connection, according to my information, consists in the fact that Brassey, representing Rothschild, has a controlling interest in Goetz & Co., while Albu & Co. have behind them the Dresdener Bank. Now Rothschild stands for the Exploration Company, which is in effect Wemher, Beit, and Rothschild, while Wemher and Beit are believed to be large owner of the Dresdener Bank. These statements are made to me on evidence which I am naturally unable to check, but I believe them to be correct, and even if only approximately true, they indicate a close consolidation of the greater part of the Rand mining industry. Outside of them, the chief businesses are J. B. Robinson, with nineteen mines, and other estates at a nominal capital of £14,317,500 and the less important Bamato firm. It is also well to bear in mind that Wemher, Beit, Rudd, and Rhodes, Bamato, and Rothschild are associated as chief owners and life governors of De Beers.

The last few years have seen large steps towards a consolidation of the entire industry under the supremacy of Eckstein, the chief instrument of which is the Chamber of Mines. The primary object of the Chamber, started by Eckstein in 1889, was to secure returns of output, wages, &c., from the various companies, and soon most of the leading companies, with the exception of Robinson, joined it. Robinson, followed by the now rising French and German companies, formed in 1895 the Association of Mines, which was in effect a rival combination. Hostilities were maintained until 1898, when Goetz and Albu were forced back into the Chamber, which has since attained a paramountcy that extends not only to the mining industry, but widely controls the industrial and indirectly the political life of Johannesburg, forming the nucleus of a monopoly which may become to the Rand what De Beers has been for some years to Kimberley. This, however, is not the place to discuss the present and probable future of the power possessed by the Chamber, and Messrs. Eckstein, who actually wield it. This brief sketch is only designed to indicate the dominance of international finance over the vast industry whose capital had recently a normal value of some £150,000,000, and which is and will remain the great source of wealth in the Transvaal. It is, I think, correct to say that the destiny of almost all these leading companies is controlled by foreign financiers. There is, moreover, no reason to believe that the capital thus wielded is chiefly owned by English shareholders. Though no means of close calculation exists, there is good reason to suppose that the French and German holdings, taken together, largely outweigh the English interest in Rand mines.

But while the power of this capitalism is based on gold, it is by no means confined to it. Whatever large or profitable interest we approach, we find the same control. The interests are often entirely severed from, and even hostile to, the mining industry, but they are in the hands of the same class. This is the case with the dynamite monopoly. Every name connected with the present and past of this scandalous economic episode is significant: Lippert, Lewis and Marks, Vorstmann, Phillip, Nobel. The rich and powerful liquor trade, licit and illicit, is entirely in the hands of Jews, from the supreme control of the liquor kings, Messrs. Lewis and Marks, down to the running of the meanest Kaffir bar. That greatest of gambling instruments, the Stock Exchange, is, needless to say, mostly Jewish. The large commercial businesses are in the same hands, in particular the important trade in horses, and other highly speculative businesses. The press of Johannesburg is chiefly their property: they control the organs of Outlander agitation on the one hand, the Star and the Leader, while the Government organ, the Standard and Diggers News, is under similar control. Nor has the Jew been backward in developing those forms of loan and mortgage business which have made his fame the world over. A rich and ably organised syndicate exists which operates through branches in all the little towns, lending sums of money or furnishing credit through retail shops, which they control, to the neigh- bouring Boers, and thus obtaining mortgages upon their farms. I am informed that a very large proportion of the

Transvaal farmers are as entirely in the hands of Jewish money-lenders as is the Russian moujik or the Austrian peasant. No one who knows the fluctuating and precarious character of Transvaal agriculture will feel surprised that the Boer should succumb to this common temptation set so carefully in his path.

It thus appears that the industrial and agricultural future of the Transvaal is already hypothecated to this small ring of financial foreigners, who not merely own or control the present values, but have, by buying up mining properties and claims of a contingent future value, secured an even more complete supremacy over the economic future. The Transvaal is a country especially adapted to the money-lender and the stock-jobber, a land of hazards and surprises, booms and slumps, where the keen-sighted speculator and the planner of bold complex combinations has unrivalled opportunities.

Dull and depressed as was Johannesburg when I visited it, the savour of gambling was in the air. Though talk of stocks and shares was in abeyance, not so the gambling side of sport. One final testimony to the supreme genius of the European speculator stood plastered upon every wall. Sweepstakes upon races are in Johannesburg not a casual caprice of a sporting few, but an important, well-organised, and enduring trade, supported apparently by a very large proportion of the men, and even the women, of the place. A "sweep" upon a single race meeting often amounts to £120,000 or £150,000, a sufficient evidence of the popularity of the demand, which extends to every class of the community. This novel industry owes its local origin to a Jew known by the name of Phillips, who kept a bar in Johannesburg. Phillips runs four big "sweeps" every year and a score of little "sweeps," which are advertised on every wall and by copious handbills. The business basis of the "sweep" is that prizes shall cover 90 per cent, of the money subscribed, the other 10 per cent, going to cover expenses of management and profits. The "industry," I am told, is a most remunerative one. Phillips has now a good handful of competitors: the names of Moss, Legate, Hess, and Herff stare upon you from the back of every newspaper. It is needless to dwell on the demoralising influence of this great and growing gambling trade. Its success is alike indicative of the place and of the people that control it.

The practical paramountcy exercised by financiers, the recognised leaders of whom are foreign Jews, over the economic interests of the Transvaal, extends also to the social and the recreative side of Johannesburg life. Many of the recognised leaders of society are Jewish. The newspapers of September 13th contained the announcement: "There will be no performance at the Empire (music-hall) to-day by reason of the Jewish Day of Atonement." The Stock Exchange was also closed upon that day.

When the British arms have established firm order, this foreign host will return with enhanced numbers and increased power. During the distress of last autumn they bought up, often for a song, most of the property and businesses that were worth buying, and as soon as settlement takes place, they will start upon a greatly strengthened basis of possession. It may be said, granting this story of a Jewish monopoly of the economic power is true, it does not justify the suggestion that the political power will pass into their hands, and that there will be established an oligarchy of German Jews at Pretoria.

But a little reflection shows that while this class of financiers has commonly abstained in other countries from active participation in politics, they will use politics in the Transvaal. They have found the need for controlling politics and legislation by bribery and other persuasive arts hitherto: the same need and use will exist in the future. Politics to them will not merely mean free trade and good administration of just laws. Transvaal industry, particularly the mining industry, requires the constant and important aid of the State. The control of a large, cheap, regular, submissive supply of labour, the chief corner-stone of profitable business, will be a constant incentive to acquire political control: railway rates, customs' laws, and the all-important issues relating to mineral rights, will force them into politics, and they will apply to these the same qualities which have made them so successful in speculative industry. In a word, they will simply and inevitably add to their other businesses the business of politics. The particular form of government which may be adopted will not matter very much. Government from Downing Street may perhaps hamper them a little more than the forms of popular representative government; but the judicious control of the press and the assistance of financial friends in high places will enable them to establish and maintain a tolerably complete form of boss-rule in South Africa.

A consideration of these points throws a clear light upon the nature of the conflict in South Africa. We are fighting in order to place a small international oligarchy of mine-owners and speculators in power at Pretoria. Englishmen will surely do well to

Anti-Semitism and the Left

recognise that the economic and political destinies of South Africa are, and seem likely to remain, in the hands of men most of whom are foreigners by origin, whose trade is finance, and whose trade interests are not chiefly British. If all I say be true, it gives no ground for any final judgment on the merits of the war. This international oligarchy may be better for the country and for the world than the present or any other rule; and England may be performing a meritorious world-service, in establishing it. But it is right for us to understand quite clearly what we are doing.[19]

It is pretty obvious why that chapter remains on Far Right and Fascist websites such as White Pride Worldwide,[20] less so why its sentiments were embraced by supposed socialists then and now. But then Hobson was a noted anti-imperialist and that excuses everything, as we will see in a later chapter.

Hobson later joined the ILP and wrote for such socialist publications such as the *New Leader*, the *Socialist Review* and the *New Statesman*. V. I. Lenin plundered his writing extensively, remarking: 'I made use of the principal English work, *Imperialism*, J. A. Hobson's book, with all the care that, in my opinion, that work deserves.'

Historians Peter Duignan and Lewis H. Gann wrote: 'Hobson's ideas were not entirely original; however his hatred of moneyed men and monopolies, his loathing of secret compacts and public bluster, fused all existing indictments of imperialism into one coherent system ... His ideas influenced German nationalist opponents of the British Empire as well as French Anglophobes and Marxists; they coloured the thoughts of American liberals and isolationist critics of colonialism. In days to come they were to contribute to American distrust of Western Europe and of the British Empire. Hobson helped make the British averse to the exercise of colonial rule; he provided indigenous nationalists in Asia and Africa with the ammunition to resist rule from Europe.'[21]

But Hobson's racism was not limited to Jews. He believed 'colonial primitive peoples' were inferior; he advocated their 'gradual elimination'. He wrote: 'A rational culture in the wide social interest might, however, require a repression of the spread of degenerate or unprogressive races.' Such a plan should be implemented following approval by an 'international political organisation'.[22] While it can be said the 1902 work reflected the Social Darwinism trend of the time, Hobson left this section mainly unchanged when he published the third edition in 1938.

The opponents of the War were united in belief that politics should be guided by moral standards, and individual character traits ascribed to the Jews included 'lust for gold', 'money-grabbing', reckless self-seeking pursuit of individual interests, greed as well as lack of ideals and true religious feelings. The only god the Jews knew, according to such arguments, was Mammon. The socialist-turned-Liberal MP John Burns and the radical Edward Carpenter, in anti-war speeches, contrasted such alleged Jewish traits with the moral superiority of the Boer farmers, ignoring their treatment of blacks and those of mixed race. In Battersea Park in May 1900, Burns described the Boers as courageous, energetic, patient and full of love for independence. He saw the Boers in a heroic battle, defending their country not so much against an army, but against militant capitalism, personified by the Jews, who allowed English soldiers to fight for their financial interests.[22] It is a theme which has been echoed on the left in countless post-imperial conflicts and has parallels with the modern left's attitude to the multiple Middle East conflicts.

John Elliot Burns (1858–1943), the son of a Scottish fitter, was born and raised in Battersea and left school at ten, eventually becoming an apprentice engineer. He was introduced to socialism by a French fellow worker who had witnessed the Paris Commune, and he voraciously read the works of Robert Owen, Thomas Paine and William Cobbett. His physical strength and booming voice made him a natural public orator. In 1881 he formed a Battersea branch of the Social Democrat Federation (SDF) and after a year working as a foreman engineer on the West African coast – where he hated the treatment of native Africans – he spent his earnings on a six months' tour to study political and economic conditions in France, Germany and Austria.[24] On his return he was elected to the SDF's executive council. In 1886 he joined a London demonstration against unemployment which resulted in the West End mayhem, during which he encouraged rioters to loot bakeries. He was arrested but acquitted of conspiracy and sedition charges. He was arrested again the following year resisting police attempts to break up an unlicensed meeting in Trafalgar Square on 'Bloody Sunday' and this time was imprisoned for six weeks. In August 1889 Burns played a major part in the London Dock Strike, by which time he had left the SDF and, with fellow socialist Tom Mann, was focusing on trade union activity as a leader of the New Unionist movement. With other London radicals such as Ben Tillett, he helped win the dispute.

In 1889, he became a Progressive member of the first London County Council and introduced a motion in 1892 that all council contracts should be paid at trade union rates. He was instrumental in the creation of the first municipal housing estate, built using a council's own direct labour force, officially opened in 1903. In 1892 he was elected MP for Battersea as the candidate of the local Liberal Association, having rejected Keir Hardie's argument for a new political party representing labour. He displayed fervent Parliamentary opposition to the war and it was on this issue that his anti-Semitism emerged.

He repeatedly referred to the 'trail of the financial serpent' and told an anti-war rally in 1900 that 'the South African Jew has ... no bowels of compassion... every institution and class had been scheduled by the Jew as his heritage, medium and dependent. Where he could not intimidate, he corrupted; where he could not corrupt, he defamed... the Boers defend their land, not from a nation armed, vindicating a righteous cause, but against a militant capitalism that is using our soldiers as the uniformed brokers' men turning out the wrong tenants in South Africa for the interests of the Jews ... with wisdom foresight and kindliness, we may yet retain South Africa for the Empire and humanity, even though we may lose it for the Jews.'[25] Later, Burns declared that 'wherever we examine, there is the financial Jew, operating, directing, inspiring the agencies that have led to this war.'[26] Burns deplored the British Army which had, in his view, been transformed from the 'Sir Galahad of History' into the 'janissary of the Jews'. In 1902, Burns further denounced 'syndicated Jews who don't fight but do know how to rob'. He remarked during a tour of the East End that 'the undoing of England is within the confines of our afternoon's journey amongst the Jews.' On another occasion he said that the 'Jew is the tapeworm of civilisation.'[27]

In December 1905 Burns entered the Campbell-Bannerman Cabinet as President of the Local Government Board, and in 1914 was appointed President of the Board of Trade in the government of H. H. Asquith, but just two days before Britain declared war on Germany, Burns resigned from the government in protest. He played no role in the war and left parliament in 1918.[28]

The socialist poet Edward Carpenter (1844–1929), an early activist for gay rights, was a regular correspondent with such socialist icons as William Morris, Keir Hardie, Annie Besant and Mahatma Gandhi.[29] After a period as a curate, he was persuaded by Henry Hyndman to join the SDF. In 1884, he left the SDF with William Morris to join the Socialist League. After inheriting a fortune, he opted for a bucolic life, but in May 1889 Carpenter wrote in the *Sheffield Independent* that the city had become the laughing stock of the civilised world. He said that the giant thick cloud of smog rising out of it was like the smoke arising from Judgement Day. It was, he wrote, the altar on which the lives of many thousands would be sacrificed. A hundred thousand adults and children were struggling to find sunlight and air, enduring miserable lives, unable to breathe and dying of related illnesses.[30] Carpenter idealised rural life and the 'masculine bond which he associated with manual labour'. Jews embodied for Carpenter everything he despised. In the tract *Boer and Briton*, Carpenter praised the Boers for leading simple lives with their cattle and for their love of the land they worked. This paradise was being destroyed, when the gold fever had turned Johannesburg into 'a hell of Jews, financiers, greedy speculators, adventurers, prostitutes, bars, banks, gaming saloons, and every invention of the devil'. The real problem laid with the leading classes in Britain, the military and the politicians, who would allow the Jews to lead them 'by the nose'. Only the working class remained 'uncorrupted' by Jewish ideas.

Many Irish nationalists including Robert Noonan, better known as Robert Tressell, the author of *The Ragged Trousered Philanthropists*, sympathised with the Boers, viewing them to be a people oppressed by British imperialism. Noonan had lived, worked and married in South Africa but did not join the pro-Boer International Brigade out of a sense of parental responsibility for his small daughter Kathleen whom he was bringing up alone. However, small groups of Irish volunteers went to South Africa to fight with the Boers, and in Britain the Pro-Boer campaign grew. The use of 'concentration' camps was rightly condemned, but the idealisation of Boer society by some leftist writers does not sit well with that society's inherently racist structure and the post-war history of repression and apartheid.

The claims of Jewish mine ownership in the run-up to the war, or alleged malevolence in propagating it, were transparent nonsense even at the time. Diamonds were first discovered in southern Africa in the mid-1860s on the farm of the de Beer family, near what is now the city of Kimberley. In 1871 the English imperialist, magnate and adventurer Cecil Rhodes bought a claim to the De Beers mine and, with this as a financial base, eventually bought up most of the diamond mines in southern Africa. In 1888 he incorporated De Beers Consolidated Mines Ltd. To keep prices high and demand steady, Rhodes also moved to take control of world diamond distribution.

By the middle of the 1890s he had formed the Diamond Syndicate, which was the forerunner of the Central Selling Organisation (CSO), a more modern group of financial and marketing organisations that came to control much of the world diamond trade. For the benefit of the ignorant, Rhodes was not Jewish, but the sickly son of a vicar.

In evidence to the 2016 Chakrabarti inquiry, Michael Meadowcroft wrote:

> ...anti-Semitism was common in the early Labour Party. Much of it came from the socialist antipathy to capitalism causing the Independent Labour Party (ILP) and, more so, the Social Democratic Federation (SDF) to make the illogical leap of equating capitalism with rich Jews. Certainly, Britain harboured a great deal of inherent anti-Semitism even though Liberal governments passed a series of Jewish emancipation acts from the 1840s onwards. It is particularly perverse for Labour to have continued this attitude after 1881 when the first impoverished Russian Jews started arriving, having fled their homeland due to pogroms kick-started by the false allegations that Jews had been responsible for the assassination of the Tsar.
>
> The SDF paper, *Justice,* carried such comments as: "Jew moneylenders now control every Foreign Office in Europe;" "It seems to be an open secret that the government of France is too much in the grip of Jews to take active measures against them as a body;" and "Modern imperialism is really run by half a dozen financial houses, many of them Jewish, to whom politics is a counter in the game of buying and selling securities and the people are convenient pawns." The ILP was also implicated with Keir Hardie's paper, *Labour Leader*, stating, "Wherever there is trouble in Europe, wherever rumours of war circulate and men's minds are distraught with fear of change and calamity, you may be sure that a hooked-nosed Rothschild is at his games somewhere near the region of the disturbances." Even within the TUC delegates expressed anti-Semitic views. At the 1900 conference, the leader of the navvies' union said, "Practically £100,000 of the taxpayers' money has been spent in trying to secure the gold fields of South Africa for cosmopolitan Jews, most of whom had no patriotism and no country."
>
> Individual socialists and Labour MPs expressed anti-Semitic views. Beatrice and Sidney Webb described Jews as a "constant influence for degradation" in their Fabian book *Industrial Democracy*. George Bernard Shaw characterised Jews as "the real invader from the East,

the Druze, the ruffian, the oriental parasite", in the *Morning Post* as late as 13 December 1925. In May and June 1891, Ben Tillett MP and Tom Mann sent letters to the *London Evening News* demanding the imposition of immigration controls against Jews. Tillett went further and not only called for the removal of Jewish workers from British soil but also blamed the then plight of the British worker on the failure of Britain's ruling class to stand up the power of the Jewish bankers. Tillett personalised his attack by denouncing Liberal MP Alfred Mond as "a German Jew". James O'Grady, Labour MP for East Leeds was another early Labour leader who expressed anti-Semitic views. Even the saintly Keir Hardie stated, "What is the need of it? Simply that men living in Park Lane, some of whom are unable to speak the English tongue, may grow rich."[31]

The combination of anti-Semitism with anti-war attacks on the government were a key part of the political debate. Susanne Terwey wrote: 'British anti-Semitism gravitated around the thus perceived sectional interests of the Jews who would realise these against the interests and at the expense of the nation; this theme was accompanied by scathing criticism of the national leadership and leading politicians who were held responsible for Jewish activities since it was government ministers who would allow the Jews to exercise their influence. In so doing, members of the cabinet and the government failed in their roles as leaders and temporary representatives of the nation.'[32]

As the war dragged into its third year, a parallel movement grew seeking ways to achieve 'national efficiency'. The journalist Arnold White was one of many who tried to redefine English society and create an ideal in which the Jews would have no place. White had won accolades when, as a Liberal candidate for Mile End, he investigated poverty in the East End. But his 1886 account, *The Problems of a Great City*, attacked the predominantly Jewish 'pauper foreigners' for uninhabitable dwellings, and dangerous anarchism.[33] After two more unsuccessful bids to become an MP in the 1890s, he campaigned against Jewish immigration from Russia, and as an agent of Baron de Hirsch he went to Russia to try to persuade the Tsar's government to establish a Jewish colony in Argentina. A eugenicist, White felt that Jewish immigration was reducing England to the world's 'rubbish heap'.[34] He argued that the problem of Jews in the UK was not 'of numbers, nor of habits, nor of occupations ... but the fact that, good, or bad or indifferent the orthodox immigrants belong to a race and cling to a community that prefers to remain aloof from the mainstream of our national life, by shunning intermarriage with Anglo-Saxons'. His treatise *Efficiency and Empire*, published in 1901, insisted that Jews represented excessive materialism and 'unearned' wealth and claimed that 'material success' was 'truly the god' of the Jews.[35] Britain was 'infected' by 'bad smart society', which was dominated by the Jews. The old elites had failed in their duty of suppressing Jewish influence. He warned that the Jewish 'island of aliens in the sea of English life' was still small but growing. The old aristocracy were guilty of admitting 'moneyed aliens who unite rapacity with display' into their midst. White concluded that it had been 'weakness, self-indulgence, want of foresight, self-respect and culture' on the part of the majority which had enabled the 'industrious' and 'unscrupulous' Jews to reach and assume their positions.[36] White advocated the creation of a new elite, young men who would take power in Parliament and in Government. This new, 'true aristocracy' would be characterised by patriotism, independence and the hostility to 'financial schemers'.[37] His 'true aristocracy' might well have worn jackboots.

The South African conflict was also marked by the idea that Jews controlled the media, a concept used by practically all who had spoken out in anti-Semitic terms during the war. Traditionally, the press had been considered by Liberals as an instrument for acceptable political education of the masses, but newspapers were increasingly run by businessmen on business principles. Jewish press barons and journalists came to personify these changes, which were attacked by Liberals, Conservatives and socialists who abhorred the way in which the government and the press whipped up nationalist feelings amongst the enfranchised but uneducated masses.[38] H. M. Hyndman repeatedly denounced what he saw as the overwhelming power of 'capitalist Jews on the London Press', believing that the 'Semitic lords of the press' had created war in South Africa.[39] Susanne Terwey wrote: 'What evolved was a concoction of attacks on Jews with criticism of a certain form of journalism symbolising the neglect of what was perceived to be the essence of the role of the political press: the education of the people, control and defence of representative democracy. In this context, Jews came to embody conscious misinformation with sectional, self-seeking interests in mind. Consequently, it was this "remorseless control" exercised by the Jews "over the expression of public opinion hostile to them" which explained to Arnold White, why the negative influence of "bad foreign Jews" and the dangers arising thereof to the Empire, had been ignored by the press.'[40]

After the war reached its messy and sordid conclusion, Jewish socialists and anarchists fought on for the interests of the working classes. In May 1904 the British premier Arthur Balfour had been pointed to a newspaper article discussing growing anti-Semitism in Britain, which led the Prime Minister to dismiss the idea publicly as 'quite untrue' in *The Times*. This provoked a sharp retort by the author Israel Zangwill who pointed to an increasing number of incidents of anti-Jewish violence and racial prejudice.[41] In 1906, the *Arbeter Fraint* group established a club for both Jewish and gentile workers. The Workers' Friend Club was founded in a former Methodist church on Jubilee Street. Rudolf Rocker befriended many prominent non-anarchist Jews in London, among them the Zionist philosopher Ber Borochov.[42] From 8 June that year, Rocker was involved in another garment workers' strike against wages that were much lower than in the rest of London even though tailoring was the area's most important industry. Rocker, appointed a member of the strike committee along with two other *Arbeter Fraint* members, was a regular speaker at the strikers' gatherings. The strike failed when strike funds ran out.[43]

In late April 1912, 1,500 tailors from the West End, more highly skilled and better paid than those in the East End, went on strike. By May, more than 7,000 were out. Under the influence of the *Arbeter Fraint* group, the East Enders decided to support the strike. Rocker saw it as a chance to attack the sweatshop system, but he was also afraid of an anti-Semitic backlash. Accordingly, he called for a general strike but that proved unsuccessful as over 70 per cent of the East End tailors were engaged in the ready-made trade, which was not linked with the West End workers' strike. Nonetheless, 13,000 immigrant garment workers from the East End went on strike following an 8 May assembly at which Rocker spoke. Not one worker voted against a strike. Rocker again became a member of the strike committee and chairman of the finance sub-committee, responsible for collecting money and other necessities for the striking workers. On 24 May, at a mass meeting held to discuss the question of whether to settle on a compromise proposed by the employers which did not entail a closed shop, Rocker's speech against proved pivotal. The bosses' proposal was thrown out with not a single vote for it, and by the next morning, all of the workers' demands were met.[44]

In the run-up to the First World War, anti-German sentiment was combined with anti-Semitism, but it was the Right who took the lead. From December 1911 onwards the Conservative editor and journalist James Leopold Maxse ranted about the pro-German intrigues of the 'international Jew', or, alternatively, the 'German Jew' in England. In his conservative monthly *The National Review*, he stepped up his game after the outbreak of hostilities in August 1914, taking his themes from the mainstream conservative press, in particular *The Times*. But his scribblings also echoed the analysis of some on the left who again blamed Jewish capitalists for the new, greater conflict and who challenged the loyalty of Rothschild and other prominent Jews at a time of war hysteria which saw the Germanic Royal Family change its name.[45]

In another echo of leftist thought, Maxse railed against the supposed influence of Jews on the governance of Britain. Feldman wrote: 'The development of modern British anti-Semitism cannot be separated from the process of democratisation and the extension of the franchise in Britain… alongside explicit worries about the state of representative democracy, its themes gravitated around demands for more responsibility, accountability, morality and transparency, and thus reflected changing expectations of those who represented and lead the nation in the wake of slow but progressing democratisation.'[46] Maxse was hardly alone and his views became almost mainstream once the Great War had erupted. In March 1915, the *Walsall Pioneer* informed its readers, about 'German Jews' who had come to England in order to influence politics in the interests of Germany.[47] While in the *Manchester Sunday Chronicle* an author with the telling epithet of 'John Briton', held that Jews as well as German Jews had – 'forced themselves into public positions and government jobs, and have then behaved in a way that no loyal and honest Englishman would behave.'[48]

Many of anti-Semitism's British advocates, including those on the left, shared at times an apprehension that the masses would not do as they were told. Brexit, anyone? Some of those authors who combined the endorsement of 'national efficiency' with anti-Semitism also questioned the value of democracy and advocated its abolition.[49]

Rudolf Rocker opposed both sides in First World War on internationalist grounds. Although most in the United Kingdom and continental Europe expected a short war, Rocker predicted on 7 August 1914 'a period of mass murder such as the world has never known before' and attacked the Second International for not opposing the conflict. Rocker with some other *Arbeter Fraint* members opened up a soup kitchen without fixed prices to alleviate the further impoverishment that came with the Great War. Rocker called the war 'the contradiction of everything we had fought for'.[50] Shortly after the publication of this statement, on December 2, Rocker was arrested and interned as an enemy alien, and *Arbeiter Fraynd* was suppressed in 1915. The Jewish anarchist movement in Britain never fully recovered from these blows.

During the First World War, In Britain, doubt was cast on the loyalty of German-Jewish immigrants as anti-German and anti-Jewish stereotypes merged in the general hysteria which enveloped British society. Old stereotypes re-emerged stronger and, for a while, more virulent. Alleged Jewish traits included criminality, clannishness, fraudulence and fast practice, materialism, and disloyalty to national interests. Jews were portrayed on the Home Front as unfair competitors for limited housing and employment. Many commentators contrasted the bad and dangerous German Jews with all other Jews. The good Jews were all patriots and loyal, the bad ones were foreign traitors and spies.[51] Around 1.5 million fought in the First World War for their respective countries. On the Allied side, at least 500,000 Jews served in the Russian Army, notwithstanding widespread Russian anti-Semitism. About 40,000 or so throughout the British Empire fought for Britain, of whom around 2,500 were killed, 1,700 decorated and 9,000 wounded.[52] And about 35,000 fought for France. After the US finally entered the war, almost 250,000 doughboys were Jewish.[53]

The Jewish contribution to the British war effort was militarily impressive. Recruitment posters written in Yiddish were plastered around London's East End. One published by the Joint Labour Recruiting Committee proclaimed: 'In England, there are thousands of Jews who should be grateful to it for freedom and justice to this country that protects them. Any appeal to passions would not be appropriate, but an appeal to honour and gratitude will look quite different.' Thousands of British-born Jews heeded such calls, but the Jewish experience in the First World War is often overlooked, given the inextricable link of the Second World War to the Holocaust.

Chief Rabbi Hertz in a special *Shabbat* prayer on the outbreak of war in August 1914 said: 'Kingdoms shake and nations tremble. The shout of the warrior and the roar of battle resounds to the ends of the earth because of the fury of the oppressor the terrors of war are upon us: they have come close to our gates.' In a statement to its readers, the *Jewish*

Chronicle proclaimed that 'England has been all she could be to Jews, Jews will be all they can be to England.' Leeds Jews rushed to join the West Riding Regiment. At a synagogue in Sunderland, a *cheder* room was taken from the children and given to the local military authorities. In Cardiff the Reverend Jerevitch urged all young people to join the Jewish division of the St John Ambulance Brigade. In Belfast the community collected £107 and handed it over to the Lord Mayor. Sir Marcus Samuel donated £1,000 to the National Relief Fund and converted his country house in Maidstone into a military hospital.[54]

Long-standing Jewish communities wanted to show their patriotism on both the front lines and the Home Front, but it has to be acknowledged that some newly arrived Eastern European immigrants had a very different attitude, and were castigated, not least by well-established Jews.[55] The *Jewish Chronicle* commented that 'Germany in this quarrel is wrong, absolutely, entirely, irredeemably wrong', yet the communal leadership still had to explain why Jews were killing each other in the mud of Flanders. University of London professor Colin Schindler wrote: 'Russian Jews perceived the Jewish national interest much more clearly than their British and German brethren. Many simply could not understand why Great Britain – which had protested on numerous occasions on behalf of the oppressed Jews of Russia and Poland – was now fighting on the side of the Tsar against civilised Germany. When Jabotinsky paid a last visit to Russia, he was called a traitor from the pulpit of Odessa's Yavneh synagogue for siding with the Tsar's ally. This feeling was accentuated by reaction to German military successes in 1914. Jews were blamed for Russian setbacks. In Poland and Lithuania, synagogues were sacked, shops were looted and Jews were hanged. Some Russian soldiers believed that pious Jews were hiding the newly invented telephone in their long beards so as to communicate with the German enemy. Jews in the revolutionary movements understood the war as one of rival imperialisms – and waited for its participants to exhaust themselves before stepping in. Zionists similarly wanted to wait and see who might win before making a move.'[56]

That changed dramatically, however, in November 1914 when Turkey entered the war on the German side. Leading Zionists reasoned that if they allied themselves with Britain, then sooner or later, a British military force would move up from Egypt to confront the Turks in Palestine. Even though a British-ruled Palestine was desirable, the majority of Zionists were not willing to gamble on a British victory. Cabinet minister Herbert Samuel within days saw a window of opportunity. An anglicised Jew who had shown little previous interest in Zionism, Samuel independently submitted a memorandum to the cabinet in January 1915. Entitled *The Future of Palestine*, it put forward 'the dream of a Jewish state, prosperous, progressive, and the home of a brilliant civilisation'.

Lloyd George and Winston Churchill were sympathetic to Zionist aspirations but motivated mainly and understandably by national interests. By late 1917, the wider war had reached a stalemate, with two of Britain's allies not fully engaged: The United States had yet to suffer a casualty, and the Russians were in the midst of a Bolshevik revolution. The British war effort would clearly be helped if British and Russian Zionists came fully on board. Zionists advocated the formation of a Jewish military force which would eventually accompany the British advance into Palestine. It was founded in 1915, in part to enable Russian immigrants to join the war effort as before conscription was introduced the following year, non-nationals who fled persecution in the early 1900s were not legally able to serve in the army. The idea of a Jewish Legion was opposed by the Board of Deputies, future Bolshevik leaders in London's East End and Lord Kitchener himself. Thirty thousand Russian-born Jews living in the UK saw the Legion as a welcome option – otherwise they would have had to fight for a Tsar who had actively condoned Jewish oppression. In Palestine the situation had become more ominous. The Turks had expelled more than 1,000 Jews and banned Hebrew signs in Jaffa. There were fears that what had happened to the Armenians at the hands of the Turks – massacre, expulsion and starvation – would also happen to the Jews of Palestine. The Jewish Legion was duly established in 1917. The Legion was the first Jewish military unit to fight for Palestine since Bar Kochba's rebellion. Sent to Palestine, the 500-strong Judean force entered Jerusalem in December with General Edmund Allenby.[57]

Jews made up four battalions of the Royal Fusiliers brought back from Plymouth and housed in the Tower of London. Preceded by the band of the Coldstream Guards, they marched through the East End into the City before service across the Channel. The German Army also recruited patriotic Jews. As a result, Jews died at Ypres and on the Somme fighting on opposite sides. Isaac Rosenberg, the Jewish war poet, evocatively wrote in 1917: 'I killed and killed with slaughter mad; I killed till all my strength was gone/ And still they rose to torture me, For Devils only die in fun.'[58]

In the Western Front trenches, 17-year-old Marcus Segal wrote a letter home to his family in Kilburn. 'I can't wait until we're together again,' he said. 'Sitting *Seder* and singing *Ma Nishtanah*.' Though aching for the comforts of faith and family, the young soldier soon adapted – even having kosher chicken dispatched from Barnet to the battlefields and building his own makeshift *succah* in the marshland. But, in 1917 at the age of 20, Segal was killed in battle. His story, like those of so many other serving Jews, was all but forgotten.[59]

Less so the fate of Lieutenant Frank Alexander de Pass, the first Jew to be awarded the Victoria Cross. Before the war, De Pass – the son of a wealthy family from Chelsea – had served in the army in India, which was a popular option for Jewish soldiers wishing to fast-track their rise through the ranks. As reported by the *London Gazette*, his VC recognised 'conspicuous bravery near Festubert, in entering a German sap [trench] and destroying a traverse in the face of the enemy's bombs – and for subsequently rescuing, under heavy fire a wounded man who was lying exposed in the open'. De Pass was killed the following day when re-entering the sap.[60]

Kosher cookery guru Florence Oppenheimer, better known by her subsequent marital name of Greenberg, qualified as a nurse and spent the war years serving on hospital ships across the Mediterranean. As well as being one of the few women, she was also the only Jew on deck. Her diary shows how life for those serving could veer from boredom to panic with the regularity of the changing tide. She wrote on 4 August 1915: 'Where are they going to take us? Do they think we all want a holiday at the government's expense? We are all thoroughly sick of it all.' Five days later, struggling to care for the influx of wounded soldiers from Gallipoli, she wrote: 'There were ten of us to look after nearly 2,000 patients... After a good wash, I felt considerably better, so I returned to my little hell once more and made the doctors go on with dressings and I went round to try to make them a bit more comfortable.'[60] Such Jewish commitment to the Allied war effort paid dividends by kick-starting the long road to the creation of an independent Jewish state. And it was Labour who began the process, albeit for complicated reasons.

In June and July 1917, the then-secretary of the Labour Party Arthur Henderson visited revolutionary Russia on behalf of Lloyd George's coalition government and was appalled at the thought that revolutionary fervour could spread to Britain. To counter Bolshevism, he reckoned, meant adopting a reformist socialist programme for the first time and make clear its war aims. The party had to reposition itself if revolution was to be avoided in Britain. Leading Fabian Sidney Webb helped draw up Labour's Memorandum on the Issues of the War. The first draft was discussed at the Labour Party conference on 10 August 1917. Section xii of the document proclaimed the party's support for Zionism: Palestine was to become 'a Free State under international guarantee'. This was nearly three months before the coalition government issued the Balfour Declaration. It was formally adopted as party policy at a joint conference of the Labour Party and the TUC on 28 December 1917. It proclaimed that the war was being fought so that 'the world may henceforth be made safe for democracy' and went on to call for 'the complete democratisation of all countries', for 'the frank abandonment of every form of imperialism', for 'the suppression of secret diplomacy', for 'the universal abolition of compulsory military service in all countries' and for 'the entire abolition of profit-making armaments firms'. The statement explicitly rejected 'the imperialist aims of governments and capitalists' in the Middle East. And Section F of the document, once again committed the party to support the establishment of a free state in Palestine 'to which such of the Jewish people as desire to do so may return and may work out their salvation, free from interference by those of alien race and religion'. Webb's principle motive was the belief that the commitment would assist the British war effort by engaging the sympathy of the Jewish community in the United States and more particularly that of the Jewish community in Russia who were seen as an important force in the revolutionary movement in that country. More generally, there was also the belief that a Zionist settlement in Palestine that was under British protection would be a strategic asset that would help bolster British power. Certainly, Webb himself had no sympathy for Zionism beyond its usefulness to the British war effort. Webb, the future Colonial Secretary, was himself capable of giving voice to anti-Semitic prejudice. He once remarked – inaccurately - on how glad he was that there were 'no Jews in the British Labour Party' and that whereas 'French, German, Russian Socialism is Jew-ridden. We, thank heaven are free', something he put down to there being 'no money in it'.[61]

Three months after the Labour resolution, the UK government followed suit. On 2 November 1917 Arthur Balfour, by now Foreign Secretary, wrote to Lord Rothschild to support the concept of a Jewish homeland in Palestine. It read: 'His Majesty's government view with favour the establishment in Palestine of a national home for the Jewish people, and will use their best endeavours to facilitate the achievement of this object, it being clearly understood that nothing shall be done which may prejudice the civil and religious rights of existing non-Jewish communities in Palestine, or the rights and political status enjoyed by Jews in any other country.'

It was the result of years of careful negotiation, ever since Turkey and the Ottoman Empire, which controlled Palestine, had entered the war on the German side. The contribution of Jewish immigrants, particularly those of Russian heritage, was a major factor. Germany had previously cornered the market in the production of acetone, an important ingredient for arms manufacture and the Jewish scientist Chaim Weizmann invented a fermentation process that allowed the British to manufacture their own liquid acetone. That breakthrough brought Weizmann to the attention of David Lloyd George when he was the munitions minister, and former premier Balfour when he was First Lord of the Admiralty. Weizmann had, by 1917, emerged as the leader of the Zionist Movement. Other Zionist leaders such as Nahum Sokolow also piled on the pressure.[62]

Balfour had long been in favour of a Jewish state, but another key factor was the desperate efforts to persuade the US to enter the war. In the War Cabinet Balfour pointed out that Jewish opinion across the Atlantic outweighed strong German-American opposition to entering the European arena on the side of the Allies. The minutes of one Cabinet session spelt that out: 'There was a very strong and enthusiastic organisation, more particularly in the United States, who were zealous in this matter, and his belief was that it would be of most substantial assistance to the Allies to have the earnestness and enthusiasm of these people enlisted on our side. To do nothing was to risk a direct breach with them, and it was necessary to face this situation.'[63] Balfour hoped that support from the world Jewish community would swing American opinion. It did, but victory was a close-run thing.

Once the Versailles peace treaty had been signed, Leo Maxse and others claimed that Jewish control over British government policy and the Premier David Lloyd George as the reasons for what they considered far too lenient terms for Germany. In late November 1918, after the signing of the armistice and in the run-up to the general election, a *Morning Post* leader expressed concern about the state of the national parliament, parties and electioneering by the people after four years of war. What would be necessary was a 'clean sweep of German-Jewish and other corrupting influences in our public life', as much as an 'independent' House of Commons working in the interest of the nation. The *Morning Post* hoped for a return to 'national politics' and in view of the upcoming peace negotiations in Paris, demanded that Britain should be represented only by men of 'British blood and feeling' with an understanding of 'national sentiments as to the peace terms'.[62] A couple of weeks later, *The Times* reproduced in one of its leaders the assumption that 'some international financiers' were said to play too great a role in the surroundings of the Peace Conference.[63]

Among the Jewish stereotypes deliberately propagated on the anti-Semitic part of the left in the wake of First World War were the following myths: Jews had started the war to bring Europe financially and politically into ruin and make Europe susceptible to Jewish 'control; and Jews exploited the misery of the war to enrich themselves. On the German Right, the myths included: Jews prolonged the war to lead the Bolshevik Revolution in furthering the aim of world revolution; with their inherited cowardice and instinctive disloyalty predisposing them against defending the nation, Jews were responsible for the pernicious malaise behind the front and stabbed the fighting troops in the back, causing the military defeat of Germany and democratic/socialist revolution; foreign Jews dominated the peace negotiations and succeeded in dividing Germans and Hungarians by artificial national borders, while their co-conspirators, the domestic Jews, misled the nation into 'surrender' and permanent 'enslavement'; and Jews controlled the complex finances of the reparations system for their own profit. Such thinking, of course, led to the Holocaust and the Second World War, and twisted leftist ideologies played at least a part in that drift into horror.

From the pro-Boer speeches to Versailles, British commentators on left and right resorted to the theme of Jewish influence in order to portray government policy as harmful and destructive to the nation and the State.[64] British political culture secured the status of the Jews as a religious minority, but the liberal-left self-image brought about a narrative according to which whatever was said about and done to Jews in Britain was not 'anti-Semitic'.

It is always problematical to impose on past societies the values of the modern age. But it is also difficult to understand, or condone, how a movement with the honourable aims of equality of opportunity and an end to imperial dominance to benefit the many, not the few, could condemn one set of prejudices and replace them with another.

4

Between the Wars

'...the art of delicate but deadly repartee'

After the Great War, anti-Semitic sentiments did fade for a period, thanks partly to a recognition among idealistic socialists that old-fashioned bigotry was not exclusive to the Right and needed to be confronted whenever it emerged from the left, and partly to the formation of Jewish trade unions and the increasing adherence of immigrant Jewish socialists to the ILP and SDF. Within the Jewish community, branches of a Jewish workers' organisation *Poale Zion* began to be established from 1903 and was affiliated to the Labour Party in 1920. *Poale Zion*, which viewed Zionism as the national liberation movement of the Jewish people, was instrumental in the Labour Party's War Aims Memorandum. From its start the Labour Party was widely supported by Jewish members and drew some of its most active leaders from the Jewish community.[1]

Zionism arose in the late 19th century in reaction to anti-Semitic and nationalist movements in Europe. In 1896, Jewish journalist Theodor Herzl published the foundational text of political Zionism, *Der Judenstaat* (The Jews' State), in which he asserted that it was the only solution to the 'Jewish Question' in Europe.[2] A year later, Herzl founded the Zionist Organisation, which at first called for the establishment of 'a home for the Jewish people in Palestine secured under public law'. Proposed measures to attain that goal included the promotion of Jewish settlement there, the organisation of Jews in the diaspora, the strengthening of Jewish feeling and consciousness, and preparatory steps to attain necessary governmental grants. Herzl died in 1904.[3]

Between the Wars

Also in 1904, Zionist leader Chaim Weizmann, later President of the World Zionist Organisation and first President of Israel, moved from Switzerland to the UK. Earlier that year, premier Arthur Balfour had successfully driven the Aliens Act through Parliament with impassioned speeches regarding the need to restrict the wave of immigration into Britain from Jews fleeing the Russian Empire.[4] Weizmann met Balfour who asked him why he had objected to an earlier scheme to create a Jewish homeland in British East Africa. Weizmann responded that he believed the English are to London as the Jews are to Jerusalem.

A law in place until the 1850s stated that no member of the Jewish religion could be elected to Parliament. Nevertheless, the bigoted Lord George Gordon, responsible for the anti-Catholic Gordon riots, converted to Judaism and in 1770 Samson Eardley, whose father was Jewish, entered Parliament. From then to 1900, 15 men with Jewish backgrounds became Conservative MPs, including premier Benjamin Disraeli, and 24 became Whig/Liberal/Liberal Unionist MPs. The trend continued into the twentieth century – between 1900 and 1939 nine Jews, including Nathan de Rothschild, became Conservative MPs, and 18, including leader Herbert Samuel, became Liberal MPs. Labour won 29 seats in 1906 and 42 in 1910, none of them taken by Jewish members. It was not until the 1922 election, after the franchise had been extended to women and some previously excluded men, that amongst Labour's 142 MPs was the party's first Jew.

Emanuel 'Manny' Shinwell was a hero of the left for most of his 101-year life. Born in London's East End to a large family of Jewish immigrants, the son of a Polish Jew who ran a small clothing shop and a Dutch Jewish mother who had been a cook. The eldest of 13 siblings, he moved to Glasgow as a boy and left school at the age of eleven. He became a trade union organiser and one of the leading figures of Red Clydeside and was imprisoned for six weeks in 1919 for his alleged involvement in the disturbances in Glasgow in January 1919. For some, perhaps, his Scottish persona outweighed his Jewish background. Shinwell served as a Labour MP from 1922 to 1924, and from a by-election in 1928 until 1931, and held junior office in the minority Labour Governments of 1924 and 1929–31.

During the 1920s, the implications of the 1917 Balfour Declaration came to the fore. It proved immensely controversial in the post-war years, and that controversy segued into Labour's first periods of power. The main issue, of course, was whether the Arab majority inhabiting

Palestine would be forced to share the lands or be dispossessed. In 1920 the Labour Party conference voted unanimously in favour of 'Palestine for the Jews', a motion proposed by the secretary of *Paole Zion*. The following year, a similar resolution proposed once again by a *Paole Zion* delegate, was carried unanimously.

In August 1920, the Palm Commission reported: 'It is said that the effect of the Balfour Declaration was to leave the Moslems and Christians dumbfounded ... It is impossible to minimise the bitterness of the awakening. They considered that they were to be handed over to an oppression which they hated far more than the Turk's and were aghast at the thought of this domination ... Prominent people openly talk of betrayal and that England has sold the country and received the price ... Towards the Administration [the Zionists] adopted the attitude of "We want the Jewish State and we won't wait", and they did not hesitate to avail themselves of every means open to them in this country and abroad to force the hand of an Administration bound to respect the "Status Quo" and to commit it, and thereby future Administrations, to a policy not contemplated in the Balfour Declaration ... What more natural than that [the Moslems and Christians] should fail to realise the immense difficulties the Administration was and is labouring under and come to the conclusion that the openly published demands of the Jews were to be granted and the guarantees in the Declaration were to become but a dead letter?'[5]

At a June 1921 meeting of the Imperial Cabinet, Winston Churchill was asked by Arthur Meighen, the Canadian Prime Minister, about the meaning of the 'national home' for Jews in the Declaration. Churchill said: 'If in the course of many years they become a majority in the country, they naturally would take it over ... pro rata with the Arab. We made an equal pledge that we would not turn the Arab off his land or invade his political and social rights.'[6] Churchill later wrote that 'there is nothing in it to prohibit the ultimate establishment of a Jewish State'. And in private, many British officials agreed with the Zionists' interpretation that a state would be established when a Jewish majority was achieved. When Chaim Weizmann met with Churchill, Lloyd George and Balfour at Balfour's home in London on 21 July 1921, Lloyd George and Balfour assured Weizmann 'that by the Declaration they had always meant an eventual Jewish State', according to Weizmann's minutes of that meeting.

Palestine's Muslim and Christian community of Palestine, almost 90 per cent of the population, naturally opposed the Declaration.

It was widely regarded as a carve-up by a European power of a non-European territory in flat disregard of both the presence and the wishes of the native majority resident in that territory. And within British military and political circles there was a general acceptance that it would eventually have to be imposed by force of arms. After a Zionist Commission parade, a delegation of the Muslim-Christian Association handed a petition to Palestine military governor Ronald Storrs saying: 'We have noticed yesterday a large crowd of Jews carrying banners and over-running the streets shouting words which hurt the feeling and wound the soul. They pretend with open voice that Palestine, which is the Holy Land of our fathers and the graveyard of our ancestors, which has been inhabited by the Arabs for long ages, who loved it and died in defending it, is now a national home for them ... We Arabs, Muslim and Christian, have always sympathised profoundly with the persecuted Jews and their misfortunes in other countries ... but there is wide difference between such sympathy and the acceptance of such a nation ... ruling over us and disposing of our affairs.'[7] In the broader Arab world, the Declaration was seen as a betrayal of the British wartime understandings with the Arabs, including those promises given by the famed Lawrence of Arabia.[8]

British public and government opinion became increasingly unfavourable to state support for Zionism. In February 1922 Churchill telegraphed Samuel, who had begun his role as High Commissioner for Palestine 18 months earlier, asking for cuts in expenditure and noting: 'In both Houses of Parliament there is growing movement of hostility, against Zionist policy in Palestine... I do not attach undue importance to this movement, but it is increasingly difficult to meet the argument that it is unfair to ask the British taxpayer, already overwhelmed with taxation, to bear the cost of imposing on Palestine an unpopular policy.'[9]

A lengthy memorandum given to the Cabinet in February 1923 laid the foundation for a secret review of Palestine policy: 'It would be idle to pretend that the Zionist policy is other than an unpopular one. It has been bitterly attacked in Parliament and is still being fiercely assailed in certain sections of the press. The ostensible grounds of attack are threefold: The alleged violation of the McMahon pledges; The injustice of imposing upon a country a policy to which the great majority of its inhabitants are opposed; and the financial burden upon the British taxpayer.'[10] Nevertheless, the Declaration was incorporated into the British Mandate for Palestine, which was finally formalised in September 1923. Unlike the Declaration itself, the Mandate was legally binding on the British government.[11]

The machinations damaged Britain's reputation in the Middle East for generations. The Declaration was also condemned in 1922 by the German anti-Semitic theorist Alfred Rosenberg in his polemic *Der Staatsfeindliche Zionismus* (Zionism, the Enemy of the State). He accused 'stab-in-the-back' German Zionists of supporting Britain in return for the promise of a homeland of their own. It was a theme which Adolf Hitler constantly repeated.[12]

Historian Elizabeth Monroe wrote that 'measured by British interests alone, it was one of the greatest mistakes in its imperial history'.[13] American academic Jonathan Schneer concluded that as the build-up to the declaration was characterised by 'contradictions, deceptions, misinterpretations, and wishful thinking', the Declaration 'produced a murderous harvest, and we go on harvesting even today'. The foundational stone for modern Israel had been laid.[14]

When in 1922, Ramsey MacDonald was returned as MP for Aberavon, the Labour *New Leader* magazine declared that his election was 'enough in itself to transform our position in the House. We have once more a voice which must be heard'.[15] MacDonald, the illegitimate son of a Scottish crofter, had with Keir Hardie and Arthur Henderson been a founding father of the Labour Party, rising to the Leadership. He had been an implacable opponent of Britain's entry into the First World War. Historian Kenneth O. Morgan wrote that 'as dissolution set in with the Lloyd George coalition in 1921–22, and unemployment mounted, MacDonald stood out as the leader of a new kind of broad-based left. His opposition to the war had given him a new charisma. More than anyone else in public life, he symbolised peace and internationalism, decency and social change ... He had become the voice of conscience.'[16] At the 1922, Labour replaced the Liberals as the main opposition party to the Conservative government of Stanley Baldwin. His new status saw him moving away from the left and he strongly opposed the wave of radicalism that swept through the labour movement

MacDonald visited Palestine in 1921 and was very impressed by the Zionist settlers he met, 'Israelites returning to Zion'. His tract *A Socialist in Palestine* was published by Paole Zion and described how the settlers were building a future in 'the home of their fathers ... in socialist fashion and upon the foundations of communal idealism'. He described them in utopian terms: 'A happy fraternal company of men and women, brown of face and sturdy of limb, everyone engaged in hard manual labour.' They had come together 'to rebuild Palestine and fence it against capitalism'. He believed that the Zionist settlement would benefit the Arabs and that already 'the Jewish worker is helping the Arab to raise his standards.'

But while his account demonstrated that MacDonald embraced the Zionist project with some enthusiasm, he was still gripped by an inclination towards vicious anti-Semitic stereotypes. He contrasted the settlers with 'the rich plutocratic Jew' who was the true economic materialist. 'He is the person whose views upon life make one anti-Semitic,' he wrote. 'He has no country, no kindred. Whether as a sweater or a financier, he is an exploiter of everything he can squeeze. He is behind every evil that governments do, and his political authority, always exercised in the dark, is greater than that of Parliamentary majorities. He is the keenest of brains and the bluntest of consciences. He detests Zionism because it revives the idealism of his race, and has political implications which threaten his economic interests.'[17] His belief that the Jewish capitalist was somehow worse than the non-Jewish capitalist dated back to the Boer War and shows that he retained the old mythologies and prejudice.[18]

The Conservative government lost a vote of confidence in January 1924 and King George V called on MacDonald to form a minority Labour government, with the tacit support of the Liberals under Asquith. The king noted in his diary, 'He wishes to do the right thing ... Today twenty-three years ago dear Grandmama died. I wonder what she would have thought of a Labour Government!' He became the first Labour prime minister and the first from a working-class background. Ten of his Cabinet appointees were also working class.

The Palestine issue was put on the back burner as MacDonald's priority was to come to terms with post-war Germany. While there were few major labour strikes during his term, MacDonald acted swiftly to end those that did erupt. When the Labour Party executive criticised the government, he replied that, 'public doles ... strikes for increased wages, limitation of output, not only are not socialism, but may mislead the spirit and policy of the socialist movement.'[19] The government lasted only nine months and did not have a majority in either House of Parliament, but it was still able to support the unemployed with the extension of benefits and amendments to the Insurance Acts and to greatly expand municipal housing for low paid workers.[20]

Labour's support for the Balfour Declaration remains a painful bone of contention on the hard left. Socialist Workers Party activist John Newsinger, joint editor of the *George Orwell Studies Journal*, wrote: 'Far from being "institutionally anti-Semitic", a much better case can be made that the Labour Party has throughout most of its history been "institutionally Zionist". The Labour Party embraced the notion of creating a Jewish state in the Middle East even before the Balfour Declaration, and thereafter regularly reaffirmed this commitment. This was a commitment shared by both the left and the right in the party, although for different reasons. The right saw a Zionist settlement and takeover of Palestine as a way of bolstering the British Empire's position in the Middle East. A Zionist settlement would be a support against Arab nationalism in the same way that Protestant Ulster was a support against Irish nationalism. The Labour left supported the Zionist cause for very different reasons. As far as they were concerned, Zionism was a movement of the left, bringing progress to a backward Middle East dominated by a landowning aristocracy that kept the great majority of the population mired in poverty. Zionism was going to inject left-wing ideas into the Middle East with Jewish workers leading the way in the fight for emancipation. The kibbutz was seen as the institution that best exemplified this. Of course, this was just so much wishful thinking, encouraged by the Zionists, but only tenable if what was actually going on in Palestine on the ground was ignored.'[21]

The Conservative government of Stanley Baldwin saw the 1926 General Strike and unemployment at over ten per cent. The May 1929 general election put MacDonald back in No 10 without a majority and relying on the support of the Liberals. The following year his administration raised unemployment pay, passed an act to improve wages and conditions in the coal industry and started to tackle slum clearances. But the government had no effective response to the economic crisis which followed the Stock Market crash.

MacDonald had disappointed the ambitious young radical Oswald Mosley by giving him the post of Chancellor of the Duchy of Lancaster outside the Cabinet, and Mosley, along with David Lloyd George and economist John Maynard Keynes, became a fierce critic of government 'inertia'. Mosley put forward a memorandum calling for high tariffs to protect British industries from international finance, nationalisation of the main industries, and a programme of public works to solve unemployment. The memorandum was signed by 15 fellow Labour MPs who should have been suspicious of his proposal to grant wide-ranging powers to the government, with only general control by Parliament, and the creation of a five-member Cabinet without specific portfolio, similar to the War Cabinet adopted during the First World War. His increasingly dictatorial tendencies were by then evident. When it was rejected by the Cabinet, Mosley resigned from his ministerial position. The Liberal-leaning *The Nation* said: 'The resignation of Sir Oswald Mosley is an event of capital importance in domestic politics ... We feel that Sir Oswald has acted rightly – as he has certainly acted courageously – in declining to share any longer in the responsibility for inertia.' He failed – but only narrowly – in a bid to persuade the Labour conference to accept his plan, and finally resigned from the party in February 1931 and formed what he initially called the New Party.

By the end of 1930, unemployment had doubled to over two and a half million. The government struggled to reconcile two contradictory aims: achieving a balanced budget to maintain sterling, and maintaining assistance to the poor and unemployed at a time when tax revenues were falling. A Treasury committee urged large public-sector wage cuts and large cuts in public spending, notably in payments to the unemployed, to avoid a budget deficit. Senior ministers such as Arthur Henderson made it clear they would resign rather than acquiesce in the cuts. MacDonald formally resigned. At the bidding of George V, a National Government was formed with the Conservatives and Liberals. MacDonald and his Cabinet supporters were expelled and quickly formed a new National Labour group, which subsequently won little support from the unions and the public. There were riots in Glasgow and Manchester. However, in the 1931 general election, the National Government won 554 seats – 473 Conservatives, 13 National Labour, 68 Liberals and various others, while Labour, now led by Arthur Henderson, won only 52. Henderson himself lost his seats in Labour's worst-ever rout.

The National Government's huge majority left MacDonald with the largest mandate ever won by a British prime minister at a democratic election, but he was ageing rapidly, and was increasingly a figurehead with a Conservative Lord President effectively in charge. MacDonald presided at the world economic conference in London in June 1933, but any chance of an effective deal to tackle the Great Depression on a global basis was torpedoed by the US. His mental and physical health declined further, and he became an increasingly ineffective leader as the international situation grew more threatening. He resigned in June 1935 in favour of Baldwin. Within months he lost his Seaham seat to Manny Shinwell. He died a lonely man reviled by his former comrades, aged 71, in 1937.[22]

The turmoil of the 1920s and 1930s in Labour's ranks had by then been exploited by a new leader who took anti-Semitism to new highs. As we have seen, Britain was rife with anti-Semitic prejudice on both the right and the left of British politics. Conservatives were, and remain, the worst offenders, but socialist double-think over comradeship and capitalism was also prevalent. The liberal economist Maynard Keynes who, after a visit to Berlin in 1926, wrote: 'If I lived there, I felt I might turn anti-Semite... It is not agreeable to see civilisation so under the ugly thumbs of its impure Jews who have all the money and the power and the brains.' George Orwell felt no compunction in displaying such prejudice in his early writings (*see subsequent chapter*). The rise of fascism abroad – Mussolini in Italy and Hitler's Nazism in Germany – and its British incarnation under former Labour MP Oswald Mosley, saw the left coming to understand the impact of totalitarianism in Europe, if not the Soviet Union.

* * *

Sir Oswald Ernald Mosley had been one of the youngest MPs, representing Harrow from 1918 to 1924, first as a Conservative, then an independent, before joining the Labour Party. He returned to Parliament as the MP for Smethwick at a by-election in 1926 and was widely regarded as a future Labour prime minister. From a prominent Anglo-Irish family, he had attacked the Conservatives, while still a Tory, over the rampages of the infamous Black and Tans in Ireland, and on the Labour benches had railed against mass unemployment and the grip of international finance. Difficult as it is to comprehend given hindsight, he was for a while regarded as a man of the left. The son of a baronet, a serial philanderer, a champion fencer, a former cavalry officer and aircraftman in the First World War with aristocratic connections and family riches, his charisma and effective debating skills were loathed by the Conservatives who branded him a class traitor. The liberal *Westminster Gazette* wrote that Mosley was 'the most polished literary speaker in the Commons, words flow from him in graceful epigrammatic phrases that have a sting in them for the government and the Conservatives. To listen to him is an education in the English language, also in the art of delicate but deadly repartee. He has human sympathies, courage and brains.'

After Mosley's split with Labour, in subsequent by-elections his New Party divided the leftist vote and allowed Conservative candidates to win. Despite this, the organisation gained support among many Labour and Conservative politicians who agreed with his economic policies, including Aneurin Bevan and Harold Macmillan. Such inclinations faded as the New Party increasingly swung towards fascism, and the party, including Mosley, lost all seats in the 1931 general election. Shortly after that defeat, the *Manchester Guardian* reported: 'When Sir Oswald Mosley sat down after his Free Trade Hall speech in Manchester and the audience, stirred as an audience rarely is, rose and swept a storm of applause towards the platform – who could doubt that here was one of those root-and-branch men who have been thrown up from time to time in the religious, political and business story of England. First that gripping audience is arrested, then stirred and finally, as we have said, swept off its feet by a tornado of peroration yelled at the defiant high pitch of a tremendous voice.'

Mosley went on a study tour of the 'new movements' of Italy's Benito Mussolini and other fascists and returned convinced that it was the way forward for Britain. He created the British Union of Fascists (BUF) in 1932, and claimed membership, at its peak, of 50,000. Despite the subject of this book, Fascist anti-Semitism was most prevalent amongst the aristocracy and Establishment figures at one end of the social scale and violent street bully boys and sectarian bigots at the other. So it is no surprise that its most prominent early supporters included the Duke of Bedford, the Earls Glasgow and Errol, Barons Redesdale, de Clifford and Russell of Liverpool, *Daily Mail* proprietor Viscount Rothermere, Group Captain Sir Louis Leisler Greig, an intimate courtier to George VI, Bank of England Director Frank Tiarks, the future traitor William Joyce, better known as Lord Haw-Haw and Belfast West Unionist MP William Allen. From the ranks of culture and sport it drew the support of racing driver Sir Malcolm Campbell, historian Major General John Fuller, England cricket team captain Arthur Gilligan, orchestra conductor Sir Reginald Goodall, the explorer St John Philby, the father of future traitor Kim, and writer Henry Williamson, best known for his environmentalist classic *Tarka the Otter*. Not so notorious at the time was Frank Clifton Bossard, a British Secret Intelligence Service agent who in the 1960s leaked classified documents to the Soviets.

What is more surprising is the handful of Labour politicians who unashamedly took the same route.

John Warburton Beckett was the son of a draper and his wife who had been born a Jew but renounced her faith to marry. He was privately educated until 14 when his father was conned out of his modest fortune by notorious fraudster Horatio Bottomley, and he worked as an errand boy.[23] After wartime army service, Beckett set up the National Union of Ex-Servicemen, which was eventually absorbed into the Royal British Legion having failed to gain Labour Party recognition. He joined the Independent Labour Party, sitting on Hackney Council from 1919 to 1922. As a Labour agent he worked closely with the young Clement Attlee. Beckett failed to capture Newcastle upon Tyne North at the 1923 general election, but took Gateshead in 1924, moving to Peckham in 1929, after which he served as an ILP whip. Noted for his fiery, passionate speeches, in 1930 he lifted the ceremonial mace in a Commons spat over the suspension of Fenner Brockway. it was wrestled from him before he could leave the Chamber. Beckett opposed the formation of the National Government, returned to the ILP and failed to hold his seat, with the vote split between three 'Labour' candidates. Supposedly retiring from politics, he visited Italy where, like Mosley, he was impressed by Mussolini's regime.[24]

On his return, Beckett joined the BUF in 1934 and become Director of Publications, editing the publications, *Action* and *Blackshirt*. He was arrested outside Buckingham Palace during the abdication crisis. When he returned to Gateshead and Newcastle upon Tyne for speaking engagements he was met with large hostile crowds and shouts of 'Traitor'.[25] He was forced to cancel one such speaking engagement near Newcastle when a crowd of around 1,000 anti-fascists rushed the stage.[26] In 1937 Mosley sacked him, and Beckett formed the National Socialist League alongside William Joyce. Disillusioned with Hitler, he left the League the following year.[27]

Robert Forgan, the son of a Church of Scotland minister, saw war service as a doctor and became Vice-President of the Medical Society for the Study of Venereal Diseases. His experience as a public health officer in the poorer areas of the city drew him to socialism and he served on the city council.[28] Forgan was godfather to Mosley's son Michael. Initially a member of the ILP, he was elected MP for West Renfrewshire in 1929, persuading the Commons authorities to install a modern ventilation system to improve health in the dust-choked corridors of power. Forgan was one of the signatories of the 'Mosley Memorandum' and he followed Mosley into the New Party. He appealed to ILP members to follow suit and acted as Chief Whip during the New Party's brief run in Parliament, losing his seat at the 1931 election along with the others.[29]

Forgan joined the BUF and was initially Director of Organisation, moving on to become an important background figure, arranging private functions with leading businessmen in an attempt to secure support for Mosley.[30] He insisted that the BUF did not exclude Jews, courted Liberal Jewish MPs and even held meetings with the leaders of the Board of Deputies of British Jews. Forgan tried to keep the BUF distinct from the Imperial Fascist League which he regarded as too ideologically 'foreign' to attract voters.[31] Mosley promoted him to deputy leader, but by 1934 he disapproved of the growing influence of BUP propaganda director William Joyce, a staunch anti-Semite, and quit the BUF.[32] Forgan's conversion to fascism had always been at best half-hearted and had more to do with his personal loyalty to Mosley, something that was largely gone by that point.[33] He took no further role in politics.

One Labour MP recruit to Mosley's cause was, however, no great surprise. Lady Cynthia Blanche Mosley, the daughter of an earl, had married Mosley in 1920 and they joined the Labour Party together in 1924. She was elected Labour MP for Stoke-on-Trent in 1929, three years after her husband has entered Parliament.[34] She followed him into the New Party despite his affair with her younger sister Lady Alexander, but did not stand in the 1931 wipe-out, and drifted away from her husband politically, having no sympathy for his move towards fascism. She died in 1933 at 34 after an operation for peritonitis.[35]

It is another uncomfortable fact for modern sensibilities that several prominent members of the Suffragette movement were at the centre of Mosley's Fascist movement. In 1914 Norah Elam shared a cell in Holloway Prison with Emmeline Pankhurst, later to stand unsuccessfully as a Conservative MP. In 1940 Elam was returned to the same prison alongside Diana Mosley. She was a militant suffragette, anti-vivisectionist and feminist who believed that Fascism would benefit all her causes. During her time as general secretary of the Women's Social and Political Union she was imprisoned three times for 'acts of terrorism' and so received the Union's hunger strike medal with three bars. In 1932 she gravitated to the BUP.

Mosley used her suffragette past to counter the criticism that fascism was anti-feminist saying that her prospective candidacy on the BUF ticket 'killed for all time the suggestion that National Socialism proposed putting British women back in the home'.[36] Mosley told a meeting in Northampton: 'Mrs Elam had fought in the past for women's suffrage ... and was a great example of the emancipation of women in Britain.'

From the start, the serial womaniser Mosley had understood the importance, after female franchise had been delivered, of the women's votes. The BUF targeted young women in recruitment drives, and not just to feed his own sexual appetites. Former suffragettes were drawn to the BUF for a variety of reasons. Many felt the movement's energy reminded them of the suffragettes, while others felt the BUF's economic policies would offer them true equality – unlike its continental counterparts, the movement insisted it would not require women to return to domesticity and that the corporatist state would ensure adequate representation for housewives, while it would also guarantee equal wages for women and remove restrictions on the employment of married women. The BUF, concerned about the impact on their ideal of white Britishness due to a falling birth rate, also offered support for new mothers while also offering effective birth control.[37]

As a Suffragette Mary Sophia Allen was imprisoned three times in 1909 for smashing windows, including at the Inland Revenue and Liberal Club in Bristol and at the Home Office.[38] At the outbreak of the First World War, she joined the Women Police Volunteers and served at Grantham and Kingston upon Hull overseeing the morals of women in the vicinity of army barracks. She became the WPV Commandant in 1920 and was sent to Germany to advise on the policing of British troops stationed there. During the 1926 General Strike she devoted her organisational skills to strike-breaking. Home Office records covering the period 1927–34 reveal that she kept dossiers on people she suspected of activities connected with vice and white slavery and was also suspected of fascist activities. She met Hitler in 1934 and discussed women police with him. She was captivated by the Fuhrer and expressed her admiration for him in public. She met Mosley at the January Club in April 1932, going on to speak at the club following her visit to Germany, 'to learn the truth about of the position of German womanhood'.[39] She was suspected of spying for the Nazis, but this was never proved. When war broke out a security review described her as a 'crank', and instead of internment she was restricted to within a five-mile radius of her Cornwall home and banned from using cars, bicycles, telephones and the wireless.[40]

Mosley faced disruption of New Party meetings and instituted a corps of black-uniformed paramilitary stewards, the Fascist Defence Force, nicknamed 'Blackshirts.' The party was frequently involved in violent confrontations and riots, particularly with Communist and Jewish groups and especially in London. At a large Mosley rally at Olympia on 7 June 1934, his bodyguards' violence caused bad publicity. This and the Night of the Long Knives in Germany in which Hitler brutally purged his 'Brownshirts' led to the loss of most of the BUF's mass support. Nevertheless, Mosley continued espousing anti-Semitism. At one of his New Party meetings in Leicester in April 1935, he stated, 'For the first time I openly and publicly challenge the Jewish interests of this country, commanding commerce, commanding the press, commanding the cinema, dominating the City of London, killing industry with their sweat-shops. These great interests are not intimidating, and will not intimidate, the Fascist movement of the modern age.'[41]

On October 4 1936, Mosley and the BUF attempted to march through an area of the East End with a high proportion of Jewish residents, and violence resulted between local and nationally organised protesters trying to block the march, and police trying to force it through, since called the Battle of Cable Street. The incident has gone into socialist history, and Jeremy Corbyn has claimed that his parents took part in routing the Fascists. The Board of Deputies of British Jews denounced the march as anti-Semitic and urged Jews to stay away, and an estimated 100,000 local residents of the area petitioned the Home Office to ban the march because of the strong likelihood of violence. That was refused and the Metropolitan Police sent a massive police escort to protect the march.[42] The local branch of the Communist Party, who had initially opposed any counter demonstration, quickly organised opposition, building barricades near the junction with Christian Street in Stepney.

Communist Party activist Reg Weston recalled: 'The fascists were assembling by the Royal Mint and police started to make baton charges, both foot and mounted, to try to clear a way for them to escort a march. They did not succeed. A barricade started to go up. A lorry was overturned, furniture was piled up, paving stones and a builders' yard helped to complete the barrier. The police managed to clear the first but found a second behind it and then a third. Marbles were thrown under the hooves of the police horses; volleys of bricks met every baton charge.'[43]

The main confrontation took place around Gardiner's Corner in Whitechapel when an estimated 20,000 anti-fascist demonstrators were met by up to 7,000 policemen, some mounted and some expressing clear Blackshirt sympathies, who attempted to clear the road to permit the march of between two and three thousand Fascists.[44] The demonstrators fought back with sticks, rocks, chair legs and other improvised weapons. Rubbish, rotten vegetables and the contents of chamber pots were thrown at the police by women in houses along the street.

Weston wrote: 'The packed crowds that day consisted of many thousands of non-Jewish Londoners. As far as the religious leaders of the Jewish community were concerned, the Board of Deputies of British Jews, their top authority, made special calls the previous week opposing any physical confrontation with the Mosleyites, urging their congregation to stay indoors. They pursued the same fatal policy that the Jewish leaders in Germany had pursued only four or five years before when faced with the Brownshirts of Hitler. We know where that led. But their followers had more sense. They came out in their thousands. The opposition in the East End itself was organised largely by the grassroots Jewish organisations, the workers' circles, the furniture and garment workers' trades unions, by the shops and the workshops. It was also organised, on almost a military scale, in the last few days by the Communists who had a great deal of influence and a vigorous membership in the area. At that time the Communist Party in Britain was a party with strong roots in the trades unions, in many workplaces and among the unemployed. A significant section of the cultural and intellectual classes also were members or sympathisers of the party. Writers, artists, actors, musicians and scientists contributed.'[45]

Police Commissioner Philip Game persuaded Mosley to disperse his Blackshirts towards Hyde Park on public safety grounds. Mosley, faced with demonstrators capable of copying his strong-arm tactics, bottled it. Weston continued: 'Back in Stepney and the East End there was almost unbelievable delight. We had won. The fascists had been defeated and humiliated. The police too and the authorities had been proved unable to protect them. Hastily a victory march had been organised to follow the route from Cable Street to Victoria Park where Mosley had planned to address his army. Hundreds joined in. Thousands stood on the pavements and in the roads, clapping and cheering as we marched on. In those days we marched, often in ranks of fours, under the leadership of the ex-servicemen of the not so far away World War I.

'Not all the bystanders clapped and cheered. At a few of the street corners in Bethnal Green and Hackney on the way – a very few – there were knots of those who jeered and spat and stretched out their right arms in salute to their leader. Mosley had his roots in the East End, not so much in the working class but in those intermediate groups, the lower, lower, middle class of costermongers, street traders, market stallmen, small shopkeepers, bookies' runners and those living by their wits... They jeered us and, strangely enough, no one retaliated – except with words. Things moved too fast.'[46]

It is important to emphasise again that the most virulent anti-Semitism existed on the Right and when Mosley tried to build a mass fascist movement in Britain, it was the left that opposed him and defeated him. Thousands of rank-and-file Labour Party members and supporters took an active part in Cable Street and other head-on confrontations, but they acted against the orders of the Labour Leadership. When the BUF held a rally in Hyde Park on 9 September 1934, the 3,000 fascists were confronted by a counter demonstration 120,000 strong. The Labour leadership had urged people to stay away. John Strachey condemned Labour's tactics at the rally: 'Stay away from the fascist demonstration; ignore fascism; it will all blow over. I believe it true to say that the Labour Party have not yet issued a single leaflet or pamphlet on the subject, and definitely tried to prevent all members of the Labour Party from taking part in a demonstration of this sort.' The same line was taken at Cable Street. While up to 300,000 anti-Fascists took to the streets to stop the march, putting up barricades and fighting the police, the Labour Party conference was meeting. Herbert Morrison, speaking on behalf of the leadership, condemned the violence which he blamed equally on the Communists and the BUF and called for new legislation to strengthen police powers. That was the Labour leadership's solution. prosecutions resulted in the imprisonment of Durham miners fighting for union recognition. Even Morrison's sympathetic biographers admit that his stance resulted in him being 'hated by many active in the Labour movement' and his advocacy of 'lectures and leaflets' to fight the fascists was regarded as 'laughable' by those 'in the thick of the disturbances'.[47] And internal party organisations that had been on the front line combating the BUF were penalised – the Socialist League was disaffiliated and the party's League of Youth was purged.

Mosley continued to organise marches policed by the Blackshirts, and a week after the battle gangs of young BUF members, taking advantage of the withdrawal of police to keep order at a communist gathering, burst into Mile End Road and smashed up Jewish shops. The government finally bowed to Labour demands and passed the Public Order Act which banned political uniforms and quasi-military style organisations and came into effect on 1 January 1937.[48] Ironically, the new law was first used against Durham miners fighting for union recognition in the London County Council elections that year, the BUF stood in three wards in East London, its strongest areas, polling up to a quarter of the vote. But by then the BUF was a busted flush outside its strongholds. After Cable Street Mosley found it impossible to book larger venues, and marches were reduced to impromptu walkabouts with Mosley shouting 'Britain First' from his loudspeaker lorry. As the fee-paying membership dwindled, Mosley made most of the Blackshirt employees redundant, having spent large amounts of his private fortune on the BUF. As the European situation moved towards war, the BUF began to nominate Parliamentary by-election candidates and launched campaigns on the theme of Mind Britain's Business. His Britain First rally at the Earls Court Exhibition Hall on 16 July 1939 was the biggest indoor political rally in British history, with a reported 30,000 attendees, but that proved to be a last gasp. After the outbreak of war, Mosley led the campaign for a negotiated peace, but after Dunkirk, the Blitz and the Battle of Britain, public opinion turned even more against him and he was interned under defence of the realm legislation.[49] The same fate met the other most active fascists in Britain, including John Beckett, resulting in the BUF's practical removal at an organised level from the UK.

The decline of the BUF can be reflected in the career of Tommy Moran. A former coal miner and engineer, he served with the infant RAF and the Royal Naval Reserve and joined the Labour Party but failed to make much impact. He joined the BUF in 1933 and organised a local branch in Derby. He became known as a robust speaker and was lured to the party's London HQ. His wife, Toni, also joined and won herself a reputation as a virulently anti-Semitic orator in the Manchester area.[50] In 1934 Mosley sent him to South Wales to recruit miners to the cause. He was not warmly welcomed the following year in Tonypandy, a location central to socialist iconography given earlier riotous clashes between striking miners and the police. Around 6,000 people gathered to hear him and other speakers, but they were stoned off the stage before he had uttered more than a few words. It marked the end of the BUF as a force in Wales. Moran was sent to more fertile territory in Northampton. He received minor head injuries at Cable Street and film cameras recorded him in the thick of several brawls.[51] He then became one of the last BUF election candidates when he stood in the 1940 Silvertown by-election in West Ham, campaigning on a platform calling for an immediate peace with Nazi Germany and won a derisory 115 votes.[52] Just before internment, he effectively took over the running of the BUF, and continued to do so behind barbed wire on the Isle of Man, his activities benignly ignored by the guards.[53]

***

Manny Shinwell, who had lost his Scottish seat at the previous contest, returned to the Commons in 1935 after defeating MacDonald for Seaham Harbour, County Durham. He campaigned vigorously for Britain to support the Popular Front government against the Fascist Franco's forces. During a heated Commons debate in 1938 he punched Tory MP Robert Tatton Bower in the face, causing internal bleeding and a burst eardrum, after Bower told him to 'go back to Poland!' Shinwell took that as an anti-Semitic remark.[54]

The number of Jews in Labour's parliamentary ranks had grown at a snail's pace since Shinwell's initial 1922 victory. Leslie Haden Guest was elected for Southwark North in 1923 and founded the Labour Party Commonwealth Group. He had converted to Judaism in order to marry but renounced that and all religious faiths in 1924.[55] Marion Phillips was elected MP for Sunderland in 1929. An immigrant from Australia, she had worked under Beatrice Webb on a Commission investigating the Poor Laws.[56] She was secretary of the Women's Labour League from 1912 and described its role as 'keeping the Labour Party well informed of the needs of women and providing women with the means of becoming educated in political matters'. In this endeavour she provoked about a quarter of a million housewives to take part in the Labour movement and helped popularise issues such as equality for women in the workplace, school meals, clinics and play spaces for children, and a more humanitarian, safety-conscious, approach to the design of homes for ordinary families. George Russell

Strauss, the son of a Conservative MP, was educated at Rugby School where he and other Jewish boys were brutalised by fellow pupils and teachers, turning him into a life-long anti-racist campaigner. He took Lambeth North for Labour in 1929, lost it in 1931, and regained it in 1934. He eventually became the longest-serving MP, leaving the Commons in 1979.[57]

Barnett Janner was born to an Orthodox Jewish Litvak family in what is now Lithuania but before his first birthday he moved to Barry, Glamorgan, where his father opened a furniture shop. A British artilleryman during the Great War, in 1921 he stood unsuccessfully for election to Cardiff city council as a candidate of the Comrades of the Great War. Three years later he had joined the Liberal Party, and in 1926 he was elected to the Board of Deputies of British Jews, subsequently becoming a member of the executive of the British Zionist Federation. He failed in his bid to be elected Liberal MP for Cardiff Central, and again in contests for Whitechapel and St George's constituency in the East End. He finally entered Parliament in 1935, standing as a Liberal and Anti-Fascist candidate; he lost it back to Labour. Within a year, Janner had joined Labour, and was quickly chosen as prospective candidate for Leicester West but the outbreak of warfare cancelled elections and he had to wait until the 1945 contest before re-entering Westminster.[58]

Samuel Sydney Silverman, later best known as a vocal opponent of the death penalty, was born into a poor Jewish draper's family in the Kensington Fields area of Liverpool. During the First World War he was a conscientious objector and served three prison sentences for his pacifism. He was elected MP for Colne in 1935. He supported the Jewish cause worldwide and the Nazi regime persuaded him to re-think his pacifist ideals.[59] Lewis Silkin, a London solicitor, was elected MP for Peckham in 1936 and later served in the Attlee government as minister for town and country planning.[60]

The up-and-down, in-and-out parliamentary careers of those listed above reflected tumultuous times. As the world fell headlong towards another global conflict, Labour and its left continued their own internal battles over Zionism, with the left regarding a Jewish state as a potential socialist paradise, and the Right championing the interests of the Arab world.

A good example of leftist divisions over Zionism is the career of Susan Lawrence, one of the earliest female Labour MPs. Born into a wealthy family and educated at Newnham College, Cambridge, she was converted to socialism and became a Labour member of the London County Council, becoming close to Sidney and Beatrice Webb. During the First World War her principal concern was improving the conditions of female factory workers. Post-war, as a member of Poplar council led at the time by George Lansbury, she defied central government and refused to set a rate, arguing that the poverty in the area meant that the poor were being asked to pay for the poor. She spent five weeks in Holloway Prison but ultimately, she and her fellow councillors' campaign succeeded – the government passed a law to equalise Poor Law rates.

In the 1923 she became one of the first three female Labour MPs but lost when the MacDonald government fell. She bounced back in a 1926 by-election. She was appointed a junior health minister in the second minority Labour Government elected in 1929 and became the first woman to chair the annual party conference in Llandudno in 1930. Like the vast majority of Labour MPs in Parliament, she refused to take part in MacDonald's National Government in 1931, and she lost her seat in the 1931 general election. In 1935, Lawrence visited Palestine and was impressed by Zionist kibbutzim and argued at a Labour conference that a socialist utopia was being created in Palestine which was benefitting all workers. But, after the government in 1936 appointed a Royal Commission under Lord Peel to investigate how the Mandate was working, in view of strife between Jews and Arabs, she wrote a memorandum for the Labour Party's Advisory Committee on Imperial Affairs stressing the problems arising for the Arabs because Jewish development was going so far, so fast. The Mandate authorities, she felt, had neglected Arab needs. She was largely ignored and spent much of the rest of her life working for the blind.

5

George Orwell and the War against Fascism

'the personal characteristics of a Jew'

As the Luftwaffe began its Blitz on London in 1940, the iconic socialist writer George Orwell heard a rumour that 'Jews greatly predominate among the people sheltering in the Tube.' He wrote in his diary: 'Must try and verify this.' Ten days later he went underground to see the crowds sheltering in Chancery Lane, Oxford Circus and Baker Street stations as the air raid sirens blared above. He recorded: 'Not all Jews, but, I think, a higher proportion of Jews than one would normally see in a crowd of this size.' He wrote that Jews 'have a way of making themselves conspicuous'.[1] His motives in investigating rumours are not clear; he must have known that civilians, Jewish or otherwise, were simply obeying instructions in terrifying circumstances during the first year of the Second World War where there was a common expectation that aerial warfare would obliterate cities and consume all within them.

By then, Orwell had established himself as the era's foremost left-wing writer despite his upper-middle class background as an old Etonian and former colonial officer. His behaviour in the Spanish Civil War, outlined in *Homage to Catalonia*, were also testament to both his personal bravery under fire and his reporting skills. But his background had imbued him with a kneejerk anti-Semitism that is clear, particularly in his early writings. After resigning as a policeman in Burma, the 24-year-old Orwell moved back to London at the end of 1927 and started investigating the reality of poverty in the capital. The following spring he moved to Paris and lived cheaply in the Latin Quarter to write in the shadows of Ernest Hemingway, F. Scott Fitzgerald and, he claimed, James Joyce.[2] Taken ill and robbed, he worked as a restaurant dishwasher before returning to his family home in Southwold. The result of his experiences was *Down and Out in Paris and London*. It made his name as a writer. C. Day Lewis wrote, 'Orwell's book is a tour of the underworld, conducted without hysteria or prejudice… a model of clarity and good sense.'[3] Compton Mackenzie wrote of Orwell's 'immensely interesting book … a genuine human document, which at the same time is written with so much artistic force that, in spite of the squalor and degradation thus unfolded, the result is curiously beautiful…'[4]

Orwell largely succeeded in portraying the grimmest of realities for those unable to get out of the poverty trap. It was also a good stab at recording the vernacular of street-level life and much of the four-letter language was toned down. What was not, however, was a three-letter word starting with J which was peppered through the book, generally reflecting the author's own prejudice rather than that of his subjects. The book, published the year Hitler came to power (1933), contains repulsive caricatures of Jews with justifications of violence in dealing with them. Writing of a Paris pawnbroker, a 'red-haired Jew, an extraordinarily disagreeable man', Orwell added, 'It would have been a pleasure to flatten the Jew's nose.' Arriving back in London he visited a coffee shop and saw that 'in a corner by himself a Jew, muzzle down in the plate, was guiltily wolfing bacon'. Others have pointed out that there is something loaded, too, about the reference to a 'muzzle', as if the man is not quite human, and the explanation for this sub-humanity has something to do with being Jewish. While the assorted, colourful, multinational lowlifes he encountered are referred to by their names, Jews are simply Jews. The anti-Semitism was noticed from the beginning, with publishers Gollancz forced to defend court challenges to the textual slurs on Jewry.

The definitive Orwell writer D. J. Taylor wrote: 'My own particular biographer's dilemma started with the discovery, in the files of the publisher Victor Gollancz Ltd, of a letter sent to Gollancz himself in the spring of 1933. The writer, Mr G. M. Lipsey, had read a copy of George Orwell's newly published *Down and Out in Paris and London*. He was furious, not only with Orwell but also with his publisher. 'On its merits or otherwise I have no desire to comment,' he commented.

'But I am appalled that a book containing insulting and odious remarks about Jews should be published by a firm bearing the name "Gollancz".' A spirited correspondence followed. There were threats of legal action, and finally the row fizzled out. Its shadow, though, hangs over much of Orwell's early writings, and indeed his whole attitude towards Jews, Jewishness and, later, the foundation of a Zionist state. Having read and annotated *Down and Out in Paris and London* half a dozen times, I was aware of the book's 'Jew' references, just as one is aware of them in, to select a random handful of Orwell's thirties contemporaries, the work of Anthony Powell, J. B. Priestley, T. S. Eliot and Graham Greene. Reading it again, in the light of the Lipsey remonstrance, I was struck by how oddly gratuitous they are.'[5]

In his journals and diaries, Orwell made numerous disparaging references to unnamed Jews. In *Burmese Days* he suggested that the only people who had benefited from the British Empire had been Jews and Scotsmen, another group he disliked. His friend the journalist Malcolm Muggeridge described him as being 'at heart strongly anti-Semitic', a man who gratuitously and repeatedly questioned his contemporaries' Jewishness and remarked on the preponderance of Jews working alongside him at the *Observer*. Orwell's diaries are also full of accusations that the Jews controlled the media.[6]

D. J. Taylor does not excuse Orwell, writing: 'One could ignore this, just possibly, if it existed in a single book. And yet for ten years the abstract figure of "the Jew" makes regular appearances in Orwell's diaries. Out tramping in the early 30s, he falls in with "a little Liverpool Jew, a thorough guttersnipe" with a face that recalls "some low-down carrion bird". Watching the crowds thronging the London Underground in October 1940, he decides that what is "bad" about the Jews is that they are not only conspicuous but go out of their way to make themselves so. He is particularly annoyed by "a regular comic-paper cartoon of a Jewess" who literally fights her way on to the train at Oxford Circus. Again, it is perfectly possible that the woman in question resembled an extra from *Fiddler On The Roof* and that the incident took place exactly as Orwell describes it. Even so, it is a safe bet that no early twenty-first century liberal will be able to read Orwell's account without clenching their teeth.' But Taylor added: 'It would be idle to classify Orwell as "anti-Semitic". He had dozens of Jewish friends and kept a vigilant eye out for evidence of anti-Semitism, both on theatre stages and in print. In fact, the complexities of what he thought and wrote about Jews defy easy summary (although it is worth pointing out that in an argument with Aneurin Bevan, he once referred to Zionists as "a gang of Wardour Street Jews" with a controlling interest over the British press).'[7]

It is easy to excuse such prejudice in a young man of his time and imbued with the standards and rhetoric of his class, and in a 1996 *Vanity Fair* column the late Christopher Hitchens wrote that Orwell 'did have a slightly thuggish side to him on occasion, making unkind remarks about "Nancy" homosexuals and (when he was younger) Jews. But he always strove to overcome these scars of his upbringing.'[8] Hitchens suggests that Orwell's antipathy toward Jews was a passing phase, an adolescent phase that he outgrew. However, Orwell's innate, inbred anti-Semitism was not confined to youthful missteps on the way to inclusive socialism. In his diaries, columns and some of his books the prejudice emerges loud and clear. Orwell never fully grew out of his ill feelings toward Jews. Even in his last years Orwell was always quick to identify people, gratuitously, as Jews, in a way in which their Jewishness is seen an explanation of their situation, actions or appearance.

From around 1940, Orwell filled a notebook with 135 names of people he considered crypto-Communists, Stalinists or fellow travellers. The list included future Labour Leader Michael Foot, the broadcaster and writer J. B. Priestly, and the historian E. H. Carr. Describing a Hollywood superstar he wrote: 'Charlie Chaplin – Jewish?' The half-Jewish poet Stephen Spender is damned as a 'sentimental sympathiser … tendency towards homosexuality'. Other long-forgotten characters on the list he described as 'Polish Jew', 'English Jew', 'Jewess'.[9] And while Hitchens later wrote: 'One of the many things that made Orwell so interesting was his self-education away from such prejudices, which also included a marked dislike of the Jews,' he added: 'But anyone reading the early pages of these accounts and expeditions will be struck by how vividly Orwell still expressed his unmediated disgust at some of the human specimens with whom he came into contact. When joining a group of itinerant hop pickers he is explicitly repelled by the personal characteristics of a Jew to whom he cannot bear even to give a name, characteristics which he somehow manages to identify as Jewish.'[10]

Only a few months after he expressed the xenophobic view that European refugees, including Jews, secretly despised England and surreptitiously sympathised with Hitler, he slammed the British authorities for squandering the talents of Jewish Central European emigré Arthur Koestler. Anshel Pfeffer noted: 'When Orwell contradicts himself, as he very often does, he tries his best to be aware of the fact and to profit from it.'[11]

However, when the Second World War broke out, Orwell did struggle both to understand his anti-Semitism and to eradicate it. In a much-quoted essay, he wrote: 'There are about 400,000 known Jews in Britain, and in addition some thousands or, at most, scores of thousands of Jewish refugees who have entered the country from 1934 onwards. The Jewish population is almost entirely concentrated in half a dozen big towns and is mostly employed in the food, clothing and furniture trades. A few of the big monopolies, such as the ICI, one or two leading newspapers and at least one big chain of department stores are Jewish-owned or partly Jewish-owned, but it would be very far from the truth to say that British business life is dominated by Jews. The Jews seem, on the contrary, to have failed to keep up with the modern tendency towards big amalgamations and to have remained fixed in those trades which are necessarily carried out on a small scale and by old-fashioned methods.

'I start off with these background facts, which are already known to any well-informed person, in order to emphasise that there is no real Jewish "problem" in England. The Jews are not numerous or powerful enough, and it is only in what are loosely called "intellectual circles" that they have any noticeable influence. Yet it is generally admitted that anti-Semitism is on the increase, that it has been greatly exacerbated by the war, and that humane and enlightened people are not immune to it. It does not take violent forms (English people are almost invariably gentle and law-abiding), but it is ill-natured enough, and in favourable circumstances it could have political results.'[12]

He went on to give examples of everyday snatches of wartime conversations he had picked up:

> Middle-aged office employee: 'I generally come to work by bus. It takes longer, but I don't care about using the Underground from Golders Green nowadays. There's too many of the Chosen Race travelling on that line.'
>
> Tobacconist (woman): 'No, I've got no matches for you. I should try the lady down the street. SHE'S always got matches. One of the Chosen Race, you see.'
>
> Young intellectual, Communist or near-Communist: 'No, I do NOT like Jews. I've never made any secret of that. I can't stick them. Mind you, I'm not anti-Semitic, of course.'

Middle-class woman: 'Well, no one could call me anti-Semitic, but I do think the way these Jews behave is too absolutely stinking. The way they push their way to the head of queues, and so on. They're so abominably selfish. I think they're responsible for a lot of what happens to them.'

Milk roundsman: 'A Jew don't do no work, not the same as what an Englishman does. "E's too clever. We work with this 'ere" (flexes his biceps). "They work with that there" (taps his forehead).'

Chartered accountant, intelligent, left-wing in an undirected way: 'These bloody Yids are all pro-German. They'd change sides tomorrow if the Nazis got here. I see a lot of them in my business. They admire Hitler at the bottom of their hearts. They'll always suck up to anyone who kicks them.'

Intelligent woman, on being offered a book dealing with anti-Semitism and German atrocities: 'Don't show it me, PLEASE don't show it to me. It'll only make me hate the Jews more than ever.'

- Orwell's acknowledgement of anti-Semitism, initially bereft of any personal *mea culpa*, paints too rosy and gentle a picture compared to the reality. Mosley and his Blackshirts may have been tucked away relatively safely in internment camps, but a visceral wish to blame the Jews for everything from bombs to food shortages was evident across Britain.
- National Archives files not released until 2018 from Winston Churchill's propaganda and censorship office showed that throughout the struggle against Hitler, British prejudice towards Jews grew relentlessly.[13] The file, entitled *Antisemitism in Great Britain*, released earlier than intended due to a Freedom of Information request from *The Times*, shows that officials confronted by reports of rising prejudice decided that Jews themselves were to blame. On 26 May 1943, Cyril Radcliffe, the ministry's Director-General, gathered his regional information officers to brief him and subsequently wrote to his minister that the only regions untroubled by anti-Semitism were north eastern England and Northern Ireland. He wrote: 'All the others showed general agreement on the fact that from the beginning of the war there had been a considerable increase in anti-Semitic feeling. They seemed to regard it as quite beyond argument that the increase of anti-Semitic feeling was caused by serious errors of conduct on the part of Jews... This view held true both of officers dealing with industrial centres and those dealing with rural areas;

it held true of officers coming from old-established Jewish centres, such as Manchester and Leeds, and officers coming from areas which had known the Jews mainly as war-time evacuees from the cities. The main heads of complaint against them were undoubtedly an inordinate attention to the possibilities of the "black market" and a lack of pleasant standards of conduct as evacuees. I reminded them that it was part of the tragedy of the Jewish position that their peculiar qualities that one could well admire in easier times of peace, such as their commercial initiative and drive and their determination to preserve themselves as an independent community in the midst of the nations they lived in, were just the things that told against them in wartime when a nation dislikes the struggle for individual advantages and feels the need for homogeneity above everything else. I thought that our main contribution from headquarters would be to try to keep before people's minds the recollection that anti-Semitism was peculiarly the badge of the Nazi.'[14]

About half of those fleeing the East End Blitz were Jews. Among prejudiced comments from provincials were that Jewish evacuees had 'extraordinary bad manners – noisy, aggressive, loud and tactless'. The worst civilian disaster of the war unleashed a wave of anti-Semitism. In March 1943, 173 people were killed in a stampede at the Bethnal Green bomb shelter in east London. The public blamed panicking Jews, although when the bodies were identified only five Jewish people were among the victims. An inquiry found the slur to be baseless. Radcliffe wrote: 'If specific stories hostile to the Jews could be traced and pinned down as untruths, such as the recent canard of the Jews being responsible for the London shelter disaster, this should be done by countering it with the individuals who were putting it about, not by giving it general publicity.'

The Times reported: 'As Mr Radcliffe's minute was being typed, in Amsterdam the Nazis began to round up Jews for the death camps. Anne Frank, still 13 and hiding in the secret annexe of a warehouse, was recording in her diary how, despite the hot weather, the family needed to light a fire each day to burn vegetable peelings. Any rubbish thrown into bins might arouse suspicions.'[13]

Churchill's first information minister was Duff Cooper, married to the society beauty Lady Diana Cooper, and their social set ranged from the Rothschilds to the Mosleys. Of the latter, he confided in his diary, 'The sight and sound of them talking their tedious twaddle makes me feel sick.' Nevertheless, the Coopers had attended the Mosleys' fancy dress barge party in Venice on 7 September 1922 which featured a guest dressed as a Venetian Jew. Cooper had been an opponent of appeasement and was the only cabinet minister to resign in protest against Neville Chamberlain's popular but doomed Munich agreement with Hitler. Cooper was alert to anti-Semitism. In the final years of peace, he warned Chamberlain's secretary of state for war, the Jewish politician Leslie Hore-Belisha, of impending bigotry. Hore-Belisha, who became a lifelong friend, wrote in his diary that Cooper predicted that 'the military element might be very unyielding, and they might try to make it hard for me as a Jew.' Once war broke out Chamberlain indeed sacked Hore-Belisha because 'there was a prejudice against him'. Hore-Belisha was then vetoed as a potential minister of information by the Foreign Office, whose attitude was summed up by the undersecretary Sir Alexander Cadogan: 'Jew control of our propaganda would be a major disaster.'[14]

An early warning was sounded of wartime British prejudice by Anthony de Rothschild who wrote to 'Dear Duff' on 26 March 1941 that: 'There is an impression that there has been of recent weeks a growth of anti-Semitism in the country and there is some reason for supposing that it may not be unconnected with enemy propaganda, although this is hard, of course, to establish. Representatives of the Jewish community in London have considered the matter and are naturally perturbed from their own point of view, but it also seems to them that developments on this line help the enemy and damage the war effort.' He suggested a radio broadcast condemning anti-Semitism as potentially destructive to Britain. But Cooper's position as minister of information was weak. John Julius Norwich recalled: 'The appointment was not a success. The press, terrified of censorship, mounted a virulent campaign against him.' Newspapers derided the ministry's social surveyors, sent out to question the public about morale, as 'Cooper's snoopers'. Four months after replying to de Rothschild, Cooper was replaced as minister of information by Churchill's friend Brendan Bracken, an Irish Catholic fantasist who entered British high society by pretending to be the orphaned son of Australians who died in a bush fire.

Meanwhile the virulent anti-Semite William Joyce, known for his catchphrase 'Germany Calling', sought to undermine British morale with broadcasts threatening bombing raids against civilian targets. His propaganda, laughed at by many, hit home for some.

A Special Branch's secret summary of anti-Jewish actions from November 1942 to April 1943 reported:

> 15 November 1942: Large numbers of an anti-Semitic stickyback portraying two Jews and bearing the words 'Britannia rules the waves – yeth, but we rule Britannia' found affixed to doors and windows of business premises in Shoreditch, east London.
>
>   1–15 January 1943: A Fascist typewritten broadsheet called *The Flame* featured anti-Semitism.
>
>   March 16–31 1943: A pamphlet by R. D. Lees, who formed a branch of the wartime far-Right movement the British National Party in Blackpool, argued that anti-Semitism was provoked by Jews. He opposed any measures for succouring Jews now under Nazi domination.
>
>   March 1943: Anti-Semitic slogans chalked and painted on walls and pavements in London districts and Old Trafford, Manchester. Reference was made to the Jewish connections of Churchill, the Foreign Secretary Anthony Eden and other public figures. At Hove, typewritten slips bearing the words 'Down with the filthy Jews' were found fixed to shop windows of a tobacconist and confectioners, the proprietor of which was Jewish, and to the windows of a Jewish hotel.
>
>   1–15 April 1943: Edward Godfrey of the British National Party bought 1,000 copies of the anti-Semitic booklet *The Truth About The Jews* published by Alexander Ratcliffe of the British Protestant League, Glasgow.
>
>   16–30 April: Anti-Semitic notices such as 'burn the Jews' were chalked on five occasions in the Paddington area of west London. Slogans were chalked on a wall in Old Trafford...

The importance attached by Cooper, at the Ministry of Information, to challenging anti-Semitism never bore fruit. Bracken would be the minister who received Radcliffe's memorandum recording that prejudice had risen throughout the war. In north-west England, police in Salford discovered a clandestine basement printing press that was flooding the market with forged clothing coupons. In a confidential memo of 17 April 1942, a regional information officer wrote: 'Since the Salford coupon case we have observed anxiety among the Jews culminating in the visit of two representative Jews to the regional office.'

Jews believed that they were being discriminated against for jobs: 'In spite of the shortage of nurses and the wishes of the Ministry of Health, local authorities are unwilling to employ Jewish girls.' The official blamed Jews for the prejudice against them: 'It appears that the Jewish leaders are so anxious to avoid admitting that "The People" have been especially blameworthy in black markets that they are unwilling to take strong spiritual and communal action. Blindness to facts and alternate periods of arrogance and whines are unlikely to endear the Jewish cause to Britain.' A London civil servant applauded the 'reasoned arguments put forward in this memorandum'.

The Ministry of Information was secretly housed away from Whitehall in the University of London's Senate House in Bloomsbury and there was hostility to an institution dedicated to such an un-British endeavour as propaganda. The ministry employed some of the finest writing talents of the age, including Laurie Lee, John Betjeman and Graham Greene. Orwell's wife worked in its censorship division, while the author himself broadcast ministry-approved propaganda at the BBC. In *Nineteen Eighty-Four* a thinly disguised Senate House served as the Ministry of Truth where Winston Smith worked. There has been speculation that Big Brother was deliberately given the same initials as Brendan Bracken.

The mothballed report showed that Jews in Britain were well aware of their fate if the Germans invaded. Some East End Jews, knowing what had been done to their compatriots by the Nazis in Germany, made ready for the coming of Hitler by carrying pellets of poison and some allegedly trekked out of London pushing handcarts containing their possessions. An Eastender born in 1902 told the Jewish Museum London's oral histories that he believed that British anti-Semites would not have bothered to gas Jews, as Hitler had done: 'I've always maintained it, if they had their way here … while you're alive, they would absolutely chop lumps off you. They wouldn't wait to put you in a gas chamber, they'd be so eager to get at you.' The British government's only wartime acknowledgement of the Holocaust came in 1942 when Anthony Eden told the Commons that 'the German authorities are now carrying into effect Hitler's oft-repeated intention to exterminate the Jewish people in Europe.' However, Victor Cavendish-Bentinck, chairman of the joint intelligence committee, regarded the reported use of gas chambers as an exaggeration by Jews 'to stoke us up'. Professor Tony Kushner wrote: 'Doubts of the atrocity stories, based on distrust of Jewish sources, continued in government circles until the end of the war.'

On 2 June 1943, as the Lvov ghetto in Poland was liquidated by the Nazis and the last of the city's 110,000 Jews were sent to a concentration camp, in Britain the noted Suffragette Margaret Corbett Ashby sounded the alarm about rising anti-Semitism in Britain. At 61, she was the *grande dame* of English liberalism and was invited to a meeting of the committee advising Bracken. She confided her concerns that Jews in Britain were facing increasing hostility and prejudice. She was heard in respectful silence, but behind her back, officials treated her warning with disdain. One unnamed civil servant, quoting the Special Branch reports listed above, wrote to a colleague: 'You will agree that there is nothing in all this to suggest anything in the nature of organised activity, at any rate on an important scale.' A scrawled response to the typed memorandum marked 'Secret' states: 'I did not think that Mrs Corbett Ashby's account showed signs of careful consideration.'

When the Ministry of Information staged a touring show, *The Evil We Fight*, highlighting Nazi atrocities in 1944, copies of a subversive pamphlet were found stuffed into exhibition screens. The typewritten, two-page tract warned that parliament was controlled by 'The City of London International Jew Finance' and rejoiced that 'Hitler is ridding the world of Jews and Judaism'. Condemning the British authorities, it said: 'They lock up Fascists who at least want Britain for the British and clear the country of these slimy, oily, greasy, immoral Jewish dagoes ... ANTI-SEMITISM MUST BE ENCOURAGED! Britain for the British and to Hell with Jews and all other alien swine.' One official wrote: 'It is my opinion that the open letter to fellow-Britons is not anti-Semitism – it is pure German propaganda. Anti-Semitism is merely a part of the whole.' Another commented in a handwritten noted that it was childish nonsense which left him quite unconcerned. At the Ministry of Information, they kept calm and carried on.

Academic Tony Kushner argued that 'anti-Semitism has not been alien to the British experience, and can indeed become respectable in times of crisis, as was the case with the internment panic in the summer of 1940. The basic difference between British anti-Semitism in the war and that of Germany or France was the role of the state. The British government, in principle, was opposed to anti-Semitism, but that this did not mean it was immune from hostility towards Jews. Indeed, its antipathy partially explains the feeble response to the crisis of European Jewry and the scale of alien internment.

The continuation of British liberal democracy has put restraints on the success of anti-Semitism without being able to destroy it'.[15]

Bernard Crick's biography claims that Orwell's newspaper writing had by 1944 shown him 'fully purged of the mild and conventional but more or less clear anti-Semitism which appeared early in *Down and Out in Paris and London* and his wartime diaries'.

In his 1945 essay *Antisemitism in Britain* Orwell wrote: 'The Jews are accused of specific offences (for instance, bad behaviour in food queues) ... but it is obvious that these accusations merely rationalise some deep-rooted prejudice. To attempt to counter them with facts and statistics is useless, and may sometimes be worse than useless.' People, he wrote, can remain anti-Semitic, or at least anti-Jewish, while being fully aware that their outlook is indefensible. If you dislike somebody, you dislike him and there is an end of it: your feelings are not made any better by a recital of his virtues. He continued: 'It so happens that the war has encouraged the growth of anti-Semitism and even, in the eyes of many ordinary people, given some justification for it. To begin with, the Jews are one people of whom it can be said with complete certainty that they will benefit by an Allied victory. Consequently the theory that "this is a Jewish war" has a certain plausibility, all the more so because the Jewish war effort seldom gets its fair share of recognition.'

Orwell pointed out that Jews were active in precisely those trades certain to arouse jealousy and hostility in war-time – selling food, clothes, furniture and tobacco, which at times of chronic shortages led to claims of overcharging, black-marketing and favouritism. And he addressed the common charge that Jews behave in a cowardly way. He wrote that the Jewish quarter of Whitechapel was one of the first areas to be heavily blitzed in 1940, 'with the natural result that swarms of Jewish refugees distributed themselves all over London'. He argued that 'one of the marks of anti-Semitism is an ability to believe stories that could not possibly be true. One could see a good example of this in the strange accident that occurred in London in 1942, when a crowd, frightened by a bomb-burst nearby, fled into the mouth of an Underground station, with the result that something over a hundred people were crushed to death. The very same day it was repeated all over London that "the Jews were responsible". Clearly, if people will believe this kind of thing, one will not get much further by arguing with them. The only useful approach is to discover WHY they can swallow absurdities on one particular subject while remaining sane on others.'[16]

Orwell wrote that there was widespread awareness of the prevalence of anti-Semitic feeling, and an unwillingness to admit sharing it: 'Among educated people, anti-Semitism is held to be an unforgivable sin and in a quite different category from other kinds of racial prejudice. People will go to remarkable lengths to demonstrate that they are NOT anti-Semitic. Thus, in 1943 an intercession service on behalf of the Polish Jews was held in a synagogue in St John's Wood. The local authorities declared themselves anxious to participate in it, and the service was attended by the mayor of the borough in his robes and chain, by representatives of all the churches, and by detachments of RAF, Home Guards, nurses, Boy Scouts and what not. On the surface it was a touching demonstration of solidarity with the suffering Jews. But it was essentially a CONSCIOUS effort to behave decently by people whose subjective feelings must in many cases have been very different. That quarter of London is partly Jewish, anti-Semitism is rife there, and, as I well knew, some of the men sitting round me in the synagogue were tinged by it. Indeed, the commander of my own platoon of Home Guards, who had been especially keen beforehand that we should "make a good show" at the intercession service, was an ex-member of Mosley's Blackshirts. While this division of feeling exists, tolerance of mass violence against Jews, or, what is more important, anti-Semitic legislation, are not possible in England. It is not at present possible, indeed, that anti-Semitism should BECOME RESPECTABLE. But this is less of an advantage than it might appear.'[17]

With little irony or self-awareness, Orwell said that there had been conscious suppression, by all thoughtful people, of anything likely to wound Jewish susceptibilities. He went on: 'After 1934 the Jew joke disappeared as though by magic from postcards, periodicals and the music-hall stage, and to put an unsympathetic Jewish character into a novel or short story came to be regarded as anti-Semitism. On the Palestine issue, too, it was DE RIGUEUR among enlightened people to accept the Jewish case as proved and avoid examining the claims of the Arabs – a decision which might be correct on its own merits, but which was adopted primarily because the Jews were in trouble and it was felt that one must not criticise them. Thanks to Hitler, therefore, you had a situation in which the press was in effect censored in favour of the Jews while in private anti-Semitism was on the up-grade, even, to some extent, among sensitive and intelligent people. This was particularly noticeable in 1940 at the time of the internment of the refugees. Naturally, every thinking person felt that it was his duty to protest against the wholesale locking-up of unfortunate foreigners who for the most part were only in England because they were opponents of Hitler. Privately, however, one heard very different sentiments expressed. A minority of the refugees behaved in an exceedingly tactless way, and the feeling against them necessarily had an anti-Semitic undercurrent, since they were largely Jews. A very eminent figure in the Labour Party – I won't name him, but he is one of the most respected people in England – said to me quite violently: "We never asked these people to come to this country. If they choose to come here, let them take the consequences." Yet this man would as a matter of course have associated himself with any kind of petition or manifesto against the internment of aliens. This feeling that anti-Semitism is something sinful and disgraceful, something that a civilised person does not suffer from, is unfavourable to a scientific approach, and indeed many people will admit that they are frightened of probing too deeply into the subject. They are frightened, that is to say, of discovering not only that anti-Semitism is spreading, but that they themselves are infected by it.'[18] In that section Orwell significantly noted that many of those who confessed to anti-Semitic tendencies belonged to the left politically.

Orwell continued: 'To see this in perspective one must look back a few decades, to the days when Hitler was an out-of-work housepainter whom nobody had heard of. One would then find that though anti-Semitism is sufficiently in evidence now, it is probably LESS prevalent in England than it was thirty years ago. It is true that anti-Semitism as a fully thought-out racial or religious doctrine has never flourished in England. There has never been much feeling against inter-marriage, or against Jews taking a prominent part in public life. Nevertheless, thirty years ago it was accepted more or less as a law of nature that a Jew was a figure of fun and – though superior in intelligence – slightly deficient in "character". In theory a Jew suffered from no legal disabilities, but in effect he was debarred from certain professions. He would probably not have been accepted as an officer in the navy, for instance, nor in what is called a "smart" regiment in the army. A Jewish boy at a public school almost invariably had a bad time. He could, of course, live down his Jewishness if he was exceptionally charming or athletic, but it was an initial disability comparable to a stammer or a birthmark. Wealthy Jews tended to disguise themselves under aristocratic English or Scottish names,

Anti-Semitism and the Left

and to the average person it seemed quite natural that they should do this, just as it seems natural for a criminal to change his identity if possible.' That last comparison seems shocking today, but it is politic to give Orwell the benefit of the doubt.

Orwell peppered his essay with personal anecdotes which hint at his previous anti-Semitism: 'About twenty years ago, in Rangoon, I was getting into a taxi with a friend when a small ragged boy of fair complexion rushed up to us and began a complicated story about having arrived from Colombo on a ship and wanting money to get back. His manner and appearance were difficult to "place", and I said to him: "You speak very good English. What nationality are you?" He answered eagerly in his chi-chi accent: "I am a JOO, sir!" And I remember turning to my companion and saying, only partly in joke, "He admits it openly." All the Jews I had known till then were people who were ashamed of being Jews, or at any rate preferred not to talk about their ancestry, and if forced to do so tended to use the word "Hebrew". The working-class attitude was no better. The Jew who grew up in Whitechapel took it for granted that he would be assaulted, or at least hooted at, if he ventured into one of the Christian slums nearby, and the "Jew joke" of the music halls and the comic papers was almost consistently ill-natured.'

Orwell wrote that literary Jew-baiting reached an 'almost continental level of scurrility' from the pens of Hilaire Belloc, G.K. Chesterton and their followers but they were carrying on a perceptible anti-Semitic strain in English literature from Chaucer onwards. He claimed that passages which smacked of anti-Semitism to contemporary eyes could be found in the works of Shakespeare, Smollett, Thackeray, Bernard Shaw, H. G. Wells, T. S. Eliot, Aldous Huxley and various others. The only English writers he could think of who, before the days of Hitler, made a definite effort to stick up for Jews were Dickens and Charles Reade.

Orwell inserted an illuminating footnote at this point: '[It is interesting to compare the "Jew joke" with that other stand-by of the music halls, the "Scotch joke", which superficially it resembles. Occasionally a story is told (e.g. the Jew and the Scotsman who went into a pub together and both died of thirst) which puts both races on an equality, but in general the Jew is credited MERELY with cunning and avarice while the Scotsman is credited with physical hardihood as well. This is seen, for example, in the story of the Jew and the Scotsman who go together to a meeting which has been advertised as free.

Unexpectedly there is a collection, and to avoid this the Jew faints and the Scotsman carries him out. Here the Scotsman performs the athletic feat of carrying the other. It would seem vaguely wrong if it were the other way about.]'

Orwell disagreed that the war on Hitler had diminished widespread anti-Semitism in England. Instead, he argued, the war had opened up a sharp division between the politically conscious and those war-weary people whose native anti-Semitism had been deepened by the nervous strain of the previous six years. Those who would never admit to anti-Semitic feelings felt them nonetheless. By now Orwell regarded anti-Semitism as a neurosis. But he understood the common perception that Jews were exploiters because 'the Jew, in England, is generally a small businessman – that is to say a person whose depredations are more obvious and intelligible than those of, say, a bank or an insurance company.' From that came the belief that Jews spread disaffection and weaken national morale. Orwell poured scorn on those intellectuals who he believed would have surrendered in 1940 and described as nonsense the belief that the disaffected intelligentsia included a large number of Jews who were the enemies of native culture and national morale.

Orwell concluded that anti-Semitism was part of the larger problem of nationalism and that Jews were historically used as scapegoats for all of society's ills. The scale of anti-Semitism is more than people care to admit but, he insisted, it was not growing and the nature of the condition differed within every individual. More dangerously, to the modern view, he went on: 'A Jew, for example, would not be anti-Semitic: but then many Zionist Jews seem to me to be merely anti-Semites turned upside-down, just as many Indians and Negroes display the normal colour prejudices in an inverted form.' And finally, he believed that while anti-Semitism could be tackled and alleviated, it could never be cured thanks to human nature.[19]

Orwell's attitude to Jews by then involved a self-aware and useful contradiction. A man can be disgusted at the sight of easily identifiable Jews while having numerous Jewish friends and even admired Jewish contemporaries, and while he knows and writes that anti-Semitism is wrong, he also acknowledges that it is ineradicable in human society, even from oneself.

Anshel Pfeffer wrote: 'Orwell accurately sketched, and in many cases foresaw the hypocrisies and contradictions of modern ideology, politics and media. For his brave refusal to conform to any party line, he paid a heavy price. After resigning from the colonial Burmese police force, he lived most of his life as an itinerant writer, forced to accept ill-paying odd jobs due to a lack of fixed income. In revolutionary Spain, he nearly paid with his life for his opposition and outspoken criticism to the communist takeover of the Republican cause. Orwell achieved critical and commercial success only when he was already dying from tuberculosis, and yet 62 years later, most of his writings still resonate clearly in a world facing the challenges he was first to detect and define.' She went on: 'Orwell was nothing if not honest, and Hitchens is right to defend him. He did try to educate himself away from his native prejudices, and even if not entirely successful in defeating them, he was scathingly honest about them. And how many other writers can we say that about? Everyone has irrational dislikes and pet hatreds, some of them morally wrong, but we either outgrow them or they evolve with us, and we have to handle them somehow. Orwell put the handling of his own feelings toward Jews on public display, an act of daring unimaginable today by any "respectable" writer. If the involuntary thought – "what is wrong with these Jews?" – goes through my mind, does that make me prejudiced? And what if I confide that thought in my diary or to a friend?" Orwell realized the ugly truth that we are all prejudiced, and tried to deal with it out in the open.'[20]

Barry Rubin noted that the essay throws a spotlight on Orwell's background and privilege which he finally had the grace to admit to: 'England was a strange mix of tolerance and intolerance in earlier years. Orwell wrote that all the Jews he knew when he was younger were people who were ashamed of being Jews, or at any rate preferred not to talk about their ancestry. He notes also though, that things considered formerly acceptable in literature and elsewhere were no longer so. Orwell noted that anti-Semitism had been driven underground by the war and that the authorities and media went out of their way to avoid offending Jews in order to establish their credentials as not being antisemites. Two-thirds of a century later, Orwell's article has some interesting things to tell us in an era when antisemitism is reviving throughout the world. Sometimes, the word "Zionist" or "Israeli" is substituted for the word "Jew". But the tip-off is that the accusations continue to be basically the same ones: allegedly hating and deliberately oppressing non-Jews, greed, conspiracy, mysterious power, irrational behaviour, and the goal of world conquest.

'The first point Orwell's article reminds us of is that no Jew really has a good sense of the extent of anti-Semitism at any given place or time. This is so simply because anti-Semitic attitudes and remarks will or won't be expressed mainly behind his back. My personal experience bears this out: overwhelmingly, the main expressions of anti-Semitism I experienced personally did not come from direct expressions but from words I overheard accidentally in nearby conversations or things non-Jewish friends told me about.'[21]

D. J. Taylor wrote that 'Orwell's fixation with doling out the word "Jew" like a kind of party badge raises fundamental questions about the social milieu he inhabited and the upbringing that put stereotypes of this sort into his head. Above all, perhaps – and this is a man regularly marked down by posterity as a secular saint – it makes him seem human in a way that much of the posthumous embalming of his reputation does not.' Orwell's *Animal Farm* and *Nineteen Eighty-Four* were, and still are, castigated by the hard left who still defend Stalin's murderous regime. And his output continues to be attacked by elements of left and right. Much of the criticism is focused on his undoubted hackery as he struggled to earn a living up against deadlines and the 'horse for courses' ethos of journalism.

Ben Judah wrote: 'There is a simplicity and a clarity to Orwell's prose. It flows nicely. But there is also nothing special about it other than the fact it has been canonised as the ultimate in English authorial excellence. This is still very much a surprise to me, because there is just so much wrong with it. Are the violent caricatures of Jews in *Down and Out in Paris and London* really defending the downtrodden in 1933? Are the rantings (against amongst others, vegetarians) in *The Road to Wigan Pier* even coherent? Were the baying hysterical yellow people forcing a European into *Shooting an Elephant* really an appropriate metaphor for colonialism in 1936? Is Julia, the paper-thin vamp in *Nineteen Eighty-Four* really a character at all?'[23]

Like any journalist, Orwell often got his forecasts wrong. He categorically announced in 1937 that 'the upper-middle class is clearly finished'. He predicted in 1941 alone that the British Empire would be converted into 'a socialist federation of states'; the London Stock Exchange would imminently be 'torn down'; Britain's country homes would be transformed into socialist 'children's camps'; and Eton and Harrow faced immediate post-war closure. As Judah pointed out, in *Nineteen Eighty-Four* Orwell had 'nothing to say about social fragmentation, financialisation, ethnic splintering, unaccountable corporations, offshore kleptocrats, or echo chambers, to name but a few. Instead, he leaves too many political minds forever chasing, Quixote-like, the totalitarian windmill of untrammeled state power. They ignore the real anaemic state before their eyes, which struggles to keep up with corporate algorithms, is unable to fulfil its promises, or tax the super-rich.' Judah added: 'Orwell was no visionary when it comes to economics, either. Recall his floating fortresses in *Nineteen Eighty-Four*, explicitly designed to eat up the surplus production of a population. His inability to meaningfully reflect on the dynamics of capitalism (beyond moralising condemnation), let alone imagine a consumer society, is a fascinating woolly mammoth frozen in ice from the post-war era. It is a reminder of how utterly written-off by European intellectuals the market economy was immediately after the war – and what a shock the 1950s consumerist take-off in living standards proved to be.' Judah concluded: 'Britain and America would benefit from reading a little less Orwell, and not just for the same reasons they would benefit from making fewer comparisons to the 1930s. Today, we need fewer morally zealous political writers on all sides – and more serious people that are honestly grappling with complexity.'

But Orwell was always an outsider, uncomfortable about the class he was born into, disdainful of working-class culture and the certainties of left-wing academia. He would have hated *Big Brother* on TV, and his new life-size bronze statue outside the BBC. But *Animal Farm* and *Nineteen Eighty-Four* have been on school curriculums for generations and have had an immense influence on the largely leftward drift of governments and social assumptions we take for granted, from the National Health Service and the welfare state to a dislike of totalitarian regimes and crypto-fascist loudmouths on both sides of the Atlantic. That is his legacy.

***

During the war Clement Attlee, Home Secretary Herbert Morrison and other Labour figures in the coalition government of Winston Churchill went along with Conservative determination to keep Jewish refugees out of Britain and its refusal to even attempt a rescue of European Jews. during the Second World War. Pamela Shatzkes wrote: 'The annihilation of European Jewry was a central German war aim; preventing it was not an Allied war aim.'[23] Indeed, rescue was seen as a positive hindrance by the Churchill government. The left's position was an unrelenting and uncompromising fight against anti-Semitism and an open-door policy to refugees from Nazi rule. The Nazis did not prohibit emigration from the territories they had occupied until August 1941 or from Germany itself until October 1941.

Growing awareness of the policy of Nazi genocide after the invasion of the Soviet Union put pressure on the Churchill government to respond. The *Daily Telegraph* reported that over 700,000 Jewish men, women and children had been killed 'in the greatest massacre in the world's history'. Five days later it carried the headline, 'More Than 1,000,000 Jews Killed in Europe' and informed its readers that it was the Nazi's intention to 'wipe the race from the European continent'.[24]

The government then came under pressure to offer sanctuary to refugee Jewish children and old people living in Vichy France. On this issue, and others, Herbert Morrison displayed arrant hypocrisy. At a Labour Party rally in London he condemned 'the infamous cruelties practised upon the men, women and children of Europe'.[25] A few weeks later, in a Home Office memorandum, he outlined his policy as 'not to admit during the war additional refugees ... unless in some quite rare and exceptional cases it can be shown that the admission of the refugees will be directly advantageous to our war effort'.[26] He told the Cabinet that letting in the Vichy refugees would 'stir up an unpleasant degree of anti-Semitism'.[27] Within weeks the Germans occupied Vichy and the door to rescue was slammed shut.

Labour MPs did their best, but wartime priorities stymied them at every turn. Sydney Silverman warned that if something was not done, 'the Jewish East End would explode with anger and frustration'. Ministers realised they had to be at least seen to be doing something. Foreign Secretary Anthony Eden, responding to a question from Silverman, condemned the unfolding Holocaust and promised retribution.[28] It was a sham, intended only to put off agitation for action. The effect however was not what he intended – it served merely, as he put it himself, 'to stimulate complaints that the government was not doing enough to help the victims of the Nazi regime'.[29]

The government established a Cabinet forum, the Committee on the Reception and Accommodation of Jewish Refugees, chaired by Attlee alongside Morrison, Eden and Tory colonial secretary Oliver Stanley. Its clandestine aim was to defend 'the British policy of inaction'.[30] At the first meeting on New Year's Eve 1942, Morrison made clear that Britain would only 'take a limited number of refugees, say from 1,000 to 2,000 but certainly not more' and they would be held on the Isle of Man 'as long as he thought necessary'.[31]

At its second meeting a week later, Stanley warned that if more Jewish refugees were allowed into Britain or Palestine then this might lead 'certain Axis countries, notably Rumania, to extrude Jews from their territories, as an alternative to the policy of extermination'. It was, he said, vital that the policy of accepting 'only the limited number of Jewish children with a small number of accompanying women from Eastern Europe should be firmly adhered to'. The British ambassador in Washington, Lord Halifax, subsequently warned him that the Nazis might change 'from a policy of extermination to one of extrusion' with the intention of embarrassing the Allies 'by flooding them with alien immigrants'. Attlee told MPs that there would be no change in the exclusionary policy because the government believed that 'the only real remedy for the consistent Nazi policy of racial and religious persecution lies in an Allied victory'.[32]

By then the Committee's real purpose had been exposed. Orwell publisher Victor Gollancz wrote a pamphlet, *Let My People Go: Some practical proposals for dealing with Hitler's massacre of the JEWS and an appeal to the British public*, a tremendous indictment of Nazi crimes and British government inaction. He rushed it into print before the end of 1942. The 32-page, threepenny pamphlet sold an astonishing 250,000 copies in three months, prompting a wave of cash offers to help feed and house Jewish refugees. The government tried to ignore it, but in March 1943 Gollancz, Labour MP Eleanor Rathbone, welfare state architect William Beveridge and others formed the National Committee for Rescue from Nazi Terror (NCRNT). A Gallup poll found strong support for rescue: 78 per cent of those questioned supported allowing refugees into the country, 68 per cent temporarily and 10 per cent on a permanent basis.[33] The Oxford Union debating society came out in favour of rescue. Gollancz proposed a motion 'that a more energetic and practical policy be pursued by the government towards the rescue of Jews in Europe'. The opposing speakers unprecedentedly crossed the floor to vote with him.[34] The Churchill government, including Attlee and Morrison, promised action but did nothing.

Clearly, anti-Semitism existed within government institutions, including the Foreign Office, and one departmental head complained in 1944: 'Why are we the tools of these people?' Whether that was overt anti-Semitism, given the attitudes of the time, remains problematical.

Shatzkes wrote that since the FO was so rarely moved to change policy in response to Jewish appeals, it is difficult to see how this judgment can be tested. Whatever prejudice there was remained concealed by the FO's refusal to move.[35]

What remains equally unforgivable, however, is the wartime government's decision to do nothing whatsoever to fight anti-Semitism on the Home Front. It would not 'allow any official discussion on the issue. The subject was banned from the popular *Brains Trust* radio show and other BBC programmes were constantly thwarted.'[36] The Home Office even refused to curb the publication of anti-Semitic propaganda during the war. Morrison, for example, refused to take any action against the Scottish ultra-Protestant Nazi sympathiser Alexander Ratcliffe when, in 1943, he brought out what was probably the first British Holocaust denial publication, *The Truth about the Jews*. Attempts to revive British fascism in the form of the British National Party and the British People's Party were allowed by the government despite protests.

Under intense Tory pressure, including from Churchill himself, Morrison released Oswald Mosley from prison on 20 November 1943, despite a tremendous wave of protest. Nine people out of ten felt that Mosley should not have been released, and a wave of angry demonstrations followed the announcement.[37] At factory meetings across the country resolutions demanding Mosley be re-imprisoned were overwhelmingly passed. When Morrison made his announcement of Mosley's release in the Commons, delegations from over 300 factories demonstrated outside, chanting 'Mosley In, Morrison Out'. The Communist MP Willie Gallacher asked why Mosley had been released while Gandhi was still imprisoned. Why indeed?

Labour remained committed to the Zionist cause in Palestine throughout the war, a commitment which was decisively reaffirmed in a party statement on 'The International Post-War Settlement', drawn up by Hugh Dalton, and issued in the spring of 1944. The section on Palestine stated that a future Labour government had 'to let Jews, if they wish, enter this tiny land in such numbers as to become a majority'. There was a necessity in Palestine 'for transfer of population. Let the Arabs be encouraged to move out, as the Jews move in'. They should be 'compensated handsomely for their land' and their 'settlement elsewhere… generously financed'. Indeed, 'we should re-examine also the possibility of extending the present Palestinian boundaries by agreement with Egypt, Syria or Transjordan'. Dalton decided to leave out a recommendation for 'throwing open Libya or Eritrea to Jewish settlement as satellites or colonies to Palestine'.[38]

The whole document was adopted as policy at the December 1944 Labour Party conference. Tory Oliver Stanley warned him that the policy was 'Zionism plus plus' and risked 'encouraging the Jews to believe that the next British Government … will do everything for them'.[39] At its May 1945 conference Labour restated its commitment yet again with Dalton looking forward to 'a happy, free and prosperous Jewish state in Palestine'. The commitment was Labour Party policy during the 1945 general election and post-election handbooks stated once again that Zionist settlers should be allowed into Palestine 'in such numbers as to become a majority' and that 'the Arabs be encouraged to move out as the Jews move in'.[41]

It was abandoned immediately the party took office. The interests of the Empire took priority over any commitment to the Zionist cause. Ministers were made aware that any attempt to implement this commitment would seriously, perhaps fatally, undermine the British position throughout the Middle East, which required Arab collaboration. It was the Labour left who took the lead in condemning the betrayal of the Zionist cause.

6

Post-war Palpitations

'a picture that will shock the world'

With the Nazis and their Axis partners defeated, the British public became fully aware of the full horror of the Holocaust in which six million Jews died, both through cinema newsreels and radio broadcasts, and the first-hand accounts of returning soldiers who had liberated Belsen and other death camps. During the summer and autumn of 1945, those atrocities confirmed, in the public mind, the justification for the previous six years of global warfare.

Not only had Labour's coalition ministers been wholeheartedly involved in the Churchill government's policy towards Jewish refugees, but they continued once they came to power in the 1945 landslide that ousted Churchill, something rarely acknowledged in Labour history. Attlee's government up to 1951 refused to let Holocaust survivors into Britain, but happily admitted – due to labour shortages in the herculean task of rebuilding Britain – over 200,000 Poles, Latvians, Lithuanians, Estonians and Ukrainians. Many were former SS from the Baltic states including an entire 8,000-strong surrendered Ukrainian Waffen SS Division. Few can doubt that anti-Semitic racism played a part in the immigration system. But the recruitment of Latvians in the British coal mines sparked outrage when local miners spotted their SS blood-group tattoos while showering. The Home Office reluctantly went along with barring men with SS tattoos from mining, but they were considered suitable 'for other occupations in Britain for which they were not obliged to remove their outer clothing'.[1] Attlee was certainly not unaware of the issue – Home Office notes showed that the recruitment had been made 'with the Prime Minister's approval'.[2] In a letter to his MP passed to the Home Office in June 1947, a Mr M. L. Hyams of Coventry wrote: 'While denying asylum to thousands of displaced persons and having no compassion on these poor, homeless, starving creatures, the British government brought into the country 8,000 bloodthirsty cut-throats, part of a German force which was guilty of the most brutal atrocities against defenceless people during the war. One can't help feeling there is something wrong with the mentality of a government, especially a socialist government which on the one hand refuses to give succour to so many helpless creatures whose only crime was they were either Jews or defied the Nazi hordes, and on the other hand opens the door of this country to scoundrels whose entry is an insult.'

Anti-Semitism had become broadly taboo as images of the death camps burned into public consciousness, but several factors emerged which saw a re-emergence of the old prejudice. The first was the bloody birth of the state of Israel. By the end of the Second World War, the Jewish population of Palestine had increased to 33% of the total population, partly due to the clandestine activities of the *Aliyah Bet* organisation which helped Jews flee the Holocaust. Britain came into fierce conflict with the Jewish community over immigration limits, as well as continued conflict with the Arab community over limit levels.

All this was taking place during the tenure of a new Labour government most focused on delivering a post-war welfare state, founding the National Health Service, rebuilding homes, transport and factories destroyed by bombing, and slowing the slide into a new economic depression. A fuel shortage during the winter of 1946–47 had led to soaring unemployment and in the spring of 1947 it peaked at 1.9 million. A harsh winter was followed by a washed-out summer, while rationing was in force, shops were struggling. People were cold and hungry, and many of those who had fought overseas remained far from home. So far, peace was delivering few benefits to a tired, broke, war-weary nation.

Labour support for Israel continued in the hope that the Labour Zionist strand in Jewish state-building would lead to socialism and development in the Middle East generally. However, Foreign Secretary Ernest Bevin was critical of Zionist goals, arguing that Jews should be convinced to resettle in Europe. One remark caused particular offence and led some critics to accuse him of anti-Semitism. American President Harry Truman was pressing Britain to immediately admit 100,000 Jewish refugees, survivors of the Holocaust who wanted to settle in Palestine. Bevin told the Labour annual conference that

American pressure to admit Jews was being applied, saying: 'There has been agitation in the United States, and particularly in New York, for 100,000 Jews to be put in Palestine. I hope I will not be misunderstood in America if I say that this was proposed by the purest of motives. They did not want too many Jews in New York.'[3] Bevin also voiced anti-Semitic canards between Jews and finance, as well as communism, and made remarks about the Jews of Europe 'pushing to the front of the queue'. During the fuel crisis he made a quip about 'Israelites', insinuating that Jewish black marketeers were hoarding fuel.

During the American controversy he insisted that he was merely restating what he said he had been told by US Secretary of State James Byrnes, but his political foe, fellow Labour MP Richard Crossman, a committed Zionist, characterised his outlook during the dying days of the Mandate as 'corresponding roughly with The Protocols of the Elders of Zion, a Tsarist fabrication written to inflame anti-Semitic prejudice'. Crossman intimated that 'the main points of Bevin's discourse were ... that the Jews had successfully organised a conspiracy against Britain and against him personally.'[4] Bevin, born illegitimately into a largely illiterate Dorset family, was notoriously plain-spoken in an often impenetrable West Country accent. His comments were ill-judged but it is doubtful that he was brazenly anti-Semitic and there is no evidence that he allowed any such prejudice to affect his political decisions. However, Hugh Dalton, Chancellor of the Exchequer in the immediate post-war government, referred to Labour Party chairman Harold Laski as the 'under-sized Semite' while also ridiculing his far left 'yideology'.[5] He also routinely referred to Africans as 'niggers' and Arabs as 'wogs'.

While the Labour government had reneged on the party's Zionist commitment, the Labour left rallied and Aneurin Bevan continued urging a pro-Zionist stance and considered resigning over the issue early in 1947. He argued in Cabinet that 'it was not necessarily true that we must avoid estranging Arab states. A friendly Jewish state would be a safer military base than any we should find in any Arab state'.[6] John Newsinger wrote: 'For Bevan and the "Tribunite left," the alliance with Zionism, complete with British military bases, remained the best way to sustain Britain's strategic position in the Middle East.'[7] Outside the government, Labour MPs Richard Crossman, Michael Foot, Ian Mikardo, Woodrow Wyatt, Sidney Silverman and others opposed the 'betrayal' of Zionism. In 1946, Foot and Crossman co-authored a pamphlet, *A Palestine Munich?*, savagely attacking the government's position.[8] Circulated at the Labour Party conference, the pamphlet emphasised Labour's longstanding commitment to Zionism, condemned the government's betrayal, apologised for Zionist terrorism and argued that a 'Judean state' would ally with Britain and 'leave in British hands the port of Haifa and such airfields and installations as we require'.[9] At the same time, *Tribune* maintained a constant pro-Zionist critique. It proclaimed that 'the Palestine tragedy represents a breakdown of social democracy. For the British forces operating against the Palestine Jews are under the orders of a British Labour Government'.[10]

In Palestine, insurgency was about to break out. The *Haganah*, the main Jewish paramilitary force, joined with the smaller militant groups *Irgun* and *Lehi* in an armed struggle against British rule which ignited the debate – still going on – about the distinction between freedom-fighters and terrorists. On July 22 1946, *Irgun* attacked the British administrative headquarters for Palestine, housed in a wing of the King David Hotel in Jerusalem.[11] Ninety-one people of various nationalities were killed and forty-six injured. The attack initially had the approval of the *Haganah* as a response to a series of widespread British raids on organisations believed to be supporting terrorism. It was characterised as one of the 'most lethal terrorist incidents of the twentieth century'.[12]

The Jewish insurgency continued throughout the rest of 1946 and 1947 despite repeated crackdowns by the British military. British efforts to mediate a negotiated solution between Jews and Arabs foundered – Jews were unwilling to accept any solution that did not involve a Jewish state and suggested a partition of Palestine into Jewish and Arab states, while the Arabs refused point blank to countenance a Jewish state in any part of Palestine, saying that the only solution was a unified Palestine under Arab rule. In February 1947, the British referred the Palestine issue to the newly formed United Nations but the Jewish insurgency continued and peaked in July 1947, with a series of widespread guerrilla raids. After three *Irgun* fighters had been sentenced to death for their role in a prison break-out in which twenty-seven *Irgun* and *Lehi* militants were freed, *Irgun* captured two British sergeants, threatening to kill them if the three men were executed. When the British carried out the executions, Irgun killed the two hostages and hanged their bodies from eucalyptus trees near Netanya, booby-trapping one of them with a mine which injured a British officer as he cut the body down. Ironically, one of the murdered sergeants, Clifford Martin, was Jewish. The hangings caused widespread outrage in Britain and tempers on the streets were ragged.

On Friday 1 August, the start of the Bank holiday weekend, the *Daily Express* reported the atrocity on its front page and published a photograph of the bodies which, it promised its readers, would be a 'picture that will shock the world'. British Jewish leaders condemned the killings, but more lurid details followed in the next day's papers. That weekend, as Walter Lever, a working-class Jewish resident of Manchester recalled, 'There was nothing to do but walk the streets... discussing the newspaper.' In Birkenhead, slaughterhouse workers refused to process any more meat for Jewish consumption until the attacks on British soldiers in Palestine stopped. Around Merseyside, fury spilt onto the streets as crowds of young men moved ominously into Jewish areas. Anti-Semitic slogans and the fascist sign were daubed on a synagogue in Plymouth. On Sunday afternoon the trouble reached Manchester where the weather had turned hot and stuffy and the pubs were running out of beer. Groups of men began breaking the windows of shops in the long-established Jewish enclave of Cheetham Hill, just north of the city centre. The city centre pubs closed early when the beer taps finally ran dry and by the evening the mob had swelled to several hundred, including some motorists who drove through the area throwing bricks from their cars. Soon the streets were covered in broken glass and stones and the crowd moved on to bigger targets, tearing down the canopy of the Great Synagogue on Cheetham Hill Road and surrounding a Jewish wedding party at the Assembly Hall, shouting abuse at the terrified guests. The next day, Lever said, 'Cheetham Hill Road looked much as it had looked seven years before, when the German bombers had pounded the city for 12 hours. All premises belonging to Jews for the length of a mile down the street had gaping windows and the pavements were littered with glass.'[13]

By the end of the bank holiday weekend, serious anti-Jewish riots had taken place in Manchester, Glasgow and Liverpool. These cities had the highest levels of unemployment in Britain and even though the disturbances initially targeted the Jews they quickly progressed to generalised looting. 'Get the Jews, get the stuff and get into the shops,' was one shout heard in Manchester. David Trilling wrote: 'Not for the first (or last) time, racism and economic exclusion combined and formed a poisonous resentment.' There were minor disturbances in Bristol, Hull, London and Warrington, as well as scores of attacks on Jewish property across the country. A solicitor in Liverpool and a Glasgow shopkeeper were beaten up. Nobody was killed, but this was the most widespread anti-Jewish violence the UK had ever seen.

In Salford, the day after a crowd of several thousand had thrown stones at shop windows, signs appeared that read: 'Hold your fire. These premises are British.' Arsonists in West Derby set fire to a wooden synagogue; workers at Canada Dock in Liverpool returned from the holidays to find 'Death to all Jews' painted above the entrance. And in Eccles, a former sergeant major named John Regan was fined £15 for telling a crowd of 700 which had smashed Jewish shop fronts: 'Hitler was right. Exterminate every Jew – every man, woman and child. What are you afraid of? There's only a handful of police.' Trilling wrote: 'Just two years after British troops had liberated Bergen-Belsen, the language of the Third Reich had resurfaced, this time at home. Anger about what had happened in Palestine was one thing, but it seemed to have unleashed something far more vicious.'[14]

Dublin-born Max Levitas, who had lived in Whitechapel since 1930, was a Communist local councillor when the 1947 riots erupted. At the age of 97, he told Trilling that although London was spared riots on the scale of those in the north, the 'hanging sergeants' incident compounded 'animosity' towards Jews in the East End. 'I opposed the hanging when I spoke at meetings, but the main fight was dealing with racism that foreigners were getting jobs and Jews were getting jobs.' He pointed out that post-war austerity was at its harshest – it was a time of hunger and poverty. Hopes that anti-Semitism, which had re-emerged during previous economic downturns, would have disappeared with the defeat of Hitler were proving short-lived. A popular stereotype persisted of Jews as 'black marketeers gaining from the war but not contributing to the effort'. Worse still, Jewish loyalty over Palestine was being questioned openly. The *Sunday Times* had addressed an editorial 'to British Jews' in which the paper accused them of failing to perform their 'civic duty and moral obligations' by denouncing the anti-British violence in Palestine.

Levitas had been part of the crowd that faced down Oswald Mosley's Blackshirts on Cable Street and, like many trade unionists, he was alarmed at the resurgence of violence. 'There was a feeling that we'd just had a war against fascism, and that we'd got to ensure that the fascists didn't do again what they did in the Thirties.' Levitas believed that one reason the fascists were kept at bay, and why east London stayed relatively calm through the late 1940s, is that the lessons of the 1930s had been learned. 'Only through the integration of society could we play a major part in stopping racism,' he told Trilling. Integration went beyond anti-fascist protest, it had to involve 'people demanding for themselves jobs, housing and education for their kids. To ensure that whatever religion you've got, whatever your colour, you play a part in society.'

Four days after its sensationalised coverage had triggered the riots, the *Daily Express* appealed for calm. 'No more of this!' it implored readers, arguing that the attacks on innocent shopkeepers had become a national disgrace. In Manchester, the violence had subsided, leaving an ugly atmosphere. 'For the rest of the week,' Lever recalled, 'one overheard behind one in the bus, over one's shoulder at the next café table, a row ahead in the cinema, whispering anecdotes and muttered abuse relating to the events of the Sunday night.' Rachel Barash, who had worked for the Jewish 'hospitality committee' that brought refugee children over from Germany and the Netherlands during the 1930s, remembered how the riots sparked a 'nasty' stand-off between boys from rival youth clubs. Until that point, the refugees, who were housed in the suburban village of Withington, had been welcomed and treated as 'our children' by their neighbours. Now Jewish boys across Manchester gathered together, ready to defend themselves.

Yet the tension dissipated almost as quickly as violence had surged; in the words of another Manchester resident, Agnes Sussman: 'It all passed over as if nothing had happened.' Dave Rich, deputy director of communications at the Community Security Trust, a charity established in 1994 to ensure the 'safety and security' of British Jews, reckoned that one reason was that there were much bigger things to worry about then. The full horrors of the Holocaust were still coming to light; efforts to establish the state of Israel were ongoing; and in Britain, for Zionist and non-Zionist Jews alike, there were more pressing economic concerns. 'Given that few people were actually hurt in the riots,' Rich said, 'it's understandable that, in the wider picture of what is on the mind of Jews at that time, it would very quickly get relegated.' Home Secretary James Chuter Ede dismissed the rioting as mere 'hooliganism ... rather than an indication of public feeling', while magistrates condemned rioters as 'un-British' and 'unpatriotic'. Rich pointed out: 'The thought that those popular anti-Jewish riots could happen two years after the Holocaust in Britain ... runs counter to the anti-fascist mythology of Britain's role in the war. Who wants to go digging that up?'

Trilling wrote: 'Yet the riots were neither an aberration nor the product of an unruly working class. Britain was experiencing an identity crisis: it had won the war but appeared to be losing the peace, with recession at home and the break-up of its empire abroad, in which the events in Mandate Palestine played only a small part. As colonised peoples increasingly demanded independence, Britain turned to a more inward-looking nationalism. Along with it came the question of who would be included and who would be left out. In 1948, with cross-party support, the Labour government passed the British Nationality Act, marking a shift from a situation where all those living in the empire – in theory, although quite evidently not in practice – were equal subjects under the Crown to one where each country in the Commonwealth could determine its own version of citizenship. Although in the years to come it would be non-white immigrants from the Commonwealth who would most strongly challenge received notions of Englishness and Britishness and who would bear the brunt of racism, Jews, too, were caught up in this, for a brief period. Yet it is best to see the events of 1947 as the end of a chapter rather than the beginning of one. A year later, the state of Israel was formed and Chaim Weizmann, who had lived and worked in Manchester, was appointed as its first president. Britain's duplicitous conduct towards Jews and Arabs since it had taken control of Palestine in 1920, the dispossession of the Palestinians and the nasty guerrilla war were events that it suited both sides to pretend had never happened. Relations were soon "normalised", and nobody cared to recall the brief moment when the messy end to a colonial misadventure was played out on British streets.' [15]

In September 1947, the British Cabinet decided that the Mandate was no longer tenable, and to evacuate Palestine. According to Colonial Secretary Arthur Creech Jones, four major factors led to the decision to evacuate Palestine: the inflexibility of negotiators on both sides who refused to compromise on their core positions over the question of a Jewish state in Palestine: the economic pressure that stationing a large garrison in Palestine to deal with the Jewish insurgency and the possibility of wider Jewish and Arab rebellions put on a British economy already strained by a World War, and the mounting criticism the government faced in failing to find a new policy for Palestine.

The Mandate collapsed into civil war as the British evacuated Palestine and refused to implement the partition resolution. Arab militias and gangs attacked Jewish areas, but in early April the *Haganah* moved onto the offensive.[16] The Arab Palestinian economy collapsed and 250,000 Palestinian Arabs fled or were expelled.

On 14 May 1948, Jewish Agency head David Ben-Gurion declared the establishment of the Jewish state of Israel. The following day, the armies of four Arab countries – Egypt, Syria, Transjordan and Iraq – invaded intent on strangling Israel at birth. A ceasefire was declared after a year of brutal fighting and temporary borders were established. Jordan annexed the West Bank, including East Jerusalem, while Egypt took the Gaza Strip. The UN estimated that more than 700,000 Palestinians were either expelled or fled from Israeli forces.[17] Some 156,000 remained and became Arab citizens of Israel.

Israel was admitted as a United Nations member in May 1949. Both Israel and Jordan appeared genuinely interested in a peace agreement but the British acted as a brake on the Jordanian effort in order to avoid damaging British interests in Egypt.[18] In the early years of the state, the Labour Zionist movement led by premier Ben-Gurion dominated Israeli politics. The *kibbutzim*, or collective farming communities, played a pivotal role in establishing the new state. Immigration to Israel during the late 1940s and early 1950s was aided by Mossad which engaged in clandestine operations in countries, particularly in the Middle East and Eastern Europe, where the lives of Jews were believed to be in danger and exit from those places was difficult.[19] An influx of Holocaust survivors and Jews from Muslim countries also helped boost the infant state's population from 700,000 to two million by 1958.[20]

In Britain and America there was a renewed sensitivity to the plight of Jews, particularly when the full scale of the Holocaust was exposed during the Nuremberg war crimes trials. David Lean's 1948 film *Oliver Twist* featured Alec Guinness as Fagin made up faithfully to replicate the caricature by the illustrator George Cruikshank in the original 1838 Charles Dickens novel, complete with long hooked nose and beard. Outrage ensued. Hollywood was so offended that the release was delayed for three years in the US; eventually only a heavily censored version was shown.[21]

Then there was a small but nasty resurgence in home-grown fascism, a trend which seems unbelievable from the modern perspective given the Holocaust, the Blitz and the long, hard, dangerous years of combatting fascism on the world stage. Although the violence in 1947 was not orchestrated by fascist political parties, it emboldened the remaining adherents. Jeffrey Hamm, a former member of the British Union of Fascists who was now in charge of the League of Ex-Servicemen, visited the north-west of England to stir up trouble. Fascists displayed copies of the *Daily Express*'s 'hanging sergeants' front page at their meetings. A shop in London run by Victor Burgess, who had been temporarily interned as a suspected enemy sympathiser under the same defence regulations as Sir Oswald and his wife Lady Diana Mosley, was issuing 'anti-Jewish propaganda', officials were told in January 1945. The Home Office was alerted but did nothing. Burgess persisted to become a notorious post-war fascist orator. Oswald Mosley had spent most of the war comfortably reading Classics in internment and, from November 1943, under house arrest. After the war, Mosley was contacted by his former supporters and persuaded to return to participation in politics. He formed the Union Movement, which called for a single nation state to cover the continent of Europe.

De-mobbed Jewish ex-servicemen, many of them committed socialists or communist, were appalled at the activities of the Union Movement and other fascist groups which engaged in rabidly anti-Semitic public speeches and violent attacks on London Jews and their property. They formed the 43 Group which had an initial membership was around 300 people, not all Jewish. Many had been decorated for bravery, including a VC for Petty Officer Tommy Gould.[22] The organisation was sometimes portrayed by its enemies as a front for either Jewish terrorists or communists but was mostly composed of British ex-servicemen who voted Labour in 1945. The Board of Deputies of British Jews worried that the 43 Group's activities could damage the Jewish community's reputation, especially given the guerrilla warfare in Palestine. The 43 Group never sought to replace the more traditional groups who preferred debate and discussion, but who had failed to stop the BUF. Instead, they aimed to prevent the Union Movement mobilising and gathering support by smashing up Mosley's gatherings and attacking fascists and anti-Semites whenever possible. Len Sherman, a martial arts expert from the Welsh Guards, told the Jewish Museum London's oral history collection: 'Any six of us was more than a match for twenty of them. We never failed, we always won. We always closed their meetings down, never failed to close a meeting down.' Activists included Merchant Navy veteran and future prolific anti-fascist writer and lecturer Morris Beckham; Gerald Flamberg, a middleweight boxing champion who had won the Military Medal at Arnhem; Battle of Britain ace Alec Carson; and future celebrity hairdresser Vidal Sassoon who, still a teenager, went on to fight with the Israeli Defence Forces. Group members broke up meetings, infiltrated fascist groups, and attacked the fascists in street fights. This led to Mosley's decision, in 1951, to leave Britain and live in Ireland. He later moved to Paris. Of his decision to leave, he said, 'You don't clear up a dungheap from underneath it'.

The 43 Group was voluntarily disbanded as its members considered that the immediate threat had passed.

Mosley's Union Movement remained active throughout the 1950s, however, and it was not until 1962, when the unrelated 62 Group was formed in the 43 Group's image, that British fascists again encountered any significant privately organised street-level resistance. The militant London-based coalition of anti-fascists was set up in response to the resurgence of fascism, particularly the creation of Colin Jordan's National Socialist Movement. It used violence against them, the remnants of Mosley's thugs, the original British National Party and the emerging National Front.[23] The Group was led by former 43 Group member Harry Bidney, a Soho night club manager, with the help of notorious hardman enforcer, Paul Nathan. Formal membership was only open to Jews, but the Group co-operated with Irish and black power activists. The Group's tactic was direct action against those it believed were organising violence against minority groups, which sometimes resulted in violent confrontations. In July 1962 this led to a riot in London's Trafalgar Square when Jordan tried to address a crowd while standing in front of a large banner which read: 'Free Britain from Jewish Control'. It also used intelligence, including informers within the fascist groups.[24]

A notable member was Gerry Gable. The son of a Jewish woman, Gable grew up in post-war east London identifying as Jewish. As a youth, he was a member of the Young Communist League and worked as a runner on the Communist Party's *Daily Worker* newspaper, leaving after a year to become a Communist Party (CP) trade union organiser. He stood unsuccessfully for the CP in May 1962 at Northfield Ward, Stamford, but left the CP because of its anti-Israel policy. Gable organised intelligence for the 62 Group on fascists, including using infiltrators to help build a defence policy for the community against fascist attacks. This led to the formation of the anti-fascist magazine *Searchlight* in the mid-1960s.

Throughout this post-war period, the left continued to be broadly pro-Israel and pro-Zionist, with the exception of CP hardliners and Stalinists, due to the view that kibbutzim were prototype socialist nirvanas, and also to respect those who had fought to establish a homeland.

The Labour left's most determined advocate of Zionism was Richard Crossman who believed that it was 'an important part of the Socialist creed' but conceded that the injustice done to the Palestinians was the lesser evil because the fact was 'that no western colonist in any other country had done so little harm, or disturbed so little the life of the indigenous people'. Zionists were bringing 'social progress' to the Middle East, 'which, in the long run, would benefit the Arab'.[25] Much later, in 1959, he spoke of what he considered the great Zionist misfortune: their colonising effort came too late to be respectable. Instead, 'they had the misfortune to come after Woodrow Wilson and Lenin had proclaimed self-determination a principle.' He complained about Attlee and Bevin having had a 'prejudice in favour of the native and against the white settler'.[26] Crossman argued that the Palestinians were never driven out but left on the orders of their leaders who he accused of unjustified scaremongering. And anyway, as he told the Commons, their homes were 'only mud huts ... terribly bad villages full of vermin'.[27] Crossman's anti-Arab and Islamaphobic prejudices were abhorrent but should not disguise the fact that the creation of Israel was enthusiastically celebrated by the Labour left. John Newsinger wrote: 'The Palestinians were disregarded as a non-people, whose fate was of no account whatsoever, compared with the establishment of Israel, "a country which was both socialist and freedom-loving". Alongside this rhetoric though, left spokesmen also argued that an alliance with Israel was the best way to sustain British influence in the Middle East.'[28]

In 1950, Woodrow Wyatt visited Israel where he saw 'democratic socialism', inspired, he believed, by 'the achievements of British socialism'. He also regretted Bevin's 'prejudice against Zionism', because 'Israel might easily have been a member state of the British Commonwealth' and, if it had been, 'action might have been taken in time to prevent the loss of Abadan oil.'[29] Newsinger wrote: 'By action, he meant military intervention. Even the Labour left saw the world through a British imperial lens.'[30]

In 1950, Morrison proclaimed that Israel was 'one of the greatest experiments in the modern world', and the Labour government formally recognised the state of Israel. Academic June Edmunds argued that concern to maintain 'a strong alliance' with the United States was behind the turnaround with Bevin himself telling the Israelis 'that his Palestine policy had been a failure'.[31] The Prime Minister Clement Attlee was himself not free of prejudice. On one occasion in March 1951 when he was considering a number of junior appointments to the government, he rejected Ian Mikardo and Austen Albu, even though they were both highly recommended, because they were Jews.

In 1956, the Labour opposition condemned British collusion in the Israeli attack on Egypt and the subsequent Anglo-French

Post-war Palpitations

Suez invasion. Labour's opposition was not motivated by any principled objection to invasion, but rather to an invasion that was not supported by the US. Then-Labour leader, Hugh Gaitskell and shadow foreign secretary Aneurin Bevan remained strong Zionists but American opposition to the 1956 Suez adventure were their main concerns. Eighty-one Labour MPs signed a Commons motion supporting Israel, and Herbert Morrison described Israeli military success as 'wonderful'. A drunken Dalton celebrated it by 'cursing the wogs'.[32] The year after the Suez invasion, the Labour Friends of Israel was established, as a demonstration that the party's condemnation of the British and French governments did not extend to Israel.

Shortly after the Notting Hill race riots, Mosley briefly returned to Britain to stand in the 1959 general election at Kensington North leading his campaign stridently on an anti-immigration platform, calling for forced repatriation of Caribbean immigrants as well as a prohibition upon mixed marriages. Mosley's final share of the vote was 7.6%.[33] In 1961, he took part in a debate at University College London about Commonwealth immigration, seconded by a young Holocaust-denier David Irving, but was treated with derision. He returned to politics one last time, contesting the 1966 general election at Shoreditch and Finsbury, and received an even more derisory 4.6% of the vote. For a while it seemed that the boil of anti-Semitism in Britain had been lanced.

With the succession of Harold Wilson to the Labour leadership in 1963, the party now had one of its most committed Zionists at the helm. Newsinger wrote: 'Actions that Labour would have condemned if carried out by any other government were either condoned, supported or ignored. At the same time, those within the party who tried to raise concerns about the plight of the Palestinians were subject to what one of their number, David Watkins MP, described as a "fascist-like reaction". They were effectively prevented from speaking in the Commons by constant barracking from their own side.'[34] The left-winger Margaret McKay, a former Communist, union organiser and, from 1951 to 1962, the TUC's chief women's officer, had a replica Palestinian refugee camp erected in Parliament Square. The party leadership was outraged. For her pains, she was inundated with 'obscene hate mail … which included packets of excreta. Far from taking steps to protect her, the party allowed her opponents within her constituency party, who ran a 'scurrilous campaign' against her (she was inevitably accused of anti-Semitism), to begin a de-selection process. She stood down as an MP in disgust in the run-up to the 1970 general election.[35]

When Julia Neuberger was a child in 1950s Britain, anti-Semitism was rarely a topic of conversation. The occasional reference would come when, driving his family around in their 'shabby Ford Popular', her father would suggest that the traffic signals were anti-Semitic if they encountered a run of red lights. Neuberger's mother escaped Nazi Germany before the war but most of her family died in the camps. Her father's grandmother found temporary refuge in the Netherlands, but later perished in Sobibor. Neuberger, who became the first female rabbi in Britain to run her own synagogue, wrote that her father's joke reflected the fact that, for many Jews, post-war Britain felt 'safe, accepting and tolerant'. She added: 'If Jews felt threatened by anti-Semitism in 1950s or 1960s Britain, we certainly were not aware of it.'

However, during those two decades, the Soviet Union spread anti-Zionist slanders to create a hotpot of fantasies about Jews, Zionists, Israel, anti-Semitism and the Holocaust which was eagerly consumed on the fringes of the radical left in Britain. Dave Rich wrote: 'By this telling, Zionism was not, as most of the left had previously thought, a legitimate expression of Jewish national longing. It was in fact a racist, colonial movement that collaborated with fascism before and during the Second World War, conspired with imperialism after it, and created an apartheid state in place of Palestine. This narrative appealed to a youthful Western left that did not remember the Holocaust, did not see Jews as victims of racism and romanticised the nationalist violence of anti-colonial liberation movements in Africa, Asia and the Middle East.

'It spread through anti-colonial and anti-apartheid networks in the 1960s, appeared in student unions in the 1970s and made its first real impact in the Labour Party during its last turn leftwards in the 1980s. That was the decade when Ken Livingstone first developed his Nazi-Zionist theories ... It was also the decade when Jeremy Corbyn arrived in Parliament as a Labour MP and sponsor of a radical anti-Zionist group, the Labour Movement Campaign for Palestine, that opposed Israel's existence and pledged to "eradicate Zionism" from the Labour Party.'[36]

The socialist academic Brendan McGeever said: 'Anti-Semitism has long been a feature of left and radical politics in Britain and across Europe. In Britain we find it in the 1890s, in the pages of Britain's first socialist newspaper, Justice – the paper of the Social Democratic Federation, Britain's first Marxist party – where articles regularly refer to Jews as financiers and international capitalists. We also see it in Keir Hardie's newspaper *Labour Leader*, which referred to hook-nosed Rothschilds. Of course we are not living in the 1890s, but the point is that anti-Semitism is not something that is external to the socialist movement. Anti-Semitism has not latched on to the left from the outside – as has been suggested in some recent debates. To varying degrees it has always had an organic presence within it. It is disappointing to see some disavow this aspect of the movement's past. Anti-Semitism and other forms of racism have always been present in the left since its inception. And there is nothing extraordinary or surprising about this given that European socialism emerged in the nineteenth century in a context of colonialism, racism, empire and a hugely exploitative capitalist society. The socialist movement absorbed elements of that mainstream culture then – and it continues to do so today. What specifically can we identify about the relationship between the left and anti-Semitism? In the visions conjured up by some socialists, Jews have often been positioned in opposition to the working class, as bearers of exploitation, or as occupying an exploitative class position. The late Moishe Postone argued that what makes anti-Semitism dangerous for the left is that it can have the appearance of being anti-hegemonic. It can take the form of a kind of fetishised oppositionalism that defines itself as being against intangible forms of global domination – something which finds expression in all kinds of political formations, not just in the left.'[37]

Part of the attraction of anti-Zionism for young lefties after the 1967 Six-Day War, and the later 1973 Yom Kippur War, was premier Harold Wilson's unequivocal support for Israel. Although he kept Britain out of the Vietnam War despite intense arm-twisting from America, he had become a hate figure amongst student radicals during violent anti-war demonstrations.

During events to mark the centenary of Wilson's birth, former Labour Party chairman Lord Tony Clarke, an ex-trade union official, said: 'I think he would be ashamed that we seem to have lost our way on Israel. His support of Israel was never in doubt. He realised the responsibility that the Labour Party had in the run-up to the creation of the state 68 years ago. Israel is built on the founding principles of socialism in this country.' Lord Clarke recalled discussing Israel with Lord Wilson while campaigning as a parliamentary candidate in 1974: 'He was very interested in my first visit to Israel just before the Yom Kippur War. He was pleased I came back full of energy to help form a Labour Friends of Israel branch in Camden. He said: "Good luck to you my boy."'

Wilson developed strong friendships with leading Zionists including Shimon Peres, who once described him as 'a true friend of Israel'. He was also close to Lady Valerie Cocks, who was the founder of Trade Union Friends of Israel, co-founder of the pro-Israel peers' group and an active LFI organiser and fundraiser during Wilson's leadership of the party. She recalled: 'He loved Israel and went on being president of LFI until he couldn't any more. He backed us in any way he could. I never had to ask him to say anything pro-Israel – it came naturally. He spoke about Israel in the most loving, warmest possible way.'

Lord Bernard Donoughue, a senior adviser to the late prime minister, recalled a conversation between himself, Wilson and his press secretary Joe Haines in Downing Street: 'It was shortly after the Yom Kippur War. Joe and I told Harold that we would happily volunteer to fight for Israel if she were under threat of extinction. Neither of us are Jewish but that was the strength of our feeling. He was very sympathetic to that point of view. He was a great supporter of Israel.'[38] Such views were increasingly anathema to a generation increasingly focused on the plight of the Palestinians and the Moslem world's growing antagonism to the West.

Less palatable to today's anti-Zionists on the left is the realisation that their near-sainted hero Tony Benn was pro-Israel during the first Wilson administration. As technology minister in 1968, Benn wrote to Foreign Secretary Michael Stewart to ask whether he should accept an Israeli invitation to give the annual Balfour Lecture. He said he had been considering a visit to Israel to discuss technological collaborations but was also critical of 'certain aspects of Israeli policy'. Benn wrote: 'I always feel sympathetic to the Jewish aspirations and would propose to devote my lecture to an examination of the contribution the Jews could make to the development of the world in the future.' Speaking at a later Jewish Board of Deputies lunch, Benn told of his 'admiration and respect' for Anglo-Jewry, and praised the community's efforts in promoting race relations. He said his mother, Lady Stansgate, had been active in the Council of Christians and Jews, and that 'the tradition of defence of the Jewish community was ingrained in my father and made him a committed friend of the Jewish people.' Much later he changed tack – hardly for the first time – and called for an end to Zionism.[39]

There was overwhelming support for Israel within Labour ranks during the 1967 Six-Day War with the left-wing Labour MP Eric Heffer urging the Israelis to hold on to their conquests. As one of the handful of opponents of Zionism within the Parliamentary Labour

Party Christopher Mayhew later observed the strength of the Zionist commitment at this time led 'to a uniquely close friendship with a foreign government which was occupying large areas of its neighbours' territory, was exercising, through measures of military government, colonial rule over a million subjects, and was openly practising racial discrimination in its immigration and housing policies'. Mayhew accelerated the rise of a radical anti-Zionism in the Labour Party with the creation of the Labour Middle East Council in 1969. He aimed to change the party's 'pro-Israel' position and was influenced by pro-Palestinian activists within the Young Liberals.[40] Mayhew had holidayed in the Soviet Union in 1934, became President of the Oxford Union and during the war rose to the rank of Major in the Intelligence Corps. Elected Labour MP for South Norfolk in the 1945 election, he served under Ernest Bevin as Under-Secretary at the Foreign Office. He lost his seat in 1950 but returned to Parliament after the death of Bevin, winning his former boss's old seat of Woolwich East in a 1951 by-election. A ferocious opponent of unilateral nuclear disarmament, he served as Shadow War Secretary from 1960 to 1961 and as a spokesman on foreign affairs from 1961 to 1964. When Labour took office in 1964 Mayhew became a junior defence minister but clashed with Harold Wilson's administration over aircraft carrier cancellations and resigned.

In 1973 Mayhew offered £5,000 to anyone who could produce evidence that Egyptian leader Nasser had stated that he sought to 'drive the Jews into the sea'. Mayhew repeated the offer later in the House of Commons[41] and broadened it to include any genocidal statement by an Arab leader,[42] while reserving for himself the right to be the arbiter of the authenticity of any purported statements as well as their meaning. Mayhew received several letters from claimants, each one producing one quotation or another from an Arab leader, all of which Mayhew deemed to be fabricated. One claimant, Warren Bergson, took Mayhew to court. The case came before the High Court and Bergson was unable to offer evidence of Nasser's alleged statement and acknowledged that, after thorough research, he had been unable to find any statement by a responsible Arab leader that could be described as genocidal.

Mayhew had been feeling increasingly uneasy with Labour policies under Wilson and in 1974 he moved to the Liberals. In the October 1974 general election Mayhew contested Bath instead of Woolwich East in order not to split his former constituency party. He was defeated. By then another pro-Palestinian was preparing to make his bid for a national voice.

7

Oh! Jeremy Corbyn

'institutionally anti-Semitic'

Jeremy Corbyn told the *Church Times* that there was a 'Jewish element in his family, probably from Germany'.[1] That was during the furore over anti-Semitism in the Labour Party under his leadership, or lack of it, and it does not take a hardened cynic to doubt the claim's veracity. But if true, it is something he kept well hidden in his youth.

Corbyn, the product of a well-off middle-class family, did not shine at the Haberdasher's Adams grammar school and, unlike his brighter siblings, was an aimless teenager who drifted into organisations with often competing aims covering nuclear disarmament, animal cruelty, communism and the Labour Party. His parents, a skilled engineer and a teacher, proposed Voluntary Service Overseas for the 18-year-old. He was flown to Jamaica on a two-year-contract to assist teaching at the exclusive, fee-paying Kingston College grammar school. He was not an effective teacher and left halfway through his second year, according to his own contradictory accounts, to see Latin America. While in Jamaica he had been attracted to both Castro's Cuba 100 miles across the water and to the Black Power movement in America, particularly Malcolm X's Nation of Islam.[2]

According to the Anti-Defamation League, the Nation of Islam 'has maintained a consistent record of anti-Semitism and racism since its founding in the 1930s'. Its literature has featured revisionist and anti-Semitic interpretations of the Holocaust, has exaggerated the role of Jews in the trans-Atlantic slave trade and, more recently accused Jewish doctors of injecting blacks with the AIDS virus.³ VSO colleagues believed that Corbyn, shy and insecure, was rebelling against his affluent background by identifying with the dispossessed and fantasised about his 'working class' roots. It is not clear whether he visited Cuba during this period, but it is feasible. He would hardly have been alone in worshipping the iconic images and propaganda of Fidel Castro and Che Guevara, posters of whom adorned the bedroom doors of many teenagers.

Academic Irving Louis Horowitz wrote: 'The Soviets provided Cuba with the model of attacking human rights activities and organisations as a necessary extension of the Jewish Zionist conspiracy. The identification of Castro with forces dedicated to the destruction of Israel was made plain in proclamation and practice. The Cuban position is that the war on terrorism is actually an example of "Liberation Imperialism".' He said that anti-Semitism is so powerfully rooted as a cultural element in authoritarian cultures that even when, as in the case of Cuban communism, it entails the tortured twisting of doctrinal elements within the Marxist-Leninist credo. Horowitz added: 'Part of the Castro attachment to communism is an overall contempt for the Jewish mini-Diaspora within the larger flight of Cubans to the United States and other places where the practice of free speech remains unimpeded.'⁴

Cuba was and remains a nation where anti-Semitism without Jews is a core belief. The Cuban National Assembly expressed its condemnation of the 'Zionist entity' as a 'horrendous and shameless action, a genocide which challenges universal public opinion, laughs at the United Nations, and threatens to invade other countries, reminiscent of the era of Nazism'.

Castro had a long gestation period under Soviet tutelage which included the Stalinist legacy in which Jews were subject to special treatment: from the denial of their special victimisation at the hands of the Nazi regime to the ousting of Jewish scholars from the sciences and a denial of emigration rights to Jews. The frequent charge of 'cosmopolitanism' in the xenophobic world of Soviet chauvinism was a virtual code word for being Jewish, or anti-national. The Soviet Press claimed that the Central Intelligence Agency was in cahoots with the 'Zionist Secret Service'. Such calumnies were repeated faithfully by the Cuban Communist Party and devoured in the bed-sit environment of Corbyn's political allies. It is certainly around this time that Corbyn's ill-informed dogma began to crystallise into something fixed and inflexible.

The fusion of Cuban foreign policy with the extremist regimes of the Middle East dates back to the ideological hardening that took place during the 1960s, shortly before Corbyn's arrival in the region. At the 1966 Havana meetings of the Tri-continental, the role of the Middle East as a bulwark against US imperialism was reaffirmed and Corbyn reputedly devoured reports of that conference during his largely-unproductive sojourn in Jamaica. The identification of Castro with forces dedicated to the destruction of Israel was made crystal clear when direct military assistance was extended to Syria during the wars of 1967 and 1973. Cuba regarded any Western attempts to counter terrorism as an example of 'Liberation Imperialism', the struggle in the Middle East was between oil rich independent nations and the US-Israeli effort to impose 'neo-liberal conquest strategies of strong states and barbarised conditions on a world scale'.[5] It was necessary to display unflinching loyalty to the dictatorial regimes in the Middle East, whether secular or clerical, and also distinguish its position from those regimes by avoiding the identification of Israel as a nation and the Jewish people as a world historic religion. The young Corbyn seems to have bought completely into this analysis and appears never to have changed his mind.

On his return to Britain, Corbyn was the only applicant for a clerical job at the London HQ of the National Union of Tailors and Garment Workers. He later exaggerated his role in fighting for low-paid workers. He claimed to have challenged bosses who had tried to cheat employees out of Christmas wages and National Insurance, bosses he labelled 'scumbags'. The union, as Tom Bower pointed out, has no record of such a dispute. The garment industry was tough, competitive and complex, but Corbyn seems to have indelibly linked unscrupulous sweatshop owners with Jewish businessmen who dominated the industry's lower end. He never understood that such an insecure industry could turn a small businessman into a production worker overnight. Bower wrote: 'Parochialism and fantasy fed the original source of his anti-Semitism – namely, as he saw it, the malign collective power of Jews.'[6] Corbyn later boasted that he had turned down the offer of a new suit from a Jewish tailor, claiming it was an attempt at bribery. He was also profoundly uneasy about the Jewish drive to succeed in order to survive. Bower wrote: 'Since he disdained materialism, culture and anything spiritual, Corbyn was an empty vessel, uneasy with a race complicated by its history of survival over two thousand years of persecution. While Jamaica was black against white ... Jews in London were the victims of discrimination by all classes of Europeans, including the working class. That truth did not quite fit the Marxist theory that Corbyn had imbibed ... workers exploited by employers who needed his protection as the first stage before eventually seizing power to govern the country.'[7]

As an organiser charged by the public sector union NUPE with boosting membership, Corbyn proved effective and tireless. To attract refuse collectors, he briefly changed his moniker to 'Jerry' but would find any excuse not to join them for a pint in the pub. During his time as a Haringey councillor, Corbyn was assiduous in cultivating the London borough's ethnic communities – Afro-Caribbeans, Asians and Greek Cypriots – but that did not extend to Orthodox Jews in Stamford Hill who had been the backbone of the local Labour party. His then-wife and fellow-councillor Jane Chapman said: 'Jeremy was conflicted because he supported Palestine and the abolition of Israel so that Palestinians could recover their homes.'[8] Corbyn regarded Israel as a bastion of American-backed imperialism, even colonialism, which to his mindset made Israel a racist state. He rejected the Balfour Declaration and dismissed the Holocaust in which six million Jews died as any justification for Jews having their own homeland at the expense, as he saw it, of others. He believed that the descendants of black slaves and dispossessed Palestinians were far more deserving of sympathy and support than death camp survivors. And he did not distinguish between Jews in London and Zionists in Tel Aviv, despite later attempts to rewrite his own history.

In the 1970s the extreme Left in Europe so embraced the conflicting causes of Middle East liberation' that in some circles even the Holocaust could be justified. Ulrike Meinhof of the Marxist Red Army Faction posed the question 'How was Auschwitz possible, what was anti-Semitism?' and stated the opinion that 'Auschwitz means that six million Jews were murdered and carted on to the rubbish dumps of Europe for being that which was maintained of them – Money-Jews.' She regarded hatred of Jews as in reality the hatred of capitalism and hence the murder of the Israeli Olympic team at the 1972 Munich Olympics was not only justified but something that could be praised. No-one is suggesting that Corbyn himself embraced or condoned such views, but they were part of the era's radical debate and dialogue.

In one respect, however, Corbyn could make common cause with the Jewish community on his patch – street opposition to the National Front. He claimed that his parents had taken part in the Battle of Cable Street against Oswald Mosley's Blackshirts. As a street-level activist he got his own chance for glory. On 23 April 1977 the National Front decided to commemorate Hitler's birthday with a march from Ducketts Common by Turnpike Lane Tube in north London down a busy London high road packed with Saturday afternoon shoppers. Corbyn, a trade union official and Labour councillor for the area adjacent to Ducketts Common, acted as the co-ordinator for all the local Haringey councillors. They had called for the NF march to be banned, recognising the provocation it was designed to be, but the police had declined. On the day, all the councillors assembled on Ducketts Common before the fascists marched, holding a giant banner making clear they stood firm against racism. But there was another group of people – anti-fascists, trade unionists, socialists – who were also determined that the NF would not march. Using his influence Corbyn was able to act as the spokesperson for both groups of people, presenting in effect a unified protest against the NF. The NF march petered out and was not repeated. That day led to the formation of the Anti-Nazi League and the first huge carnival in conjunction with Rock Against Racism at Victoria Park in May 1978. *Morning Star* journalist Keith Flett wrote: 'We should remember Corbyn's role in some of the events that led to the birth of the anti-racist and anti-fascist movement that did much to stop the NF from becoming, as it threatened to in the late 1970s, a major political force.'[10] However, it can still be argued that Corbyn's motivation was more to do with anti-fascist activism and organisation rather than any great concern with the safety of the Jewish community.

During this and subsequent periods, Corbyn would see first-hand how Militant and other extremist tendencies were able to take over a party, or union, or local authority branch using tactics of smear, direct insult and intimidation. In party branches from Liverpool to London, the Jewish community – with some high-profile exceptions – tended towards moderation. They were most concerned with the mundane job of representing local families and aspiring to provide decent housing, schooling and jobs, rather than supporting freedom fighters in Latin America or establishing nuclear-free zones or arguing about the factional differences between Marxism, Trotskyism, Stalinism and every other 'ism' in the book. That made them, to the Militant mindset that Corbyn embraced with zero sense of irony, 'class traitors' or stooges of capitalism, the CIA and the 'secret state'. Any who did not support the Trotskyist analysis 100 per cent were dismissed as apologists for colonialism, as were those who only agreed 70 or 80 or 90 per cent. The 1970s was a turbulent time, of course, but under Corbyn's tenure, street cleaning and school improvements were miles below Chile solidarity on his order of priorities. Former comrades, however, recall that Corbyn shunned face-to-face confrontations with those he considered enemies – Jewish or otherwise – but created the climate in which others could do the dirty work for him. This allowed him 'deniability' in the rare examples when the tactics of bullying and abuse became public.

While at Haringey, Corbyn agreed with the Trotskyist Ted Knight's refusal to welcome the successful 1976 Israeli special forces rescue of hostages held at Entebbe airport in Uganda. At subsequent elections, local Jews boycotted Knight and by extension his 'henchman' Corbyn. Corbyn's attitude towards Africa during this period and after is instructive. His hatred of 'colonialism' on that continent was, and is, shared by many, but he never seemed to grasp the fact that post-war administrations for many and varied reasons granted independence to 700 million people over just two decades. Corbyn, like many, protested against apartheid South Africa and the Ian Smith regime in post-UDI Rhodesia. Like many, he applauded the negotiated independence which led to Zimbabwe, but rarely acknowledged that Robert Mugabe turned from freedom fighter to corrupt and vicious dictator. In Corbyn's circle, Mugabe's attack on Britain as a country run by liars and scoundrels struck a loud note. But they were deaf when he also blamed the dominance of Britain's 'gay mafia' and when he told his cowed Cabinet that if it hadn't been for Mrs Thatcher 'none of you would be sitting here today.' Such things did not gel comfortably with the mindset that all victims – black, brown and Muslim – must be supported. But not Jews.

Before Labour's 1979 election defeat and the Thatcher era, Corbyn, George Galloway and Gerry Healy of the Workers Revolutionary Party (WRP) discussed the creation of the *Labour Herald* as a platform for extreme left views bankrolled by Iraq's Saddam Hussein and Libya's Muammar Gaddafi.[11] Healy, well-known for personal thuggery and anti-Semitism, regarded his constantly fracturing splinter of the left as his personal fiefdom. John Lister, expelled from the WRP in 1974, concluded: 'Healy was a crook and a political charlatan, who preserved his position as General Secretary of the WRP by resorting to the most bureaucratic and anti-democratic measures, who stubbornly opposed any campaigning for women's liberation or gay rights, who habitually subjected women "comrades" to sexual abuse, who sold out the WRP's formal principles and programme for Middle East oil money and who has done more than anyone to degrade the reputation of Marxism and Trotskyism in Britain.'[12] But Corbyn regarded Healy's socialist credentials as impeccable.

Corbyn's failure to reconcile conflicting stances is most noticeable in his avowed pacifism and his long support for the IRA, Hezbollah, Hamas and other terrorist organisations. Throughout the 1970s and subsequent decades he proved himself an apologist for terrorism in at least tacitly supporting the IRA's violent efforts to achieve a united Ireland. Just three weeks after the Brighton bomb in which Margaret Thatcher narrowly avoided death but five others were not so lucky, Corbyn met Sinn Fein's Gerry Adams and two convicted IRA volunteers in Westminster. His explanation – the need to open dialogues on all sides of the Ulster Divide – may have seemed admirable but his invitations clearly favoured the Republicans. He and Ken Livingstone had previously met Adams and the 'dialogue' was continued up to the Good Friday peace agreement delivered by Tony Blair with no help from Corbyn. Livingstone, as leader of the Greater London Council, had tried to offer £53,000 of ratepayers' cash to the Troops Out movement and had declared that 'what Britain has done for the Irish nation' was 'worse than what Hitler did to the Jews'.

Corbyn voted against the 1985 Anglo-Irish Agreement, saying, 'We believe that the agreement strengthens rather than weakens the border between the six and the 26 counties, and those of us who wish to see a United Ireland oppose the agreement for that reason.' In 1986, Corbyn joined a demonstration protesting against the trial of a group of IRA members including the Brighton bomber Patrick Magee[13] who would be found guilty of murdering five people. After refusing police requests to move from outside the court, Corbyn and 15 other protesters were arrested for obstruction and held for five hours before being released on bail but not charged. Following the 1987 Loughgall ambush, in which eight IRA members and one civilian were shot dead by the British Army in an operation to defend a police station, Corbyn attended a commemoration by the Wolfe Tone Society and stated 'I'm happy to commemorate all those who died fighting for an independent Ireland.'[14]

In the early 1990s, MI5 opened a temporary file on Corbyn to monitor his links to the IRA. The Metropolitan Police's Special

Branch scrutinised Corbyn for two decades, as he was 'deemed to be a subversive', someone who might 'undermine ... Parliamentary democracy'.[15] He appeared at a number of Republican protest events. According to *The Sunday Times*, following research in Irish and Republican archives, Corbyn was involved in over 72 events connected with Sinn Féin, or other pro-republican groups, during the period of the IRA's paramilitary campaign. In 2017 Corbyn said that he had 'never met the IRA', and Shadow Home Secretary Diane Abbott explained the apparent lie, saying that although he had met members of the IRA, 'he met with them in their capacity as activists in Sinn Fein.'[16]

In tandem with his activities on behalf of Irish terrorists, Corbyn supported those who overtly wanted to destroy Israel and its people. He supported the campaign to overturn the convictions of Jawad Botmeh and Samar Alami for the 1994 bombing of the Israeli Embassy in London. Both had admitted possessing explosives and guns but denied they were for use in Britain. Corbyn signed five early day motions in support of their case between 2002 and 2006. The convictions were upheld by the High Court of Justice in 2001 and by the European Court of Human Rights in 2007. In 1982 the *Labour Herald*, co-edited by Livingstone, printed a cartoon captioned 'The Final Solution' depicting Israeli premier Menachem Begin dressed as a Nazi officer crushing Arab corpses under his jackboot. The magazine accused Zionists of collaborating with the Nazi regime and exploiting 'the sympathy stirred up' by the Holocaust. Corbyn's contribution to the debate was to condemn the British government's failure to support 'the inalienable rights of the Palestinian refugees'.

Throughout the 1980s, Corbyn continued to display rampant hostility to a Zionist Israel, both in the causes he espoused and the people he mixed with. The latter included the playwright Jim Allen who collaborated with film director and left-wing icon Ken Loach. Their most controversial project was Allen's stage play, *Perdition*, which dealt with an allegation of collaboration between Hungarian Zionists and the Nazis during the Holocaust. The play was due to open at the Royal Court Theatre in January 1987 but was cancelled 36 hours before the opening night. Lord Goodman wrote: 'Mr Jim Allen's description of the Holocaust can claim a high place in the table of classic anti-Semitism.'[17]

More pernicious an influence, however, came from Tony Greenstein who orchestrated the Labour Movement Campaign on Palestine

(LMCP) which saw Israel as an 'apartheid state' which had no right to exist. Israel's defeat of the 1973 Arab invasion, its military and economic dominance in the region, and the occupation by settlers of the West Bank remained factors feeding the hostility towards the Middle East's only functioning democracy. Corbyn sponsored the LMCP's campaign to 'eradicate Zionism' by replacing Israel with Palestine. The organisation said, with Corbyn's apparent approval, that 'Zionism is inherently racist.' In 1984 Corbyn chaired a conference blaming the Labour Party for 'colonising' Palestine, sponsored a newsletter calling for the expulsion of *Poale Zion*, the only Jewish group affiliated to the party, and supported the expulsion of Jewish societies by student unions.[18] A Labour campaigner of the time, Harry Fletcher, said that Corbyn was 'institutionally antisemitic' – he simply subscribed, without any thought of his own, to left-wing prejudices of the era.

Corbyn was slavish in his support for Tony Benn, the era's biggest icon of the left, whose leadership bids failed but who succeeded in undermining successive Oppositions during the Thatcher years. Benn had been sympathetic to Israel while a minister but hardened his stance to suit shifting left-wing fashions. He became a Palestine Solidarity Campaign (PSC) member and one of Britain's most vocal Israel critics. He appeared to equate Israel's approach in the West Bank with the Holocaust, accused the country of ethnic cleansing and war crimes, backed calls for a boycott, and said the Israeli ambassador should be expelled from the UK following the Cast Lead operation in Gaza in 2009. He said at a PSC event in January 2011 that he did not believe in a two-state solution. 'The answer is a single state where Jews and Palestinians live together. To do that we have to dissolve Zionism,' he said.[19] Corbyn agreed.

Meanwhile, Israel gave anti-Zionists such as Corbyn a lot more ammunition, much of it legitimate from most viewpoints. The Cast Lead Israeli military offensive in Gaza resulted in the death of between 1,100 and 1,400 Palestinians and 13 Israelis. The election of Menachem Begin's *Likud* party saw the emergence of messianic nationalism, Thatcherite economic policies, the decline of the Israeli Labor Party and the occupation of the West Bank and the Gaza Strip. In Britain the Labour view of Israel shifted amongst its upper echelons towards sympathy for the concept of Palestinian statehood.[20] The broad membership, however, retained sympathy for Israel, particularly among older people with vivid memories of

Oh! Jeremy Corbyn

death camp newsreels. That eventually resulted in more balanced support for a two-state solution. Nevertheless, the sharp shift to the right in Israeli politics, together with a rise of broad anti-colonial politics, saw the left's attitudes hardening, a trend which Corbyn was happy to give voice to.[21]

A pivotal shift in the left's anti-Semitic attitude towards even greater hard-core antipathy came in 1982 with the Sabra and Shatila massacre of several hundred Palestinian and Lebanese Shi'ite civilians in a refugee camp outside Beirut by the Phalanges Christian militia allied to the Israeli Defence Forces which the previous year had invaded the south of the country. The sight of Jews nodding through Christians to slaughter Muslims was an event which shamed all involved, including Israel. It boosted the anti-Zionist instincts of the far-left in Britain while leaving moderates distinctly queasy. To the people surrounding Corbyn it was a propaganda gift. In 1983, a commission chaired by Sean MacBride, the human rights activist and winner of both the Lenin Peace Prize and the Nobel Peace Prize, assistant to the UN Secretary General and President of the United Nation General Assembly, concluded that Israel as the camp's occupying power, bore responsibility for the violence. His commission also concluded that the massacre was a form of genocide.[22] To Corbyn the verdict of an Irish freedom fighter endorsed his condemnation of Israel. What he never accepted, but MacBride did, was that Israel did respond emphatically to what was undoubtedly a shameful episode. Its Kahan Commission found that Israeli military personnel, aware that a massacre was in progress, had failed to take serious steps to stop it. The Commission deemed Israel indirectly responsible, and Ariel Sharon, then defence minister, bore personal responsibility 'for ignoring the danger of bloodshed and revenge', forcing him to resign.[23] But to the mindset of Corbyn and his narrow band of cronies, Israel never admitted its 'war crimes', which made them racists and capitalists and colonialist and every other epithet that could be thrown at them.

Following Shatila, *Radio Havana* stated that 'not even the Nazis undertook a retaliation of such proportions against a civilian population.' The response to guerrilla insurgency in the Gaza region was seen 'as the army of Israel proceeding with its work of extermination' and identified this struggle as 'part of the fascist designs over the Palestinian people. And 'the Zionist regime has shielded itself behind the kidnapping of an Israeli soldier to intensify their genocide of the Palestinians.' Cuba's essential ploy was to identify the Israeli response to the Hezbollah forces in Southern Lebanon as itself genocidal. The Cuban Ministry of Foreign Affairs stated that 'the real purpose are the hegemonic plans of Tel Aviv and Washington to dominate all the energy resources in the area.' Corbyn, by then a regular visitor to the island, agreed, believing that the emphasis on petroleum resources as the real source of the conflict in the Middle East accords well with the Marxist view that all conflicts in which 'imperialism' engages are motivated by economic self-interest. The Cuban statement goes some way towards explaining Corbyn's opposition to the EU: 'The armaments with which this genocide is being committed are supplied by the United States ... With rare exceptions, the European Union has served as an accomplice and has accepted the bland statements imposed by the Empire on the other side of the Atlantic.' The supposed linkage of Europe to America was seen as 'the shameful and cowardly passivity of the European Union'.

After Castro's death, Corbyn said it marked 'the passing of a huge figure in modern history, national independence and twentieth century socialism'. He added that 'for all his flaws' Castro would be remembered as an 'internationalist and a champion of social justice'. Typically, Crorbyn did not spell out what the 'flaws' were.

The Labour Committee on Palestine was formed in June 1982 to challenge the Labour Middle East Council, which supported a two-state solution, and to oppose the 'Zionist state as racist, exclusivist, expansionist and a direct agency of imperialism'. Ken Livingstone and Ted Knight of Lambeth borough council were early supporters; the chair was former British Anti-Zionist Organization (BAZO) activist Tony Greenstein. The new committee backed a resolution at the 1982 Labour Party conference to recognise the Palestine Liberation Organization (PLO) as the 'sole legitimate representative of the Palestinian people'. To the embarrassment of the party leadership, the conference passed the resolution.[24]

Labour academic Paul Keleman has argued that there is no evidence that anti-Semitism played any role in the left's changing perceptions of the Israeli Palestinian conflict in that period.[25] Daniel L. Staetsky, a senior research fellow for the Institute for Jewish Policy Research, also reported that anti-Semitism on the left was no higher than that of the general population.[26] But animosity grew, thanks in part to perception that much of the Jewish population had supported Margaret Thatcher, especially in her own seat of Finchley.[27]

In 2000, the Jewish anti-Zionist Paul Eisen, who had declared at numerous public meetings that the Nazis had not killed six million Jews, called at Corbyn's home and asked him to support Deir Yassin Remembered (DYR), an organisation set up to commemorate the 1948 massacre by Jewish terrorists of around 100 Palestinians near Jerusalem. Eisen recalled: 'I'd hardly begun my feverishly rehearsed pitch before his chequebook was on the table.'[28] Eisen later denied that he was a 'Holocaust-denier', rather a 'revisionist'. In 2008 he explained: 'That Jews suffered greatly from 1933–45 is not in question but the notion of a premeditated, planned, and industrial extermination of Europe's Jews with its iconic gas-chambers and magical six million are all used to make the Holocaust not only special but also sacred. We are faced with a new, secular religion, a false God with astonishing power to command worship. And, like the Crucifixion with its Cross, Resurrection etc, the Holocaust has key and sacred elements – the exterminationist imperative, the gas-chambers and the sacred six million. It is these that comprise the holy Holocaust which Jews, Zionists, and others worship and which … the revisionists refuse.'[29] So that's clear then.

What is really clear, yet again, is that Corbyn never seemed to detect even a whiff of hypocrisy or double standards – never mind breaches of party policy – when he was feted at rallies organised by Muslim organisations which rejected democracy, secularism, socialism or equal rights for women and homosexuals. When he was challenged on such matters, he simply fell back on Lenin's supposed, but highly doubtful, maxim that socialists would be given a free pass if they aligned themselves with any group, however unsavoury, dedicated to roughly similar goals.

In the first week of September 2001, Corbyn welcomed motions at the UN World Conference Against Racism in Durham, South Africa, which identified Zionism as the world's worst sort of racism and described the Moslem world's most repressive and totalitarian regimes as the 'good oppressed' because they were victims of Anglo-US imperialism. Placards were waved reading 'Kill All Jews' and 'The Good Things Hitler Did'. The following week Osama bin Laden's men piloted airliners into New York's World Trade Center and the Pentagon, killing almost 3,000 civilians. With by-now-predictable double-think, Corbyn condemned mass murder but held America and Britain responsible for the atrocity and said that Israel's occupation of the West Bank had 'driven' decent Moslems to terrorism. Corbyn advocated a zero response by the West.

Corbyn joined with CND general secretary Kate Hudson, *Morning Star* communist journalist Andrew Murray, the noted Trotskyist

Lindsey German and others to create the Stop the War Coalition. German had at the Durham conference said: 'I am not prepared to regard the state of Israel as somehow a viable presence.' What could have been an ineffective, divisive grouping was transformed by a flood of Moslem activists. They took note of Corbyn's comments that 'the Israeli tail wags the American dog' and that Israel was the 'keystone' of global imperialism – and promptly elected him vice-chairman. For a hard core, the aim was not so much preventing the loss of life inevitable in any war, rather the destruction of Western liberalism.

Premier Tony Blair rejected the Stop the War Coalition's argument that the invasion of Afghanistan would not bring peace or justice, and it has to be accepted that that view was proved correct both in that conflict and the subsequent American-led invasion of Iraq. So too were their suspicions over the 'dodgy dossier' on Saddam Hussein's military capacity used as the main excuse for the Iraq enterprise. On February 15 2003 at least 750,000 people – and perhaps as many as one million – joined a Stop the War demonstration in London partly organised by the Muslim Association of Great Britain which, it has been alleged many times, has connections with the Muslim Brotherhood, a terrorist organisation held responsible for suicide bombings and murders intended to enforce Sharia law. Some on the left were dubious about such a connection but were overruled before the demonstration by Corbyn, Murray and German.[30] In any case, Blair ignored the protest, the war went ahead, and he won the subsequent general election. Stop the War did, however, raise Corbyn's profile and gave him the beginnings of the public recognition that he craved.

Stop the War activists, and general disquiet over the Iraq conflict and No 10's 'dodgy dossier' deployed as a justification, heightened tensions between Islamic and Jewish communities, particularly in inner-city areas. One victim was Oona King who in 1997 had become only the second black woman, after Diane Abbott, to become an MP. The trouble was, she also had a Jewish heritage. In her maiden speech, King described the racial abuse she and her family had suffered as a child. She referred to herself as 'multi-ethnic', representing 'a truly multicultural constituency where hardship and deprivation gave birth to Britain's greatest social reforms'.[31] Her work on various committees covering Bangladesh and genocide in Rwanda saw her selected in 2003 as one of '100 Great Black Britons'. But her antipathy to the murderous regime of Saddam Hussein meant she felt she had no alternative but to vote in favour of the American-led invasion that toppled the dictator, although she was also appalled at the lack of planning for the war's aftermath.[32]

At the 2005 general election, her Bethnal Green and Bow seat, with a population of approximately 45,000 Muslim residents, was 'Respect' Leader George Galloway's best chance to defeat a Labour candidate. It proved a single-issue campaign which King described as 'one of the dirtiest ... we have ever seen in British politics'. King complained of 'quite disturbing' anti-Semitic and racial abuse, and an activist close to Galloway was overheard saying that they were going to 'get rid of the black Jew'.[33] She was pelted with rotten vegetables and eggs during a memorial service commemorating the Second World War German bombing of a block of flats that had predominantly Jewish victims.[34] King claimed it was a deliberate part of Respect's campaign, but Galloway and his spokesman denied any accusation of racial abuse. Both candidates were given police protection, King after her car tyres were slashed and Galloway after receiving a death threat.[35] King lost the seat by 823 votes, a 26.2% swing from King to Galloway. King said that, whilst her support for the war in Iraq had been a major issue, false claims in the Bangladeshi press that she wanted to get rid of *halal* meat had played a part in her defeat.[36] In 2010, King unsuccessfully challenged Ken Livingstone for the Labour Party nomination in the London Mayor contest, but Livingstone accused her of using inappropriate methods of obtaining email addresses of Labour Party supporters, something she vehemently denied. She was created a life peer and switched to a career in the media. Another effective Labour campaigner had been lost.

Corbyn continued to espouse the Palestinian cause. If he had confined himself to their right to exist, function and prosper, that would by normal political standards be honourable. The Palestinians had clearly had a raw deal. What was unacceptable was his embrace of factions whose preferred tactics were violence and whose oft-stated aim was the total destruction of the 'illegal' state of Israel. Corbyn repeatedly invited the most zealous anti-Zionists to his Westminster office, while not extending the same courtesy to prominent Jews.

He first denied on BBC Radio 4 meeting Moslem extremist Dyab Abu Jahjah, invited to address a Stop the War rally denouncing Israeli, American and British imperialism. Jahjah was arrested on suspicion of terrorist activities on his arrival at Heathrow Airport but Corbyn persuaded Home Secretary Jacqui Smith to let him through.

Pressed on his meeting, Corbyn said: 'I do not know who this person is.' He was shown a photograph of himself with Jahjah in the House of Commons, and promptly lost his rag. Bower wrote: 'Depicted as a friend of extremists, the man who prided himself on never losing his temper became noticeably irate for the first time in public. A new truth about Corbyn emerged. His nature was to reject any blame for an error. When exposed, he lost his temper.'[37] Another visitor was Islamic Movement in Israel leader Raed Salah who had likened Jews to 'monkeys' and 'bacteria'. Salah had been convicted in Israel for publicly claiming that Jews had drunk the blood of non-Jewish babies or eaten it baked in bread – a centuries-old smear. He also insisted that 9/11 was a Jewish plot. Asked if he had made a misjudgement in meeting Salah who he welcomed as a 'very honoured citizen' in 2011, Corbyn replied: 'We had quite a long conversation about multi-faith objectives.'

Corbyn never even tried to distance himself from such racist lunacy as that espoused by Salah and Jahjah. Indeed, he described the Reverend Stephen Sizer, an Anglican vicar banned from social media by the Church of England over his support for tweets claiming that Israel ordered the attacks on the twin towers, as a 'hero' for standing up to Zionism. In 2009 he told a Gaza-supporting rally of the tears he shed when told by his 'good friend' Ewa Jasiewicz about the appalling conditions in Gaza. Jasiewicz was best known for daubing graffiti on the walls of the Warsaw Ghetto from which 400,000 Jews had been taken to their deaths, and who had advised Palestinians to 'bump off' Israeli politicians.[38]

On 3 March 2009, Corbyn pronounced: 'It will be my pleasure and my honour to host an event in Parliament where our friends from Hezbollah will be speaking. I have also invited our friends from Hamas to come and speak.' Corbyn claimed that Britain had made a 'big, big historical mistake' in labelling Hamas a terrorist organisation; it was merely an 'honest' outfit committed to resisting Zionist imperialism. He urged the UK government to negotiate directly with Hamas and Hezbollah to 'bring about long-term peace and social justice'. He ignored Hamas's charter which promised to give five million Jews in Israel the option of either fleeing or being pushed into the sea. The military wing of Hamas had launched rocket attacks against Israeli civilians and soldiers, engaged in suicide bombings, and hit targets as far away as Tel Aviv and Haifa. The attacks on civilians have been condemned as war crimes and crimes against humanity by Human Rights Watch and other monitoring organisations.[39] It is frankly inconceivable that Corbyn was unaware that both outfits were committed to destruction rather than peace and justice. Israeli Ambassador to London Mark Regev said: 'You've had too many people on the progressive side of politics who have embraced Hamas and Hezbollah. Both of them are anti-Semitic organisations, you just have to read Hamas's charter and it's like chapters straight out of the *Protocols of the Elders of Zion*. I'd ask the following question: if you're progressive, you're embracing an organisation which is homophobic, which is misogynistic, which is openly anti-Semitic, what's progressive about that?' He added that the left was 'in denial' about the scale of the problem.[40]

On Holocaust Memorial Day 2010, Corbyn hosted a Commons protest to compare Gaza to Auschwitz in which the anti-Zionist death camp survivor Hajo Meyer spoke of the 'misuse of the Holocaust for political purposes'. It is doubtful that Corbyn saw any irony.[41] Meyer said: 'Judaism in Israel has been substituted by the Holocaust religion.'[42] When asked about his involvement with the meeting, Corbyn said: 'Views were expressed at the meeting which I do not accept or condone. In the past, in pursuit of justice for the Palestinian people and peace in Israel/Palestine, I have on occasion appeared on platforms with people whose views I completely reject. I apologise for the concerns and anxiety that this has caused.' By then, Corbyn's support for downtrodden Palestinians had again taken him into the dangerous arms of Iranian-financed Hamas and Hezbollah which between them had 60,000 well-armed militia in Gaza, Lebanon and the immediate region.

Much later, in 2016, Corbyn was under pressure over his choice of company and told MPs investigating accusations of anti-Semitism in the Labour Party that he regretted calling Hamas and Hezbollah 'friends'. Giving evidence at the home affairs select committee, he said: 'The language I used at that meeting was actually here in parliament and it was about encouraging the meeting to go ahead, encouraging there to be a discussion about the peace process. It was inclusive language I used which with hindsight I would rather not have used. I regret using those words, of course.' Corbyn was challenged about the views of his communications director, Seumas Milne, who had praised Hamas for their 'spirit of resistance' at a rally and who had 'chanted that they will not be broken'. Corbyn said he was unaware of the incident.

Corbyn was a long-time supporter of the Islamic Human Rights Commission (IHRC), seen by many as a front for the Iranian regime. Founded in 1979, it has four directors: Chairman Massoud Shadjareh described the late supreme leader Ayatollah Khomeini as 'a torch light for the whole of mankind' and spoke of the Islamic Republic's record of 'standing against injustice' as 'the only nation standing against oppression, against tyranny, in line with the wishes of Iranians and the overwhelming majority of people in the region and beyond'. Arzu Merali, the research director, co-wrote a paper with Shadjareh, which spelt out that the real enemy was the West, adding, 'we are all Hezbollah'. Another director, Sajed Reza Ameli, is the Tehran-based secretary of the Iranian policy unit the Supreme Council of the Cultural Revolution. And the fourth director is Nazim Ali who at a rally days after the Grenfell Tower fire disaster blamed 'Zionists who give money to the Tory party to kill people in high-rise blocks. Corbyn said that IHRC 'represents all that's best in Islam'. He added: 'I like the way it works. I like the sense of values around it.' When asked about the regime's suppression of women's right, including the arrest of a woman who dared attend a football match, Corbyn did not respond. He received almost £20,000 for appearances on the Iranian state-funded Press TV, according to the Register of Members' Interests. Press TV had its British licence revoked in 2012 after it broadcast an interview carried out under duress with a detained journalist.

Corbyn hosted an Iranian TV discussion programme which was used as a platform to promote Zionist conspiracy theories. When one contributor referred to the BBC as 'Zionist liars' Corbyn asked if he had 'used his right as a licence-payer to complain about their coverage'. When Osama bin Laden was killed by US special forces in May 2011, Corbyn told Iranian broadcasters that the killing was 'a tragedy that would make the world a more dangerous place'. Tory premier David Cameron, at his party's annual conference, condemned his stance, to polite applause. At a rival conference nearby young Corbyn supporters screamed 'Jewish Tory scum' at Blairite Labour delegates. Others sent online abuse to mainly female delegates; Jess Philips was told: 'Kill yourself, you bigoted scum.' Characteristically, Corbyn stayed silent. Bower wrote: 'Letting others attack his enemies was a win-win tactic.'[43]

In January 2014 Corbyn joined an all-party Parliamentary trip to Iran, flying business class despite his initial objection. The delegation aimed to consider abuses of human rights, but Corbyn remained silent during meetings with officials about the regime's executions of homosexuals, juvenile drug-users and political opponents, or the suppression of women and minorities.[44]

The Arab Spring, the fall of Gaddafi in Libya, brutal wars across the region and the rise of the ISIS death cult appear to have change Corbyn's simplistic views of the Middle East not one iota – it was all the fault of Zionists, the American military machine, British colonialism and international capitalist conspiracies. Asked if he would condemn British Moslem volunteers to ISIS, currently engaged in mass rape, sexual slavery, public beheadings and drowning and burning opponents in cages, he replied, 'it's wrong to make value judgements.' Of ISIS tactics, he told the Russian TV channel *RT*: 'Yes, they are brutal. What they have done is quite appalling; likewise what the Americans did in Fallujah and other places is appalling.' His biographer, Tom Bower, wrote: 'In Corbyn's eyes, there was a moral equivalence between the American army using excessive force against organised Sunni and Shia terrorist armies in Iraq that were responsible for planting huge bombs in Baghdad and other cities, and ISIS pushing gays off tower blocks.'[45]

In January 2011, a motion was submitted to rename Holocaust Memorial Day as 'Genocide Memorial Day' so that it would reflect the truth that not all Nazi victims were Jews. Corbyn put his name to it. Karen Pollock, chief executive of the Holocaust Educational Trust later said: 'Holocaust Memorial Day already rightly includes all victims of the Nazis and subsequent genocides, but the Holocaust was a specific crime, with anti-Semitism at its core. Any attempt to remove that specificity is a form of denial and distortion.'[46]

That same year Corbyn was engaged in another telling controversy, although its implications would not emerge for several years. The radical writer John Atkinson Hobson of the Manchester Guardian covered the Boer War and in 1902 published *Imperialism: A Study*. (*See Chapter 3*) Corbyn wrote the foreword for a republication in which he described it as 'a great tome' and 'brilliant'. He may have missed the section that asserted that global finance was controlled 'by men of a single and peculiar race, who have behind them many centuries of financial experience' who 'are in a unique position to control the policy of nations'.[47] When the row broke out, Corbyn responded that the language used to describe minorities in Hobson's work is 'absolutely deplorable', but asserted that his foreword analysed 'the process that led to the First World War' which he saw as the subject of the book and not Hobson's racist language. To be fair, Hobson was also cited and praised by previous Labour leaders, including Gordon Brown who described Hobson as 'probably the most famous Liberal convert to what was then literally "new Labour"'. But the incident exposed Corbyn's propensity to honour heroes without bothering to check what they had actually said, done and written.

The following year saw an incident which, when it was exposed six years later, threw up questions about his eyesight and possibly his sanity. The 2012 Freedom for Humanity was a street mural painted in east London by American artist Mear One. The artist admitted it depicted an 'elite banker cartel' of the Rothschilds, the Rockefellers, the Morgans and others sitting around a Monopoly-style board game places on the backs of semi-naked black men. The mural – always intended to be a temporary installation, was removed by Tower Hamlets council following complaints by residents. Local Mayor Lutfer Rahman said 'the images of the bankers perpetuate anti-Semitic propaganda about conspiratorial Jewish domination of financial and political institutions'. The artist denied that but even the most cursory examination showed that the Jewish caricatures resembled the imagery used by *Der Sturmer* in Nazi Germany. Corbyn, who responded to a Facebook post from the artist, criticised its removal, asking: 'Why? You are in good company. Rockerfeller (sic) destroyed Diego Viera's mural because it includes a picture of Lenin in 1934.'[48] Later, when his response was finally reported, Corbyn's spokesman issued a statement: 'Jeremy was responding to concerns about the removal of public art on grounds of freedom of speech. However, the mural was offensive, used anti-Semitic imagery, which has no place in our society, and it is right that it was removed.' In his own statement, Corbyn said, 'I sincerely regret that I did not look more closely at the image I was commenting on, the contents of which are deeply disturbing and anti-Semitic. The defence of free speech cannot be used as a justification for the promotion of anti-Semitism in any form. That is a view I've always held.'[49] Many doubted that claim. Karen Pollock of the Holocaust Educational Trust said that the mural was 'indefensible' as it 'was blatantly anti-Semitic, using images commonly found in anti-Semitic propaganda – it is impossible not to notice'.[50]

In a January 2013 meeting in Parliament, the UK Palestinian Authority representative Manuel Hassassian said that Jews are 'the only children of God ... because nobody is stopping Israel building its messianic dream of Eretz Israel [the Land of Israel].' A few days later at an event at Friends House convened by the Palestinian Return Centre, Corbyn defended Hassassian's comments on the history of Palestine. Deploying his trademark heavy-handed sarcasm, he said that those comments were 'dutifully recorded by the thankfully silent Zionists' in the audience. Corbyn went on to say that these 'Zionists' had approached Hassassian and 'berated him afterwards for what he had said', and that they had 'two problems': 'One is that they don't want to study history and secondly, having lived in this country for a very long time, probably all their lives, they don't understand English irony either. Manuel [Hassassian] does understand English irony and uses it very, very effectively so I think they need two lessons which we can help them with.'[51] When a tape of his speech emerged, historian Deborah Lipstadt asserted that Corbyn had crossed the line from anti-Zionism to anti-Semitism. Corbyn responded that he was using Zionist 'in the accurate political sense and not as a euphemism for Jewish people'. A Labour spokesperson said that parts of the speech which contextualised Corbyn's language were 'edited out of the footage ... He had been speaking about Zionists and non-Zionist Jews and very clearly does not go on to use Zionists as any kind of shorthand for Jews'. That became a common defence but cut little ice even with those who had previously been staunch Corbyn defenders. One of them was *The Guardian*'s Simon Hattenstone, who wrote: 'It is unclear what the irony in question is. But it is irrelevant. To generalise about any race or religion is discriminatory. And if there were ever a clear example of somebody conflating Zionist with Jews, this appears to be it. Let's play the traditional "swap the minority" game. Instead of "Zionists" let's make it, say, Muslims or African-Caribbeans or Asians or Irish needing lessons in history or irony. Not nice, eh? And what exactly does he mean by Zionists who have spent all or most of their lives in this country? Today the party insisted that Corbyn had been quoted out of context and that he had been referring to "Jewish and non-Jewish activists". Maybe. But it sounds pretty much like he was talking about British Jews to me. Let's look closely at the words used by Corbyn: These British Zionists don't study history, and they don't understand irony (ironic coming from one of the greatest literalists British politics has produced). In other words, they are uneducated, they have failed to integrate or assimilate, they are outsiders, they don't belong, they need to be taught a lesson. Sorry, Jeremy, this is the language of supremacism.'[52]

In 2014, Corbyn and some of his staff had been members of three private Facebook groups, including *Palestine Live* and *History of Palestine*, containing anti-Semitic posts. A spokesman said that Corbyn had been added to the first two groups by others, had little involvement in them, and had either left them already or left following the reports. The Labour Party stated that a full investigation would be undertaken, and action taken against any member involved.[53] But *The Sunday Times* uncovered over 2,000 examples of anti-Semitic, racist, violent threats and abusive posts in Corbyn-supporting private Facebook groups, including frequent attacks on Jews and Holocaust denying material.[54] Many of the posts criticised Labour MP Luciana Berger and Jonathan Arkush, president of the Board of Deputies of British Jews. A Labour Party spokesperson said the groups 'are not officially connected to the party in any way'. Subsequently, Corbyn deleted his own personal Facebook account that he had set up before becoming Labour leader, although his official page remained.[55]

The former Archbishop of Canterbury, Lord Carey of Clifton, said of Corbyn: 'The weakness of his statements can give the impression that he is, deep-down, somebody who doesn't like Jewish people. I hope he might say that's not the case, but I feel he's not giving clear leadership to his own party in condemning from within his own ranks people who speak out against Jewish people.' He added: 'I would encourage socialists and those in the Labour Party to pay attention to what they say about racism and about the influence of Jews within their own party.' Columnist Sean O'Grady of *The Independent* wrote that for a long time he had given Corbyn the benefit of the doubt on the issue, but finally he wrote: 'When you start to add it all up, though, you do start to wonder what's going on in his head. Particularly, you wonder whether, in fact, all Corbyn's political prejudices – against American "imperialism", Nato as an "occupying force", about international finance capitalism, for Hezbollah and Hamas – are just fanning out, or feeding in, to one unifying theme: an unacknowledged anti-Semitism. The best that can be said is that he is so dim he probably doesn't even realise it, but that may be too generous.'[56]

Irving Horowitz wrote: 'Anti-Semitism is so powerfully rooted as a cultural element in authoritarian cultures that even when, as in the case of Cuban Communism, it entails the tortured twisting of doctrinal elements within Marxism-Leninism. Its leaders will sacrifice the ideology to the reality. The fusion of Jihadist acts of revenge and terror, the instance on the supreme role of Islamist belief as a test of moral worth, and the virtual negation of popular rule as a test for regime worth, all become part of the common struggle against Israel as a nation and Judaism as a cultural tradition. For a world that has witnessed the horrors of the Holocaust in Nazi Germany and the systematic decomposition of Jewish life in Bolshevik Russia, the new wave of warfare upon the singular democracy in the Middle East and the calumny heaped upon its people – even by European powers that should now know better – is a grim reminder that moral progress lags far behind technological advances.'[57]

At a constituency level, Corbyn has taken up some local Jewish causes, with mixed results. University of Buckingham politics professor Geoffrey Alderman wrote:

> For whilst it's one thing to accuse him of being 'soft' on anti-Semitism, tolerating it and even befriending some of its exponents, it's quite another to level the charge against him personally. What truth – if any – could there possibly be in such an accusation? The fact of the matter is that Corbyn has an impressive record of supporting Jewish communal initiatives. For instance, he was recently supportive of Jewish efforts to facilitate the speedy issue of death certificates by the north London coroner. In 2015 he took part in a ceremony in his Islington constituency to commemorate the founding of the North London Synagogue. In 2010 he put his name to an Early Day Motion (tabled by Diane Abbott) calling on the UK government to facilitate the settlement of Yemeni Jews in Britain.
>
> In 1987 the West London Synagogue approached Islington Council with a startling proposal: to sell its original cemetery to property developers, destroying the gravestones and digging-up and reburying the bodies lying under them. This cemetery (dating from 1840) was not merely of great historic and architectural interest – in the view of orthodox Jews, the deliberate destruction of a cemetery is sacrilegious. So when Islington Council granted the planning application, a Jewish-led and ultimately successful campaign was launched to have the decision reversed. I was part of that campaign. So was Jeremy Corbyn. Meanwhile, the then-leader of Islington Council (1982–92), whose decision to permit the destruction of the cemetery was eventually overturned, was none other than Margaret Hodge (though it is unclear whether she personally was in favour of

the proposal). I have deliberately omitted from this discussion any consideration of Corbyn's attitude to Zionism and whether anti-Zionism is inherently anti-Semitic. All I will say here – as a proud Zionist – is that in my view context is, again, paramount. I will agree that from time to time, as backbench MP and party leader, Corbyn has acted unwisely. But the grounds for labelling him an anti-Semite simply do not exist.[58]

Rhea Wolfron, a Jewish member of Labour's ruling body, wrote: 'I've had the honour of working closely with Jeremy Corbyn, one of the most principled people in politics. As a former member of the Jewish Leadership Council Board, I can't be dismissed as someone on the fringes of the Jewish community, as many of my friends and comrades have. Criticising the actions of the Israeli government is not anti-Semitic. As a Jewish person who is critical of some Israeli government policies, I find this suggestion deeply offensive. Many of us are aware that there is a political discourse that surrounds Israel and the Occupation that is toxic and sometimes crosses the line into anti-Semitism. Criticising the Israeli government's actions does not mean you are denying Israel's right to exist. Jeremy has been clear that he is committed to working towards a just and viable settlement of the conflict, with a secure Israel alongside a secure and viable state of Palestine, as set out in Labour's manifesto.'

She said that a 'conflation of anti-Semitism with criticisms of the Israeli government undermines the fight against anti-Semitism and distracts us from challenging this evil in our society. But this isn't to say that anti-Semitism doesn't exist within the Labour Party. It does and Jeremy made his commitment to eliminating it absolutely clear. When I have faced anti-Semitism, whether within or outside of our movement, Jeremy has been an ally, Jennie has been an ally, as have many other Labour comrades. Anti-Semitism exists on the left, as it exists in society but this does not mean anti-Semitism is more of a problem on the left.' She went on: 'Many left-wing Jews have grown up struggling to find our place in the community. We've found places in youth groups or other organisations or built our own communities, but now that fight is feeling insurmountable. Recently I've seen my friends cast out, subjected to daily abuse and even told they just aren't Jewish. This level of vitriol doesn't allow for well-meaning or constructive conversation; without which we stand no chance of truly eradicating the evil of anti-Semitism in our society.

Anyone who knows, has met, or worked with Jeremy Corbyn, as I have, knows that he does not have a prejudicial bone in his body, and is utterly committed to tackling anti-Semitism, as he is all forms of discrimination and oppression, which he has fought against all his life. My commitment to Labour is unwavering and I am proud of the work that Jeremy is doing to tackle anti-Semitism in politics and wider society.'[59]

The Canary's Frea Lockley reported 'concrete' proof that Corbyn was not anti-Semitic. Top of the list was Corbyn's 2016 visit to the Terezin concentration camp in the Czech Republic. Ahead of the visit, he told the *Independent* that, the memorial is 'a vital reminder of the genocidal crimes carried out during the Second World War and the dangers that far-right politics, anti-Semitism and racist scapegoating pose to society'. It was allegedly his 'third visit to such a camp, all of which were largely unreported in the most read UK papers'. Lockley wrote: 'In fact Corbyn's commitment to peace and global human rights has been internationally recognised. In 2013, he was awarded the Gandhi Foundation International Peace Award. Then in 2017, he received the Séan MacBride Peace Prize. Again, neither of these awards gained wide recognition in the mainstream media.

'Corbyn has a noteworthy track record of opposing anti-Semitism through parliamentary procedures too. These include: In 1990, he stood behind concerns about the "dissemination of anti-Semitic and racist materials" and challenged the lack of prosecution over sharing known anti-Semitic publications. Corbyn signed an Early Day Motion (EDM) in 2003 condemning "terrorist, anti-Semitic attacks" against two synagogues. This EDM also criticised "a dramatic increase in anti-Semitic incidents against the UK Jewish community and ... rise in support for the BNP". It rejected "those who cynically exploit differences of opinion over Israel and Palestine to promote anti-Semitism". The EDM called for the government to "institute a zero-tolerance policy to combat anti-Semitism, Islamophobia and racism in all its forms". In 2009 he signed an EDM to challenge the rise of anti-Semitism in UK universities. He also signed an EDM criticising online anti-Semitism in the same year. In 2013, Corbyn signed an EDM to condemn "all forms of racism and anti-Semitism in sport".'[60] Putting a signature to an EDM (Early Day Motion) is, however, the least onerous and time-consuming part of an MP's job.

Possibly an explanation of why Corbyn and his supporters are so blind to their biases can be found is a *New Statesman* article by Alan Johnson, senior research fellow at the Britain Israel Communications and Research Centre (BICOM). He quoted the British novelist Howard Jacobson's question: 'Why can't we oppose the inequities of a society weighted in favour of wealth, and all the trash that wealth accumulates, without at the same time having to snuggle up to Putin, pal out with Hamas, and make apologies for extremists?' Johnson said: 'One answer to the Jacobson Question has been offered by Yasmin Alibhai Brown, a defender of Corbyn. His "tendency for unchecked inclusiveness", as she delicately puts, is due to his "naivety". But that explanation will not do. We won't find the answer in one man's naivety, especially not one with a lifetime of political experience behind him. We must go deeper, reading Corbyn's undoubted tendency to snuggle, to pal out and to apologise as a symptom of an intellectual and political malady: the long-term ideological corruption of that part of the left in which he was formed. This corrupting ideology can be called "campism". It has caused parts of the left to abandon universal progressive values rooted in the Enlightenment and sign up instead as foot soldiers in what they see as the great contest between – these terms change over time, as we will see – "Progressive" versus "Reactionary" nations, "Imperialism" versus "Anti-Imperialism", "Oppressed" versus "Oppressor" peoples, "The Empire" versus "The Resistance", or simply "Power" versus "The Other". Again and again, the curse of campism has dragged the political left down from the position of intellectual leader and agenda-setter to that of political irrelevance, or worse, an apologist for tyranny. Only when we register the grip of this ideology will we understand why some leftwingers march around London waving placards declaring "we are all Hezbollah now!".'

Johnson reckoned that in the twentieth century, it took the form of Stalinism, a social system that was at once anti-capitalist and totalitarian, and that spread a set of corrupting mental habits that utterly disorientated the left. He said: 'Clinging to the dogma that it must have been some kind of socialism that had replaced capitalism, many imagined themselves to be involved in a "great contest" between the capitalist camp and the (imperfect) socialist camp. And that ruined them. They became uncritical supporters of totalitarianism – notwithstanding their knowledge of the show trials, mass killings, gulags, political famines, and military aggressions; notwithstanding the fact that they themselves were not totalitarians. The result was the slow erasure of those habits of mind, sensibilities and values of an older left-wing culture rooted in the Enlightenment. In its place the Stalinist-campist left posited lesser-evilism, political cynicism, power-worship, authoritarianism, and sophisticated apologias for tyranny.'

He concluded: 'The result has been immense political disorientation, political cross-dressing, and moral debasement across swathes of the left. How else to explain the leftwing social theorist Judith Butler's astonishing claim that, 'understanding Hamas, Hezbollah as social movements that are progressive, that are on the left, that are part of a global left, is extremely important'? When we understand how campism creates that kind of ideology-saturated and captive mind, we can better understand Corbyn's choice of comrades and answer the Jacobson Question. The commitment to oppose every projection of force by the West as malign underpins Corbyn's commitments to unilateral nuclear disarmament and withdrawal from NATO, his attitude to the IRA, and to Putin, and his false equating of the actions of Isis and the coalition in Iraq.'

Johnson quoted the Community Security Trust: 'I am sure that Corbyn would be the first to condemn Holocaust denial. The problem is not that Corbyn is an anti-Semite or a Holocaust denier – he is neither. The problem is that he seems to gravitate towards people who are, if they come with an anti-Israel sticker on them.' Johnson added: 'Hezbollah comes with the mother of all anti-Israel stickers. That is why – although Corbyn knows that it is a radical Shia militant group that has subverted Lebanese democracy, actively supported Bashar al-Assad's brutality in Syria, and seeks the destruction of Israel – he nonetheless tells the left that Hezbollah are our 'friends'.

'Hamas too. Yet Corbyn knows that Amnesty International believes Hamas to be guilty of war crimes, torture, abductions, and summarily killing civilians. He knows that when five Jews praying in a synagogue were murdered, along with the heroic Druze policeman who came to their aid, in 2014, Hamas welcomed the attack, calling it a "quality development". The problem is not that Corbyn agrees with what all these people say. It is that he agrees with who they are: the Resistance to Empire. The apologies and the contortions and the evasions all begin there. The concern here is not that Corbyn indulges in anti-Semitism. He does not. At best, he is an innocent abroad who – oddly, in the age of "Google it!" – can't seem to work out who is who, or what is what.'

And the openDemocracy blogger Keith Kahn-Harris also expressed scepticism about Corbyn's explanation of his choice of comrades:

'Although he has defended his contacts with Islamists, the IRA and others as a contribution to peace-making, Corbyn does not have the deep relationships across the spectrum [or] the even-handedness that this would entail. [He] 'is constantly predisposed to be at least convivial towards a broad swathe of those who see themselves as opposed to the West. Much of what appears to be [Corbyn's] openness does indeed reflect engrained political pathologies.'

A *Jerusalem Report* opinion article also tried to get to grips with Corbyn's mindset: 'Jeremy Corbyn is an exponent of a hard-left political agenda peculiar to Britain. It is based on a particular view of the British class system, its colonialist past and capitalism. He opposes the lot. Everywhere Corbyn sees victims of over-wheening colonial exploiters or unscrupulous big business, and clearly feels a bond of sympathy with all who claim to be struggling against them, no matter how ruthless their methods. A fashionable new-wave philosophy called "Intersectionality" has captured the left-wing in the UK and Antifa in the USA. Intersectionality holds that there is a link between all manifestations of oppression, however diverse, and therefore between all victims. Female victims of sexual inequality have a bond with black victims of racial inequality and with victims of lesbian, gay, bisexual and transgender inequality, and so on. Intersectionality decrees that Palestinians are quintessential victims, and that their villainous oppressors are Israel, which it accuses of every sort of monstrous criminality including genocide. The logic of intersectionality decrees that anyone who opposes racism, homophobia or sexism must necessarily oppose Israel. That diktat is easily extended to all who support Israel, and by a further extension all Israelis, most of whom happen to be Jews. This is how eminent academics have come to refuse to engage professionally with their Israeli counterparts, while stoutly maintaining that they are not anti-Semitic in doing so.'[61]

So, is Jeremy Corbyn anti-Semitic and therefore racist? He and his acolytes reject the very idea as unthinkable. 'Anyone who knows Jeremy knows there isn't a racist bone in his body' is a common mantra amongst the Corbynista set. But a person is judged by the company he keeps and the things he says, and there is plenty of evidence above to the charge. If it walks with bigots, talks like a bigot and acts like a bigot, it is most probably a bigot. The only thing that is clear is that he doesn't believe it himself. But as we have seen, Corbyn is hardly blessed with self-knowledge. My own view is that Corbyn has such a narrow world view, pretty much unchanged since his teens and reinforced by a life happiest spent in meetings with the like-minded and demos against capitalist and colonialist demons, and surrounded by acolytes who boost his own smug certainties. He has fooled himself into believing in conspiracies, many of them involving Jews. He has been hood-winked by brighter people and justifies socialising with terrorists and their sympathisers by his constant refrain that he is committed to peace through dialogue. In fact, he contributed nothing positive to peace in Northern Ireland or the Middle East. In the former case, the hard work was done by the likes of John Hume and David Trimble, Mo Mowlam, Tony Blair, Bill Clinton and many others who despised Corbyn's brand of tokenism in a complicated cause. In both the case of Northern Ireland and the Middle East the question of whether, through supporting often-conflicted 'freedom movements' and praising anti-Zionist fanatics, there is blood on his hands can never be proven. Either way, he would have contributed more to peace by going to the pub with off-shift binmen.

Corbyn, in his utterances, has always displayed ignorance about socialist history. He is notorious for showing little inclination for reading books. Like many better-read colleagues, he has been highly selective in his understanding of Marx. He appears to know little of the work of the Jewish diaspora in building socialist movements from their beginnings on the fringe to the creation of the Labour Party itself. He appears oblivious to the part played by Jewish millionaires in the funding of the Russian Revolution or the part, albeit for less than honourable motives, that Joseph Stalin played in the creation of Israel. And for someone who claims always to side with dispossessed refugees, he has shown little interest in the history of Jews fleeing persecution before, during and after the Holocaust.

Another thing which remains crystal clear is that he has shown no leadership in his supposed efforts to root out anti-Semitism among his most fervently racist supporters. His intellectual shortcomings evinced in his misreading of history has played a part in that, of course. But another major factor is his see-sawing between causes dear to the metropolitan elite in his Islington power base and the shilly-shallying which exposes the myth that he is a man who has always stuck to his principles. The obvious case is Brexit – Corbyn voted against the then-Common Market in 1975 and consistently opposed greater integration in the decades that followed. He then campaigned for Remain in 2016 referendum, then supported Commons moves to establish a permanent customs union and maintain close alignment to the single market. Then he belatedly swung behind a second referendum to overturn the original decision, while pledging that as prime minister he WOULD take Britain out of the EU. Maverick Tory columnist Peter Oborne, previously a believer in Corbyn's integrity and commitment to just causes, wrote: 'Corbyn will soon have taken more positions on Brexit than there are in the Kama Sutra.'[62] His fence-sitting on that and other issues such as the HS2 high-speed rail link exposed a weak man held hostage by the fanatics that surround him. Which goes a long way to explain his self-denial on anti-Semitism.

The ordure really hit the fan after Corbyn snatched the Labour Leadership, but it took a while. Jeremy Corbyn got a rock star reception at the 2017 Glastonbury Festival telling the enthusiastic crowd that millions of young people who voted for him would not be silenced or side-lined. His popularity at Worthy Farm could be measured by the number of pro-Corbyn banners on display and Corbyn T-shirts. They easily outnumbered those for the biggest names on the musical bill – Radiohead, Foo Fighters and Ed Sheeran. And the chant 'Oh, Jeremy Corbyn' rang round the world's biggest greenfield festival. There would be no repeat performance at subsequent festivals as more people saw through his façade. And a major factor in that was a perfect storm over anti-Semitism.

8
Labour Pains

'clear evidence of ignorant attitudes'

A membership surge prompted by Ed Miliband's party rule change admitting 'three-pound entryists' in August 2015 saw Jeremy Corbyn emerge as the surprise front-runner in the upcoming elections for the Labour Party leadership. It was not long before numerous anti-Semitism issues came back to haunt him.

The *Jewish Chronicle* quizzed him over his past platform-sharing with 'Holocaust deniers, terrorists and some outright anti-Semites'. Corbyn responded his oft-repeated mantra that his relationship with Hezbollah and Hamas was part of his 'search for peace' in the Middle East. The newspaper pointed to his failure to object to anti-Semitic banners and posters that were a prominent feature of London Quds Day rallies supported by the Stop the War Coalition, of which Corbyn had been national chair since 2011.[1] The *Chronicle* also asked him about Deir Yassin Remembered, an organisation commemorating the massacre of over 100 Palestinian villagers in 1948 founded by Holocaust denier Paul Eisen.[2] Up to 2013, Corbyn and Jewish Labour MP Gerald Kaufman had attended some of the group's annual events. Corbyn insisted that such attendances had taken place before Eisen had made his views known publicly, and that he would not have associated with him had he known.[3] That was another occasion in which Corbyn either had a faulty memory, or was remarkably ill-informed, or was being economical with the truth. Eisen's views had been well known in political circles since at least 2005 and he had written an essay on his website in 2008 entitled 'My life as a Holocaust denier'.[4]

Chronicle editor Stephen Pollard contacted Carmen Nolan, Corbyn's media spokesperson offered him a right-of-reply article, but Corbyn declined. Pollard pressed Nolan on why Corbyn had professed friendship with Hamas. The outcome was that Corbyn responded to seven detailed questions with evasive answers. Nolan explained: 'He's attended countless meetings and he cannot check the background of everyone he's met.'[5] His former lover and Labour MP Diane Abbott defended Corbyn by branding those who challenged his version of recent history part of a 'Westminster elite' opposed to his anti-austerity agenda.[6] Forty-seven prominent Jewish activists, including Selma James and Miriam Margolyes, signed a round-robin letter criticising the *Jewish Chronicle*'s reporting.[7] Such verbal fight-backs branding critics as class traitors and accusing journalists of fake news – scams which Donald Trump later used instinctively – became a common tactic in Camp Corbyn. They were deployed regularly after Corbyn's September coronation as Leader.

A major player in Corbyn's successful Leadership campaign was Jon Lansman, formerly Tony Benn's chief fixer in the 1980s. He was raised in an Orthodox Jewish family in North London, and his father was a Conservative councilor in Hackney. At 16 he visited Israel and worked on a *kibbutz* in the Negev. He recalled: 'It was actually a very politicising experience. When I did my *bar mitzvah* I saw myself as a Zionist and I think after I went there I felt it less. I was more interested in the *kibbutz* and what I liked about it was the pioneering spirit, the sense of community and radicalism of it.'[8] Lansman volunteered for Corbyn's leadership campaign and was the sole director of Jeremy Corbyn Campaign 2015 (Supporters) Ltd, an official campaign company that held data collected by volunteers and activists.[9] His reputation as an activist was based on hard work, commitment and occasionally dodgy practices – he posted a Twitter link on Facebook depicting rival Labour candidate Liz Kendall as a future Tory leader. Corbyn's spokesperson was forced into a rebuttal, saying: 'We discourage all Jeremy Corbyn supporters from joining in with spoof websites or social media.'[10] Kendall and another Leadership rival, Yvette Cooper, were Twitter-spammed with abusive epithets, including 'witch' and 'c***', which Lansman condemned.

Following Corbyn's election, Lansman co-founded the campaign group Momentum to promote the radical socialism that the new Leader claimed to advocate and represent. When worries about anti-Semitism surfaced, Lansman wrote on his *left Futures* blog that the use of the term Zionist to describe supporters of the government in

Israel was 'counter-productive'. He cited one poll of British Jews which found that 71% favoured a Palestinian state and 75% opposed the Israeli settlements, while 68% still identified as Zionists.[11] He said that a 'rational debate about how to change the terms of the current debate' requires an acknowledgement 'that people on the left may also demonstrate some prejudice of their own'. In a January 2016 interview, asked about attitudes to Israel in the Labour Party and the attitudes of Jews towards it, said: 'Yes, of course the vast majority of British Jews are supportive of Israel as a Jewish state – and actually so is Jeremy – but they are far from supportive of all aspects of what is currently happening there. I think Jews in Britain want peace too. I think Jeremy's message of fairness for the Palestinians is not something that will be rejected by the Jewish community.'[12] Lansman later became exasperated by the language and activities of the Corbyn-supporting group Jewish Voice for Labour. (*see following chapter*) Lansman's organisational skills and obvious integrity contributed to the continuing upsurge in membership, particularly among young people drawn to Corbyn's banner. The organisation he helped to create, however, remains more problematic.

From its inception, Momentum polarised opinion across the centre and left within Labour. It swiftly built up a grassroots organisation pledging support for Corbyn but was seen by many as a second-generation Militant Tendency, partly due to its tactics of swamping local parties in a bid to deselect moderates. Lansman, however, and other founders took as their inspiration the Greek movement *Syriza* and *Podemos* in Spain, both of which used grassroots organisation to counter austerity.[13] Later they took note of such progressive platforms as that run in the US to build support for the socialist Bernie Sanders.[14] Momentum impressed many with its skilful deployment of social media to target marginal seats and to produce budget information videos which went viral. Within three years it had attracted 20,000 Labour Party members.

Sabotage attempts by splinter hard-left groups such as the Alliance for Workers' Liberty (AWL) – which described Momentum as being 'politically conservative' and claiming the group's leadership were 'avoiding any criticism of or going beyond what party leadership has said and done'[15] – were seen off. Centre Labour MPs warned that such organisations as the Socialist Workers Party (SWP) might seek to infiltrate Momentum, but Lansman and company promised to resist any such entryism.[16] However, Labour MP Owen Smith, later to launch an unsuccessful challenge to Corbyn's Leadership, accused Momentum of using the same tactics as Militant.[17] Oliver Kamm wrote: 'Like the Trotskyists of a generation ago Momentum is an entryist organisation that's parasitic on the Labour host. This time, though, the far left has managed to gain control of the party structures and is intent on making life tough for Labour MPs.' A Labour councillor said: 'I think Momentum in Liverpool is a mask for Militant. There are decent Momentum people and then there are the others who have their own agenda.' But former Labour MP Peter Kilfoyle, who had acted as enforcer for the Labour leadership against Militant on Merseyside in the 1980s as the party's north-west regional organiser, rejected the comparison, instead describing Momentum as fulfilling the same kind of role on the left of the party as Progress did on the right.[18] Labour's deputy leader Tom Watson said on TV: 'They look like a bit of a rabble to me, but I don't think they are a problem for the Labour Party.'[19] Former sports minister Gerry Sutcliffe coined the description, which stuck in New Labour circles, of 'Trendy Wendies and Nigels' which referred to the alleged dominance of 'university lecturers with nice lifestyles who want a revolution in which others pay the price'.[20]

Momentum called for its membership to lobby Labour MPs 'to support Corbyn, not Cameron, over Syria' on Twitter in line with Corbyn and the Stop the War Coalition's opposition to bombing ISIS centres. Some Labour MPs criticised Momentum's move to lobby on party political grounds before the Labour Party's official position on military action had been decided.[21] In the 2016 elections for the NEC, Momentum won six key supporters. Although some of the Momentum high command came from Jewish backgrounds, many members appear to have been unaware of the point at which their version of anti-Zionism became anti-Semitism.

Social media, so ably used by Momentum and the other Corbynistas, became the source of a tsunami of anti-Semite allegations in the early years of his Leadership. Journalists trawled websites to find tweets and Facebook pages which showed, at best, incredible naivety and, at worst, sickening prejudice. An early such scandal under the Corbyn leadership probably fell into the first category.

Naz Shah ticked many boxes when she took the Bradford West constituency in May 2015 with a majority of 11,420 over the former maverick Labourite George Galloway, at 42 becoming one of just nine Muslim Labour MPs. Born locally, at 12 she was sent to Pakistan for an arranged marriage. When she was 20, her mother was convicted of murdering her abusive partner and served seven years imprisonment.[22] Before her election, Shah worked as a carer for disabled people, as an NHS Commissioner and chaired the mental health charity, Sharing Voices Bradford. She revealed that in a 2012 byelection she had voted for Galloway, the man she eventually beat.[23]

In April 2016, blogger Paul Staines discovered that she had in August 2014 reposted a Facebook entry from the anti-Zionist academic Norman Finkelstein satirically promoting the relocation of Israel to the US. Commenting on that post, Shah said: 'problem solved' and suggested the plan might 'save them some pocket money' by ending US aid for Israel.[24] When the story erupted, Finkelstein said that his post 'was, and still is, funny. Were it not for the current political context, nobody would have noticed Shah's reposting of it either. Otherwise, you'd have to be humourless. As crazy as the discourse on Israel is in America, at least we still have a sense of humour. It's inconceivable that any politician in the US would be crucified for posting such a map.'[25] Finkelstein claimed that Labour Right-wingers were using the scandal to undermine Corbyn, Finkelstein asked 'What are they doing? Don't they have any respect for the dead? ... All these desiccated Labour apparatchiks, dragging the Nazi holocaust through the mud for the sake of their petty jostling for power and position. Have they no shame?'[26] Shah herself responded that her views on Israel had moderated in the 20 months since the post. She stepped down from her unpaid post as John McDonnell's Parliamentary aide, but somehow kept her seat on the home affairs select committee which was itself probing the alleged rise of anti-Semitism in the UK.[27] Under increased media pressure, Corbyn condemned her social media comments as 'offensive and unacceptable'. Shah was suspended from the Labour Party[28] but reinstated ten weeks later after the National Executive gave her a formal warning, told her to apologise for bringing the party into disrepute, and warned that if there was another incident, she would be expelled. She complied and claimed that the damaging row was caused by her own 'ignorance'. She said that her post was anti-Semitic but she was not.[29]

Shah bounced back and nearly doubled her majority at the snap June 2017 election, but showed that on social media she had learnt few lessons from the Finkelstein stramash. That August she retweeted and liked a tweet from a parody account on a child sex scandal involving Muslim men which read: 'Those abused girls in Rotherham and elsewhere just need to shut their mouths. For the good of diversity'. Shah deleted the retweet but the damage was done. Her spokesperson said: 'This was a genuine accident eight days ago that was rectified within minutes.' She told reporters that she had been working for 'over 20 years on the issues of child abuse, violence against women, and grooming. She has and will continue to advocate for all victims, and work towards eradicating this evil from society.'[30] A survivor of the abuse scandal called for Shah to resign.[31] Equality and Human Rights Commission chief executive Rebecca Hilsenrath said the MP 'should know better'. But again, lessons do not appear to have been learnt. After Winnie Mandela's death in April 2018, Shah tweeted Mandela's infamous quote endorsing the 'necklacing' – execution by rubber tyres filled with petrol – of opponents. Shah later deleted the tweet without comment.[32] A few months later Shah was appointed Shadow Women and Equalities minister. Within Corbyn's orbit pretty much any mistakes can be forgiven if the perpetrator is on-side.

By the time of the Shah rumpus, the Labour Party had suspended 56 members – 0.012% of the party membership – for statements alleged to be anti-Semitic, pending investigation.[33] Ken Livingstone defended Shah and said he had never heard anti-Semitic comments from Labour members. Livingstone added: 'When Hitler won his election in 1932 his policy then was that Jews should be moved to Israel. He was supporting Zionism before he went mad and ended up killing six million Jews.' Momentum's Lansman was quoted as saying: 'A period of silence from Ken Livingstone is overdue, especially on anti-Semitism, racism and Zionism. It's time he left politics altogether.'[34] Labour MP John Mann publicly confronted Livingstone in a stairwell in front of a news camera crew, calling him a 'Nazi apologist' and a 'fucking disgrace'.[35] Labour's chief whip Rosie Winterton, told Mann it was 'completely inappropriate for Labour members of Parliament to be involved in very public rows on the television'. Livingstone was suspended for a year. In a subsequent hearing in April 2017 the NEC deemed him guilty of prejudicial and detrimental conduct and banned him from standing for office or representing the party at any level for a further year.[36] He later resigned from the party, saying: 'I do not accept the allegation that I have brought the Labour Party into disrepute – nor that I am in any way guilty of anti-Semitism. I abhor anti-Semitism, I have fought it all my life and will continue to do so.'[37]

From May 2016, Labour was embroiled in numerous parallel investigations, claims and counter-claims over alleged anti-Semitism. Momentum vice-chair Jackie Walker was investigated over private comments she made on Facebook exaggerating the role of Jews in the

Right: Karl Marx.

Below right: Friedrich Engels.

Below left: Henry Irving as Shylock.

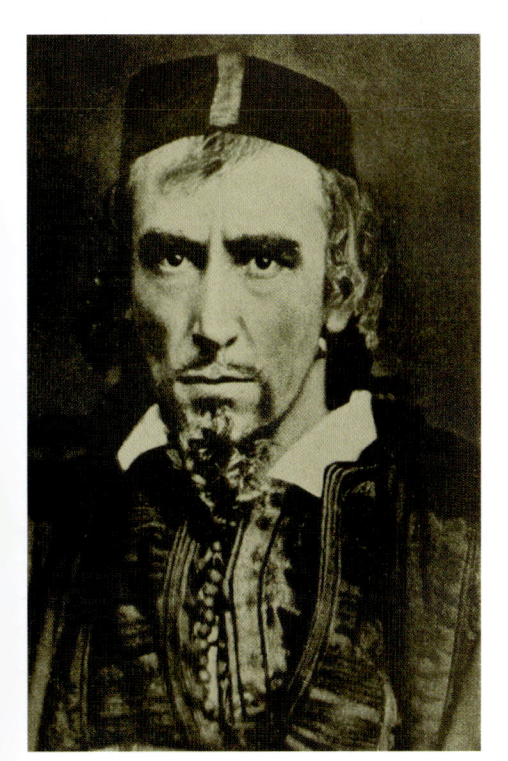

Above left: Keir Hardie.

Above right: H. M. Hyndman.

Below: The trenches of the First World War. (National Library of Scotland)

Manny Shinwell. (London School of Economics Library)

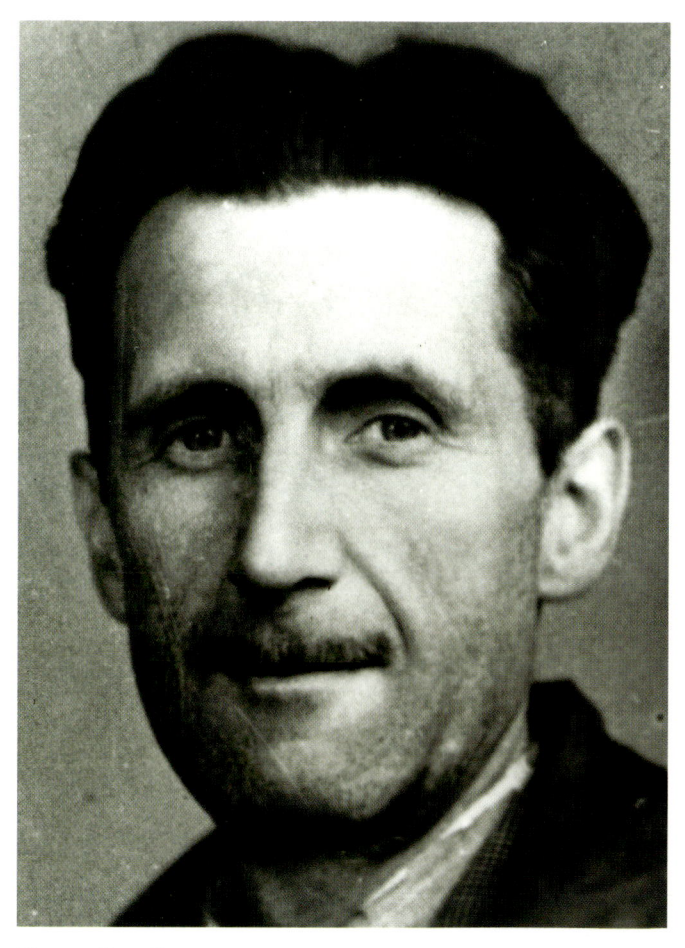

George Orwell.

Left: Oswald Mosley. (Library of Congress)

Below: A mural marking the Battle of Cable Street.

Clement Attlee, Harry Truman and Josef Stalin in 1945 at Berlin conference. (Library of Congress)

British paratroopers enforcing a curfew in Tel Aviv after the King David Hotel, which housed the British administrative headquarters for Palestine, was bombed by the Irgun in July 1946. (National Library of Israel)

Harold Wilson. (National Archives and Records Administration)

Fidel Castro. (Library of Congress)

Margaret Hodge. (Institute for Government)

Louise Ellman. (Courtesy of Rob Carney)    Luciana Berger. (Policy Exchange)

Ken Livingstone. (Brisbane City Council)

Shami Chakrabarti. (Courtesy of the Bar Council under Creative Commons BY-ND 2.0)

John Mann MP. (UK Government)

Above: A highly controversial mural painted by American artist Mear One in East London. When it was removed, Corbyn offered his sympathies to Mear One, saying that the artist was in 'good company'. (Courtesy of Bablu Miah under Creative Commons 2.0)

Left: Corbyn at the 'Rage Against Israel' rally in 2010. (Courtesy of Maddy Cozins under Creative Commons 2.0)

Below left: Corbyn at a No More War event in 2014. (Courtesy of Garry Knight under Creative Commons 2.0)

Atlantic slave trade. Walker claimed mixed Jewish and African descent, her mother being a black Jamaican Sephardi Jew and her father from an Ashkenazi Jewish family who had fled pre-Revolutionary Russian *pogrom*s. In Walker's Facebook account, a private discussion from that February was recorded in which the debt owed to the Jews because of the Holocaust was raised. Walker responded: 'Oh yes – and I hope you feel the same towards the African holocaust? My ancestors were involved in both – on all sides as I'm sure you know, millions more Africans were killed in the African holocaust and their oppression continues today on a global scale in a way it doesn't for Jews ... and many Jews (my ancestors too) were the chief financiers of the sugar and slave trade which is of course why there were so many early synagogues in the Caribbean. So who are victims and what does it mean? We are victims and perpetrators to some extent through choice. And having been a victim does not give you a right to be a perpetrator.'[38]

The Israel Advocacy Movement uncovered her private comments, the *Jewish Chronicle* published them and then notified the Labour Party.[39] She was suspended by the party, pending investigation. Lansman slammed 'a lynch mob whose interest in combatting racism is highly selective'. The investigation was wrapped up after a few weeks with no disciplinary action taken.[40] Walker said: 'Yes, I wrote "many Jews (my ancestors too) were the chief financiers of the sugar and slave trade". These words, taken out of context in the way the media did, of course do not reflect my position. I was writing to someone who knew the context of my comments. Had he felt the need to pick me up on what I had written I would have rephrased – perhaps to "Jews (my ancestors too) were among those who financed the sugar and slave trade and at the particular time/in the particular area I'm talking about they played an important part"... [My claim] has never been that Jews played a disproportionate role in the Atlantic Slave Trade, merely that, as historians such as Arnold Wiznitzer noted, at a certain economic point, in specific regions where my ancestors lived, Jews played a dominant role "as financiers of the sugar industry, as brokers and exporters of sugar, and as suppliers of Negro slaves on credit".'[41] She dismissed subsequent claims that her comments were reminiscent of the Nation of Islam's anti-Semitic take on the slave trade. Walker, who has joint British-US nationality, said that 'the Nation of Islam is an anti-Semitic group which seeks to set Jewish and Black people against each other. Any examination of my work, my writing, my life, would make clear my opposition to this ideology.'[42]

During the September 2016 Labour Party conference, Walker attended a training session on anti-Semitism for party members held by the Jewish Labour Movement (JLM). She said, during a section on school security, 'I was a bit concerned by your suggestion that the Jewish community is under such threat that it has to use security in all its buildings. I have a grandson, he is a year old. There is security in his nursery and every school has security now. It's not because I'm frightened or his parents are frightened that he is going to be attacked.' After the meeting, she said, "I did not raise a question on security in Jewish schools. The trainer raised this issue, and I asked for clarification, in particular, as all London primary schools, to my knowledge have security and I did not understand the particular point the trainer was making. Having been a victim of racism, I would never play down the very real fears the Jewish community have, especially in light of recent attacks in France.' In the session, there was a discussion on the definition of anti-Semitism set out by the JLM and Walker, claiming to speak as an anti-racism trainer, said: 'I still haven't heard a definition of anti-Semitism I can work with.' JLM chair Jeremy Newmark said that 'I am appalled that somebody ... would come to a training session designed to help party activists address anti-Semitism and use the occasion to challenge the legitimacy of the training itself.'

At the event, Walker also said: 'Wouldn't it be wonderful if Holocaust Memorial Day was open to all peoples who've experienced holocaust?' When others shouted that it did include other genocides, she responded, 'In practice, it's not actually circulated and advertised as such.' Later, she asked why Holocaust Memorial Day only concerns genocides committed since the 1940s, thereby excluding 'the African holocaust' during the slave trade. She also said: 'I would never play down the significance of the Shoah. Working with many Jewish comrades, I continue to seek to bring greater awareness of other genocides, which are too often forgotten or minimised. If offence has been caused, it is the last thing I would want to do and I apologise.'[43] The party suspended her from membership pending an investigation. Walker again insisted her words had been taken out of context and no further action was taken following the investigation.[44] But Walker was removed from her Momentum position, while remaining on its steering committee, after the TSSA union threatened to withdraw funding.[45] Lansman called Walker's comments 'ill-informed, ill-judged and offensive', but not anti-Semitic.[46] The Momentum committee stated that, although it 'does not regard any of the comments she appears to have made, taken individually, to be anti-Semitic ... the Committee does consider her remarks on Holocaust Memorial Day and on security of Jewish schools to be ill-informed, ill-judged and offensive. In such circumstances, the Committee feels that Jackie should have done more to explain herself to mitigate the upset caused.' The Committee stated that 'Jackie should not be expelled from the Labour Party.'

In March 2017, Glasgow Friends of Israel and Labour Against Anti-Semitism sought unsuccessfully to prevent her speaking on 'Palestine: Free Speech and Israel's Black Ops' at Dundee University. A similar event at Aberdeen University was cancelled. Labour Against Anti-Semitism described her talk as 'part of an increasing normalisation of anti-Semitic hate speech that has to be confronted and eliminated' and that it 'threatens the safety of Jewish students' and therefore the university was 'failing in its duty of care'. Walker responded that there was a difference between being pro-Palestine and anti-Zionist, and anti-Semitic, and that she and her partner were Jewish.[47] A number of prominent left-wing activists defended Walker, including film director Ken Loach, a Corbyn favourite, who said she should be allowed to play a significant role in the party,[48] and Noam Chomsky who said 'I wholeheartedly support the right of anyone to criticise Israel without being branded anti-Semitic. That goes in particular for Jackie Walker.'[49] Despite such high-profile backing, later that month, Walker was suspended from the Labour Party pending investigation, for a second time, with the NEC referring her case to the party's National Constitutional Committee. Never one to keep her head down, Walker meanwhile performed *The Lynching*, her one-woman show about her experience, which premiered at the Edinburgh Festival Fringe in August 2017. The Board of Deputies of British Jews wrote to the city council to express their concern that the show was being mounted on council-owned facilities.

In September 2018, Jewish Voice for Labour sponsored a premiere of the documentary film *The Political Lynching of Jackie Walker* close to the venue of the Labour Party conference was being held nearby. The 200-strong audience were evacuated because of a bomb scare. JVL said the film 'is an incisive and chilling exposé of attempts to silence critics of Israel, in particular those who support the socialist project of Labour leader Jeremy Corbyn. It connects the global struggle against racism and the far right with the Palestinian cause.'[50] Another film, *Witch Hunt*, on the accusations of anti-Semitism against Walker and others during Corbyn's leadership, premiered in Broadstairs in February 2019.

Labour MP Chris Williamson booked a Parliamentary room to show it, but the screening was cancelled after a complaint from the Board of Deputies. A Labour spokeswoman said: 'It's completely inappropriate to book a room for an event about an individual who is suspended from the party and subject to ongoing disciplinary procedures.' The film's promoters said the cancellation was due to intimidation.[51]

After a March 2019 hearing, Walker was finally expelled from the Labour Party for 'prejudicial and grossly detrimental behaviour against the party'.

* * *

Following the 2016 suspensions, Corbyn commissioned an inquiry into anti-Semitism and other forms of racism headed by the renowned barrister Shami Chakrabarti, the former head of the human rights advocacy group Liberty. As that organisation's director, she campaigned against what the pressure group saw as the 'excessive' anti-terrorist measures that followed the September 11 2001 attacks on the US. She was a former member of the breakaway Social Democrat Party and was shortlisted in the *Channel 4* Political Awards 2006 for the 'Most Inspiring Political Figure' title, coming second to celebrity chef Jamie Oliver and above then-premier Tony Blair, David Cameron and Bob Geldof.[52] Chakrabarti was on the governing board of the London School of Economics when it accepted a £1.5 million donation from Saif al-Islam Gaddafi, the son of the Libyan dictator. She insisted she did not attend the 2009 Council meeting which approved the donation and that she 'only subsequently raised concerns about links with Mr Gaddafi, given his father's appalling regime'. She went on to state that she did not think 'the decision in question resulted from anything other than a naive assessment, made in good faith, of the democratic reforming ambitions of the dictator's son'.[53] Nevertheless, the LSE Director resigned and Chakrabarti was accused of hypocrisy by the Student Rights project of the Henry Jackson Society for being 'the director of a human rights group while legitimising murderous regimes'. Chakrabarti asked the Metropolitan Police to investigate the legality of the donations. Chakrabarti admitted to feeling 'bucketfuls' of embarrassment and shame about the affair and in April 2013 her spokesman confirmed that she had severed all ties with the LSE.[54] On her appointment to the 2016 inquiry, she joined the Labour Party, insisting that she had members' interests and values at heart. Chakrabarti criticised the Conservatives for not conducting their own enquiry into Islamophobia.

Announcing the inquiry, Corbyn said that he was determined to expunge racism from the party: 'Labour is an anti-racist party to its core and has a long and proud history of standing against racism, including anti-Semitism.' The inquiry's remit was to decide how best could tackle racism, including both anti-Semitism and Islamophobia. Chakrabarti would speak to various groups, including the Jewish community. She would then report back to party officials within two months and set out guidelines on acceptable behaviour and language.[55] It was widely expected to focus on the cases of Shah and Livingstone. Chakrabarti had two deputy chairs: Jan Royall, who was also investigating allegations of anti-Semitism at Oxford University Labour Club, and David Feldman, director of the Pears Institute for the Study of Anti-Semitism. In 2007, Feldman was a signatory to Independent Jewish Voices, which in May 2016 described some allegations of anti-Semitism within Labour as 'baseless and disingenuous'.

Chakrabarti refused to investigate most individual complaints of the most rabid alleged anti-Semitic attacks, describing them as 'unhappy incidents', refused to define anti-Semitism and refused to address any distinction between anti-Semitism and anti-Zionism. She ignored the Corbynista demonisation of Israel. She interviewed Corbyn and said: 'I put to Jeremy the list of people he had met and shared platforms with in the past, and he had good answers. He was searching for peace and trying to get reconciliation.' He was not anti-Semitic but a 'passionate' supporter of Palestinian rights. She discussed her findings with Seamus Milne but denied that he had vetted her report. An 'insider' quoted by Bower said: 'In Shami's opinion, she had delivered what Milne required to end the dispute. But she had failed to grasp the seriousness of the Jews' despair. She was out of her depth.'[56]

The inquiry's findings were speedily published at a Labour Party event on June 30. The report made 20 recommendations on tackling instances of racism, including: abusive references to any particular person or group based on actual or perceived physical characteristics and racial or religious tropes and stereotypes, should have no place in Labour Party discourse – such epithets includes terms such as 'Zio' and 'Paki'; Labour members should resist the use of Hitler, Nazi and Holocaust metaphors, distortions and comparisons in debates about Israel-Palestine in particular; there should be procedural rule changes to improve the party's disciplinary process and the adoption and publication of a complaints procedure; the appointment of a general counsel to the Labour Party to give advice on issues including disciplinary matters and to take responsibility for instructing external lawyers; the party should increase the ethnic diversity of its staff; and the report rejects the idea of a lifetime membership ban from the party for anyone deemed to have used racist language, and suggests no retrospective action i.e. against comments made prior to the inquiry. The report concluded that the party 'is not overrun by anti-Semitism, Islamophobia, or other forms of racism', but has suffered from an 'occasionally toxic atmosphere' and 'too much clear evidence [of] ignorant attitudes'.[57]

The response from the Jewish community was initially one of cautious optimism. Chief Rabbi Ephraim Mirvis urged 'full and unhesitating implementation of [its] findings'.[58] Feldman said: 'This is an important document at a time, when more than ever, we need to stand firm against all forms of racism and intolerance. The report marks a positive step towards ensuring that the Labour Party is a welcoming place for all minority groups. It recommends steps to ensure that members act in a spirit of tolerance and respect, while maintaining principles of free speech and open debate. The recommendations are constructive and provide a sound basis on which the party can move forward.'[59] Jeremy Newmark, chair of the Jewish Labour Movement, said: 'It's a strong platform for the party to ... set a gold standard in tackling racism and anti-Semitism.' All-party Parliamentary Group on Anti-Semitism chair John Mann called it 'hugely significant'. Another specialist academic, Keith Kahn-Harris, said that Chakrabarti had 'delivered a report that, while not the last word on the subject, does at least deserve to be discussed seriously and calmly'.[60] Some hope of that, as it proved.

At the report's launch, Jewish Labour MP Ruth Smeeth was accused by activist Marc Wadsworth from the pro-Corbyn group Momentum Black ConneXions of working 'hand-in-hand' with the right-wing media.[61] Smeeth burst into tears but Corbyn passed her by with only a smirk. Smeeth criticised Corbyn for not speaking out in her defence, saying: 'It is beyond belief that someone could come to the launch of a report on anti-Semitism in the Labour Party and espouse such vile conspiracy theories about Jewish people, which were ironically highlighted as such in Ms Chakrabarti's report, while the leader of my own party stood by and did absolutely nothing ... a Labour Party under his stewardship cannot be a safe space for British Jews.' Almost two years after the incident, Smeeth was accompanied by a cordon of around 40 Labour MPs and peers to a hearing of Labour's

National Constitutional Committee (NCC) into Wadsworth's conduct.[62] Wadsworth was expelled for bringing the Labour Party into disrepute.

Corbyn said that he would put his weight behind an 'immediate implementation of the Chakrabarti report's recommendations. But he undermined Jewish confidence in his sincerity with comments which some saw as comparing Israel's actions to those of ISIS. He told activists that 'our Jewish friends are no more responsible for the actions of Israel or the Netanyhu government than our Muslim friends are for those various self-styled Islamic states or organisations'.[63] Chief Rabbi Mirvis said the remarks were 'offensive', and 'rather than rebuilding trust among the Jewish community, are likely to cause even greater concern'. A Corbyn spokesman said that he 'was explicitly stating that people should not be held responsible for the actions of states or organisations around the world on the basis of religion or ethnicity'.[64]. Chakrabarti defended Corbyn, saying: 'I read the leader's speech five minutes before we went into the main room ... I listened very carefully to what he said. He reflected my report ... His point was: when you have Jewish neighbours or friends, or Muslim neighbours or friends and something bad happens in the world, don't ask them to be the first to explain or defend or condemn.'[65] The report's initial guarded welcome swiftly turned to anger over failures to deliver.

For some that was confirmed when Corbyn announced Chakrabarti as the only Labour appointment to the House of Lords in David Cameron's post-Brexit vote resignation honours list in the following weeks. Some Labour MPs said that undermined the credibility of the whole exercise. The Community Security Trust, which monitors anti-Semitism in Britain, said the move was 'a shameless kick in the teeth for all who put hope in her now wholly compromised inquiry into Labour anti-Semitism'. Marie van der Zyl, vice-president of the Board of Deputies, called it a 'whitewash for peerages scandal'. Corbyn's spokesman said that Chakrabarti was 'an ideal appointment to the Lords'.[66] In October she was elevated to Corbyn's Shadow Cabinet as Shadow Attorney General. Author Howard Jacobson called her inquiry 'a brief and shoddy shuffling of superficies' that 'spoke to very few of the people charging the party with anti-Semitism and understood even fewer of their arguments'. He suggested that the peerage showed contempt for those who had raised issues over anti-Semitism in the party.[67]

The cross-party home affairs select committee called Corbyn, Chakrabarti and Livingstone to give evidence in a separate, wider investigation of anti-Semitism. Its report described the Chakrabarti Inquiry as 'compromised' and found that 'the failure of the Labour Party consistently to deal with anti-Semitic incidents in recent years risks lending force to allegations that elements of the Labour movement are institutionally anti-Semitic'. It criticised the leadership for allowing Labour to become 'a safe place for those with vile attitudes towards Jewish people'. However, the committee concluded that '...there exists no reliable, empirical evidence to support the notion that there is a higher prevalence of anti-Semitic attitudes within the Labour Party than any other political party'.[68] The committee said that Chakrabarti had been 'insufficiently open' in her answers to them over when she was offered her peerage, criticised the party's handling of the report and earlier allegations and complaints and suggested that Corbyn lacked understanding of 'the distinct nature of post-second-world-war anti-Semitism'. Corbyn insisted the criticism of Chakrabati's independence was unfair, saying he had appointed her after the completion of the report based on her legal and campaigning experience and accused the select committee of 'political framing'. Livingstone claimed the report had been 'rigged'. And Chakrabarti said that on anti-Semitism Labour was not 'much worse than any other party'. Later she accepted that some recommendations had not been implemented and said that the new Labour Party general secretary, Jennie Formby, would make this a priority.[69]

During the 2017 snap general election called by the hapless Theresa May in a failed bid to win a majority for her flawed Brexit deal, Jewish Labour Movement chairman Jeremy Newmark said that 'Jeremy Corbyn appears to have failed to understand the nature of contemporary anti-Semitism in the same way that it's understood by most of its target group'. Labour MP Wes Streeting said: 'I don't think many Jewish voters in my constituency have been very impressed with the way the Labour Party as a whole have responded.' But he denied that Corbyn was anti-Semitic.

The day after a live TV head-to-head with Mrs May, judged a no-score draw, Corbyn appeared on *Women's Hour* to talk about his chosen subject, childcare. He stumbled when presenter Emma Bartlett asked him how much 30 hours of childcare cost, faffing around with his notes. Within minutes social media was alive with attacks on Barnett calling her a Jew and 'Zionist shill'.[70]

At that election Corbyn confounded many critics by denying Mrs May an overall majority, but it was far from the triumph painted by his diehard supporters. Around 26% of Jewish voters voted for Labour. Analysis suggests that, in the five UK constituencies where more than 10% of the population identify as Jewish – Finchley and Golders Green, Hendon, Hertsmere, Hackney North and Stoke Newington and Bury South, Labour's vote share increased by seven points, almost three points less than the national average. However, this includes an above-average swing to Labour in Hackney North and Stoke Newington. The significance of the Jewish vote was argued to have manifested in the 'Bagel belt', consisting of four seats in north-west London with a dense Jewish population: Finchley and Golders Green, Hendon, Chipping Barnett and Harrow East.[71] While the swing to Labour in Chipping Barnet was above the national average, it was much lower in the other three constituencies, and Labour failed to capture them. The anti-Semitism row may well have cost Corbyn the election.

In September 2017, Unite the Union general secretary Len McCluskey said that the row 'was created by people who were trying to undermine Jeremy Corbyn'. He stated that he had never heard anti-Semitic language at a party meeting, adding: 'Unfortunately at the time there were lots of people playing games, everybody wanted to create this image that Jeremy Corbyn's leadership had become misogynist, had become racist, had become anti-Semitic and it was wrong.'[72]

In October 2017, Labour Against the Witch-hunt was formed to oppose what they saw as unjustified disciplinary action against Labour activists accused of anti-Semitism. However, Jon Lansman categorised anti-Semitism in the Labour Party into three forms: petty xenophobic remarks, of which he '[doesn't] think there's much'; old-school blood libel anti-Semitism, which is 'extremely rare'; and reaction to the Israeli-Palestinian tensions whereby, 'we all understand that when that conflict heats up, it results in dreadful anti-Semitism. It shouldn't result in that, but it does'.[73]

During the 2017 Labour Party conference, new rules proposed by the JLM and supported by Jeremy Corbyn were adopted on hate speech. Previously, party members could not be disciplined for 'the mere holding or expression of beliefs and opinions'. Under the new rules, those who express anti-Semitic or other forms of hate speech, including racism, Islamophobia, sexism and homophobia, or other 'conduct prejudicial to the party', could be disciplined. Jewish authors Howard Jacobson, Simon Schama, and Simon Sebag Montefiore wrote: 'We are alarmed that during the past few years, constructive criticism of Israeli governments has morphed into something closer to anti-Semitism under the cloak of so-called anti-Zionism,' further stating: 'Although anti-Zionists claim innocence of any anti-Semitic intent, anti-Zionism frequently borrows the libels of classical Jew-hating,' and adding: 'Accusations of international Jewish conspiracy and control of the media have resurfaced to support false equations of Zionism with colonialism and imperialism, and the promotion of vicious, fictitious parallels with genocide and Nazism.'[74]

Corbyn's defenders again cited his record of campaigning against racism and supporting Jewish communal initiatives. They pointed out that he took part in a ceremony in his Islington constituency to commemorate the original site of the North London Synagogue and his visit to the Theresiennstadt Ghetto.[75] But incidents from Corbyn's past, particularly during his time as a backbencher, (*see previous chapter*) came back to haunt him. His January 2010 co-chairing, during the UK's Holocaust Memorial Week, of a talk by anti-Zionist Auschwitz survivor Hajo Meyer who compared Israel to the Nazis, drew particular odium. Louise Ellman told the BBC that she was 'absolutely appalled' at Corbyn for his action.[76]

Corbyn's 2011 signing of a Commons motion to rename Holocaust Memorial Day resurfaced, as did Corbyn's 2011 foreword to the republication of John A. Hobson 1902 book claiming that finance was controlled by Jews, as uncovered in 2019 by Conservative peer Daniel Finkelstein.[77] Perhaps the biggest own goal came with Corbyn's 2012 efforts to prevent the removal of the street mural painted in east London by American artist Mear One (*see previous chapter*), and when in March 2018, Labour MP Luciana Berger attracted a torrent of abuse for asking Corbyn why he had questioned the mural's removal.

The media coverage over the mural was followed by an open letter from the Board of Deputies of British Jews and the Jewish Leadership Council stating that Corbyn was 'repeatedly found alongside people with blatantly anti-Semitic views', concluding that Corbyn 'cannot seriously contemplate anti-Semitism, because he is so ideologically fixed within a far-left worldview that is instinctively hostile to mainstream Jewish communities'.

The letter said in full:

Today, leaders of British Jewry tell Jeremy Corbyn that enough is enough. We have had enough of hearing that Jeremy Corbyn "opposes anti-Semitism", whilst the mainstream majority of British Jews, and their concerns, are ignored by him and those he leads.

There is a repeated institutional failure to properly address Jewish concerns and to tackle anti-Semitism, with the Chakrabarti Report being the most glaring example of this. Jeremy Corbyn did not invent this form of politics, but he has had a lifetime within it, and now personifies its problems and dangers. He issues empty statements about opposing anti-Semitism, but does nothing to understand or address it. We conclude that he cannot seriously contemplate anti-Semitism, because he is so ideologically fixed within a far-left worldview that is instinctively hostile to mainstream Jewish communities. When Jews complain about an obviously anti-Semitic mural in Tower Hamlets, Corbyn of course supports the artist. Hizbollah commits terrorist atrocities against Jews, but Corbyn calls them his friends and attends pro-Hizbollah rallies in London. Exactly the same goes for Hamas. Raed Salah says Jews kill Christian children to drink their blood. Corbyn opposes his extradition and invites him for tea at the House of Commons. These are not the only cases. He is repeatedly found alongside people with blatantly anti-Semitic views, but claims never to hear or read them.

Again and again, Jeremy Corbyn has sided with anti-Semites rather than Jews. At best, this derives from the far left's obsessive hatred of Zionism, Zionists and Israel. At worst, it suggests a conspiratorial worldview in which mainstream Jewish communities are believed to be a hostile entity, a class enemy. When Jeremy Corbyn was elected leader of the Labour Party, Jews expressed sincere and profound fears as to how such politics would impact upon their wellbeing. Our concerns were never taken seriously. Three years on, the party and British Jews are reaping the consequences. Routine statements against anti-Semitism "and all forms of racism" get nowhere near dealing with the problem, because what distinguishes anti-Semitism from other forms of racism is the power that Jews are alleged to hold, and how they are charged with conspiring together against what is good.

This is not only historic, or about what Jeremy Corbyn did before being party leader. It is also utterly contemporary. There is literally not a single day in which Labour Party spaces, either online or in meetings, do not repeat the same fundamental anti-Semitic slanders against Jews. We are told that our concerns are faked, and done at the command of Israel and/or Zionism (whatever that means); that anti-Semitism is merely "criticism of Israel"; that we call any and all criticism of Israel "anti-Semitic"; that the Rothschilds run the world; that Isis terrorism is a fake front for Israel; that Zionists are the new Nazis; and that Zionists collaborate with Nazis.

Rightly or wrongly, Jeremy Corbyn is now the figurehead for an anti-Semitic political culture, based on obsessive hatred of Israel, conspiracy theories and fake news that is doing dreadful harm to British Jews and to the British Labour Party. Jeremy Corbyn is the only person with the power to demand that it stops. Enough is enough.

Corbyn's reply, again in full, was:

Thank you for your letter to the Labour Party concerning anti-Semitism issued as a press statement last night. First of all, let me acknowledge the anger and upset that provoked it, and repeat my offer of an urgent meeting to discuss the issues you have raised as soon as possible. I stated yesterday, and repeat today, that I will not tolerate any form of anti-Semitism that exists in or around our Party and movement. I am committed to eliminating anti-Semitism wherever it exists.

As I told the Labour Party conference in 2016, anti-Semitism is an evil that led to the worst crimes of the twentieth century. Prejudice and hatred of Jewish people has no place whatsoever in the Labour Party, and every one of us has a responsibility to ensure it is never allowed to fester in our society again.

I recognise that anti-Semitism has surfaced within the Labour Party, and has too often been dismissed as simply a matter of a few bad apples. This has caused pain and hurt to Jewish members of our party and to the wider Jewish community in Britain. I am sincerely sorry for the pain which has been caused, and pledge to redouble my efforts to bring this anxiety to an end. While the forms of anti-Semitism expressed on the far Right of politics are easily detectable, such as Holocaust denial, there needs to be a deeper understanding of what constitutes anti-Semitism in the labour movement. Sometimes this evil takes familiar forms – the east London mural which has caused such understandable controversy is an example. The idea of Jewish bankers and capitalists exploiting the workers of the world is an old anti-Semitic conspiracy theory. This was long ago, and rightly, described as "the socialism of fools". I am sorry for not having studied the content of the mural more closely before wrongly questioning its removal in 2012.

Newer forms of anti-Semitism have been woven into criticism of Israeli governments. Criticism of Israel, particularly in relation to the continuing dispossession of the Palestinian people, cannot be avoided.

Nevertheless, comparing Israel or the actions of Israeli governments to the Nazis, attributing criticisms of Israel to Jewish characteristics or to Jewish people in general and using abusive phraseology about supporters of Israel such as "Zio" all constitute aspects of contemporary anti-Semitism. And Jewish people must not be held responsible or accountable for the actions of the Israeli government.

The Labour Party has always opposed anti-Semitism, old and new, and always will. We are proud of our deep historical links with Jewish communities, and to have fought alongside generations of Jewish men and women against fascism, prejudice and discrimination. This is a part of our common heritage from which we will never be separated. But I acknowledge that anti-Semitic attitudes have surfaced more often in our ranks in recent years, and that the party has been too slow in processing some of the cases that have emerged. Early action has nevertheless been taken, and we will work to speed up procedures, to deal with cases of anti-Semitic abuse or attitudes.

I am committed to making our party a welcoming and secure place for Jewish people. Zero tolerance for anti-Semites means what it says, and the party will proceed in that spirit. That demands among other things the overdue full implementation of the recommendations of the Chakrabarti report, including a programme of political education to increase awareness and understanding of all forms of anti-Semitism. The battle against anti-Semitism should never become a party political issue. It must unite all of us if we are both to honour the memory of the victims of the bestial crimes of the twentieth century and build a future of equality and justice for all. In that spirit, I must make it clear that I will never be anything other than a militant opponent of anti-Semitism. In this fight, I am your ally and always will be.

Following the letter exchange, hundreds of people outside Parliament Square protested 'Enough is Enough' against anti-Semitism in the Labour Party, demanding that Corbyn does more to tackle anti-Jewish feeling in Labour Party ranks. JVL organised a smaller counter-demonstration.[78] A JVL spokesman said after the event: 'There is a massive difference between saying that more needs to be done within the party and a demonstration like this which is implicitly trying to force him [Corbyn] out ... This protest is unnecessary, inflammatory and politicised.' The organisation said that it was 'appalled' by the Board of Deputies' letter, saying: 'They do not represent us or the great majority of Jews in the party who share Jeremy Corbyn's vision for social justice and fairness. Jeremy's consistent commitment to anti-racism is all the more needed now.' JVL chair Jenny Manson defended Corbyn, saying he had taken 'enormously strong action' to deal with the issue in his party.[79]

In August 2018 Corbyn's recorded comments about Jews lacking a sense of irony surfaced and sparked another rumpus.[80] His comments were accused by some of being barely coded anti-Semitism, including by Labour MPs Luciana Berger, Wes Streeting, Mike Gapes and Catherine McKinnell, and political strategist John McTernan. A number of Conservative MPs reported Corbyn to the parliamentary standards watchdog over the comments.

***

It was not just on the national stage that Corbyn's fan club, including Momentum, pursued those MPs it considered 'moderate' or 'Blairite' or 'Zionist'. Anyone who had been part of the Blair/Brown administration which had given Labour 13 years in power, brought relative peace to Northern Ireland, introduced paid holidays for part-time worker and the national minimum wage, embarked on the biggest school-building programme in generations, and slashed hospital and GP waiting times, was fair game. If they were Jewish, that was a bonus.

One of the most ferocious centres of bigotry and intimidation wasin and around Liverpool, previously the hotbed of the Militant Tendency ousted in the mid-1980s when then-Labour Leader Neil Kinnock took them on with his 'black taxi' conference speech. One of their top targets was Dame Louise Ellman, the Manchester-born President of the Jewish Labour Movement, chair of the Labour Friends of Israel, and of the All-Party Britain-Israel Parliamentary Group. The *Times of Israel* called her 'tough-as-nails' and 'an unabashed friend of Israel'. She had a parliamentary reputation as a highly effective campaigner prepared to perform in the unglamorous role of a backroom operator. She had been a party member since 1963, was elected a councillor in 1970, became a council leader in 1981 and entered Parliament in 1997. For nine years she chaired the influential transport select committee holding governments to account on such issues as rail links, speed that kills, the closure of Coastguards stations and related issues. She consistently opposed spending cuts across education, the health service, policing and the post office network. She fought long and hard to win justice for Liverpool football fan Michael Shields, wrongly convicted in a Bulgarian court, and lobbied for Gillian

Gibbons, a teacher jailed in Sudan for blasphemy, who was pardoned. She was consistently re-elected with solid majorities in working class Liverpool Riverside and had never faced any serious challenge from left or right. That all changed in 2015. After Corbyn became party Leader she had to get used to being called a 'bitch' at riotous local party meetings.

Her cardinal sin was to have been one of the first to protest against the anti-Semitism displayed from 2001 by the Stop the War Coalition which included distributing magazines featuring cartoons portraying Jews with large noses pulling the strings of politicians, media bosses and bankers, waving placards with swastikas, and opposing Israel's right to exist. When she denounced such activities on BBC Radio 4, she was threatened with libel by the Muslim Association of Britain, a branch of the Muslim Brotherhood. In a Christmas 2003 Commons debate she complained about a 'rising tide of anti-Semitism'. Jews were being targeted by Stop the War activists as an elite who had stolen wealth from the masses. She blamed Islamist groups for 'inciting racial hatred' against Jews under the umbrella of anti-Zionism. *The Guardian* published letters denouncing her for identifying Muslims as anti-Semitic and endorsed a complaint that all dispossessed Palestinians were victims of Zionism. She clashed with anti-Zionist and Jewish Labour MP Gerald Kaufman who had a track record of wooing Muslim voters in his Manchester constituency. Corbyn wrote in the *Morning Star* that Israel was 'wagging the American dog' and was reportedly heard mocking Ellman as 'the Honourable Member for Tel Aviv', although he later denied that.[81]

From 2015 her constituency party membership soared from 500 to 2,700, and most of the new members seemed obsessed with Israel. Ellman recalled: 'During my time serving on and leading Lancashire County Council, and from 1997 serving as MP for Liverpool Riverside, I was not subjected to anti-Semitism locally. Party meetings focused on the things that matter most to people – housing, the health service, transport, education, care for the elderly and so on. The vast majority of members supported my efforts to make life better for my constituents. All that changed the moment Jeremy Corbyn became Labour Leader. There was a huge influx of new members who didn't want to talk about such issues – all they wanted to do was barrack me about my support for Israel.

'Every month I would produce a detailed report on my parliamentary activities on behalf of my constituents. I demanded extra funding for local schools, a new Royal Liverpool Hospital, better train services for

Liverpool, decent treatment for refugees, a reversal of local government funding cuts but they were more interested in interrogating me about Israel and claiming I supported repression in Palestine. That was not true – it is a complex situation and there needs to be justice on all sides. I have always supported a two-state solution directly negotiated with an independent Palestine, a secure Israel and a just settlement for refugees. I was abused on social media being called a 'JLM's bitch' and a 'racist supporter of Israeli child abuse' – a reference to arrests on the West Bank. I suspected the new members were from Momentum acting like a party within a party.

'The atmosphere became so poisonous that sometimes I thought they were going to physically attack me. One person asked me how did it feel as an elected member of a democratic party to represent the "fascist" government in Israel? During a discussion on the bombing of an ISIS factory in Syria, I was asked if I had seen a video online which proved that Israel had funded ISIS. I was asked if I would withdraw my support for attacking ISIS in case this hurt an Israeli soldier. Another person said that Israel was responsible for anti-Semitism. I felt these were anti-Semitic attacks on me.'[82]

Dame Louise asked for a Labour Party inquiry, but this was initially rejected.[83] She was not surprised. However, in September 2016 the tactics being deployed by hard-left activists to deselect her and seize control of the Riverside party were revealed by leaked documents showing how Momentum in Liverpool organised recruitment drives and set up secret forums to devise strategies for wresting control. The main aim of the Corbyn-supporting group was to take over the executive of the party and oust the moderate MP. The group made plans to bolster its numbers in the constituency party before elections for local party officers, and to try to influence the constituency's MP and councillors. Remarks on one document made clear that the Momentum branch's objectives centre on 'obtaining a new executive committee at the forthcoming AGM, one which will better reflect the political objectives of the membership, and better respect internal party democracy'.[84]

At the same time, it was revealed an off-the-books investigation into the activities of Jeremy Corbyn supporters had been carried out, infiltrating their meetings and private Facebook groups with the aim of leaking the findings to the press. The blogger Guido Fawkes obtained a 19-page document titled 'An investigation into far-left infiltration of the Labour Party in Liverpool since September 2015'.

The investigators 'found a way into secret Facebook and *Google* groups that Momentum were using locally to coordinate and plan'.[85]

In her submission to the Chakrabarti Inquiry, Ellman wrote:

> I am deeply disturbed by the hesitant and inconsistent way in which the Labour Party is addressing current displays of anti-Semitism among its members. I am also concerned about the party's reluctance to recognise anti-Semitism as a distinctive, unacceptable prejudice in its own right. Doing so does not undermine the importance of combatting all forms of racism wherever they are found. It acknowledges the urgent need to address the specific problem currently facing the Labour Party. A policy of zero tolerance is required.
>
> The party's inconsistency is demonstrated with the contrasting cases of Naz Shah MP and Jackie Walker. Naz Shah has apologised for her actions and is seeking to educate herself about anti-Semitism. I welcome this. At the time of writing this submission she remains suspended from the Labour Party. In contrast, Jackie Walker has refused to apologise for promoting the anti-Semitic lie that Jews were the major financiers of the African slave trade. This was first put forward by Louis Farrakhan, as the leader of the Nation of Islam. He is banned from entering the UK. This untruth is backed by far-right figures, including KKK clansman David Duke. Despite her refusal to apologise, Jackie Walker has been speedily readmitted to the party without any explanation as to why this decision has been taken. This situation is made even worse, as she has now not only re-iterated her position, she now alleges that a conspiratorial smear campaign organised by supporters of the Israeli government, investors in the arms trade and the far right is responsible for the allegations of anti-Semitism.
>
> This is a totally untenable position. The far-left is meeting the far-right in promoting anti-Semitic conspiracy theories! This cannot be acceptable. What has the Labour Party come to? It is deeply problematic that neither Jeremy Corbyn nor his office have denounced the widespread allegations that claims of anti-Semitism in the Labour Party are cover for a smear campaign against our leader.
>
> I am a longstanding Labour Party activist. I joined the party in 1963 and have held elected office continuously since 1970; from 1970–97 as a member of Lancashire County Council, between 1981–97 as leader of Lancashire County Council; as chair of the north-west Labour Party between 1993 and 1998. Since 1997 I have

been the Labour and Co-operative MP for Liverpool Riverside. During this period, I have experienced a handful of isolated instances of anti-Semitism in the party. I have never encountered anything remotely approaching the scale of ideologically driven prejudice evident in recent months.

The indecisive reaction and attempts to minimise the problem have fuelled the views that anti-Semitism is endemic in the Labour Party and is regarded as being of little consequence. This situation has serious consequences. I am deeply concerned that the longstanding association between the Jewish community and the Labour Party is disintegrating. Labour is rapidly becoming regarded as hostile territory, a no-go area, for Jewish people unless they are willing to disassociate themselves from the mainstream Jewish community. Citing Jewish people or groups whose opinions differ from the overwhelming majority of the community does not change this dire situation. Indeed, any efforts by the Labour Party to disparage widespread, genuine concerns will simply exacerbate the situation.

Concern about anti-Semitism in the Labour Party is not confined to the Jewish community. Many people throughout the UK and from a wide variety of backgrounds are appalled. As complaints about anti-Semitism towards me are currently being investigated, it is not appropriate to discuss them in this submission. I do, however, wish to place on record that I have found these incidents to be deeply disturbing. I ask you to consider this submission as part of the context in which you propose appropriate recommendations for tackling anti-Semitism in the Labour Party. New rules are required, clear boundaries must be set and strong action taken. The current situation presents a serious challenge to the party's values, integrity and electability. The future of the Labour Party as a credible, inclusive, mainstream party campaigning for social justice is at stake.[86]

In October 2016 the NEC acknowledged that Liverpool Riverside CLP had experienced 'growing and significant tensions between members over the last 12 – 18 months' and an investigation was launched after the party received a series of complaints of 'uncomradely behaviour, endemic behavioural problems within meetings and incidents of anti-Semitism'. The investigation received written statements signed by ninety-six members of the constituency party used as the basis for a report – but the report remained unpublished. It did, however, confirm many of the explosive allegations made and which can now be revealed. In its opening paragraph it acknowledged: 'Tensions have developed between a large group of members and the CLP Executive Committee, with numerous allegations and counter-allegations being investigated.' It went on:

> During the course of interviews, several members stated categorically that, faced with the prospect of a CLP meeting, they would not feel comfortable attending with five members citing fears for their own or others' physical safety. Those still attending made it very clear that they will stop attending meetings if things continue unchanged. Several recollections brought members to tears. Older members likened the environment in the CLP today to that faced in Liverpool when the Militant Tendency was at the height of its power. This investigation received many reports from members who described the CLP as being characterised by a "toxic atmosphere", "fear" and "intimidation like a punishment cell".
>
> At the heart of these accusations lies a tension between a vocal group of regular CLP attendees and the CLP executive. The EC has, as a matter of course, met very infrequently for several years as there has been no need for regular meetings. Despite the rise in membership, they have continued to meet sporadically, which has caused frustration amongst many members who feel that they should meet regularly in order to administer the CLP more effectively. This has resulted in an acrimonious atmosphere at most meetings over the last 18 months, attested by members on both sides of the disagreement. The EC has indeed struggled to administer the CLP effectively. There have been several meetings, particularly the All Member Meeting on July 1st 2016, where members not appearing on CLP membership lists have arrived without proof of membership. Difficulties have arisen where the EC has had no choice but to let such people in due to the administrative difficulties of checking every attendee's name at a meeting where attendance has far exceeded any precedent. Additionally, where people have arrived at meetings whose membership could not be verified, tension has arisen over the prescience of meetings amongst those who have not received meeting notifications and subsequent suspicion of extra-party organising.
>
> The Chair and Secretary have been the target of a great deal of abusive behaviour from a number of members. The decisions they have made during meetings have often been met

with derision and anger, even where those decisions have been made in the face of indignant attendees numbering well over 100. Both sides have failed to communicate effectively with each other, but the uncomradely behaviour displayed towards the EC, typified by a "them and us" mentality, has fallen short of the standard expected of party members and has contributed to ill-feeling within the constituency.

Several individual incidents are alleged to have taken place at meetings – including members being told to "fuck off" for expressing their views, one member physically threatening the MP, and several members alleged to have been shouted at or harassed during meetings. This investigation received reports from several members that every meeting in the last *circa* 18 months has featured uncomradely behaviour in the form of "shouting down" of speakers, heckling, jeering, threats and a "baying" atmosphere from a group of members who greet opinions they do not share with sardonic remarks. Several reports detailed members having to leave meetings due to the stressful atmosphere, while others refused to return to meetings.

Tensions have been stirred in the last 12 months as a result of the promulgation in the media of several reports regarding Liverpool Riverside CLP. Several members expressed grievances with these reports – not only based on their alleged basis in untruths, but also because they felt aggrieved at what they perceived as attacks on them through the media. Members from both sides of the argument have appeared in local and national press outlets. This press attention has been regrettable as it has brought the local party into disrepute in the public eye, though the author of the anonymous document initially found in several national media outlets has not been possible to trace.

This investigation has found there to be a problem with behaviour and atmosphere within the CLP. particularly during All Member Meeting. Elected representatives of the party are routinely harassed, and media attention has heightened this enmity. Additional difficulties have arisen from the fact that the location used for the meeting of July 1st – a well-known local centre which is one of the few remaining suitable venues for the size of the CLP's membership – has since refused to allow the party use of Its premises due to the unpleasant nature of that evening. The meeting "ended in chaos" involving a vote of no confidence In the

Chair and the incumbent breaking down in tears amidst a great deal of shouting and personal abuse. The atmosphere in meetings is evidently at best unpleasant and at worst an acerbic one, and the high number of first-time attendees unwilling to return or longstanding members unwilling to continue their attendance Is indicative of an endemic problem. This investigation finds that a great deal of these issues have come as a result of the difficulties in managing such large numbers at All Member meetings. There is little doubt that the EC has struggled to communicate effectively with the membership which has been growing apace, and Is hoped that me recommendations of this report help the newly elected EC (post-AGM) to tackle the administrative problems faced by the current EC as well as lessen the impact of any uncomradely incidents or difficult atmospheres within meetings.

There have been CIP meetings during which anti-Semitic incidents are alleged to have taken place. These have arisen as a result of Interrogations of the MP over the Israel. Ahead of each meeting the MP circulates a written account of her Parliamentary work. The investigation reviewed these reports and found sparse mention of the Middle East, but members attested unanimously that a significant proportion of each meeting is given over to intense questioning on Israel from the floor following the MP's report. It would appear that the issue arises without fail in CLP meetings – regardless of the MP's report – often as a platform to attack the MP. This has, on occasion, spilled over into incidents which have drawn allegations of anti-Semitism, particularly where some members have felt that others are holding the MP – a Jewish woman – personally accountable for the actions of the Israeli government. Three individual incidents were reported to this investigation as having taken place in the public forum of CLP meetings, with over ten subsequent complaints received about online comments or comments made or overheard in private in the context of CLP meetings. The most extreme of these involved one member describing Zionism as "a danger to the Jewish people" and a "negation of the principles of Judaism itself", and explicitly suggesting Israeli responsibility for ISIS, Hamas and Al Qaeda. Such interventions have been met in meetings with perceptible shock and denouncements, but the atmosphere of meetings is such that these reactions have been "shouted down". Incidents of online abuse have included members stating that the MP's voting record is "enough to incite anti-Semitism", that the MP's ethnicity has contributed to her having a "major blind spot on the Israel-Palestine conflict, and that the MP is "JLM's bitch". One member remarked in a meeting that Israel was "responsible for the global rise in anti-Semitism", while another made comparison between the so-called "terror tunnels" in the Gaza Strip and the tunnels in the Warsaw Ghetto used by Jews to escape Nazi terror. This investigation found that the members involved in making these statements demonstrated little regard for other members and no consideration as to whether such statements might cause grave offence. First-hand witness statements received by this investigation allege that other examples of incidents and comments alleged to have been made within the context of CLP meetings and online activity include the following: Every Jew is a "Zio-fascist" if they support Israel's existence; Israel has no right to exist. Jews bear an individual and collective responsibility for the actions of the Israeli government. Israel and Zionists "created ISIS for their own purposes"; Israel is funded by America at the behest of the "Jewish lobby", "other Zionists" are targets "when they can be identified" and "deserve to feel uncomfortable" in CLP meetings.

Several submissions to this inquiry have denied the presence of any anti-Semitism in the CLP, whereas others have said variously that "as a Jew I am seriously considering whether I can continue to be a member of the Labour Party' and "I am Jewish and I have been put off going to local meetings". This investigation finds that whilst there is not an endemic anti-Semitism problem within the CLP, there have been incidents where criticism of Israel has been framed in language which can be deemed anti-Semitic and has caused offence to other members. This has contributed to an environment in which Jewish members have taken legitimate offence at a select few egregious statements and have been unwilling to continue any association with the party. Individual disciplinary cases will be taken where appropriate to ensure that no member feels uncomfortable attending party activity. Furthermore, the aforementioned "obsession" with questioning the MP over Israel – an exercise which takes up CLP time and puts off the majority of members who do not come to meetings to discuss the Middle East – is carried out by a minority and has contributed to a fragmented and hostile atmosphere within the CLP.

The report's conclusions were:

> There can be no doubt that Liverpool Riverside CLP has experienced severe difficulties over the last year and a half, exacerbated by the public playing out of tensions between some members and the MP and elected representatives of the party. Meetings have been typified by tensions and uncomradely behaviour, while incidents of anti-Semitism seem to have occurred with troubling regularity. The investigation has made explicit to all members its aim of finding a way for the CLP to return the effective campaigning force which has delivered outstanding election results over the last twenty years in local and national elections. It has sought to find a way to settle differences between members, ensure that the causes of tensions are removed, and to forge an environment in which no single member is uncomfortable in or deterred from party activity. It is believed that some of these difficulties can be resolved through the lessening of the administrative and emotional strain on the EC to both deal with a very large membership and also to deal with an incredibly difficult atmosphere. It is believed that where this report has mentioned failings on the part of the EC, these can in part be mitigated by the great emotional stress these members have been under, feeling threatened and, in one instance, "terrified every time my phone rang". The recommendations are deemed not only necessary, but an effective way of resolving the burden on the EC whilst encouraging mass participation across the constituency. They are aimed at easing structural and administrative difficulties arising from a vast membership as well as ensuring that uncomradely behaviour is negated and that the conditions of meetings can be managed better and conducive to comradely debate and spirited campaigning.[87]

The report's recommendations included: all role-holders in Liverpool Riverside should receive training on organisational matters, including formal meeting structures and internal ballot best practice; and branch delegates to sign the membership code of conduct and guidelines on conduct.

Ellman was made a Dame Commander of the Order of the British Empire in the Queen's Birthday Honours List in June 2018 for parliamentary and political services. To Momentum activists that proved a red rag. The following month one of Jeremy Corbyn's closest allies defended Labour activists who use language 'perceived as anti-Semitic' at a packed meeting of Momentum supporters in Liverpool. Derby North Labour MP Chris Williamson spoke out after a member of the Sefton Constituency Labour Party, known only as Jack, defended a suspended NEC member. Jack, claimed that 'Israeli foot soldiers' were attempting to 'take our democracy away from us'. He was given a standing ovation, and the loudest cheer of the night, when he told the gathering: 'What could be a greater threat to our democracy than a foreign government who is trying to veto the person we want for prime minister? Of course, I'm talking about the Israelis with their foot soldiers in Labour - the LFI, the JLM. They are trying to take our democracy away from us. I was disappointed in the Labour Party's reaction to the smears that have been thrown at the Labour Party. I was disappointed this morning – I was furious this evening because Pete Willsman was forced to retract the statement he made.' To loud applause, Williamson urged the audience to be 'brave' in the face of 'sinister' action taken against such 'activists in the Labour Party'. He said that some in the party had 'allowed their passion to run away' and expressed themselves in 'a light which could be perceived as anti-Semitic ... I don't believe they are anti-Semites.'

An undercover reporter for the *Jewish Chronicle* wrote: 'When Williamson returned to speak he failed to challenge the anti-Semitic conspiracy theory that had been given rapturous applause from the audience. The MP, a former shadow fire and emergency services minister under Corbyn, said: "I understand the reasons why some feel cowered. I think it was wrong to take the action we did against Ken Livingstone ...We should have drawn a line in the sand. Ken has spent his life fighting bigotry, anti-Semitism and racism". Mr Williamson also attacked the Board of Deputies and the "self-appointed" Jewish Leadership council. He said: "They don't speak for all Jews in this country – there's Jewish Voice for Labour, there's the Jewish Socialist Group, there's non-aligned Jews." Admitting "we need to be careful of the language we use", he suggested those who did use anti-Semitic language should have "political education" with regional officers urged to "put your arms around these people". I'd arrived at the event at the Quaker Meeting House in Liverpool city centre earlier that evening. Staff offered a friendly welcome and directed me to the upstairs room in which the meeting took place – but outside the door of the first-floor office a woman who said she was from Merseyside Momentum quizzed me on how I knew about the event. I said I had seen an advert on Facebook and had been visiting Liverpool on business and thought I would enjoy hearing Mr Williamson speak about "democratic reforms" in Labour before returning to London. She told me to take a seat inside.

'During the event, speakers including Walton MP Dan Carden repeatedly attacked the Parliamentary Labour Party. And there was widespread anger from the audience about "smears" that have dogged Mr Corbyn's leadership. Mr Williamson suggested the "ruling class are throwing everything" at the Labour leader to stop him coming to power. He also said he supported mandatory deselection of MPs. At one stage the chair of Ellman's Riverside Constituency Labour Party (CLP) called for her to be replaced. Other speakers – including Nina Houghton, secretary of Luciana Berger's Wavertree CLP, and the chair of Walton CLP, Mary Doolin, also backed calls for the deselection of elected representatives. Ms Houghton, who declared herself to be a feminist, claimed that Liverpool's Jewish female MPs were not pro-women enough. She also backed calls for greater representation of BAME (Black, Asian and minority ethnic) individuals in Liverpool Labour – but faced embarrassment when a black woman in the audience pointed out that the entire panel of speakers was white.'

Jennifer Gerber, director of Labour Friends of Israel, told the newspaper: 'It is absolutely disgraceful that a Labour Party member would accuse fellow members of having dual loyalty, indulging in the language of anti-Semitic conspiracy theories. Sadly, the use of such anti-Semitic tropes is becoming increasingly normalised and it is troubling that Chris Williamson MP, having heard these remarks, did not take the opportunity to condemn them in any way. LFI will be lodging formal complaints against the individual who made these comments with both the Labour Party and Momentum.'[88]

In March 2018 Riverside CLP member Kayla Bibby posted graphic anti-Semitic imagery from a white supremacist US website, in particular a Facebook image of the Statue of Liberty being covered by an alien 'facehugger' emblazoned with a Star of David, the international symbol of the Jewish faith, saying: 'The most accurate photo I have seen all year!' But Bibby, who is a member of Ellman's local party, received only a formal warning, known as a 'reminder of conduct', and was not ordered to undertake any training on anti-Semitism. Ellman complained that her case had not been dealt with strongly enough and the issue erupted again when Bibby was a delegate at that September's party conference in Liverpool. It emerged that, despite Corbyn's claims to be tackling anti-Semitism nationally, just 12 members had been expelled since the previous April for abuse linked to or driven by Jew hatred. Hundreds of cases were not progressed to full disciplinary hearings and many dealt with only by similar 'reminders of conduct'.

Ellman complained to general secretary Jennie Formby about the lack of tough action, pointing out that Bibby had never been suspended, and had not apologised for her conduct. In her reply, Formby said: 'The party staff and the NEC Disputes Panel members who deal with each case have the benefit of all the relevant evidence, which generally includes the material originally complained of and any response by the member to enquiries made in the course of investigation. That contrasts, of course, with the position of those who pen speculative and often anti-Labour comment in the media about the party's internal processes.'

Nowhere near satisfied by that response, the MP authorised *HuffPost UK* to publish the offensive image to underscore how disturbing it was and raised the case during a heated meeting of the Parliamentary Labour Party (PLP). Fellow MPs were shocked by types of imagery and articles that were posted on the notorious American website 'Incogman'. *Huffpost* was then passed evidence that Bibby had approached the website to explicitly ask permission to use the anti-Semitic imagery, which had accompanied an article titled 'Bloodsucking Alien Parasites Killing America'. The website is viciously racist and homophobic and among its recent articles have been a string of anti-Semitic diatribes. Its contents are so graphic that the site is blocked by the UK parliamentary authorities. During the PLP meeting, Ellman distributed a dossier containing some of the imagery to fellow MPs. Among the headlines were 'Jew Judge Forcing Christians To Give Kids To Fags', 'Jew Lawyer Trains Rapefugees How To Act Christian'.

Bibby had been named as a potential candidate for the city council elections in a booklet drafted by the party's Liverpool Local Campaign Forum (LCF), was excluded from the candidate list, and failed in her appeal against that decision. She was belatedly suspended from the party. Ellman said: 'I welcome the fact that the Labour Party have taken action at last, but it is shameful that I had to pursue the case in this way and expose the party's shortcomings. Further investigations must take place while the suspension occurs. This should not be the end of it, but it's an important first step. Somebody who acted in this way should have no place in the Labour party.'

Bibby told *HuffPost UK*, via email: 'The Labour Party now has a modern and well-functioning disciplinary process as you will know and I am of course delighted that this is being looked into, as I'm sure you are. Any speculation in relation to the matter would prejudice the outcome of any investigation and therefore it is not reasonable for me to comment further.' Those close to Bibby suggested last year that she had posted the image because she thought the blue Star of David was a symbol of Israel and her point was about the state of Israel rather than Jews as a race.[89]

Despite the toxic atmosphere, Louise Ellman remained within the Labour Party until she could take the abuse no longer. She conceded, however, that she did not receive the level of anti-Semitic abuse suffered by nearby Liverpool MP Luciana Berger who did jump ship.[90] Although some allies acknowledged that her youth and relative naivety played a part, the foul treatment meted out to her led to prison terms.

Berger entered Parliament aged 28 in 2010 when she took the Labour seat of Liverpool Wavertree vacated by Jane Kennedy. She was the great-niece of trade union and Labour movement legend Manny Shinwell, the War Secretary in the Attlee government. Berger said of her Jewish upbringing: 'I went to the synagogue a lot, and I was part of a strong community. One of its values, "Tikkun Olam", literally means "repairing the world", and it instilled strong values in me at quite young age.'[91] After a private education she became a student activist and co-convened the NUS Anti-Racism/Anti-Fascism Campaign.[92] She worked as a consultant for the Treasury and the NHS during the last part of Tony Blair's government and ran a non-profit campaigning and education organisation working with democratic socialists and trade unions for peace and security in the Middle East. She was the Director of Labour Friends of Israel from 2007 to 2010.

From the start she ran into trouble from local activists who claimed she had been imposed on them by New Labour through the use of an all-women shortlist. She said: 'As a university student and activist, I was attacked from all quarters from the far-Right to the far-left. When I was selected as a Labour council candidate in 2009, people publicly challenged how I could possibly represent anyone from the Bengali community because of my faith and since my selection and election as the Member of Parliament for Liverpool, Wavertree, I have received a torrent of anti-Semitic abuse.'[93] She later recalled that when first put forward as a candidate, 'I never thought I'd be described on BBC News as "a Jewish MP". What other MPs are defined by their faith?'[94] But her career swiftly progressed under Ed Miliband who appointed her a junior shadow minister for energy and climate change. She faced some criticism in September 2011 from the Jewish community in Liverpool and supporters of Israel for not using her position to defend Israel. After 16 months in Parliament, she had not mentioned Israel in any of her parliamentary interventions.[95]

In October 2013, Berger was appointed shadow minister for Public Health following a shadow cabinet reshuffle. After Corbyn's election as leader, Berger was made shadow minister for Mental Health, a post that did not have a governmental equivalent. She resigned in June 2016 in the mass resignation of shadow ministers from the Labour front benches over deep concerns about Corbyn's leadership.[96] Her action, and her appointment as parliamentary chair of the Jewish Labour Movement, resulted in an upsurge of hostility.

Berger had already been targeted by far-Right groups who sent her cartoons of herself wearing a concentration camp uniform and yellow star. Police warned her not to travel home alone. In October 2014, Garron Helm, a member of the neo-Nazi National Action youth group, was imprisoned for four weeks after he sent an anti-Semitic tweet to her. He served two weeks before being released.[97] Similar messages were posted to her on Twitter. According to Berger, 'at the height of the abuse, the police said I was the subject of 2,500 hate messages in the space of three days', using the same hashtag.[98] She was forced to install security measures in her Liverpool and London homes and accused Twitter of insufficient action to counter the problem. During the 2015 general election, a UK Independence Party parliamentary candidate was suspended from the party after sending an allegedly anti-Semitic tweet to Berger. Joshua Bonehill-Paine, a supporter of Helm and a self-described far-right anti-Semite, was convicted of racially aggravated harassment of Berger and was sentenced to two years. John Nimmo was sentenced to 27 months in prison after pleading guilty to nine charges, including sending Berger death threats and anti-Semitic messages signed 'your friend the Nazi'.[99] Jack Coulson, a teenager obsessed with neo-Nazism and who allegedly had told an acquaintance that he was going to kill Berger, was jailed for eight and a half months for possessing a document for terrorist purposes.

Then-Labour leader Ed Miliband wrote on Facebook that the 'shocking attacks' on Berger and others 'highlighted the new channel by which anti-Semites spread their views'. He went on: 'The recent spate of incidents should serve as a wake-up call for anyone who thought that the scourge of anti-Semitism had been defeated and that the idea of Jewish families fearful of living here was unthinkable. Some have told me how, for the first time in their lifetime, they are scared for their children's future … Others have expressed a general unease that this rise in anti-Semitism could signal that something has changed, or is changing, in Britain. As the son of Jewish refugees from the Holocaust who found a home in Britain, I am immensely proud of our country's record for diversity, tolerance and respect.'[100]

Anti-Semitic abuse and threats from the far-Right may, unfortunately, come with the territory for a female Jewish MP. But after Berger asked Corbyn's office in March 2018 about the Mear One mural, she received further online abuse which she believes came from the left.[101] The heavily-pregnant MP wrote: 'Last week I received a torrent of abuse from people purporting to be of the left. One person told me: "Momentum will be watching you Luciana." One email urged me to "resign or perhaps kill yourself so that an actual Labour MP can take your place, Tory c***".' Some had accused her of 'faux anti-Semite outrage' over the Mear One issue, while further attacks focused on the 'truth' that banks were run by Jews. It was falsely suggested that Berger was a 'paid-up Israeli lobby operative' – while further of abusive messages included menacing threats of deselection from people at least purporting to be supporters of Momentum. She also revealed staff working at her constituency office had faced a barrage of abusive telephone calls. She added: 'Their time last week was largely taken up with contending with people calling my office and literally screaming down the phone. They've had to give statements to the police about the threats they've been on the receiving end of, and been exposed to violent emails and messages on my social media. I'm very concerned about the impact it has had on them'[102]. After the murder of fellow Labour MP Jo Cox, Berger was emailed a picture of a large machete and told that she would get it just as Cox got it. On another occasion a letter was hand-delivered to her office saying she would be stabbed and have acid thrown in her face.

Berger was applauded by members on all sides of the Commons after she spoke of the abuse she had endured over the course of her adult life. She said she received her first piece of hate mail aged 19, which described her as a 'dirty Zionist pig'. Standing in front of the 'More in Common' memorial plaque to Jo Cox, she said:

'Here starts my 18-year experience of contending with anti-Semitism.' She has since been attacked by the far-Right and far-left, later saying anti-racism is a central Labour value and there was a 'time not long ago when the left actively confronted anti-Semitism'. She added: 'One anti-Semitic member of the Labour Party is one member too many. And yes, as I've said outside this place in Parliament Square, and it pains me to say this proudly as the chair of the Jewish Labour Movement, in 2018 within the Labour Party anti-Semitism is more commonplace, is more conspicuous and is more corrosive. That's why I have no words for the people who purport to be both members and supporters of our party, who use that hashtag JC4PM, who attacked me in recent weeks for my comments, they attacked me for speaking at the rally against anti-Semitism, they've questioned my comments where I questioned comments endorsing that anti-Semitic mural, who say I should be deselected or called it a smear.' People have accused her of being a traitor, an 'absolute parasite', and told her to 'get out of the country and go back to Israel'. She said the 'hurt and anguish' of the Jewish community must be understood and taken seriously. Berger went on: 'My party urgently needs to address this issue publicly and consistently. We need to expel those people from our ranks that hold these views – including Ken Livingstone. We have a duty to the next generation. Denial is not an option. Prevarication is not an option. Being a bystander who turns the other way is not an option. The time for action is now. Enough really is enough.'[103]

In February 2019, Berger's Liverpool Wavertree constituency announced that two motions of no confidence in her had been submitted, both condemning her for 'continually' criticising the Labour Party leader. The second motion was proposed by a local member who had previously described her as 'a disruptive Zionist' and had accused her of 'spouting rubbish about anti-Semitism to take the heat [out] of her commitment to the murdering government of Israel'.[104] Local members claimed that one of Berger's critics had posted on Facebook that the MP should be 'exposed for the disruptive Zionist she is', and that evidence of anti-Semitism had undermined what some viewed as legitimate criticism. The local party executive said it had not control over motions submitted by members and very little choice on whether to debate 'legitimately-submitted motions'. They went on: 'We strongly reject the media inaccuracies and the accusations of political bullying, for simply adhering to party rules and doing our jobs. Furthermore, we as an executive have always and continue now to express total solidarity with Luciana as a victim of misogyny and of anti-Semitism – coming mostly from the far Right. Our chair is himself Jewish and the suggestion that the CLP executive is in any way a party to bullying and anti-Semitism is a false and slanderous accusation.' Mealy-mouthed, to say the least, but such statements seem part of a deliberate campaign to kill by a thousand cuts the hopes and aspirations of a sitting MP.

Admittedly both motions were eventually withdrawn, but only after Berger was defended by major party figures. Deputy leader Tom Watson defended Berger in the Commons, saying she had 'our solidarity, our support, as she battles the bullying and hatred from members of her own local party. They bring disgrace to the party I love.' He told BBC One's *The Andrew Marr Show*: 'She's being bullied. That motion should never have been moved in her local party, the meeting to hear it should never have been scheduled.' He said Corbyn had 'made it clear these things are not done in his name', and they 'are not helping him, they are harming the reputation of the Labour party'. Shadow health secretary Jonathan Ashworth said Berger had his 'full support', adding: 'It's clear we need to go further and faster in dealing with anti-Semitism in the Labour Party – one anti-Semite in the Labour party is one too many'. Tony Blair called Berger's treatment 'shameful', and said: 'The fact that someone like Luciana Berger – who is a smart, capable, active member of parliament doing her best for her constituents – the fact that she should even be subject to a no-confidence motion with this type of allegation swirling around is shameful for the Labour party.'[105]

In February 2019, Berger and six other MPs resigned from the Labour Party in protest at Corbyn's leadership, citing disagreements over the handling of Brexit and mishandling of anti-Semitism within the party. Two weeks later she gave birth to her second child, who was called Zion. She and the others to break away formed The Independent Group, later renamed Change UK. She accused the Labour leadership of a 'hierarchy of racism' within which anti-Semitism is deemed less bad than other forms of prejudice. 'They have betrayed its (Labour) history as an anti-racist party,' she said. 'I did everything in my power to challenge it ... and yet it got worse. I resent that so much of my time was consumed with this. I got into politics to fix things and yet I couldn't fix my own party. My values stayed the same – I didn't leave the Labour Party, it became a shell of what it was when I joined as a student.'[106] Cultural journalist David Levesley wrote: 'The resignation of Berger from the Labour Party is a sad mark of how toxic anti-Semitism on the left has become. But her time in the party should be remembered for a lot of other amazing speeches and accomplishments. Luciana Berger has made her way into the headlines, more often than not, as a frequent critic of the Labour Party's handling of anti-Semitism and someone who is open about her own experiences with it. But she is also an MP of great moral fibre, a mother and a poster child for resilience and fortitude with a long record of being on the right side of history. Berger has consistently pushed for progressive social policy and given long-term support for gay rights. She has been a frequent supporter of the EU and has consistently voted against the bedroom tax and for a more robust support system for people on benefits. She has, equally, frequently voted for higher taxes on banks and their staff's bonuses and supported the mansion tax throughout. She has always voted to replace Trident and has consistently voted against tuition fees and academy schools.'[107] Berger left Change UK after the breakaway party fared badly in European elections, and in September 2019 joined the Liberal Democrats.

Momentum and the hard-left claimed her defections had proven their case that Berger had always been in the Labour Party under false pretences. And her decision to switch three times in a year may have been a bit rough on Labour voters in Wavertree who at the 2017 election had given her a 29,466 majority. But Ben Rich, chief executive of the radical centre think tank, Radix, and previously chief of staff to then-Lib Dem Leader Tim Farron, wrote in the *Jewish Chronicle*: 'Luciana Berger MP's decision to join the Liberal Democrats has the potential to change everything. And I am not just talking about the fortunes of one political party. For years, the Lib Dems struggled to handle the abject and increasingly bizarre comments of Jenny Tonge and David Ward, the erstwhile MP for Bradford East. Support for the Palestinian cause lapsed all too quickly into anti-Semitism. And yet, even at the height of these troubles, few seriously argued that these fringe figures represented the party as a whole.

'Contrast that with the Labour Party under Jeremy Corbyn: the fish rots from the head. As Luciana sadly came to realise, anti-Semitism was endemic within those now leading her party and it could no longer be her home. She was not alone. Jewish voters appeared to be boxed in. In 2017, around three-quarters clearly felt they had no choice but to vote Conservative because of Labour institutional anti-Semitism and the Lib Dems' lack of progress.

'And yet surely this was a temporary aberration. While our community's commitment to self-improvement and enterprise led some to conclude that the Conservative Party (at least under Mrs May) best represented their values, others see our Jewish values best represented in the commitment to education, social justice, community-building, internationalism and a two-state solution of the left and centre-left. Those – such as Luciana – from this proud left tradition, who probably comprise roughly half our community, were left politically homeless by the Corbynista takeover. A handful soldiered on but the vast majority were left without a political vehicle through which to promote their own best interpretation of Jewish social and religious values.'

He went on: 'The political debate has also moved on. The societal divisions laid bare by Brexit have become ever more entrenched, unleashing a wave of intolerance and authoritarianism. It is an understatement to describe this as "unsettling" for any minority community. The disdain for our political traditions and the direct attempts to undermine our Parliamentary sovereignty, the deployment of mass rallies and chanting and even the adoption of a language of political violence are all too reminiscent of other times. In such circumstances it is simply wrong any longer to sit on the sidelines and say "I lack a political champion. I'll wait and see. I despair". There is too much at stake.

'Luciana has clearly reached the same conclusion and her decision not only gives permission to other Jews who share her values to make the same move but impels us to follow. This is not a time to sit on the political sidelines and wait to see how things turn out. By joining the Liberal Democrats, Luciana has raised her standard for the battle ahead – and Jews on the left of British politics now need to flock to it. Anti-Semitism is often described as the "canary in the coalmine" for a society in trouble but the Jewish community can also be a lion. We have the capacity to lead the fight for a more just, open, inclusive and tolerant society – if we so choose – verbally, financially and practically.'[108]

That may have been a blatant Lib Dem bid to attract disaffected voters, but the overall analysis is largely correct. The Labour Party of Clement Attlee and Nye Bevan, the socialist movement of Robert Noonan, and the trade union traditions of Jack Jones, would not recognise many of those who attempt – and sometimes succeed – to drive out MPs because they do not fit exactly their narrow-minded template.

And the treatment of Ellman and Berger was spurred on social media by keyboard Corbinistas not just because they were Jewish, or critical of Corbyn, or lukewarm on Brexit, but also because they were women. Such vile tactics were also employed by against such difficult women as Yvette Cooper, Liz Kendall, Emma Lewell-Buck, and Helen Jones who spoke of the 'culture of contempt' among those surrounding Corbyn. Jones added: 'The truth my party ignores is that women Labour MPs, however well respected they are, often face bullying and harassment in their constituency parties.' Shadow minister Tracey Brabin, in most other respects a Corbyn loyalist, conceded that 'an element of misogyny' is at play. *Times* columnist Clare Foges wrote: 'The hard left lionises men such as Julian Assange, who spent seven years holed up in the Ecuadorean embassy in the face of sex assault allegations in Sweden; Ken Livingstone, who as London Mayor welcomed Yusuf at-Qaradawi, a Muslim cleric who was accused of supporting wife-beating and the stoning of gays; Red Ken's old mate Gerry Healy, leader of the Workers Revolutionary Party, who was accused of "gross sexual abuse" (allegations dismissed by Livingstone as an MI5 conspiracy). How could the so-called progressives have such blind spots?'[109] The answer is that misogyny and anti-Semitism have traditionally been a stick to beat uppity women with.

Once again, it has to be stressed that the right was also guilty of violent and threatening misogyny, especially when Brexit was involved. Heidi Allen, after she had quit the Conservative party, was stalked by a former soldier Brexiteer who tweeted that he would bring a rope to the scaffolding outside her home. She said: 'It's like warfare. You are in a camp: you are either a Remainer or you are a Brexiteer... It's become very nasty and MPs are right in the centre of that,' she told *The Times* colour supplement. 'I've had endless death threats by email. One of them said, "Novichok coming soon".' Outside Parliament on College Green, thugs shouted 'Gas Gina' while lawyer Gina Miller, who had launched a court challenge to Brexit, was being interviewed. Rhodri Philipps, the 4th Viscount St Davids, offered a £5,000 bounty to anyone who ran her over. The hard-right were a constant source of ideas for the Twitter-obsessed hard-left, not for the first or last time.

Dame Louise Ellman faced yet another challenge from within her Liverpool constituency party – opponents arranged a vote of no confidence on the Jewish day of *Kol Nidre*. The Jewish Labour

Movement, which is the community's only affiliate to the party, said that the scheduling of the vote 'is truly despicable'. A statement added: 'This is racially motivated targeting and bullying of a Jewish MP – a perfect example of how the party is institutionally racist towards Jews. This isn't the first time that Liverpool Riverside has sought to silence, sideline or sack Dame Louise for speaking truth to power and calling out racism. The General Secretary, Jennie Formby, must step in now and put this rotten CLP into special measures.' JLM added that they will 'be asking the EHRC [Equality and Human Rights Commission] to consider this example of institutional anti-Semitism and the leadership's reaction to it as part of its inquiry'. Board of Deputies' president Marie van der Zyl condemned the timing of the vote: 'That a Jewish MP should be threatened with a vote of no confidence tabled for Yom Kippur – the holiest day in the Jewish calendar – when she has no opportunity even to respond, ought to be a source of deep shame for the Labour Party. Louise Ellman has fought bravely against anti-Semitism in her own party, and she should be applauded, not vilified.'[110]

After years of abuse, Ellman quit the Labour Party in spectacular fashion, saying Jeremy Corbyn was 'not fit' to become prime minister. After 55 years as a party member she said she 'can no longer advocate voting Labour when it risks Corbyn becoming PM', adding anti-Semitism had become 'mainstream' in Labour under his leadership. 'With a looming general election and the possibility of him becoming prime minister, I feel I have to take a stand,' she said. The Labour Party had 'become a very extreme and uncomfortable place, with no room for dissent. It's now come to a situation where the Equality and Human Rights Commission is conducting a statutory investigation into the Labour Party to establish whether it is intuitionally anti-Semitic.'[111] 'This is extremely distressing, indeed I found it very traumatic, and I think it does mean that the Labour Party under Jeremy Corbyn is simply not fit,' she added. She now had 'no political home' and stressed she had no intention of defecting to another political party, as other former Labour MPs had done, and hoped to be able to return to Labour under different leadership. She described her decision as 'truly agonising, as it has been for the thousands of other party members who have already left'.[112] In her resignation letter, Ellman said: 'Jewish members have been bullied, abused and driven out.' She added: 'A party that permits anti-Jewish racism to flourish cannot be called anti-racist. This is not compatible with the

Labour Party's values of equality, tolerance and respect for minorities. My values – traditional Labour values – have remained the same. It is Labour, under Jeremy Corbyn, that has changed.'

Labour MP Wes Streeting laid the blame firmly at Corbyn's door: 'Labour's leader knew what was happening to Louise. He was asked to intervene. He chose not to. That is what institutionalised racism looks like.' Former shadow Home Secretary Yvette Cooper said: 'Am just despairing at the way Louise Ellman has been treated and am sickened to the stomach at the response from some in our party to her resignation. It shames us all that we've lost her.'[113] Hilary Benn called Dame Louise an 'outstanding' MP, telling the BBC: 'I think it is a terrible shame that Louise feels she has had to come to this decision. It's clear from reading her letter that she has agonised over this and I think it shows there is a continuing problem which the party needs to get to grips with. I think all of us need to do more to confront this.' And Ruth Smeeth MP said: 'Dame Louise Ellman's resignation is a tragic loss to our movement. She is an inspiration. She has been a Labour activist for over fifty years and has dedicated her life to our movement. I am devastated that she has left the Labour Party. That another Jewish woman has been hounded out of our party. There is no justification for the anti-Jewish hate and abuse that she has suffered. The leadership of the Labour Party should be ashamed that this is happening on their watch. I am truly disgusted. Personally, I'm staying to fight for the soul of the Labour Party. But tonight I lost an ally and a friend.'

True to form, however, social media continued to kick her with a tsunami of tweets. A Corbyn-supporting Facebook group described her as 'a vile creature and a compulsive and pathological liar. Let's hope the Labour (sic) cleanses itself of the Zionist domination that plagued the party since 1945.'[114] A party spokesman said: 'Jeremy Corbyn and the Labour Party are fully committed to the support, defence and celebration of the Jewish community and continue to take robust action to root out anti-Semitism in the party and wider society.' A constituency party spokesperson came out with the familiar mantra that Ellman had jumped before she was pushed. For decent Labourites, the agony continued.[115]

9

Post-natal Blues

'...the debate has become toxic.'

While three successive Tory-led administrations were in turmoil over Brexit – Labour admittedly had its own divisions on that issue – Corbyn's Opposition in part failed to exploit that because of the parallel civil war over anti-Semitism. In that, as in other arenas, Corbyn failed to show leadership even after a furious John McDonnell warned that the issue was out of control.

Momentum continued to blame 'Blairites' for the venomous nature of the debate. That proved risible, but Corbyn had long lost control and his attempts to persuade the Jewish community of his good intentions also proved too little and too late. Former Chief Rabbi Lord Jonathan Sacks said: 'I think that some of the anti-Semitism was hidden and it's simply become liberated from the constraints of various taboos. How has Jeremy Corbyn dealt with anti-Semitism in the Labour Party? I feel that this is a genuine stain on the fabric of British political life. To find something as manifestly evil as anti-Semitism and not deal with it? Jews must not be left to fight anti-Semitism alone.'[1]

It quickly became clear that the Chakrahbarti inquiry had solved nothing and every week through 2018 and 2019 brought more turmoil, investigations, claims and counter-claims. The *Sunday Times* reported that it had uncovered over 2,000 examples of anti-Semitic, racist, violent threats and abusive posts in Corbyn-supporting private Facebook groups, including frequent attacks on Jews and Holocaust denying material. The 20 largest pro-Corbyn private Facebook groups, which have a combined membership of over 400,000, were reported to have as members 12 senior staff who worked for Corbyn and shadow Chancellor John McDonnell.

Faced with a seemingly never-ending row, Corbyn said: 'I'm not an anti-Semite in any form' and claimed that he challenges 'anti-Semitism whenever it arises and no anti-Semitic remarks are done in my name or would ever be done in my name'. Corbyn also said that he would not tolerate antisemitism 'in and around' Labour. 'We must stamp this out from our party and movement,' he said. 'We recognise that anti-Semitism has occurred in pockets within the Labour Party, causing pain and hurt to our Jewish community in the Labour Party and the rest of the country. I am sincerely sorry for the pain which has been caused.'[2] That April, Corbyn attended a 'third night' Passover Seder celebration held by the radical Jewish group Jewdas, which had suggested that allegations of anti-Semitism within Labour are a political plot aimed at discrediting the party as well as tweeting that Israel is 'a steaming pile of sewage which needs to be properly disposed of'.[3] Corbyn was criticised for attending by the Jewish Leadership Council, while the Board of Deputies of British Jews said: 'If Jeremy Corbyn goes to their event, how can we take his stated commitment to be an ally against anti-Semitism seriously?'[4] Charlotte Nichols, Young Labour's women's officer and member of Jewdas, commended Corbyn for attending, arguing that it was 'absolutely right' for Corbyn to 'engage with the community at all levels' and that many of the event attendees are absolutely part of the 'mainstream community'.[5]

That same month, following a meeting with Corbyn, the Jewish Leadership Council and the Board of Deputies said, 'We are disappointed that Mr Corbyn's proposals fell short of the minimum level of action which our letter suggested. In particular, they did not agree in the meeting with our proposals that there should be a fixed timetable to deal with anti-Semitism cases; that they should expedite the long-standing cases involving Ken Livingstone and Jackie Walker; that no MP should share a platform with somebody expelled or suspended for anti-Semitism; that they adopt the full International Holocaust Remembrance Alliance definition of anti-Semitism with all its examples and clauses; that there should be transparent oversight of their disciplinary process.'[6] Corbyn however described the meeting as 'positive and constructive' and re-iterated that he was 'absolutely committed' to rooting out anti-Semitism in the Labour Party.[7]

In April 2018, the Israel Labor Party under Avi Gabbay announced it would cut ties with Corbyn and his office due to their handling of anti-Semitism, but still retain ties with the UK Labour Party as a whole. In a letter to Corbyn, Gabbay wrote of 'my responsibility to acknowledge the hostility that you have shown to the Jewish community and the anti-Semitic statements and actions you have allowed'. In September 2018, Femke van Zijst, spokesperson of the Labour Party of the Netherlands, declared that her party found 'recent reports worrisome' about Corbyn and the growth of anti-Semitism in the UK Labour Party.

In August 2018, it emerged that Corbyn had also been present at a wreath-laying at or near the graves of Salah Khalaf and Atef Bseiso, key members of the Black September terrorist group behind the 1972 Munich Olympics massacre. Photographs disproved initial attempts by Corbyn supporters to deny the story. A Labour spokesperson said that 'a wreath was laid on behalf of those at the conference to all those who lost their lives, including families and children'. But BBC film showed that at the ceremony Corbyn stood in a designated confined covered area where all dignitaries typically stand during such ceremonies, which also covers the graves of Bseiso and Khalaf.[8] Corbyn said that he had been present during commemorations where a wreath was laid for Palestinian leaders linked to Black September but did not think that he had actually been involved.[9] A Labour spokesperson stated that Corbyn 'did not lay any wreath at the graves of those alleged to have been linked to the Black September Organisation or the 1972 Munich killings. He of course condemns that terrible attack, as he does the 1985 bombing'. The Labour Party lodged a complaint over the reportage of the event to the press watchdog, but it was later dropped.[10]

Over a year earlier, Labour had adopted the International Holocaust Remembrance Alliance (IHRA) Working Definition of Anti-Semitism. Later Sir Stephen Sedley, a former appeal court judge and a visiting professor at Oxford University, said: "Anti-Semitism, where it manifests itself in discriminatory acts or inflammatory speech, is generally illegal. Criticism of Israel or of Zionism is protected by law. The IHRA working definition conflates the two by characterising everything other than anodyne criticism of Israel as anti-Semitic". Labour formally adopted the definition at its September 2017 Conference. Jewish Voice for Labour Jonathan Rosenhead described it as intentionally 'vague', allowing for 'the protection of Israel' via 'a side door' and thus 'encouraging the presumption that criticism of Israel is likely to be anti-Semitic'.[11] The organisation saw the change as an 'anti-democratic restriction on political debate' and offered its own definition.[12] Thirty-nine left-wing

Jewish organisations in 15 countries, including six in the UK, declared that the definition was 'worded in such a way as to be easily adopted or considered by western governments to intentionally equate legitimate criticisms of Israel and advocacy for Palestinian rights with anti-Semitism, as a means to suppress the former' and that 'this conflation undermines both the Palestinian struggle for freedom, justice and equality and the global struggle against anti-Semitism. It also serves to shield Israel from being held accountable to universal standards of human rights and international law'.[13] Writer Antony Lerman said: 'Jewish leaders claim exclusive rights to determine what is anti-Semitism, potentially putting Jewish sentiment above the law of the land. The fundamental principle that IHRA is so flawed it should be abandoned, not tinkered with. The answer to hate speech is more speech, not suppression of offensive views.'

Labour's national executive committee (NEC) adopted a new code of conduct defining anti-Semitism for disciplinary purposes, intended to make the process more efficient and transparent. It included the IHRA definition, but amended or omitted four of the eleven examples used, all relating to how criticism of Israel could stray into anti-Semitism and added three others. Two examples were described not as anti-Semitic, but as wrong: 'Accusing Jewish citizens of being more loyal to Israel, or to the alleged priorities of Jews worldwide, than to the interests of their own nations', and 'comparisons of contemporary Israeli policy to that of the Nazis'. The omitted examples were 'the existence of a state of Israel is a racist endeavour' and 'requiring higher standards of behaviour from Israel than other nations'.[14] General secretary Jennie Formby said the code supplemented the definition 'with additional examples and guidance', creating "the most thorough and expansive Code of Conduct on anti-Semitism introduced by any political party in the UK'. NEC member Jon Lansman said: 'Clear and detailed guidelines are essential to ensure that anti-Semitism isn't tolerated, while protecting free speech on Israel's conduct, within a respectful and civil environment. This is what Labour's code of conduct provides.'[15]

The Board of Deputies of British Jews and the Jewish Leadership Council disagreed, saying that the new rules 'only dilute the definition and further erode the existing lack of confidence that British Jews have in their sincerity to tackle anti-Semitism within the Labour movement'. Veteran Labour MP Margaret Hodge called Corbyn a 'fucking anti-Semite and a racist'.[16] Law lecturer Tom Frost said the code ignored the Macpherson Principle that 'a racist incident is any incident which is perceived to be racist by the victim or any other person.'[17]

On 16 July, over 60 British rabbis said that Labour had 'chosen to ignore the Jewish community', that it was 'not the Labour Party's place to rewrite a definition of anti-Semitism', and that the full definition had been accepted by the Crown Prosecution Service, the Scottish Parliament, the Welsh Assembly and 124 local authorities. Later in July, in an unprecedented move, three UK Jewish newspapers, The *Jewish Chronicle*, *Jewish News* and the *Jewish Telegraph*, carried a joint editorial saying that a Corbyn government would be an 'existential threat to Jewish life' in the UK. The former chief rabbi Lord Jonathan Sacks in turn stated that Labour's anti-Semitism was causing British Jews to consider leaving the country. The newspapers also stated: 'Had the full IHRA definition with examples relating to Israel been approved, hundreds, if not thousands, of Labour and Momentum members would need to be expelled.' A Labour spokesman said the party posed 'no threat of any kind whatsoever to Jewish people'. (2018)

Human rights solicitor Geoffrey Bindman said that 'the new code of conduct on anti-Semitism seeks to establish that anti-Semitism cannot be used as a pretext for censorship without evidence of anti-Semitic intent in line with the view of the all-party Commons home affairs select committee in October 2016 that the IHRA definition should only be adopted if qualified by caveats making clear that it is not anti-Semitic to criticise the Israeli government without additional evidence to suggest anti-Semitic intent ... Far from watering down or weakening it, Labour's code strengthens it by addressing forms of discrimination that the IHRA overlooked.' Philosopher and scholar of anti-Semitism Brian Klug said, 'The IHRA code is a living document, subject to revision and constantly needing to be adapted to the different contexts in which people apply its definition. This is the spirit in which the drafters of Labour's code have approached their task.' Historian Geoffrey Alderman wrote: 'This Labour Party row will not be settled by relying on a flawed and faulty definition of anti-Semitism.'[19]

In August 2018, Corbyn conceded that anti-Semitism was a 'problem that Labour is working to overcome'. He said that some criticism of Israel may stray into anti-Semitism at times, but denied that all forms of anti-Zionism were inherently racist, and pledged to 'root out anti-Semitism' within the party, saying, 'People who dish out anti-Semitic poison need to understand: You do not do it in my name. You are not my supporters and have no place in our movement.'[20] In the same month, Corbyn said that the notion that he or Labour posed an 'existential threat' to British Jews was 'overheated rhetoric', but agreed that factions of the

Labour Party had issues with anti-Semitism and that there was work to be done for Labour to regain the trust of British Jews.[21]

The following month, all 11 examples were accepted by the NEC, while Jeremy Corbyn said that they would not prevent criticism of the Israeli government or advocating Palestinian rights. The Media Reform Coalition examined over 250 articles and broadcast news segments covering the issue and found over 90 examples of misleading or inaccurate reporting. The research found evidence of 'overwhelming source imbalance', in which Labour's critics dominated coverage which failed to include those defending the code or critiquing the IHRA definition, and omitted contextual facts about the IHRA definition, concluding these were 'systematic reporting failures' disadvantaging the Labour leadership.[22]

At the Labour party conference, Corbyn said he wanted Labour and the Jewish community to 'work together and draw a line' under anti-Semitism. He went on to attack the record of the Conservative Party for accusing Labour of 'anti-Semitism one day, then endorse Viktor Orban's hard-right government the next day'.[23] In February 2019, Corbyn reiterated: 'As leader ... I wish to set out my own commitment along with that of the wider shadow cabinet as the leaders of the Labour Party in parliament to root out anti-Semitism. I am determined we will defeat racism wherever we see it and I know that anti-Semitism is one of the oldest, nastiest and most persistent forms of racism.'[24] A week later, he said in parliament, "anti-Semitism has no place whatsoever in any of our political parties, in our lives, in our society'.

Later, Corbyn said: 'While other political parties and some of the media exaggerate and distort the scale of the problem in our party, we must face up to the unsettling truth that a small number of Labour members hold anti-Semitic views and a larger number don't recognise anti-Semitic stereotypes and conspiracy theories. The evidence is clear enough. The worst cases of anti-Semitism in our party have included Holocaust denial, crude Jewish-banker stereotypes, conspiracy theories blaming Israel for 9/11 or every war on the Rothschild family, and even one member who appeared to believe that Hitler had been misunderstood. I am sorry for the hurt that has been caused to many Jewish people. We have been too slow in processing disciplinary cases of mostly online anti-Semitic abuse by party members. We are acting to speed this process up. People who hold anti-Semitic views have no place in the Labour Party. They may be few – the number of cases over the past three years represents less than 0.1% of Labour's membership of more than half a million – but one is too many.'[25]

The party, however, could not heal all wounds. Labour peer Peter Hain and former Israeli negotiator in peace talks Daniel Levy argued that 'actually the problem is political, and therefore requires a political not simply a procedural solution.'[26] In July 2019, Labour MP Clive Lewis wrote: 'Expulsions alone will not solve Labour's anti-Semitism crisis. Political education about anti-Semitism can help to ensure a socialist politics based on real equality becomes the common sense across the party.'[27] Labour appointed a liaison officer to improve the party's relationships with the Jewish community and issued an online leaflet entitled *No Place For Antisemitism* alongside related documents and videos, as the launch of a programme of educating members on oppression and social liberation, and to help them confront racism and bigotry. This was promoted to all party members by an email from Corbyn.

In April 2018, the then-new Labour general secretary, Jenny Formby, had announced that a team of lawyers had been seconded to handle disciplinary cases and that a new post of in-house general counsel had been advertised 'to advise on disciplinary matters and improvements to our processes'. Lansman wrote that leaked emails '... suggest that former compliance unit officials from the Labour right may have delayed action on some of the most extreme and high-profile anti-Semitism cases, including Holocaust denial, allowing a backlog of cases to build up that would damage the party and Jeremy's leadership.'[28] In September, the NEC approved a doubling of the size of the party's key disciplinary body, the National Constitutional Committee, in order to speed up the handling of anti-Semitism claims. In February 2019, Formby noted that the Governance and Legal Unit had suffered during 2018 from a high level of staff sickness and departures, which was addressed in part by secondments. She also said that the unit was now back to full strength and that the size of the unit would be more than doubled. In July, a Labour spokesperson said that the rate at which anti-Semitism cases have been dealt with had increased fourfold after Formby took up her position in May 2018. The NEC agreed to speed up determination of the most serious cases by giving a special panel comprising the General Secretary and NEC officers the authority to consider these cases and expel members where appropriate, rather than requiring the cases to be referred to the quasi-judicial National Constitutional Committee.[29]

Formby told Labour MPs that, of the complaints about anti-Semitism received by the party from April 2018 to January 2019, 400 related to individuals who were not party members. In a further 220 cases, Labour had found that there was insufficient evidence of a breach of party rules. Some of the remaining 453 complaints, i.e. those where there was sufficient evidence of a breach of party rules, related to social media posts dating back a number of years. These 453 complaints received over the ten-month period represented 0.06% of Labour's 540,000 membership.[30] Investigations had resulted in 12 expulsions and 49 resignations from the party and 187 formal warnings, while some complaints received recently were still under investigation. Some Labour MPs questioned the accuracy of the data. That summer, Formby provided updated disciplinary figures regarding complaints of anti-Semitism and committed to regularly publishing statistics. During the first six months of 2019, 625 complaints about members had been received, some members being the subject of multiple complaints, and 116 members suspended. A further 658 complaints were received about people who were not members.[31] Of the complaints received relating to members, Labour decided that 100 lacked sufficient evidence and 163 showed no rule breaches, 90 received formal warnings or reminders of conduct and 97 had been referred to the National Constitutional Committee, which has the power to expel members. 146 cases were still being processed. NEC Antisemitism Panels had met six times and made 190 decisions, compared with 2 and 8 in the same period the previous year. The National Constitutional Committee had concluded 28 cases and made 8 expulsions with another 12 members resigning, compared with 10, 7 and 3 in the same period the previous year.[32]

However, such claims that Labour was indeed rooting out anti-Semitism through disciplinary procedures were undermined by a July 1919 edition of the BBC's *Panorama* entitled 'Is Labour Anti-Semitic?' Produced by John Ware, it included a devastating claim by former staff that, in the first half of 2018, senior Labour figures had interfered in the complaints process while new senior officials in their department downgraded outcomes for anti-Semitic behaviour. Labour denied that there was interference and said the former staff included those who had 'personal and political axes to grind'. The party added, 'The *Panorama* programme was not a fair or balanced investigation. It was a seriously inaccurate, politically one-sided polemic, which breached basic journalistic standards, invented quotes and edited emails to change their meaning.'[33] The BBC responded that 'the investigation was not pre-determined, it was driven by the evidence.' Labour later submitted a formal complaint about the programme to the BBC, one of around 1,600 received.[34] But that complaint would rebound on Labour at a crucial time (*see next chapter*). Staff members represented by the GMB trade union voted overwhelmingly to call on the party to be consistent in supporting whistle-blowers wherever they worked and to apologise to their former colleagues.

In May 2019, following complaints submitted by the Jewish Labour Movement and the Campaign Against Anti-Semitism, the Equality and Human Rights Commission (EHRC) launched a formal investigation into whether Labour had 'unlawfully discriminated against, harassed or victimised people because they are Jewish': specifically, whether 'unlawful acts have been committed by the party and/or its employees and/or its agents, and; whether the party has responded to complaints of unlawful acts in a lawful, efficient and effective manner'. In 2016, Labour MP Harriet Harman had expressed concern about the suitability of its chair, David Isaac, given his principal role as an equity partner at a City law firm that advises the Conservative government, Pinsent Masons. Previously, in September 2017, the EHRC chief executive, Rebecca Hilsenrath, had demanded a zero-tolerance approach to anti-Semitism in the Labour Party and swift action by the leadership to deal with it. Antony Lerman, former founding director of the Institute for Jewish Policy Research, raised concerns that such a statement made Hilsenrath unsuitable to lead a probe into Labour. He wrote: 'Prior to investigation, is it not worrying that the ceo already claims to know what the Labour Party needs to do?'[35] Formby asked that a request by Labour deputy leader Tom Watson to Labour parliamentarians, asking that complaints about anti-Semitism be copied to him for monitoring, be disregarded on the grounds that this would disrupt the official process and be in breach of data protection law. Shadow Chancellor John McDonnell looked forward to the investigation's conclusions stating: 'I want it quicker actually, I need it speeded up. Let's learn the lessons and then also work with the organisation to implement what recommendations they bring forward. On that basis I'm hoping we'll get a clean bill of health but more importantly we can become much more effective at tackling not just anti-Semitism but racism, both in our party and society overall.'[36]

Jewish Voice for Labour produced a dossier for the EHRC in response to its request for evidence in relation to its investigation. JVL holds that without making public the complaints and Labour's response when the EHRC shared them ahead of launching the investigation, 'the EHRC have violated the Equality Act 2006 which requires that they specify who is being investigated and "the nature of the unlawful act" they are suspected of committing, both required by its own terms of reference.'[37]

Throughout Corbyn's era, a welter of fringe organisations were formed largely to defend and laud their leader against charges of anti-Semitism and denigrate anyone who doubted his greatness or fitness to govern. Inevitably, they were generally on the extreme left, made up of veteran agitators with a sprinkling of academics included for intellectual clout, and they were very wary of publishing details of their memberships, which are thought to be tiny. Surprisingly to many, several of these groupings, often allied to Momentum, are purportedly Jewish while being vehemently anti-Zionist, and have often raised the loudest voices to keep controversies as heated as possible, as we have seen above.

Jewish Voice for Labour (JVL) was formed in July 2017 as an organisation for Jewish members of the Labour Party who do not go along with the much bigger Jewish Labour Movement (JLM). One of its aims is to 'to oppose attempts to widen the definition of anti-Semitism beyond its meaning of hostility towards, or discrimination against, Jews as Jews'.[38] Jenny Manson, an activist in Jews for Justice for Palestinians and a former Labour councillor, was elected chair. Manson said the organisation is 'not anti-Zionist' but was 'an alternative voice for Jewish members of Labour' who do not support the JLM's 'profoundly Zionist orientation'.[39] Secretary Glyn Secker wrote that JVL has 'established a very different, authentic, radical, and socialist Jewish narrative to that promulgated by the Jewish Labour Movement and Labour Friends of Israel'.[40] Co-Chairs Jenny Manson and Leah Levane 'contend that the JLM cannot represent all Jewish members of the Labour Party when it is committed "to promote the centrality of Israel in Jewish life" as well as the wider Jerusalem Programme of the World Zionist'.[41] The organisation's motto is 'Always with the oppressed; never with the oppressor', taken from a quote by Marek Edelman, the last surviving commander of the Warsaw Uprising.

JVL's most vocal supporters have strong links to Corbyn's inner circle. Unite the Union's Len McCluskey, for example, welcomed it as a 'positive move forward'.[42] David Rosenberg, author and founding member of the Jewish Socialists' Group, described JVL as 'a broader, more inclusive, more open-minded group – not fixated on defending Israel…'[43] Corbyn himself said JVL are 'committed to fighting anti-Semitism and making sure there is a Jewish voice in the party. We already have the Jewish Labour Movement. JVL was established last year and I think it is good that we have organisations within the party that are giving that voice to people.'[44]

Not surprisingly, more mainstream outfits disagreed. JLM referred to it as an 'extreme fringe'.[45] Board of Deputies President Marie van der Zyl referred to it as 'a tiny organisation whose odious views are representative of no-one but themselves'.[46] And elements of Momentum are sceptical. Founder Jon Lansman, at the Limmud Festival, said that JVL 'is an organisation which is not just tiny but has no real connection with the Jewish community at all' and 'it doesn't represent the Jewish community in a way that JLM clearly does represent the Labour wing of the Jewish community.' Lansman also argued that 'the most influential anti-Semitism-deniers, unfortunately, are Jewish anti-Zionists.'[47]

JVL can, however, be fairly judged by its actions. As seen above, it defended Ken Livingstone and supported Jackie Walker, claiming she was the victim of a 'vituperative campaign ... based on this sliver of quasi-fact'.[48] It opposed the Working Definition of Anti-Semitism being formally adopted by the Labour Party for disciplinary purposes as 'attempts to widen the definition of anti-Semitism beyond its meaning of hostility towards, or discrimination against, Jews as Jews'. JVL challenged 'unjustified allegations of anti-Semitism' which are 'used to undermine Jeremy Corbyn's leadership'.[49] JVL complained to BBC director-general Tony Hall about the Corporation's 'lack of impartiality and inaccuracies' and 'biased' coverage of Labour MP Margaret Hodge's allegations of anti-Semitism against Jeremy Corbyn.[50] It rejected suggestions that comparisons between Israel and 'features of pre-war Nazi Germany' or apartheid-era South Africa were 'inherently anti-Semitic', arguing: 'Drawing such parallels can undoubtedly cause offence; but potent historical events and experiences are always key reference points in political debate. Such comparisons are only anti-Semitic if they show prejudice, hostility or hatred against Jews as Jews.'[51] Its guidelines on anti-Semitism included the view that 'Jews, Israelis and Zionists are separate categories that are too frequently conflated by both supporters and critics of Israel. This conflation can be anti-Semitic. Holding all Jews responsible for the actions of the Israeli government is anti-Semitic. Many Jews are not Zionist.' It published an open letter calling the party under Corbyn an 'a crucial ally in the fight against bigotry and reaction' and noted Corbyn's consistent campaigning in support of 'initiatives against anti-Semitism'. It conceded, however, that there was a 'disproportionate focus on anti-Semitism on the left, which is abhorrent but relatively rare.'[52]

The Jewish Socialists' Group (JSG) was born in the mid-1970s in Manchester and Liverpool to oppose the National Front on the streets and support the Anti-Nazi League. It was a founding member of the International Jewish Peace Union. But its laudable aims were soured by intellectual conflict with the Jewish communal leadership and in particular, the Association of Jewish Ex-Servicemen. Its main contribution to the issue of anti-Semitism within Labour was its April 2016 statement: 'Accusations of anti-Semitism are currently being weaponised to attack the Jeremy Corbyn-led Labour party with claims that Labour has a "problem" of anti-Semitism ... This is despite Corbyn's longstanding record of actively opposing fascism and all forms of racism and being a firm a supporter of the rights of refugees and of human rights globally.'[53]

The London-based group Jewdas was described in *The Guardian* as a Jewish hipster organisation engaged in political, cultural and artistic activities.[54] The *Jewish Chronicle* saw it as a 'Jewish diaspora group, known for its far-left anti-Zionism'.[55] In May 2015, the group launched its inaugural Birthwrong trip to Andalusia, Spain, parodying Birthright Israel's heritage trips for young adults from the Jewish diaspora. Advertised as 'a trip for anyone who's sick of Israel's stranglehold on Jewish culture and wants to get away on a raucous holiday', the itinerary included: 'See Maimonides! Get pissed! Do some Jewish tourism! Spend Shabbat with Andalusian Jews! Shvitz in a hammam! Visit a communist village! Get pissed!'[56] Jewdas took part in protests against neo-Nazi demonstrations in north London, and against a far-right rally against Syrian refugees arriving in Dover.[57] It snatched widespread media attention for organising an event called *The Protocols of the Elders of Hackney* with a flyer parodying traditional anti-Semitic images. Four members of the group were arrested.[58]

Independent Jewish Voices (IJV) was launched in 2007 by 150 prominent British Jews including Nobel laureate playwright Harold Pinter, historian Eric Hobsbawm, lawyer Sir Geoffrey Bindman, film director Mike Leigh and actors Stephen Fry and Zoe Wanamaker. They said it was 'born out of a frustration with the widespread misconception that the Jews of this country speak with one voice – and that this voice supports the Israeli government's policies'.[59] IJV stated it was founded 'to represent British Jews ... in response to a perceived pro-Israeli bias in existing Jewish bodies in the UK', and, according to Hobsbawm, 'as a counter-balance to the uncritical support for Israeli policies by established bodies such as the Board of Deputies of British Jews'.[60] The group's Declaration said: 'We are a group of Jews in Britain from diverse backgrounds, occupations and affiliations who have in common a strong commitment to social justice and universal human rights. We come together in the belief that the broad spectrum of opinion among the Jewish population of this country is not reflected by those institutions which claim authority to represent the Jewish community as a whole. We further believe that individuals and groups within all communities should feel free to express their views on any issue of public concern without incurring accusations of disloyalty. We have therefore resolved to promote the expression of alternative Jewish voices, particularly in respect of the grave situation in the Middle East, which threatens the future of both Israelis and Palestinians as well as the stability of the whole region.'[61]

Although themselves often divided on individual cases, such groups have generally insisted that accusations of anti-Semitism against the Labour Party are, firstly, to conflate anti-Semitism with criticism of Israel in order to deter such criticism and, secondly, to undermine Corbyn's leadership.

By 2019 there had been a long fightback by those who saw themselves as being unfairly attacked for anti-Semitism, and by those who supported them. In February Labour MP Chris Williamson MP was suspended and investigated after he was recorded defending the party's record on combating anti-Semitism.[62] The Labour Party in Northern Ireland (LPNI) released a statement opposing the second suspension of Williamson on the grounds that it was 'arbitrary and unreasonable' and stated that the 'allegations of rampant anti-Semitism in the Labour Party' have led to detailed research and a number of investigations being conducted to ascertain the truthfulness of the claims. Some of the research has been conducted by world renowned Jewish organisations, with no affiliation, support for, or loyalty to the UK Labour Party. Despite their clear objective and independent credentials, their findings have been almost universally ignored by the UK media.' It then went on, 'It is a fair comment to say that the Labour Party does not have any form of particular problem with anti-Semitism. It is also fair to say that Labour Party members are not to blame for the narrative that suggests that there is a particular problem with anti-Semitism in the party. It logically follows that members of the Labour Party should not feel that they should be apologetic about something that has been shown to be false.'[63]

Pro-Corbyn websites, such as *The Canary*, were the target of an advertising boycott campaign by Stop Funding Fake News, which said that *The Canary* 'regularly publish fake news and attempt to justify anti-Semitism' and that two of its writers had made anti-Semitic comments. The campaign was backed by *Countdown* TV presenter Rachel Riley, while *The Canary* called the accusations a smear and those behind the campaign 'political Zionists'.[64] Riley accused Jeremy Corbyn of 'giving voice to holocaust denial' after a Twitter row with George Galloway. The 32-year-old also accused the former Labour MP of being 'anti-Semite scum', telling him to 'f***off'.

A number of individuals using Twitter to respond to criticism of Labour were criticised by the Community Security Trust for claiming that allegations of anti-Semitism in the party are 'exaggerated, weaponised, invented or blown out of proportion, or that Labour and Corbyn are victims of a smear campaign relating to antisemitism'.[65] A separate analysis of social media activity by Labour Party members, based on fourteen case studies, showed a pattern of greatly increased references to Israel, anti-Semitism and British Jewry following Corbyn's election as leader.[66] The report suggested that the reason is the influence of 'radical extremists' at a time when the Labour Party membership expanded hugely.[67] An alternative theory is that the increase in such material was, at least in part, a response to the high and sustained level of critical media coverage of anti-Semitism allegations. In June 2019, Labour peer Peter Hain and former Israeli negotiator in peace talks Daniel Levy claimed that the effect of Labour's stance on anti-Semitism has been 'to empower apologists for totally unacceptable Israeli government attacks on Palestinians and the steady throttling of their rights – allowing those apologists to scale new heights in their dishonest attempts to label criticism of such Israeli policy as "anti-Semitic".'[68]

In August 2015, dozens of prominent Jewish activists signed an open letter criticising the *Jewish Chronicle* for what they viewed as its 'character assassination' of Corbyn. They wrote: 'Your assertion that your attack on Jeremy Corbyn is supported by "the vast majority of British Jews" is without foundation. We do not accept that you speak on behalf of progressive Jews in this country. You speak only for Jews who support Israel, right or wrong.' They continued: 'There is something deeply unpleasant and dishonest about your McCarthyite guilt by association technique. Jeremy Corbyn's parliamentary record over 32 years has consistently opposed all racism including anti-Semitism.'[69]

Richard Kuper, spokesperson for Jews for Justice for Palestinians, said that, while 'there is some antisemitism in and around the Labour party – as there is in the wider society in Britain, there is clearly also a coordinated, willed and malign campaign to exaggerate the nature and extent of anti-Semitism as a stick to beat the Labour party' under Corbyn. In the same month, Ian Saville, a Jewish Socialists' Group and Labour Party member, said he was 'disturbed' by the way anti-Semitism had 'been used to attack the left in the Labour Party'.[70] The Jewish Socialists' Group said that anti-Semitism accusations were being 'weaponised' in order to attack the Jeremy Corbyn-led Labour party with claims that Labour has a "problem" of anti-Semitism'. It added, 'a very small number of such cases seem to be real instances of anti-Semitism. Others represent genuine criticism of Israeli policy and support for Palestinian rights.' The statement concluded: 'The Jewish Socialists' Group sees the current fearmongering about anti-Semitism in the Labour Party for what it is – a conscious and concerted effort by right-wing political forces to undermine the growing support among Jews and non-Jews alike for the Labour Party leadership of Jeremy Corbyn, and a measure of the desperation of his opponents.'[71]

Eighty-two 'Jewish members and supporters of the Labour party and of Jeremy Corbyn's leadership' wrote an open letter stating that they 'do not accept that anti-Semitism is rife in the Labour party' and that 'these accusations are part of a wider campaign against the Labour leadership, and they have been timed particularly to do damage to the Labour party and its prospects...'[72] Jewdas suggested that the allegations are aimed at discrediting the party and called the reaction to them a 'bout of faux-outrage greased with hypocrisy and opportunism', saying it was 'the work of cynical manipulations by people whose express loyalty is to the Conservative Party and the right wing of the Labour Party'.[73] Joseph Finlay, the former deputy editor of the *Jewish Quarterly* magazine and co-founder of several grassroots Jewish organisations, described Corbyn as 'one of the leading anti-racists in parliament', adding that: 'Anti-Semitism is always beyond the pale. Labour, now a party of over half a million members, has a small minority of anti-Semites in its ranks, and it suspends them whenever it discovers them. I expect nothing less from an anti-racist party and an anti-racist leader.' He continued, 'There are many threats to Jews – and we are right to be vigilant ... The idea that Britain's leading anti-racist politician is the key problem the Jewish community faces is an absurdity, a distraction, and a massive error.'[74]

The Palestinian-Israeli Socialist Struggle Movement said that they 'view Corbyn as a strong opponent of anti-Semitism and see the attacks being made on him for what they are – attempts to discredit a left-wing politician who has put forward a manifesto seen by capitalists as too radical in favour of working class interests ... The smear campaign against Corbyn is a dangerous attempt to sabotage the struggle for left and socialist solutions.'[75]

Over 200 Jewish members and supporters of the Labour Party signed a letter published in *The Guardian*, calling the party under Corbyn an 'a crucial ally in the fight against bigotry and reaction' and Corbyn's campaigning consistently in support for 'initiatives against anti-Semitism'. They also welcomed Labour's support for 'freedom of expression on Israel and on the rights of Palestinians'. They felt that the 'disproportionate focus on anti-Semitism on the left, which is abhorrent but relatively rare'.[76] Andrew Feinstein, executive director of Corruption Watch pointed out that 'only a very small percentage of Labour members hold anti-Semitic views and a YouGov poll in 2015 found Labour displayed the second least amount of any political party, second only to the Liberal Democrats. In 2017, two years into Jeremy Corbyn's leadership, the extent of anti-Semitism in Labour had actually dropped, according to polling.'[77] Gabor Mate, Canadian psychologist and writer, Jewish holocaust survivor and former Zionist, when asked about allegations of anti-Semitism in the Labour Party said: '...The whole anti-Semitism charge, when it comes to the Palestinian issue, is simply a way to intimidate and silence critics of horrendous Israeli policies.'[78]

Independent researcher Jamie Stern-Weiner's review of the cases of anti-Semitism found that some were represented in the media in a way that treated comments about 'Zionists' as being the same as Holocaust denial and comments about anti-Semitic conspiracy theories.[79] Israeli historian and Oxford University Professor of International Relations Avi Shlaim argued that 'charges of Jew-hatred are being deliberately manipulated to serve a pro-Zionist agenda'.[80] Norman Finkelstein said: 'The only plausible answer is, it's political. It has nothing whatsoever to do with the factual situation; instead, a few suspect cases of anti-Semitism – some real, some contrived – are being exploited for an ulterior political motive. As one senior Labour MP said the other day, it's transparently a smear campaign.'[81] John Newsinger, professor of history at Bath Spa University, wrote: 'There has been a sustained attempt made to discredit the Corbynites by alleging that they are somehow responsible for the Labour Party having a serious problem with anti-Semitism, that the Labour left and the left outside the Labour Party is, in fact, anti-Semitic ... There are two points worth making here: first that the allegations are politically motivated smears, perpetrated by people completely without shame, and second that they do considerable damage to the real fight against anti-Semitism.'[82] Noam Chomsky said: 'I wholeheartedly support the right of anyone to criticise Israel without being branded anti-Semitic.'[83]

Forty-two senior academics wrote condemning anti-Corbyn bias in coverage of the debate and suggested that 'dominant sections of the media have framed the story in such a way as to suggest that anti-Semitism is a problem mostly to do with Labour and that Corbyn is personally responsible for failing to deal with it. The coverage has relied on a handful of sources such as the Board of Deputies, the Jewish Leadership Council and well-known political opponents of Corbyn himself.' They continued: 'It is not "whataboutery" to suggest that the debate on anti-Semitism has been framed in such a way as to mystify the real sources of anti-Jewish bigotry and instead to weaponise it against a single political figure just ahead of important elections. We condemn anti-Semitism wherever it exists. We also condemn journalism that so blatantly lacks context, perspective and a meaningful range of voices in its determination to condemn Jeremy Corbyn.'[84] One of the academics, Jane Dipple of the University of Winchester, was herself investigated by her university and the Labour Party over allegedly anti-Semitic posts on Facebook. In August 2018 the university said that Dipple no longer worked there but refused to say if she had been sacked or if she had resigned.[85]

Israeli historian and socialist activist Ilan Pappe stated that 'Corbyn is not an anti-Semite and the Labour Party, until his election, was a pro-Israeli bastion' and 'there is anti-Semitism among all British parties – and much more on the right than on the left.' He continued: 'It is not the Labour Party that is infested with anti-Semitism; it is the British media and political systems that are plagued by hypocrisy, paralysed by intimidation and ridden with hidden layers of Islamophobia and new chauvinism in the wake of Brexit.'[86] Stephen Sedley dismissed the charge that the Labour Party is 'institutionally' or 'culturally' anti-Semitic. He wrote that 'an undeclared war is going on inside the party, with pro-Israeli groups such as the Jewish Labour Movement seeking to drive out pro-Palestinian groups like the Jewish Voice for Labour by stigmatising them, and Corbyn with them, as anti-Semitic.' He believes that outside bodies like the Board of Deputies of British Jews and the Jewish Leadership Council – 'neither noted for balanced criticism of Israel' – weigh in, aided by 'generous media coverage'.[87]

Scholar of anti-Semitism Brian Klug wrote: 'It's paradoxical if, at the moment Labour wakes up to the necessity of combatting anti-Semitism in its ranks, it is shouted down because of its failure to deal with it in the past.' In October 2018, he wrote: 'It appears that two different objectives are being conflated by Jewish leadership: confronting anti-Semitism and toppling Corbyn.'[88] Lorna Finlayson, a lecturer in political philosophy at the University of Essex, said that 'no one has yet produced any evidence either that anti-Semitism is more prevalent in the Labour Party than elsewhere in British society (within the Conservative Party, for instance), or that its incidence within Labour has increased since Corbyn became leader.' But in September, Professor Rebecca Ruth Gould, a literary theorist, said that 'Labour must recognise the internal diversity of the Jewish community and not allow a political faction to silence other points of view, as is happening now to an unprecedented degree.'[89]

Writer Antony Lerman wrote: 'It's hard to believe, after the battering Labour has experienced over the issue of anti-Semitism in the party since Jeremy Corbyn was elected leader and the fact nothing the party has done has succeeded in fully placating its critics, that officials expected anything approximating universal approbation. But the new code [of conduct] had barely seen the light of day before it was being condemned in the harshest terms by all and sundry.' In September, he noted 'The default mode of almost all the mainstream media is to take as given that the party is institutionally anti-Semitic ... the ever wilder doubling-down on painting Corbyn an anti-Semite and the increasingly desperate attempts to oust him from the leadership using hatred of Jews as a weapon with which to achieve this.'[90]

Author Lev Golinkin wrote that 'the same leaders and institutions who are up in arms over Britain's Labour Party have failed, over and over, to express appropriate outrage' and 'a case can be made that for many of these institutions, people like Corbyn and Farrakhan are manna from heaven, because they allow them to show the world how fiercely they fight anti-Semitism without actually having to do so in places where it's inconvenient.'[91] Israeli journalist and author Gideon Levy called Corbyn 'a paragon of a leftist, one who has fought his whole life for the values he believes in'. He added: 'Leave the incitement campaign against Corbyn and wish him luck: He's a man of conscience, and I hope he'll be Britain's prime minister. It could be good for Israel as well.'[92] Writer Richard Seymour wrote: '...allegations that Labour is institutionally anti-Semitic, or that Corbyn himself is a racist, cut against, rather than with, the grain of what people already suspect to be true. Those who dislike Corbyn overwhelmingly think he's a politically correct peacenik, not a Jew-hater.'[93]

American scholars Noam Chomsky and Norman Finkelstein, called the criticism of Corbyn and Labour 'insane' and 'hysteria' and led by powerful interests, with Chomsky arguing that the aim is to undermine Corbyn's attempt to create a political party responsive to the electorate, and Finkelstein asserting that, given the lack of evidence, the campaign was a calculated hoax.[94] In May 2019, Finkelstein called the allegations of anti-Semitism 'witch-hunt hysteria'. Chomsky said: 'The way charges of anti-Semitism are being used in Britain to undermine the Corbyn-led Labour Party is not only a disgrace but also ... an insult to the memory of the victims of the Holocaust.'[95]

Israel-based journalist Jonathan Cook noted that a Labour Party report by Jennie Formby providing numbers on Labour anti-Semitism cases 'decisively undercut' the claims of Corbyn's critics 'not only of endemic anti-Semitism in Labour, but of any significant problem at all'.[96] In April 2019, historian and University of Buckingham Professor of Politics Geoffrey Alderman wrote that Corbyn 'has an impressive demonstrable record of supporting Jewish communal initiatives'. In May, he wrote that 'I will agree that from time to time, as backbench MP and party leader, Corbyn has acted unwisely. But the grounds for labelling him an anti-Semite simply do not exist.'[97]

However, Mark Seddon and Francis Beckett concluded that 'the debate has become toxic. It's all abuse and bullying and point-scoring. It long ago ceased to concentrate on the protection of British Jews on one hand, and the creation of a better and more equal society in Britain on the other.'

A YouGov survey commissioned by the Campaign Against Antisemitism (CAA) found that supporters of the Labour Party were less likely to hold anti-Semitic views than those of the Conservative Party or the UK Independence Party (UKIP), while those of the Liberal Democrats were the least likely to hold such views.[98] Further analysis of the survey data revealed that, among Labour Party supporters, anti-Semitism had declined between 2015 and 2017.[99] A study into contemporary anti-Semitism in Britain by the Institute for Jewish

Policy Research found that 'Levels of anti-Semitism among those on the left-wing of the political spectrum, including the far-left, are indistinguishable from those found in the general population. Yet, all parts of those on the left of the political spectrum – including the "slightly left-of-centre", the "fairly left-wing" and the "very left-wing" – exhibit higher levels of anti-Israelism than average.' It went on: 'The most anti-Semitic group on the political spectrum consists of those who identify as very right-wing: the presence of anti-Semitic attitudes in this group is 2 to 4 times higher compared to the general population.'[100] It continued: 'However, in relation to anti-Israel attitudes, the very left-wing lead: 78% (75–82%) in this group endorse at least one anti-Israel attitude, in contrast to 56% in the general population, and 23% (19–26%) hold six to nine such attitudes, in contrast to 9% in the general population. Elevated levels of anti-Israel attitudes are also observed in other groups on the political left – the fairly left-wing and those slightly left-of-centre. The lowest level of anti-Israel attitudes is observed in the political centre and among those who are slightly right-of-centre or fairly right-wing.' The report, however, found that '...anti-Israel attitudes are not, as a general rule, anti-Semitic; but the stronger a person's anti-Israel views, the more likely they are to hold anti-Semitic attitudes. A majority of those who hold anti-Israel attitudes do not espouse any antisemitic attitudes, but a significant minority of those who hold anti-Israel attitudes hold them alongside anti-Semitic attitudes. Therefore, anti-Semitism and anti-Israel attitudes exist both separately and together.'[101] The study stated that in 'surveys of attitudes towards ethnic and religious minorities ... the most consistently found pattern across different surveys is heightened animosity towards Jews on the political right...' and that 'the political left, captured by voting intention or actual voting for Labour, appears in these surveys as a more Jewish-friendly, or neutral, segment of the population.'

But another YouGov poll of 1,864 British Jewish adults found that 83% felt that the Labour Party was too tolerant of anti-Semitism among its MPs, members, or supporters. A poll by *The Jewish Chronicle* found that just 13% of Jews intended to vote for Labour, and that, when asked to rank the degree of 'anti-Semitism among the political party's members and elected representatives' between 1 (low) to 5 (high), Jews ranked Labour at 3.94, compared with 3.64 for UKIP, 2.7 for the Liberal Democrats, and 1.96 for the Conservatives.[102]

In September 2018, a Survation survey found that 85.9% of British Jews considered Jeremy Corbyn anti-Semitic, and 85.6% considered the Labour Party to have 'high' or 'very high' levels of anti-Semitism within the party's members and elected representatives.[103]

In May 2016, a YouGov poll had found that 49% of Labour members felt that the party did not have a problem with anti-Semitism, 47% agreed that it was a problem, but 'no worse than in other parties', while 5% thought that anti-Semitism is a bigger problem in Labour than in other parties. In March 2018, a poll showed 77% of Labour members believed the charges of anti-Semitism to be deliberately exaggerated to undermine the leader or stop criticism of Israel, while 19% said it was a serious issue.[104] However, a July 2019 poll by YouGov among Labour Party members found that 70% of members thought that anti-Semitism in the party was a 'genuine' problem.[105]

The damaging rows continued as political and parliamentary life was otherwise paralysed by Brexit. There was a series of MP resignations quite apart from the Change UK cabal, and most involved some degree of unease about anti-Semitism. Bassetlaw MP John Mann used his exit from the Commons to criticise Corbyn's record as leader, and directly blame him for the party's anti-Semitism crisis. Mann – standing down after 18 years as an MP – accepted a full-time post as the government's 'anti-Semitism tsar'. He said he could not campaign for Corbyn knowing he could become prime minister and said he would 'never forgive' him for allowing the party to be 'hijacked' by anti-Semites. He said: 'Corbyn has given the green light to the anti-Semites and, having done so, has sat there and done nothing to turn that round.'[106] The chair of the all-party group on anti-Semitism went on: 'The party will not survive the erosion of its principles and its soul by this racist infiltration. Every time I go into a meeting with a group of Jewish people, I wince when they raise the issue of the Labour Party and Corbyn. He has not just hijacked my political party; he has hijacked its soul and its ethics. I will never forgive him for that. I could not have stood at the next election and looked people in the eye and answered the question they ask an awful lot – "if I vote for you, I'm also voting for Jeremy Corbyn as prime minister." I'm not prepared to lie to my voters and tell them that Corbyn is appropriate as prime minister. Because I don't think that he is.' He added: 'The mass growth of anti-Semitism is driving many Jewish people to question whether they have a future in this country.'[107] Mann, who had previously worked for the engineering union and the TUC, had opposed the Militant Tendency as national trade union officer for the 1997 general election. From the get go, Mann had been an opponent of Corbyn's 's leadership.[108]

Although anti-Semitism is no laughing matter, some did snigger at the title of 'tsar' that Mann was given. Giles Coren wrote: 'I'm sorry but anti-Semitism TSAR. Have these people no ear for nuance at all? The tsars were the most anti-Semitic people ever. The tsars basically invented anti-Semitism. Almost every Jew in this country (the Corens amongst them, of course) fled here because of pogroms powered by tsarist anti-Semitism. If there had been no tsars there would literally be nobody for the Corbynite left to laugh and sneer at and blame for everything. We'd all still be in Russia. And dead, of course, because of Hitler.'[109]

Birkenhead MP Frank Field resigned the Labour whip over a 'culture ... of nastiness'.[110] Christine Shawcroft, the recently appointed head of the party's disputes panel, resigned after it emerged she had opposed the suspension of Peterborough council candidate Alan Bull, for what she called 'a Facebook post taken completely out of context and alleged to show anti-Semitism'. She later said that she had not seen the 'abhorrent' Facebook post in question. Bull, in 2015, had shared in a closed Facebook group an article suggesting that the Holocaust was a hoax to 'invite discussion and debate'. Bull later said: 'I'm not an anti-Semite, I am not a holocaust denier – I support equal rights for Palestinian people.'[111]

Dudley MP Ian Austin resigned Labour to sit as an Independent in February 2019. His adoptive father was a Czech Jew who had himself been adopted by an English family on the Nazi invasion of his homeland.[112] Austin had been one of Gordon Brown's closest lieutenants, both at the Treasury and as prime ministerial aide. At the 2010 election he kept his marginal seat while his three neighbouring Labour MPs lost theirs. He served as a shadow minister for culture, media and sport, then work and pensions. In June 2012, he had apologised after claiming falsely that the Palestinian human rights group Friends of Al-Aqsa had denied the Holocaust happened in an article he wrote on the Labour Uncut website the previous year, accepting that the offending material had been written by an unconnected individual.[113] On the education select committee he was critical of Corbyn's approach, calling for him to stop acting like a 'student union president'.[114] Austin was reprimanded by the Speaker for heckling Corbyn by shouting 'sit down and shut up' and 'you're a disgrace', as Corbyn criticised the 2003 invasion of Iraq in his response to the publication of the Chilcot Inquiry. Austin described

Russia as 'a fascist, homophobic dictatorship' and suggested the England team boycott the 2018 FIFA World Cup.[115] In July 2018, Austin was put under investigation by the Labour Party for allegedly using abusive language towards the party chairman Ian Lavery. General Secretary Jennie Formby dropped the inquiry after Austin was reprimanded by the Chief Whip. All of which – together with his membership of Labour Friends of Israel – made him a hate figure in the Corbynista ranks. A Labour motion stripped Austin of membership of the foreign affairs select committee. He claimed that Corbyn wanted 'to boot me off this committee because I stood up against racism'.[116] Theresa May's government promptly appointed him trade envoy to Israel. Austin later explained: 'Corbyn's leadership, mixing incompetence and dogma, stretched my loyalty beyond breaking point.'[117]

When Corbyn U-turned on a 2019 election date because of parliamentary paralysis over Brexit, Austin wrote that the Corbynistas 'always back the wrong side, whether it is the IRA, Hamas or Hezbollah, who they describe as friends. No previous Labour Leader would have supported brutal totalitarian dictatorships like the ones in Cuba or Venezuela that have no regard whatsoever for the rule of law. No previous Labour Leadership would have allowed a party with a proud history of fighting racial prejudice to have been poisoned by racism – which is what happened under these people – against Jewish people, to the extent that members have been arrested on suspicion of racial hatred, and the party itself has become the first in history (with elected representatives in parliament) to be investigated under equalities laws by the Equalities and Human Rights Commission.' He added: 'These people, and the people around them, are a million miles away from the traditional mainstream, decent politics of the Labour party. They have poisoned a once-great party with extremism…'[118] To Momentum and Corbyn's inner circle, the loss of such MPs was a bonus. Corbyn cheerleader Andrew Murray, in his new book *The Fall and Rise of the British Left*, claimed that the 'anti-Semitism furore' reflected the Establishment's alarm at Corbyn's rise to power. The electorate were unconvinced.

At the 2018 annual Labour Party conference, Luciana Berger was given police protection because of the anti-Semite threats made against her. The following year's shindig saw Labour Friends of Israel scrap plans for a stall in the conference complex because it couldn't guarantee the safety of those staffing it. And the Jewish Labour

Movement attacked a decision to hold a debate on revised party rules on anti-Semitism on a Saturday – the Jewish Sabbath.

Social media was blamed for much abuse, including the trolling of Jewish women such as Rachel Riley who dared to challenge the Corbynite agenda. In September 2019 the Center for Countering Digital Hate (CCDH) reported that online abuse of public figures was damaging public discourse. It conceded that the worst offenders were on the fascist right but did not let off the left. Its advice was to ignore such abuse because retweeting in disgust simply gives the oxygen of publicity to the abusers. That was akin to blaming rape victims for their abuse – just forget about it and move on. But the report's authors did have a point in that online abuse, by its nature secretive, confuses the debate. Hugo Rifkind pointed to a well-respected London Jewish barrister accused online of being a 'hater of Leftist Jews'. The perpetrator was uncovered as a fellow Jewish barrister in the same Chambers who may or may not have been motivated by personal ambition. Who knows?[119]

The blitz on Jewish or Jewish-supporting MPs was stepped up as Britain geared up for another snap election due to premier Boris Johnson's moronic machinations over Brexit. Veteran Labour MP Dame Margaret Hodge, a Jew, faced a reselection contest in her east London constituency, having been highly critical of Corbyn's leadership and the party's response to complaints of anti-Semitism. She said: 'At a vital time for the country, with a general election looming, we should be focusing our efforts on holding Boris Johnson and the Tories to account.' Mike Katz, chairman of the Jewish Labour Movement, said the trigger ballot vote was a 'shameful moment for a party which claims to embody the values of equality and diversity. Margaret Hodge has been a steadfast campaigner against racism, fascism and intolerance throughout her political life. She saw off the BNP in Barking and has over the last few years been determined in her opposition to anti-Semitism within the Labour Party. She has been the target of vicious smears, derision and anti-Semitism, because she has been resolute in her opposition to anti-Jewish racism.' Labour's former deputy leader Harriet Harman said she was 'dismayed more than I can say' by the vote. She tweeted: 'Margaret Hodge, scourge of tax avoiders, racists and anti-Semitism. Champion of progressive policies. Hyperactive local MP. Surely this cannot stand!' A party source said there was nothing to suggest the vote had anything to do with anti-Semitism.[120]

10

The End?

'They may be kidding themselves.'

As the clock ticked towards Boris Johnson's 'do or die' Halloween 2019 Brexit deadline, Jeremy Corbyn finally allowed his troops to support a snap December 12 general election. He launched the campaign on October 31, the day that the prime minister had said he would rather be 'dead in a ditch' than remain in the EU.

Corbyn, aware of public dissatisfaction with his own confused position on Brexit, aimed to focus on domestic issues such as the NHS and an attack on rich, tax-dodging 'elites'. Within the Corbyn inner circle there was an assumption that the voters would blame the Tories alone for the Brexit-dominated 'zombie parliament', and for almost a decade of Tory paralysis over care for the elderly and a housing market that excluded younger generations from the property ladder. The fact that Theresa May and Johnson had reneged on repeated EU exit deadlines would also, they believed, gift them victory, as would the interventions of Donald Trump. Corbyn said: 'This election is a once-in-a-generation chance to transform our country and take on the vested interests holding people back.' Given recent events, there was fat chance of that tactic being wholly successful. Corbyn and his party were again engulfed in the anti-Semitism row which they had allowed to fester.

That row merged with wider dissatisfaction which had less to do with such policies as re-nationalisation of rail, power, postal and other services, more with questions of competence, security and leadership. The week before, a Survation poll suggested that under Corbyn, Labour's support had plunged to just 7 per cent among Jewish voters. Further polling has suggested that most British Jews ranked Brexit as their main concern ahead of the election – with anti-Semitism their next most pressing issue.[1] And yet another found that 47 per cent of British Jews had seriously considered emigrating if Corbyn got the keys to No 10.

A *Jewish Chronicle* leading article said: 'Two years ago, when Britain last elected a government, a case could be made that a Labour vote did not entail putting Jeremy Corbyn into Downing Street. Few believed Labour capable of winning 30 per cent of the vote, let alone winning the election. There was a view that one could safely vote Labour without risking a Corbyn government. That turned out to be erroneous. By winning 40 per cent of the vote, Labour showed it was certainly capable of winning.

'That means that there is now every chance that, on December the 13th, Britain could wake up with its first ideologically anti-Semitic prime minister. And it is no longer possible to fudge the issue. A Labour vote means only one thing: a vote to make Jeremy Corbyn PM. Labour "moderates" who have spent the past four years tweeting their support for the Jewish community and professing their supposed opposition to their party's institutional racism have now been exposed as careerists who regard their party's racism as a price worth paying for their own status as MPs.

'By standing as Labour candidates, they are asking voters to support them in making Britain's most prominent anti-Semite our prime minister. What a shameful state for British politics – indeed for Britain itself. This is an epochal election … The impact of a Labour victory is almost unimaginable for our community – or would be, if we did not already know the attitude of the Labour leadership towards Jews and its support for anti-Semites. The prospect is truly frightening.'[2]

A week later the *Chronicle* published an even more devastating leader on its front page aimed at all Britons, not just Jews: 'The vast majority of British Jews consider Jeremy Corbyn to be an anti-Semite. There is racism on all sides of politics and it must be called out wherever it is found. History has forced our community to be able to spot extremism as it emerges – and Jeremy Corbyn's election as Labour leader in 2015 is one such example. Throughout his career, he has allied with and supported anti-Semites such as Paul Eisen, Stephen Sizer and Raed Salah. He has described organisations like Hamas, whose founding charter commits it to the extermination of every Jew on the planet, as his "friends". He has laid a wreath to honour terrorists who have murdered Jews. He has insulted "Zionists" – the word used by anti-Semites when they mean "Jew" because they think it allows them to get away with it – as lacking understanding of "English irony".'

'There were some who hoped that he might change as leader. The opposite has happened. The near total inaction of Mr Corbyn and the rest of the Labour leadership in dealing with anti-Semites in the party has both emboldened them and encouraged others. Indeed, Mr Corbyn and his allies have actively impeded action against the racists. Instead of listening to and learning from mainstream Jewish bodies such as the Board of Deputies and Jewish Leadership Council, Mr Corbyn has treated them and their recommendations with contempt – and given support to fringe organisations set up solely to deny the existence of Labour anti-Semitism. Is it any wonder Jews worry about the prospect of Mr Corbyn as prime minister?'[3]

Lord John Mann, by now actively engaging as the government's independent adviser on anti-Semitism, wrote an even more damaging opinion piece: 'The Jewish community is spread across nearly every single parliamentary constituency in the UK. It has built a strong and proud record of engagement with public and civic life. British Jews are simply citizens, rightly and properly active in our participatory democracy. However, Jews are disproportionately targeted in turbulent political times, and against the current backdrop in Britain, anti-Semitism is rising. Jews feature in the conspiracies and lies drawn on by populists as part of their "us versus them" talk. To that end, the Jewish community has a responsibility, as we all do, to shun, to protest and to cast out anti-Semites. The best way to do that is at the ballot box ... Whatever your party, however you vote, make anti-Semites pay the price for their decision to seek public office.'[4]

Jewish Labour Movement (JLM) chair Mike Katz wrote: 'For most Labour activists, general elections are a time of frenetic activity. Certainly that's been the case for me and many of my fellow Jewish Labour Movement members in recent years. But this election, it's different. At our AGM in April, our members unanimously adopted policy deeming Jeremy Corbyn unfit to be prime minister as a result of his abject failure on anti-Semitism ... From murals and wreaths to Livingstone and Walker and Williamson, there are too many shameful examples to list; itself damning evidence of the moral slide, from a party that fights intolerance to one that tolerates casual racism against Jews.

'Labour's crisis of anti-Semitism stems from a failure of leadership by Jeremy Corbyn. Many Jews are genuinely concerned about what Corbyn as prime minister may mean for them, their families and the community.

Our attempts to engage in good faith and propose the actions necessary to tackle anti-Jewish racism have been rebuffed time and time again. Instead of implementing an independent disciplinary process we've seen delay, obfuscation and botched decision-making. Political interference is endemic and used to protect the leadership's friends and allies, rather than ensure the party is a safe space for Jews.

'Our Labour values have not changed, nor have our support for Labour policies. But we can't support a leader who has failed so utterly to tackle racism in his party and ensure it is a safe space for us. Fighting racism, prejudice and intolerance remain at the heart of our Labour values. It is the failure of the leader and his supporters to live these values which has led us to this.'

He confirmed that JLM said its members will not be campaigning for Labour MPs at the election 'unless in exceptional circumstances and for exceptional candidates', including its parliamentary chair Ruth Smeeth and those 'who've been unwavering in their support of us'. The organisation stressed that their stance 'does not mean that we no longer support the Labour Party's policies and its historic values, nor do we wish to see Boris Johnson or Jo Swinson in Downing Street'. The JLM added: 'The last four years have been catastrophic for Jews in the Labour Party. Nevertheless, the Jewish Labour Movement has kept true to our Labour values and resolved – for now – to stay and fight racism, rather than disaffiliate and walk away.' At the 2017 election, JLM had organised more than 50 campaign activities across six electoral regions and in marginal seats.[5]

Former Tony Blair speechwriter Philip Collins wrote: 'When representatives of a religious or ethnic minority are warning that your party is regarded in their community as a menace, then you ought to vote for someone else. This really ought to be a bedrock principle. Louise Ellman and Luciana Berger left the Labour Party because they regarded it as anti-Semitic and that the rot started at the top, with Jeremy Corbyn. Yet this is a man that Labour MPs, who tweeted their anguish at the departure of their colleagues, are demanding that we install as prime minister. They may not have him on their election leaflets. They may be kidding themselves. They're not kidding me.'[6]

It got worse. In the crucial London battlefields, the Jewish vote was by now split in multiple directions. Lee Harpin wrote: 'Many in the community could automatically be expected to vote Conservative – particularly with the assurance that it might be the best way to prevent Mr Corbyn reaching Downing Street. But the re-emergence of

The End?

the Liberal Democrats as a political force has excited many who are angered by the Tory Party's direction over Brexit.'[7]

Dame Margaret Hodge also insisted she would carry on fighting anti-Semitism 'from inside' the Labour Party. Having only just overcome an attempt to deselect her from her Barking seat, she said: 'I know that argument but I'm quite clear I must campaign for the Labour values that brought me into the party. I campaign on those values of anti-racism. I will never stop calling out anti-Semitism. I just won't. I think it's really important that me and Ruth Smeeth stay fighting from the inside. We are both tough individuals and neither of us will be frightened of them.'[8]

Leading Rabbi Dr Jonathan Romain took the unprecedented step of writing to his congregation urging them to vote for whatever political party stands the best chance of beating Corbyn's Labour candidates in the forthcoming general election. The Maidenhead synagogue minister revealed he had sent the letter to 823 families who are members of the Berkshire *shul* across 16 different constituencies suggesting that 'a Corbyn-led government would pose a danger to Jewish life as we know it.' Rabbi Romain said he had decided to send out the letter despite receiving a negative reaction from rabbinic colleagues who had said he should not be party political.

In his letter, Rabbi Romain wrote: 'I should stress that the problem is not the Labour Party itself, which has a long record of fighting discrimination and prejudice, but the problem is Jeremy Corbyn. Corbyn-led Labour, has at best, let anti-Semitism arise within its ranks, or at worst, has encouraged it. This has never happened under any previous Labour leader, whether under Tony Blair on the right, Neil Kinnock in the centre or Michael Foot on the left, so the finger of responsibility really does seem to point to Jeremy Corbyn.'

Pointedly, the rabbi suggested to *shul* members: 'If you, too, think that a Corbyn-led government would pose a danger to Jewish life as we know it ...whether it be utterances that cause Jews to feel victimised, less secure and no longer at ease ... or maybe even legislation that restricts Jewish life or relations with Israel in some way, then you may wish to vote to ensure Labour does not gain your local seat.'[9]

Later a second rabbi, Yuval Keren, also urged his congregation to vote tactically to deny Corbyn power, saying his party was 'riddled with anti-Semitism'. Keren, of the Southgate Progressive Synagogue, wrote: 'Since Jeremy Corbyn's assumption of Labour leadership, the attitude of the party towards British Jews has changed dramatically ... If you believe that a Corbyn-led government would be detrimental to

Jewish life as we know it, you should put aside all other considerations and vote for the party that is most likely to defeat Labour in your local constituency.'[10]

The BBC rejected Labour's formal complaint over the Panorama investigation into the party's anti-Semitism crisis. Corbyn had spearheaded a full-scale offensive on the claims made in the show, which saw former party staffers blow the whistle on the party's problems tackling anti-Jewish racism, accusing the Corporation of allowing a broadcast with 'many, many inaccuracies'. But its executive complaints unit, the highest disciplinary body, concluded there was no case to answer. The verdict further embarrassed Corbyn just as he launched his election manifesto. Labour's lengthy complaint had singled out the presenter, investigative reporter John Ware, for criticism – accusing him of holding 'hostile' views of Corbyn.[11] A BBC insider said: 'It was felt that John Ware had gone out of his way to put every allegation made in the show to Labour well ahead of the programme being aired. In fact, it emerged that Labour themselves sat on the allegations for some time, before launching an extraordinary attack on John's credibility as a journalist.'[12] Such tactics of first ignoring and then smearing journalistic efforts had become a Corbynista trademark.

The Corbinista Left carried on as before, seemingly oblivious to the damage done. Birkenhead members overwhelmingly backed a motion calling for suspended MP Chris Williamson to be 'immediately' reinstated. At the CLP meeting called to discuss tactics following veteran MP Frank Field's decision to stand as an Independent in part because of its false claims about links between the Israeli government and Isis, only a handful of members voiced opposition to the motion among the 50 present. Williamson – who had been accused by the Board of Deputies of 'Jew baiting' – lost a High Court bid to be reinstated in Labour after he was suspended. Birkenhead CLP members also supported a letter written by a hard-left activist, investigated over anti-Semitism claims, which stated that 'pro-Israel Labour MPs' would 'prefer a pro-Israel Conservative government to a socialist Labour government, critical of Israel'.[13]

Corbyn supporters also made further advances in parliamentary selections in Rother Valley, Bassetlaw, Nottingham East, Poplar and Limehouse. In Luciana Berger's former Merseyside constituency of Wavertree, Unison North West regional convenor Paula Barker was selected. Barker, whose supporters included Momentum, Unite, Unison, and the CWU, won 86 per cent of the membership vote, coming far ahead of her two 'right-wing' opponents.[14]

Jonathan Freedland wrote: 'The timing of a pre-Christmas election shouldn't bother too many JC readers. When it comes to preparing for the holidays, December is hardly Jews' busiest month. Even so, the prospect of an election in the season of nativity plays and mince pies will, I suspect, be filling Jews with a special kind of dread. For if we accept that, ultimately, a Westminster election is a binary choice that will see either Boris Johnson or Jeremy Corbyn in Downing Street, then many Jews will reckon they're being presented with two options that are both painfully hard to stomach.'

He went on: 'I've spoken to ordinarily calm, cool-headed people whose palms grow clammy as they work through the scenarios. The prospect of Corbyn in front of that shiny black door makes them shudder. Again, we hardly need to spell out why. Jews have developed a shorthand for discussing Corbyn's record. Say "the mural" or "English irony", and most will understand exactly what you mean. If this were all in the past, maybe some British Jews – especially those horrified by Brexit – would be prepared to look past it. But the way Corbyn's Labour party has handled anti-Semitism within its ranks has only deepened the alarm. And yet many Jews also fear a hard Brexit under Boris Johnson. They look at the choice confronting them and worry that they are being asked to choose between the devil and the deep blue sea.'[15]

And it got worse and worse. Virtually every day the Corbynista record on anti-Semitism reared its ugly head. On BBC's *The Andrew Marr Show*, John McDonnell was shown front pages of the *Jewish Chronicle*, the *Jewish News* and the *Jewish Telegraph* warning that Corbyn in No 10 would threaten the way of life for British Jews. He said: 'I'm so sad. I just want to reassure them we're doing everything we can … We're also doing everything we can to educate our own members … All the things they've asked us to do, we're doing and that we will enable us to reassure the Jewish community that actually the Labour Party will ensure our society creates a safe and also a decent environment for them and for everybody else.'[16] The Board of Deputies swiftly tweeted: 'John McDonnell's claim that Labour is doing all the things [we] asked over anti-Semitism stretches credulity. If Mr McDonnell really wants to show he's serious about tackling anti-Semitism, he will resign from the Labour Representation Committee which campaigns against disciplinary action for anti-Semites…'[17]

Tom Watson quit as Labour's deputy leader and announced he would not stand again as an MP. Although his resignation letter was cordial towards Corbyn, a key factor in his decision was the failure to tackle anti-Semitism. At the 2019 Labour annual conference,

Momentum had orchestrated a botched attempt to abolish the deputy leadership, a move which Watson described as a 'drive-by shooting'. Watson's many 'sins' included his calls for a second referendum on Brexit, his alleged leadership ambitions and his recognition that the anti-Semitism fracas was deeply damaging. In the end the Jewish founder of Momentum, Jon Lansman, became the scapegoat of that debacle. But implicated were Corbyn's most senior aide, Seamus Milne, and his sidekick James Schneider, together with Corbyn 'gatekeeper' Karie Murphy. Almost overnight, that damaging row was overshadowed when it emerged that another close Corbyn aide, policy chief Andrew Fisher, author of Labour's 2017 election manifesto, had quit. In his resignation messages, Fisher denounced that Corbyn team that he had been part of for a 'lack of professionalism, competence and human decency'.[18] And it was that innate lack of decency within Corbyn's posh, privileged and Marxist inner circle which allowed anti-Semitism to fester for so long.

Ian Austin urged Labour voters to support Boris Johnson in the general election, largely because of failures to tackle anti-Semitism, saying that Corbyn was 'completely unfit' to be PM.[19] In a later interview with the *Jewish Chronicle*'s Lee Harpin, he fought back tears as he paid an emotional tribute to his Jewish refugee father who died just after his split with Labour: 'In the last conversation I had with Dad he said to me: "I am really proud of you. And I really approve of all the decisions you have taken".' Austin said his father, who arrived in Britain from Czechoslovakia in 1939 aged 10 and never saw his mother and sisters again as they were murdered in the Treblinka death camp, understood his reasoning.

Austin, who was influential in securing government funding of the work of the Holocaust Educational Trust (HET) while working as a special adviser to former PM Gordon Brown, said the moment that led to him really contemplating how he could remain in Labour took place in 2018 as he joined the March of the Living event in Poland. 'We were in a hotel before going to Auschwitz,' he recalled. 'I was introduced to a survivor in a wheelchair as "the MP Ian Austin". He looked at me asked: "For what party?" I replied "Labour" and I will never forget his words. He said to me "Are you not ashamed to be in the Labour Party with all the anti-Semitism?" I knew then I had to do more about this. I knew it was going to come to the point where I had a big decision to make.' Asked if he felt that comparisons between the situation in the UK with that of Germany in the 1930s was valid,

The End?

he said: 'I would not say this is Germany in the 1930s. But it is important to recognise that the Holocaust did not start with the industrial slaughter of six million Jews. It started with words, with prejudice, conspiracy theories. We saw a community being treated differently and we saw politicians turning a blind eye.'[20]

Meanwhile, Chris Williamson was finally banned from standing as a Labour MP and announced he would stand as an Independent, having for years denounced anyone who split from the Corbynista agenda.[21] Clacton Labour candidate Gideon Bull pulled out of the election race after calling a Jewish councillor 'Shylock'. He said he did not realise the Shakespearean character was a Jew. Scottish Labour candidate Kate Ramsden quit when it emerged that she had compared Israel to a child abuser. She had written: 'To me the Israeli state is like an abused child who becomes an abusive adult.' It emerged that in 2015 another Labour hopeful, Zarah Sultana, had tweeted about 'celebrating' the deaths of Tony Blair and Israeli leader Benjamin Netanyahu.[22] Did anyone tell such people to stop digging?

Corbyn insisted that the party had candidate selection processes in place where 'due diligence' was in place to weed out anti-Semitism. He said: 'I have introduced very strong procedures into the party. We go through it, we go through due diligence on candidates and where there are questions, they are brought before a group to answer those questions and then decisions are made. In some cases, candidates are removed.'[23] However, the veracity of that was put in doubt as more Labour candidates, generally on the Left, were also exposed for alleged anti-Semitic leanings. Momentum-backed Ali Milani, challenging Boris Johnson in Uxbridge, had claimed that the 9/11 terror attacks were 'false flag' operations masterminded by the US government. He later apologised for his remarks. Kate Linnegar standing in North Swindon posted messages about 'Holocaust mongers' and liked a post entitled *How Israel lobby manufactured UK Labour Party's anti-Semitism crisis*. She was also accused of propagating material which blamed a 'smear campaign' for the row and a post which 'compared the actions of Israel to Nazi Germany'. She too apologised.[24] North West Cambridgeshire Labour candidate Ed Murphy share social media images of a flag on which the Star of David was replaced by a skull-and-crossbones. In a 2014 tweet, deleted when it emerged during the election campaign, he posted: 'Israel a terrorist state? And Israeli military ... are international pirates.' Bassetlaw candidate Keir Morrison retweeted messages in support of Chris Williamson, saying Labour had been 'too apologetic' in response to the anti-Semitism storm which in any case, he said, was a 'media myth'.[25]

Islington councillor Claudia Webbe, a close Corbyn ally, was propelled into the safe seat of Leicester East vacated by Keith Vaz who stood down after a rent boy and drugs scandal. It emerged that in 2006, she wrote a letter to *The Guardian*, saying Livingstone's four-week suspension as London Mayor 'smacked in the face of true democracy'. The Jewish Labour Movement said Webbe's selection was part of Labour's continued attempts to 'select candidates with a dodgy track record on defending anti-Semitism'. It said: 'Claudia Webbe defended Ken Livingstone and as chair of the party's disciplinary body promoted the view that elites were making false allegations against Jeremy Corbyn.' And it added that 'the figures who've enabled our discrimination are being rewarded with seats.'[26]

Labour candidate Alana Bates, contesting the Conservative/Liberal Democrat marginal seat of St Ives in Cornwall, played guitar in the band *The Tribunes* that performed a song including the words 'Justice should not have to wait, Israel's an apartheid state, Justice should not have to wait, Israel is a racist state'. Bates said: 'It's not a political manifesto. I didn't write it for a start. It's a song. At no point during the song does it say Jewish people out of the Middle East. At no point does it talk about Jewish people at all. It's about Israel. The song says that Israel is a racist state. I would personally say that the government policies of Israel are racist.' She removed the song from digital platforms on the advice of Labour HQ.[27]

Other parties saw anti-Semitic skeletons emerge from the cupboards of parliamentary candidates. The Scottish National Party dropped its candidate for the key target seat of Kirkcaldy pending disciplinary action after it emerged he had shared a post on Facebook in 2016 which included an image of billionaire George Soros as a puppet master controlling world leaders.[28] Graham Cushway, the Brexit Party candidate for Brighton Kemptown, co-founded a Luftwaffe-themed metal band in which performed wearing SS-style clothing and Iron Crosses. He played bass for *Stuka Squadron* – so named after Junkers Ju 87 dive bomber planes used in the Second World War.[29] Jonathan Metliss, a member of the Board of Deputies defence committee, allegedly stormed into the offices of Luciana Berger and allegedly branded her 'evil' and a 'disgrace' for standing as a parliamentary candidate against the local Tory.[30]

The End?

In Corbyn's own constituency of Islington North, there were mixed messages about the impact of the anti-Semitism row on his own re-election chances. Local Rabbi Mendy Korer, who had remained on good terms with Corbyn while maintaining an apolitical stance publicly, said: 'One of his strong points has been his commitment to supporting the local community as a constituency MP.' He added that Corbyn had attended Jewish events in the borough 'come rain or shine', including the menorah lighting that now attracts the second biggest crowd after Trafalgar Square. He said: 'Most Jews here are living an integrated lifestyle and they are more likely to encounter crimes like phone snatching or knife crime than anti-Semitism. My role on a local level is about nurturing the community and making Judaism proudly available to anyone that chooses.' But when pressed on his cautious approach, he added: 'We need to appreciate the kind of borough Islington is. The people here are cosmopolitan, international and entrepreneurial and they might not have the same concerns as other Jews.'

That caution was not wholly shared by a middle-aged Jewish resident who suddenly felt isolated when surrounded by neighbours with Labour posters in their windows. 'What has happened in the Labour Party has soured my friendships with people I live side by side with,' she said. 'They know I am Jewish and I care about anti-Semitism in the party but they believe it is all a conspiracy and propaganda to stop Corbyn from winning.' She told the *Jewish Chronicle*: 'I am passionate about social issues but I can't bear to see him get anywhere near government.'[31]

Diane Abbott defended Hackney North and Stoke Newington which has a high proportion of Charedim and Left-leaning Jews, but even here the anti-Semitism row had an impact. Rabbi Avraham Pinter, the principal of Yesodey Hatorah Senior Girls' School, said: 'The community here has tended to vote Labour. People are confused about what to do in this situation. There is no question Diane Abbott is opposed to anti-Semitism – nobody doubts that. There is just concern that, has she always recognised it?' Rabbi Herschel Gluck, a Charedi stalwart, defended Ms Abbott if not Labour, saying that in her 32 years as MP she had been 'an extremely good, very helpful local MP'.[32]

During an increasingly lacklustre campaign, Corbyn was hit by more incidents from his terrorist-hugging past. *The Golam* Twitter account revealed that in 2011 he met a representative of the Popular Front for the Liberation of Palestine – General Command, a group with alleged links to Hamas. The Beirut meeting occurred when Corbyn was part of a delegation to Lebanon. PFLP-GC, a proscribed terrorist organisation, is committed to the destruction of Israel and is opposed to any negotiation with Israel. Its attacks included the May 1970 Avivim massacre in which twelve people were murdered, including nine children, when two rocket-propelled grenades were fired at a school bus on its way to class. A 2018 US State Department report said: 'Since the early 1990s, the group has primarily focused on supporting Hizballah's attacks against Israel, training members of other Palestinian terrorist groups, and smuggling weapons.'[33]

Twenty-four public figures wrote a round-robin letter declaring they would not vote Labour because of the party's problem with anti-Semitism. The signatories include novelists John Le Carré, Fay Weldon and William Boyd, actors Joanna Lumley and Simon Callow and former head of the Commission for Racial Equality Trevor Phillips. Their letter said the election for British Jews 'contains a particular anguish: the prospect of a prime minister steeped in association with anti-Semitism. Under Jeremy Corbyn's leadership, Labour has come under formal investigation by the Equality and Human Rights Commission for institutional racism against Jews. Two Jewish MPs have been bullied out of the party. Mr Corbyn has a long record of embracing anti-Semites as comrades.' They said that as an issue, anti-Semitism has been relegated by Brexit. 'But anti-Semitism is central to a wider debate about the kind of country we want to be. To ignore it because Brexit looms larger is to declare that anti-Jewish prejudice is a price worth paying for a Labour government.' Opposition to racism 'cannot include surrender in the fight against anti-Semitism,' they wrote. 'Yet that is what it would mean to back Labour and endorse Mr Corbyn for Downing Street.'[34]

Their letter was belatedly followed by protestations from established 'luvvies' in the Corbyn fan club – the usual suspects such as film director Mike Leigh and comic actor Steve Coogan – who, like Corbyn, appears to blame all society's ills on the media – plus stand-up Rob Delaney and Hollywood star Mark Ruffalo, notable for playing *The Incredible Hulk* and featuring in the *Avengers* film franchise.[35] Enough said.

Former Labour minister Joan Ryan, who earlier in the year 'with sadness but firm resolve' left the party after more than 40 years, also declared she would not vote for it under Corbyn. Brought up amid Lancashire's Irish working-class community, she said she had learnt

The End?

two crucial lessons: 'The dignity of work, and the evils of racism and prejudice'. She went on: 'I felt I had no choice but to leave a party overwhelmed by fear and hatred, poisoned by prejudice against Jewish people, and a vicious bully of its internal critics. At the heart of the problem is Jeremy Corbyn.' During the 1980s she worked as a historian at the Imperial War Museum, charged with capturing the stories of civilians in the Second World War. 'I spoke with many Holocaust survivors, hearing horrific accounts of their time in ghettos, on forced marches and in the Nazi extermination camps,' she said. 'The experience cemented my belief that the evil of anti-Semitism must never again be allowed to poison political discourse in this or any other country. Yet in Corbyn's Labour, that is precisely what has happened. It is truly shaming...'[36]

- And it continued to get worse. When Corbyn addressed the Confederation of British Industry in London about workplace diversity, a young woman asked him: 'What are you going to be doing, personally, to demonstrate ... that Labour isn't just for the many and not the Jew?' Corbyn, clearly uncomfortable with what his supporters later described as an 'ambush', said: 'I've spent my life opposing racism in any form. Be it done by the far-right or by the random attacks on individuals, or against a man that was murdered outside my house because he happened to be a Muslim and there happened to be a racist person driving a vehicle that thought it was OK to drive in a crowd of worshippers. Just as much as those people that attack synagogues, daub fascist graffiti over them, or attack Jewish people in this country, the USA or anywhere else, have no place whatsoever in a civilised society.' He added: 'The history of the Jewish people has been one of the most unbelievable and egregious – [with] attacks on them in central Europe throughout the early part of the twentieth century, which of course ended with the Holocaust and all the horrors that went with that. That is where racism leads you to if you don't challenge it in the first place.'[37]

- Jewish comic actress Maureen Lipman revived her character Beattie – star of the BT adverts in the 1980s and 1990s – for a video attacking Corbyn's Labour. Beattie spoke to her friend Nora over the phone, telling her: 'My mother always said, "this is a kind and a decent country. They will always do the decent thing". "Well if that's the case, why would anybody vote for this Labour Party?"' She continued: '"Of course, we were all Labour, everybody voted Labour. I voted Labour all my life. You know what my late husband said? If you're Jewish, they gave you your Labour Party badge the day after your circumcision. They gave with one hand, they took with the other. But this lot ... this lot's not Labour. They're not socialists. You know what they are, Nora? They're extremists, that's what my Melvyn says, and he's not often wrong."' The two-minute video was produced by anti-extremism campaign Mainstream, led by former Labour MP Ian Austin.[38]

As we have seen, during the election campaign Labour certainly did not have a monopoly on anti-Semitic tropes. Three Conservative election candidates were investigated over allegations relating to their social media use. The probe came after Boris Johnson told reporters that 'if anybody is done for Islamophobia, or any other prejudice or discrimination in the Conservative Party they are out first bounce.'[39]

• An SNP candidate dropped over alleged anti-Semitic comments won a Westminster seat despite the party's withdrawal of support. Neale Hanvey, candidate for the Kirkcaldy and Cowdenbeath constituency was dropped in the run-up to the poll after social media posts he made two years ago came to light. Hanvey wrote to Jewish groups in a bid to make amends.[40]

• The co-founder of Extinction Rebellion sparked fury by saying the Holocaust was 'just another f***ery in human history'. In an interview with German newspaper *Die Zeit*, Roger Hallam said: 'The fact of the matter is, millions of people have been killed in vicious circumstances on a regular basis throughout history.' The subject came up when he said during the interview that people should fight climate change with the same emotion as people regard Auschwitz, the largest Nazi camp where more than a million Jews were murdered. 'Emotionality is the only way you can get people to do something,' he said. When a *Die Zeit* journalist suggested the *Shoah* was unique, he said: 'There are various debates as to whether the Holocaust is unique or not. I know that that's the conviction in Germany. But with all respect I don't agree with it.'[41]

• The Hope Not Hate organisation uncovered tapes which showed Brexit Party leader Nigel Farage appearing to endorse 'New World Order' conspiracy theories linked to anti-Semitism. In an interview with *Revelation TV*, an evangelical Christian channel, he claimed firms such as Goldman Sachs 'see the European Union as basically the forerunner of global government'. He added: 'It's pretty clear who the enemy is as far as I'm concerned – the enemy are these giant multinational businesses [who] are prepared to basically take down

The End?

our democratic systems ... If you really look at it: what percentage of the UK actually believe in the United States of Europe, actually believe in this New World Order?' Anti-Semitism watchdog the Community Security Trust said Farage's language were 'familiar code words for anti-Semitic conspiracy theories'.[42]

The main parties clashed bitterly over alleged racism, with tempers reaching boiling point. Seconds after appearing on Sky TV, Foreign Secretary Dominic Raab and Shadow Transport Secretary Andy McDonald confronted each other. Talking over each other for close to a minute, McDonald said of the Tories' refusal to launch a full inquiry into Islamophobia: 'You're actually putting it into the long grass, you're refusing to do it ...' Raab replied: 'Two parties in this country's history have been investigated by the Equalities and Human Rights Commission (EHRC) – Labour under Corbyn and the BNP (British National Party). Answer that.'[43]

During the *BBC Question Time* forum involving the four main leaders, Corbyn suffered a toe-curling exchange when a man in the audience told him: 'I heard you talk about free speech and standing up for human rights. I have two young daughters and what terrifies me is some of the Labour MPs, some of the female MPs, and the misogyny that has happened in the Labour Party ... I am willing to give you the benefit of the doubt in terms of maybe people aren't doing it in your name. But I look at a video of Ruth Smeeth online where she was in a press conference with you and Ruth Smeeth, a Jewish MP, was heckled out of the press conference and there you are at the end of the press conference chatting happily to that same heckler. I don't buy this whole nice old grandpa. I see that video and that tells me all I need to know and I am terrified for my daughters because I see what you did in that video. I don't understand how you can say you stand up for human rights and free speech when that is how you support a Labour MP at a Labour press conference. I think that is disgraceful.' Corbyn responded: 'Nobody should suffer any abuse in public life or privately.' The audience member hit back: 'Watch the video.'[44]

Corbyn unveiled Labour's race and faith manifesto, saying: 'In government, Labour will do everything necessary to guarantee the security of the Jewish community, defend the Jewish way of life and the right to live it freely, and to combat rising anti-Semitism in our country and across Europe.' Proposed measures included changing the law to include attacks on places of worship as a specific aggravated offence; working with social media firms to combat the rise of anti-Semitism online; an independent review into the threat of far-right extremism and how to tackle it; reviewing the national curriculum to ensure it teaches about racism, anti-Semitism, Islamophobia, xenophobia and black history, and to continue education about the Holocaust; and ensuring coroners services meet the needs of faith communities, with 'out of hours' services to ensure quick burials when required, allowing some Jewish and Muslim families to bury loved ones in accordance with their religious practice.

Strategists believed that would end the party's anti-Semitism furore, but it quickly proved a forlorn hope. Overnight Chief Rabbi Ephraim Mirvis launched another stinging attack on Labour's record under Corbyn, claiming the party is not doing enough to root out anti-Jewish racism – and asked people to 'vote with their conscience' in the general election. He said that 'a new poison – sanctioned from the very top – has taken root' in the party. Labour's claim it had investigated all cases of anti-Semitism in its ranks was a 'mendacious fiction', he added. In his article, the Orthodox Chief Rabbi of Great Britain and Northern Ireland – who is the spiritual leader of the United Synagogue, the largest umbrella group of Jewish communities in the country – said that raising his concerns 'ranks among the most painful moments I have experienced since taking office'. But he claimed 'the overwhelming majority of British Jews are gripped by anxiety' at the prospect of a Labour victory. He wrote: 'The way in which the leadership of the Labour Party has dealt with anti-Jewish racism is incompatible with the British values of which we are so proud – of dignity and respect for all people. It has left many decent Labour members and parliamentarians, both Jewish and non-Jewish, ashamed of what has transpired.' The Chief Rabbi claimed the response of Labour's leadership to threats against parliamentarians, members and staff has been 'utterly inadequate' and said it 'can no longer claim to be the party of equality and anti-racism'.

BBC religion editor Martin Bashir wrote: 'This is a sweeping and unequivocal condemnation of Labour's leadership, its treatment of Jewish parliamentarians and its handling of allegations of anti-Semitism. It's also highly unusual for such an intervention by the leader of a religious denomination during a general election campaign. The Chief Rabbi has pastoral oversight for a large proportion of people who identify as Jewish in the United Kingdom. Last week, the Archbishops of Canterbury and York appealed to voters and politicians to 'honour the truth' and 'challenge falsehoods'

The End?

but there was no specific criticism of individual candidates nor their party leaders. But the Chief Rabbi's article asks if Jeremy Corbyn is fit for high office and calls on voters to consider what the result of this election "will say about the moral compass of this country"? Last year, three Jewish newspapers – T*he Jewish Chronicle*, *The Jewish News* and *The Jewish Telegraph* – published exactly the same front cover on 25 July, arguing that a Labour government under the leadership of Jeremy Corbyn would prove "an existential threat" to British Jewry. The Chief Rabbi, in this highly critical column, is saying much the same.'

Corbyn, in a subsequent car-crash interview with Andrew Neil, declined four times to apologise to the British Jewish community, saying only that he was 'determined that our society is safe' for 'all faiths'. Labour activists admitted Corbyn's performance was 'truly horrific' as they vowed to 'push images and stories with positive messages' to deflect from the 'awful' appearance.

BBC political editor Laura Kuenssberg wrote after the interview: 'The Labour leader stuck resolutely to his formula that he abhors all forms of racism. He visibly means that. Yet many people watching tonight may have felt it uncomfortable that a simple apology seemed to stick in his throat. The other problem for the Labour Party is that the action they say that they have taken firmly, and now speedily, has not brought a resolution. Labour has been struggling with this for more than three years. That is despite repeated and serious promises to sort it out. Inevitably, that raises questions about how capable the leadership is of getting to grips with tricky and sensitive issues.'[45]

The Archbishop of Canterbury, Justin Welby, said Mirvis felt he had 'no choice' but to speak out despite the natural inclination for faith leaders to 'keep schtum' during an election campaign. Citing the Church of England's own process of reckoning over child abuse, he said the public acknowledgement of past mistakes by institutions was vital but it was only the first step in a process of healing. 'Just sorting it out internally is not always the answer,' he said. 'Just doing the right thing was not enough – people needed to know and feel that things had changed.'[46]

The timing of the Chief Rabbi's intervention ahead of the supposedly flagship launch of Corbyn's anti-racist manifesto launch predictably drew an ungracious response from the dwindling Corbyn faithful, some of whom claimed that Mirvis was a Tory determined to wreck Labour's chances. Covering the Tottenham launch, political sketch-writer Quentin Letts wrote: 'The Chief Rabbi's intervention had created a sullen, vehement mood. Here was the Corbyn Labour Party in the raw. Mr Corbyn himself turned up an hour late, amid rumours that he had been delayed by crisis talks with aides. He looked dented.' Leicester East candidate Claudia Webbe, herself accused of anti-semitism, 'moved mirthlessly among the troops, doing silent air kisses with thickset stooges. Her face was set in a mask – a glowering, waxen half-smile. Ms Webbe became absorbed in her mobile phone, tapping mirthlessly at its screen.'[47]

Suspicions of a crisis meeting appeared to be confirmed when John McDonnell did something that his supposed boss had refused to do – he apologised for Labour's handling of the whole anti-Semitic issue. And Corbyn's failure to apologise contrasted with Boris Johnson's apology for the 'hurt and offence' that has been caused by Islamophobia in the Tory Party.[48]

Former Labour Home Secretary Charles Clarke joined the chorus of disapproval over Corbyn's performance. He said: 'My expectation of Jeremy Corbyn is very low ... but it was a disgraceful performance. He has to go through a process of apology ... but in fairness that's only a small part of it – it's about the whole conduct of the Labour party in dealing with anti-Semitism.'[49]

The Labour leader insisted in the ITV leaders' debate that the party had 'investigated every single case' raised by complainants. Jonathan Goldstein, chair of the Jewish Leadership Council, insisted that he had not, despite Corbyn's claims of talking to all sides, met him for over 18 months. He said: 'We have sought many times over the course of the past years to build bridges with the leadership of the Labour Party. You will recall back in April 2018 we met with Jeremy Corbyn and the leadership group. We were told we would be invited back so that we could continue to build bridges. I'm still waiting for that invitation...'[50]

Several days after the Andrew Neil interview, a clearly rattled Corbyn finally gave something approaching an apology. Asked repeatedly on ITV's *This Morning* by presenter Phillip Schofield to apologise, Corbyn said anti-Jewish racism was 'vile and wrong' and would not be tolerated in any form under a future Labour government. He said internal processes for dealing with anti-Semitism cases were 'constantly under review' and his door would be open to Rabbi Mirvis and other faith leaders to discuss their concerns if he entered Downing Street. After a tetchy studio exchange, Corbyn

The End?

finally said: 'Our party and me do not accept anti-Semitism in any form. Obviously I am very sorry for everything that has happened, but I want to make this clear – I am dealing with it, I have dealt with it. Other parties are also affected by anti-Semitism. Candidates have been withdrawn by the Liberal Democrats, the Conservatives, and by us, because of it. We just do not accept it in any form whatsoever.' As always, Corbyn's response was qualified, and said with exasperation, and raised the question of why it had taken so long to deliver anything approaching a simple 'sorry'. And only when pushed into a corner.[51] Corbyn's claim that he had 'dealt with' the problem was greeted with incredulity. Board of Deputies president Marie van der Zyl said: 'Mr Corbyn has not dealt with it in the past few years; whether he will deal with it now remains to be seen.'[52]

When a home-grown Islamic convicted terrorist released under licence killed two on or around London Bridge before being shot dead by police, Corbyn initially rejected the understandable reaction that the killer should not have been out and about, particularly when it quickly emerged that 74 people jailed for terror offences and released early will have their licence conditions reviewed.[53] Horrified aides, including some from the Momentum corner, insisted he praised the security, police and emergency services and the civilians who had tackled the terrorist on the bridge. He did so, but could not resist a caveat blaming Donald Trump, Tory cuts and long-standing injustice for the war on terror. He added: 'That's why Labour supports an end to half a century of Israeli occupation and the illegal settlements in occupied Palestinian territory…'[54] In Corbyn's mind any condemnation of murder must be qualified by a defence of Islamic extremism, however deranged, and a barely disguised attack on Israel's right to exist.

By then, the election was clearly running away from him, despite the heavily orchestrated ecstasy which greeted him on the streets when securely surrounded by youngish members of Cult Corbyn. Former Labour minister for Europe Denis MacShane told a Roman Catholic readership that Jews had been among the greatest activists, philosophers and writers on the Left, adding: 'That Jeremy Corbyn has turned so many of them against Labour is, as Talleyrand said of one of Napoleon's impulsive judgements, "worse than a crime, it's a blunder".'[55]

Nearly 100 prominent Liverpool figures signed a declaration condemning anti-Semitism, saying that Jewish former MPs Luciana Berger and Dame Louise Ellman were left to 'walk alone' over the party's failure to address it. Among the rabbis, politicians and academics who signed the Liverpool Against Anti-Semitism declaration were Rabbi Ariel Abel, of the city's Princes Road Synagogue, and legal expert Professor Bernard Jackson. It read: 'Liverpool has a proud history of mobilising against racism and a proud history of solidarity with the victims of racism. Over the past few years we have seen a string of anti-Semitic incidents culminating in 2019 with the successive resignations from the Labour Party of two Liverpool MPs, Luciana Berger and Louise Ellman. They both denounced institutional anti-Semitism in the Labour Party and a culture of bullying, bigotry and intimidation in their local CLPs. This should have been a turning point. Instead, they were largely allowed to "walk alone". We, citizens of this city, Jewish or not Jewish, want to express our profound disquiet and regret at these events as well as our solidarity with Luciana and Louise. We will not tolerate anti-Semitism and we will not tolerate the accommodation of anti-Semitism. We commit to hold to account, to educate and to mobilise. Today, we reclaim Liverpool's proud history.' Raphael Levy, one of the community activists behind the declaration, said he hoped it would 'put a marker in the sand' over how the city feels about Labour's anti-Semitism problem. He added: 'We hope people will take it into account but that doesn't mean we are anti-Labour. The question of anti-Semitism shouldn't be brushed under the carpet.'[56]

And when it seemed that it really could not get any worse, it did. With just a week to go before polling, an online leak revealed that 70 serving and ex-Labour officials had given sworn statements to the Equality and Human Rights Commission (EHRC) investigation. They formed part of a submission from the Jewish Labour Movement asking the EHRC to urge Labour to acknowledge it has become 'institutionally anti-Semitic' and needs to change. Jeremy Corbyn had made Labour a 'welcoming refuge' for anti-Semitism and the party is 'no longer a safe space for Jewish people'. The organisation – affiliated to the party for a century and representing about 2,500 members – argued that anti-Semitic conduct has become 'pervasive' in recent years. It also claimed there were no reliable figures for how many cases of anti-Semitism still have to be dealt with by the party's complaints team, despite Corbyn's insistence that processes have been speeded up. The JLM reported that 136 complaints were outstanding in October, while around 100 allegations were not logged in the system at all. Labour responded that those figures were inaccurate, but it had not provided any official statistics on the issue since July. The JLM submission included a signed affidavit from a former Labour official who alleges they were asked to transfer details of complaints being investigated at Labour's headquarters to Corbyn's office.[57]

Compiled over 13 months up until November, the 53-page dossier concluded the Labour Party had seen a 'relentless flow' of anti-Semitic incidents. Some of the allegations had been in the public domain for months, but the largely unnamed personal accounts in the JLM dossier were damning: at Labour's 2017 conference, a member said he shared a table with two delegates he did not know who agreed Jews were 'subhuman', 'didn't deserve to be allowed to define what constitutes anti-Semitism' and should be 'grateful we don't make them eat bacon...' One person listed 22 examples of anti-Semitic abuse directed at him at local party meetings, including being called 'a Tory Jew', 'a child killer', 'Zio scum', being told 'he's good with money', 'to shut the f*** up, Jew' and 'Hitler was right'. South Tottenham's membership secretary objected to member applications from 25 ultra-orthodox Jews and required home visits to their houses. A party member said: 'The only reason we have prostitutes in Seven Sisters is because of the Jews.' Margaret Hodge, after writing a *Sunday Times* article, received Facebook messages from Corbyn-supporting groups calling her a 'Zionist b****', and referring to 'Zionist remedial cancer', 'damaging Labour in the interests of Israel' and 'under the orders of her paymaster in Israel'. A Labour member said at a local meeting other members defended a person who repeated 'the over-representation of Jews in the capitalist ruling class that gives the Israel-Zionist lobby its power'. A parliamentary candidate described witnessing a member tell a Jewish councillor to 'go home and count their money' after they were deselected. At a conference fringe event a speaker said they had the right to discuss whether the Holocaust happened – nobody called out the behaviour and a member said US police who killed black teens were probably trained in Israel. A 2017 parliamentary candidate said he received a large amount of anti-Semitic commentary on social media, including: 'You and your Zionist cult are NOT welcome. This is London. Not Tel Aviv.' One member said he was leafleting for a rule change to prohibit all types of discrimination and was called racist and members said they would not support the change because JLM was 'financed and controlled by the Israeli government'. One former staffer at the Leader's Office said he was subjected to an 'inquisition' about being Jewish, including

Anti-Semitism and the Left

his views on Israel. According to another former Labour official, senior members of Corbyn's team described calls for Ken Livingstone to be expelled as part of a 'Jewish conspiracy'. A sixth form student said he was forced to leave the Labour Party Forum's Facebook group shortly after joining after members searched his account for links to Jewish organisations and accused him of being a Zionist operative. Labour MP Ruth Smeeth was called a 'yid c***'.

Suggesting cover-ups by members of Corbyn's office, the dossier claimed senior staff requested the party revoke the suspension of a member for anti-Semitic posts because he was 'on friendly terms with the leader'. One staff member said: 'It became increasingly common for those under investigation to email the Leader of the Opposition or a member of the National Executive Committee and, if they were high status enough, the case would disappear.' The dossier claimed there was a culture of anti-Semitism in the party which top party officials are 'ignoring, denying, relativising and accepting'. Corbyn was personally accused of 'publicly supporting anti-Semites and anti-Semitic tropes' under a party 'cast in his image' that is now 'institutionally antisemitic'.[58]

An increasingly rattled Corbyn denied that Labour has become a 'welcoming refuge' for anti-Semites. He told the BBC: 'When I became leader of the party there were no processes in place to deal with anti-Semitism. We introduced an education process, so that party members understood the hurt that can be caused by [it] ... I think we've got processes in place that have improved it a great deal.'[59]

Corbynista strategists convinced themselves that their leader had put the anti-Semitism row to bed – they couldn't have been more wrong. In the last dying days of the contest it – once again – got much worse with three more hammer-blows to his claims that he had 'sorted' the problem with his disciplinary measures.

First, the Simon Wiesenthal Centre, the world's leading Nazi-hunting organisation, appeared to name Corbyn the worst anti-Semite on the planet. The human rights body said: 'No one has done more to mainstream anti-Semitism into the political and social life of a democracy than the Jeremy Corbyn-led Labour Party. Members and staff who have dared to speak out against the hate were purged, but not those who declared "Heil Hitler" and "F*** the Jews".' Rabbi Marvin Hier said: 'If it wasn't for Winston Churchill and Britain leading the fight against Nazism in the Second World War who knows if the Allies would have won? Britain was at the forefront of defeating Hitler and now, on the 75th anniversary of the liberation of Auschwitz, the person who wants to sit in Winston Churchill's chair at No 10 is fostering antisemitism. If Mr Corbyn wins he will make Britain a pariah on the world stage. It will be a disaster for democracy.' On hate issues, Corbynistas rated higher than Hamas and a 'Hitler worshipper' who opened fire on a synagogue; the 2018 front-ranker was another gunman who gunned down 11 Jews at another US synagogue. A Labour spokesman said: 'This ranking is ridiculous and grossly offensive. Putting Jeremy Corbyn at the head of a list containing neo-Nazi synagogue shooters is a transparent political attack and has nothing to do with tackling anti-Semitism.'[60]

• Then it was reported, contrary to Corbyn's claims of zero tolerance to anti-Semitism, that at least 30 candidates have been linked to the deepening scandal in the party. Nineteen of the election hopefuls were first-time candidates, with half of them having faced claims directly. But four candidates were axed following anti-Semitism-related issues since the election was announced. A Labour Party spokesman said: 'There are a number of Conservative, Lib Dem and SNP candidates who have made anti-Semitic comments, including one Tory candidate who said events in the Holocaust were "fabricated". In government, Labour will introduce education on anti-Semitism, Islamophobia, xenophobia and racism in the national curriculum to tackle prejudice in our society.'[61]

• Corbyn's denials were exposed by a *Sunday Times* inquiry which uncovered a leaked dossier from Labour's own disciplinary department suggesting it had been overwhelmed with complaints that remained unresolved for up to three years. A leaked audio recording from a disciplinary committee session in October included an official complaining that the vast majority of 130 complaints logged for 18 months remained outstanding. In some of the complaints Labour members were accused of using such terms as 'bent nose liars', likening Jewish people to killer viruses and calling for the 'extermination of every Jew on the planet'. A Nottingham member wrote that 'Jews represent a viral infection that needs to be completely eliminated.' It took the party ten months to expel that member. Another was allowed to remain in the party after confronting a councillor at a Labour meeting and shouting that he 'licked the bum of Jews for money'. And another posted on Facebook that the Red Sea was the ideal destination to get rid of the Jews 'who are a cancer on us all', adding: 'No need for gas chambers anyway – gas is so expensive and we need it in England.' It took eight months for him to be expelled. Other members' posts included claims that Jews were behind the 9/11 attacks, that 'IRA murderers took their cue from Jews,' that 'Zionist scumbags' had taken control of the party and the economy, and that photographs of Jewish victims of the Nazi death camps had been faked. There were further references to 'Swindler's List', 'assaults on boy children' and 'Black Death'. The secret files showed that half of the cases dealt with resulted in either a mere warning or no action at all. Crucially they covered the period June 2018 to October 2019, well after the appointment of Jennie Formby as Labour's general secretary. Corbyn's high command had insisted that she had done much to tackle the problem and implement the strict disciplinary procedures constantly referenced by Corbyn, but the leaked files showed a system at best in disarray, at worst being shuffled into the sidings. Dame Louise Ellman said: 'This reduces to rubble my party's claim that anti-Semitism in the party is being dealt with. It is beyond belief that members can make statements of Holocaust denial and call for Jews to be completely exterminated yet remain in the party for months or years or receive a mere slap on the wrist.'[62]

Shadow Chancellor John McDonnell apologised to the Jewish community for 'the suffering we've inflicted on them'. Asked whether anti-Semitism will be part of the reason if Labour loses the election, he replied: 'I worry that this has had its effect. We've done everything I think we can possibly do. We've apologised to the Jewish community. We've always got to learn lessons, of course we have – all political parties. Because it isn't just the Labour Party.'[63] But pressed by Andrew Marr, McDonnell said he will remain president of the far-left Labour Representation Committee (LRC), which has dismissed allegations of Labour anti-Semitism as 'propaganda' used by the 'ruling class' to attack Corbyn.[64]

More than 3,000 people gathered in Parliament Square to stand against anti-Semitism. People held signs that said 'together against anti-Semitism' and 'solidarity with British Jews', as the clock ticked towards polling day. Although no speaker directly mentioned Corbyn or Labour, the event had obvious political undertones. Robert Rinder, the lawyer, TV personality and grandson of a Holocaust survivor, gave an emotional speech in which he warned that Jews had sat 'for too long in fear', and 'what starts with the Jews never ends with the Jews,' adding '… what starts with a mural ends up in murder.' The rally, Rinder said, was 'not about politics but there are certain things which disqualify you from the leadership of this country', adding that being Jewish in Britain today should not have to be 'an act of courage'. Actress and writer Tracy-Ann Oberman listed to the crowd some of the hate-filled rhetoric to which she had been subjected since she began speaking out against anti-Semitism on social media. She said she hoped 'the political class would deal with this kind of thing', but instead, the Jewish community was currently caught between the hard left and the far right, and that misogyny was bound up with the abuse. Fiyaz Mughal, founder of Muslims Against Anti-Semitism, received cheers when he declared: 'Britain is not Britain without Jews.'[65]

Corbyn then claimed that many Jewish people feel 'very at home and very happy' in the party, and that many Jewish Labour members had told him 'thank you for the processes put in place, thank you for the education processes you've put in place'. He continued: '[When] I became leader of the party, there weren't any proper processes in place for dealing with any accusations against any members. I set up those processes. I also set up a fast-track process and an education process to deal with [it]. So I have made sure that has happened.' That was immediately challenged when *Channel 4 News*' fact checking service reported that, despite being proposed in July, the fast-track process had only been used in one anti-Semitism panel meeting held in early November.[66]

And his claims were, to say the least, thrown into doubt when Corbyn addressed a rally on Bristol's College Green and confronted with Jewish students from the city's university about alleged anti-Semitism. One of the protesters told the *Jewish Chronicle* that she was called a 'filthy Jew' who should go back to where she belonged. Former Union of Jewish Students President Hannah Rose shared a video of the counter demonstration, where people chanted 'from Kashmir to Palestine, occupation is a crime'. The footage showed a man wearing a Labour sticker, telling the students: 'You're the killer of Palestinian people ... you're an absolute disgrace.' Another protester said she was called a 'puppet of the Zionist media' by one supporter, who asked one of her friends 'if the Israeli government were paying us to be there'. Another man was shown to approach a protester, telling him: 'You're a pr**k, what are you doing? You're friends of the f**king media, man. Siding with the Tories.' And yet another protester was told by people who identified themselves as Labour supporters 'you're a filthy Zionist.' She said: 'None of us mentioned Israel once. When I was speaking to these people they just couldn't understand why calling me a filthy Zionist was anti-Semitic.'[67]

Polling day on 12 December 2019 saw such ignorance bearing bitter fruit.

As exit polls pointed, accurately as it turned out, to a thumping majority for the Tories, Ken Livingstone said, with no apparent sense of irony or self-knowledge, that 'the Jewish vote' was not 'very helpful'.[68] For once, he was right as overnight the scale of Labour's disastrous showing became clear, losing seats across former Labour heartlands in the North and Midlands, handing Boris Johnson a Commons majority of 80 and putting the Conservatives back in power for five more years.

In Finchley and Golders Green, a 25 per cent Lib Dem surge for Luciana Berger and a collapse of the Labour vote meant that the sitting Tory kept his seat. In Chipping Barnet former Cabinet minister Theresa Villiers, who had campaigned against anti-Semitism, confounded pollsters by hanging on despite a strong Labour challenge. She said: 'I call on Labour during this period of reflection to root out anti-Semitism. They haven't done so.' She added that the issue had been raised with her on the campaign trail by Jews and non-Jews – and said that the resurgence of hate in politics must be considered alongside radical policies and Brexit in Labour's heavy defeat.[69] That view was echoed by failed candidates who reported that anti-Semitism was mentioned on doorsteps as much as Brexit, including constituencies with negligible Jewish populations.

Polly Toynbee wrote: 'Corbyn came weighted with baggage too heavy for a Hercules to shift: the IRA, the Hamas friends, Venezuela. But anti-Semitism was the accusation he could not shift. I am certain he sees no stain of it in himself, refusing to comprehend it and so could not apologise. Failure to purge every case left candidates on the doorstep dumbstruck when anyone said, "I can't vote for an anti-Semite".'

Corbyn duly announced that he would be standing down from the Leadership but gave no firm timescale. True to form, Corbyn refused to take the blame for the party's most disastrous general election defeat for 80 years, with 59 fewer MPs, or set a date for his departure. Instead he blamed Brexit and the 'personal abuse' he had taken from the media. Exit polling demolished his defence, revealing that far more voters turned against Labour because of its leader (43 per cent) than because of its pro-referendum Brexit policy (17 per cent).[70]

Toynbee spoke for many when she wrote of Boris Johnson: 'Given the worst choice in history, the public preferred him to his opponent. How bad did Labour have to be to let this sociopathic, narcissistic, glutton for power beat them? That's the soul-searching question every Labour member, office-holder and MP has to ask. Labour was disastrously, catastrophically bad, an agony to behold. A coterie of Corbynites cared more about gripping power within the party than saving the country by winning the election. The NEC, a slate of nodding Corbynite place-persons, disgraced the party with its sectarian decisions. Once it was plain in every poll and focus group that Corbynism was electoral arsenic, they should have propelled him out, but electoral victory was secondary.'[71]

Baroness Jenny Tonge, who quit the Lib Dems after being suspended in 2016 in part because of her vocal anti-Israel stance, bitterly said: 'The Chief Rabbi must be dancing in the street. The pro-Israel lobby won our general election by lying about Jeremy Corbyn.'[72]

The direct impact of the Jewish vote may not have been pivotal in more than a dozen seats. Britain's Jewish community numbers little more than a quarter of a million, one of the reasons why Corbyn's strategists initially treated them with such disdain. Nationwide, the Tory share of the vote went up by just over one per cent, while Labour's plummeted and, with the exception of Putney, failed to take target seats. Given that, tactical voting proved supreme. Broadly, the Brexit vote was retained pretty solidly by the Tories thanks to Nigel Farage's decision not to challenge incumbents, while the Remain vote was split between Labour and the Lib Dems, to the detriment of both. But in a wider sense it can be argued that anti-Semitism did play a major part in robbing Corbyn of the key to No 10. During a truly bizarre election campaign in which old loyalties and certainties were confounded, the issue of trust became paramount. Across the UK the 'nosepeg' was used by voters who didn't much like or trust the main candidates. They were faced with Boris Johnson, whose relationship to the truth is akin to that of Donald Trump, and Jeremy Corbyn who constantly – when away from adoring supporters and toadies – displayed the American President's lack of self-knowledge. All three do not seem capable of recognising their own character flaws and narcissistic self-delusion.

Corbyn's strategists took northern and midlands seats ravaged and almost destroyed by Tory policies in the 1980s and 1990s for granted. These are working class areas where socialism and patriotism are not mutually exclusive, unlike the views of metropolitan elite around Corbyn. They have been let down so many times by both Conservative governments and Labourites who equate the Union flag with imperialism, disdain the armed forces in which many of the target electorate's sons and daughters serve, and who put ideological purity ahead of the day-to-day concerns of hard-pressed families. They know prejudice when they see it and didn't need to be Jewish to recognise it.

In Corbyn's case, anti-Semitism tropes ruined his self-image as a tireless anti-racist – witness his testy, cringing avoidance of questions when taken from his natural habitat on the stumps to the forensic atmosphere of broadcasting studios. A key moment in the campaign was when a *BBC Question Time* audience member said he could no longer 'buy' Corbyn's self-serving PR as a kindly grandpa. That was an indication of how the row had gone well beyond the Jewish community into the wider electorate understandably confused over who they should trust, or who deserved their trust. The electorate were presented with a choice between two untrustworthy frauds, one of them already in No 10 and the other happiest protesting outside No 10.

The dilemma was summed up half-way through the campaign by 86-year-old Molly Bennett from Meon Valley near Southampton. Asked how she would vote, she replied: 'Well, I know who I'm not voting for. The red man (Corbyn). He doesn't like the Jewish people and I don't agree with that. I normally vote Conservative, but I can't bear the buffoon. (Johnson).'[73] She wasn't that much impressed by the Lib Dems either.

Corbyn was just about the only Labour Leader in living history who could not beat Boris after nine years of austerity-driven Conservative government. Dame Margaret Hodge, who won re-election in Barking, said: 'A year ago I was one of four strong, hardworking Jewish women serving in the Labour Party as MPs. Today as I wake up, I'm the last one standing. Two were driven out of the party. The third one, Ruth Smeeth, who has fought valiantly, lost her seat last night. And I think that in itself says a lot about what the party felt in relation to its attitude to Jews and therefore the nastiness which the party has become.' Smeeth lost her Stoke-on-Trent North seat despite campaigning so honourably to weed out anti-Semitism. She told the BBC: 'Its seismic... the end.'[74]

Afterword

'the slop in which anti-Semites feel at home.'

As we have seen, anti-Semitic tropes have been evident from Marx and Keir Hardie to George Orwell and Jeremy Corbyn. The puzzlement which Corbyn and his coterie of metropolitan elitists greet charges of anti-Semitism and racism can be summed up as: 'I'm Left so I must always be right.' And that in turn is part of a wider malaise which sees Stalinist intimidation as a legitimate response to any and all criticism. In that sense, anti-Semitism is just a symptom of the disease.

The Left has been a force for great good in Britain but has always contained a minority driven by rabid class hatred. It has been most virulent in those from privileged backgrounds who instinctively deny their own roots but who rarely understand the realities faced by decent working-class communities. For a few generations, the politics of bile were generally confined to endless meetings in back rooms – Jeremy Corbyn's natural milieu – and were relatively harmless. But social media gave the haters a wider and more instant bite, together with the trend back towards deselection of sitting Labour MPs. In that febrile environment, anti-Semitism and other prejudices thrived.

In an analysis of Orwell's *AntiSemitism in Britain*, editor Ben Cohen wrote: 'Since 1945, British society has changed dramatically. Those who occupy the "nationalist" end of its political spectrum – particularly those urging withdrawal from the European Union – do not, by and large, succumb to the temptations of Jew-baiting, though there are exceptions. Rather, it is those who describe themselves as 'internationalists' who are the most vulnerable. This is the direct consequence of a doctrinaire "anti-imperialism" that begins and ends with solidarity with one (and only one) people – the Palestinians – and which regards Jews as an integral component of the superstructure of white, colonial privilege.'[1]

In his analysis of the same essay, Barry Rubin wrote: 'Another theme is the need of anti-Semitism to camouflage itself. Notes Orwell, "Above a certain intellectual level people are ashamed of being anti-Semitic and are careful to draw a distinction between 'antisemitism' and 'disliking Jews.'" Today the same role is played by the effort to make a distinction between the systematic hatred and slander of Israel and its supporters, and anti-Semitism. There always has to be some rationale for why it is an acceptable slur or hatred. Here, too, Orwell pointed out that this hatred is not easily combatted. To attempt to counter them with facts and statistics is useless. He views anti-Semitism as an emotional choice not shaped by rationality. Today, too, there is a war that frightens many in the West that can be called a "Jewish war", in that if it were not for Israel's existence one might believe there wouldn't be international terrorism or a threat from radical Islamism. Anti-Semitism is still seen as a shameful thing and thus it must be disguised by rationalisations, which today focus on Israel and those who support it. At the same time, though, it draws on all the traditional images and themes and is much more common than is thought.'[2]

However, a 2019 study blamed the media for the Labour anti-Semitism furore. Its search of national newspapers for coverage that mentioned Corbyn, Labour and anti-Semitism between 15 June 2015 and 31 March 2019 showed five and a half thousand articles. TV news bulletins, programmes and social media were not included. The survey found that on average people polled believed that around a third of Labour Party members had been reported for anti-Semitism – in fact it was under one per cent. Its authors said: 'As a left-wing political party, it is at the core of Labour's mission that it must be anti-racist. In that sense, one case of anti-Semitism is too many. But the huge disparity between public perception and the actual number of reported cases must make this one of the worst public relations disasters that has been recorded. It raises the question of why the party was so unable to deal with the issue.'[3]

Emma Goldberg wrote: 'Combatting anti-Semitism when it appears isn't just an act of defence for the Jews; it is an essential part of the larger struggle to end white nationalism in all its forms ... Personal commitment to fighting anti-Semitism stems less from a particular tie to the Jews and more from the understanding that tolerating any form of bigotry is a boon for all white nationalists. To refuse to deal with any ideology of domination, moreover, is to abet it. Contemporary social justice movements are quite clear that to refuse anti-racism is an act of racism; to refuse feminism is an act of sexism. To refuse opposition to anti-Semitism, likewise, is an act of anti-Semitism. Anti-Semitism, on its own, is an ugly force – but it is most potent when used to grease the engines of white supremacy writ large.'[4]

Actress Tracey-Anne Oberman, best known for her role in *Eastenders*, resigned from the Labour Party in 2016 due to its delay in concluding the disciplinary process against Ken Livingstone and suffered a Twitterstorm of racial abuse. At the 2019 election she described herself as 'politically homeless'. Her grandmother escaped tsarist Russia pogroms to come to England, and with her husband fought against Moseley's Blackshirts. She said: 'Jewish people were drawn to Labour because it protected minorities – it put a protective arm around them. It was the party of tolerance, of unity and equality.' Her grandparents 'would find it unfathomable to think that in 2019 I am having to fight such hatred and intimidation – and from the left, not the far-right. They would be horrified by some of the Nazi-like tropes and language used. The politics of the left has become so confused that I don't know who or what it represents anymore.'[5] Fair comment.

During the election campaign, you would have thought that the hate-mongers, left and right, would have had the sense to at least keep quiet. You would be wrong, and that strikes at the heart of some who claim to be Corbyn-friendly. *Jewish Chronicle* reporter Rosa Doherty wrote that before the contest was called, she already had the overwhelming feeling that this election was going to be a struggle. She wrote: 'I started to realise just how exhausting it was going to be when a family member, who is not Jewish and who is pro-Corbyn shared a picture of Neturei Karta, a tiny Strictly Orthodox sect, along with the caption that they were the "real Jews" because of their support for the Labour leader. Oy vey, I thought as I whatsapped my mum furiously about how ignorant the individual had been. I can't tell you how much fun it is trying to explain who the Neturei Karta are and how impossibly unrepresentative of the rest of us they are – and why it is probably just a teeny bit racist to share pictures of visibly Jewish men just because you think they agree with your narrow world-view. And then, adding that the only reason they support your precious leader is because they oppose the creation of a state of Israel until the coming of the Messiah. I search for the funny side because it is essential for my mental health. And I know that, as my mum always reminds me, I would not be me without the wonderful diversity gifted to me at birth.

'But it's not just family. And it's not just me. As a Jewish friend sympathised, "my Facebook is full of Jews putting up stuff about Jezza and all their mates piling in saying he's a good bloke, and the anti-Semitism is all made up as a smear, and then it kicks off." He may as well have been speaking for me. More than 80 per cent of the content on my Facebook feed should come with a trigger warning. Here's a post from a trustafarian, who wouldn't know a *siddur* from a synagogue. He's sharing Jewish Voice for Labour links with the self-appointed authority of a rabbi. And here are people complaining about Jews having a "monopoly on media coverage" or "ulterior motives" in the election. These are people I know. Or do I? Maybe I should just ignore it, again and again. But how can I leave the misinformation to go unchallenged? All these quandaries race though my mind when I came on to Facebook. I often wonder, before social media, how people discovered that the people they like were bigoted lunatics. Nowadays, you don't need to wait years to discover that a friend is a raging homophobe, racist or anti-Semite. You just follow their Twitter feed and see their mental word vomit exploding all over the page.'

She added: 'I have always felt aligned with the Labour party and socialist values. It was only when I started writing about, documenting and experiencing anti-Semitism, particularly within the Labour Party, that I started to feel there was something about me that fundamentally doesn't belong. It is never what I think about education, social housing, or supporting people who need help, that makes me feel a little out of place. It is the really simple fact that I think Jewish people should not have to hide or denounce integral parts of their Jewish identity in order to fit in. But when it comes to anti-Semitism it is not a simple difference of opinion. If you dismiss the Jewish community's experience of racism in the context of the Labour party and the election, I just can't have a genuinely friendly relationship with you. How could I?'[6] Such dilemmas are possibly the most long-lasting effects of the anti-Semitism which Corbyn and the leadership has at least allowed to fester for so long. Hardly comradely, is it?

The explosion in Labour's membership which Corbyn initially achieved was impressive, as was his appeal to younger and first-time voters. But here was another problem caused by a young generation who, in some cases, put style over substance without any real idea of the implications. The sociologist David Hirsh argued that pro-Palestinianism is a cipher for others to project their identity onto; there is an 'intense personal payoff' from self-conscious anti-Zionism, which produces a 'feeling of inner cleanliness'. In other words, 'The ugly surge in left-wing anti-Semitism over the past few years assumes a connection with support for the Palestinian cause, yet in reality there is plenty of evidence to suggest that these people are not really concerned with the Palestinians but are merely using them for their own selfish interests.' It is part of a broader trend; their politics are more a part of their identity than a programme for improving the world. He went on: 'It is not so much what they believe in, but rather who they are, and causes such as anti-Zionism are analogous to a favoured sports team or brand of clothing. This is why anti-Zionism in particular is so attractive – it is entirely cost free. For well-educated, middle-class professionals, opposition to Israel holds no jeopardy: they will not need to pay any more tax or suffer discrimination in access to jobs or education. It allows privileged white people in Britain and America to pretend they are Oliver Tambo or Nelson Mandela, without actually putting themselves at risk or effecting any benefit to Palestinians.'[7]

Under Corbyn, the true Left of radical campaigning and genuine anti-racism has been bastardised into a hate cult distinguished by repellent self-righteousness. Corbyn's cronies, more than willing to act with venality when it suits them, have told themselves that if you say you are on the side of the poor and the downtrodden, anything goes. Anyone who disagrees is so obviously on the side of the imperialist, the fat cat bankers and hedge fund managers, the exploiters driven by greed alone to make their billions. David Aaronovitch wrote: 'Under Corbyn, that self-righteousness has intoxicated the troops. From what I can see from their publications and demeanour they genuinely believe that anyone with a contrary is irredeemably morally deficient.'[8] Again, such smug certainty is worthy of the barely literate Donald Trump.

What distinguishes Corbynista anti-Semitic prejudice from knee-jerk Tory Islamophobia is that their belief that Israel is an imperialist creation feeds into their conspiracy theories that Jewish capitalism has a malign influence not just in the oppression of Palestinians, but everywhere. *Times* columnist Philip Collins wrote: 'Take all these views and heat them to boiling point and I think you create a brew of anti-Semitism. Or at least the slop in which anti-Semites feel at home.'[9]

And finally, we must come back to Jeremy Corbyn himself. It is true that he denounced anti-Semitism in robust terms during electioneering at times he deemed to be appropriate and electorally advantageous but has never denounced himself for sharing platforms with virulent anti-Semites, both domestic and foreign. He has launched half-hearted inquiries into anti-Semitism but not into the selection processes which have produced proven bigots as candidates. His get-out line is always that he believes in party democracy and all this is nothing to do with him. Me racist? Don't be daft. Anti-Semitic? Just another media slur. He has never admitted culpability for the excesses done in his name. In columnist Hugo Rifkind's memorable phrase, he is 'like a pop diva who studies her nails while her record company throws her hometown friends out of the afterparty'.[10]

Another aspect is indelibly linked to Corbyn's world view, pretty much unchanged since his youth, illustrated by his long-standing opposition to, and contempt of NATO, the brainchild of Clement Attlee and Ernest Bevin. They saw it as an alliance which, after the Second World War and the defeat of Nazism, would provide mutual security and a bulwark against future expansion by totalitarian states. Corbyn, in a 2011 speech, described it as 'an attempt to create an empire of the mind. The hard power of their [American] weaponry, the malign influence of the CIA, and its creation of pliant and friendly governments actively suppressed and subjugated people in the poorest countries of the world'.[11] In his mind, and that of Hobson a century earlier, such bodies were merely a weapon of colonialism and capitalism, and that imperialism was made possible by the power of capitalists to make the state provide military protection for their overseas investments. And, of course, the Jewish diaspora were heavily involved in all that. One of Corbyn's right-hand men, Andrew Murray, described the fall of the Berlin Wall as 'a historic set-back for human progress'. At a stroke, the Corbynistas shredded the legacy of Attlee, Bevin and even Michael Foot.

The question most asked, including some from within his own coterie, is whether the anti-Semitism shown in what he has said and the company he has kept, is down to blinkered ignorance or cynical personal ambition or self-deluding racism. My own view, for what it's worth, is: all three. History has shown us that they go hand in hand. And none have a legitimate place in Britain's Labour Party.

On a personal note, I will die as a man of the Left, believing in a concept based on decency and a pragmatic view that the ideals of justice and equality of opportunity can only be achieved if they are the will of the people. Not by narrow-minded, hate-filled bigotry. In the 2019 election I refused to break the habit of a lifetime and voted Labour, but despite Corbyn, not because of him. Members of my extended family, the children and grandchildren of coal miners, broke with family tradition and ignore the sound of ancestors whirring in their graves. Alan Johnson, widely seen as the best leader Labour never had, said of Corbyn: 'Everyone knew that he couldn't lead the working class out of a paper bag.'

With the polling slips only just going into landfill sites, however, a tsunami of tweets showed that the bigotry is still there. Corbynistas blamed 'Blairites', the media, and, of course, 'traitors' who betrayed the vision of their Dear Leader ... anyone but themselves. John McDonnell, just before he stood down as a potential successor, had the grace to admit that Labour faces a 'long haul' in the next bid to gain power following its fourth election defeat in a row, but insisted that Corbyn had been 'the right leader' for the party. Once again there was talk of betrayal and the impact of the wicked media. The real betrayal, however, goes beyond that of the Jewish community who historically did so much to birth and sustain the Labour and trade union movement. It is the betrayal of struggling communities and families who face the prospect of another five years of Boris Johnson and, given his track record, the stark reality of his soon-to-be-broken promises on the NHS, schools, policing and welfare. Labour under Corbyn handed power on a plate to a premier – even more posh, privileged and self-entitled than Corbyn – who understands the greed of the super-rich far more than the daily travails of the poor. And that is sickening. No wonder true socialists are howling with rage. Including me.

Jason Cowley, editor of the Leftist *New Statesman* which refused to endorse Corbyn during the campaign, wrote: 'My politics are sceptical, and I value independence of thought, the spirit of criticism and a willingness to debate. I also value human decency. And I believed that Corbyn was unfit to be prime minister because of his indulgence of, and reluctance to apologise for, anti-Semitism in Labour, his refusal to take a stance on Brexit and his toxic associations with extremists over several decades. That Labour should be led by such a man was unconscionable ... It gives me no pleasure to have been proved right about Corbyn's Labour. And now the hollowed-out party must grapple with the bitter truth that it has created the conditions for another long period of Conservative rule, when the circumstances for a revival of the left could not have been more propitious.'[12]

Within hours of the election John Mann, the government's independent adviser on anti-Semitism, announced he was launching a probe into the role of far-Left websites in the growth of Jew-hate in the UK. He had previously said: 'When Corbyn goes the problem doesn't go with Corbyn.'[13] The Twittersphere duly went beserk after the results came in – one from an Irish journalist said: 'It's a great result for Zionism. Monsters are roaring their support.' Another read: 'Fascism begins in the UK today.' The eventual bowing out of Corbyn and McDonnell may change little as their cronies retain control of the party's power structure, including the NEC and officials who incubated anti-Semitism. Jewish columnist Gilliam Merron wrote of the forthcoming Labour Leadership ballot: 'Whenever it comes, this leadership election will be viewed, at least by some, as an opportunity for the Labour party to make a clean break from the last four and a half years, entering a new chapter. But while many within our community will doubtless be happy to see the back of Mr Corbyn, we know that the issues within the party will not simply cease to exist when he departs.'[14] Given the excuses deployed by Cult Corbyn, that could well prove an understatement.

Bertolt Brecht wrote after the defeat of Nazism: 'For though the world has stood up and stopped the bastard, the bitch that bore him is in heat again.'

Notes

1. Bad Marks

1. McLellan, 2-4
2. Wheen, 10
3. *Dictionary of National Biography, Volume 37* (Oxford University Press, 2004) 57-58
4. McLellan, 14
5. Calhoun, 23
6. The Communist Manifesto
7. Macoby, 44-46
8. *Soviet Jewish Affairs Journal*, 14:1, 1974
9. *Ibid.*
10. Greenblatt, 291-307
11. Quora, 20 17
12. *Journal of the History of Ideas*, 164
13. Mehring, 100-101
14. Hampsher-Monk, 496
15. Wheen, 58
16. *Engage Journal 3*, September 2006
17. *New York Daily Tribune*, January 4 1856
18. MEKOR IV, 490, August 25 1875
19. *The Philosopher's Magazine*, March 23 2015
20. Marx-Engels Correspondence, Volume 3, 82
21. *The Western Socialist, No 1*, 1960
22. *The Philosopher's Magazine*, March 23 2015
23. *Die Deutsche Ideologie*, 162
24. *Neue Rheinische Zeitung*, April 29 1849
25. *The Western Socialist, No 1*, 1960
26. *Ibid.*
27. Kluger, 121
28. Bernstein, 184
29. *New York Times*, August 18 2007
30. *Salford Star*, issue 6, winter 2007
31. *Arbeter-Zeitung, No 19*, May 9 1890
32. Jacobs, 400
33. Sibernica, 41
34. *Leo Baeck Institute Yearbook*, XVI 1971, 124
35. Jacobs, 401
36. *Ibid.*
37. *Der Sozialdemokrat*, October 5 1882
38. Jacobs, 403
39. *The Spectator*, April 4 2018
40. Sacks, 98-108

2. Shylock, Fagin and the Children of the Ghetto

1. *Guardian*, November 3 2007
2. *Times Literary Supplement*, July 6 2011
3. *Quest*, issue 3, July 2012
4. *The Merchant of Venice*, Act III, scene I
5. Adler, 344-350
6. Adler, 341
7. *Guardian*, November 25 2003
8. Granach, 276-277
9. *The Alternative* website, June 2017
10. Marlow, 132
11. *Pickwick Papers*, 632-637
12. Irving Howe, Introduction to 1982 Bantam Classic edition of *Oliver Twist*
13. *La Scena Musicale*, September 29 2005
14. Howe, Introduction
15. Johnson, January 1 1952
16. *La Scena Musicale*, September 29 2005
17. *Ibid.*
18. Johnson, January 1 1952
19. Wheeler, 81
20. *Guardian*, January 24 2006
21. M.I.A. *Encyclopaedia* home page
22. Fishman, 239
23. *Daily Telegraph*, October 2 1888
24. Kershen, 133-143
25. Zangwill's *Spitalfields* app, August 2016
26. Ibid.
27. Ibid.

3. When Two Tribes Go to War

1. Feldman, 266-267
2. Feldman, 94-120
3. Feldman, 268-290
4. *Quest*, July 12 2012
5. Wistrich, 203-205
6. Hirschfield, 95-112
7. Morgan, 89-90
8. *Justice*, 1884
9. Judd and Sturridge, 242
10. *New Stateman*, March 26 2018
11. *Patterns of Prejudice*, 363
12. *Encyclopaedia Britannica*, 12th edition, 1922
13. *Justice*, June 17 1899
14. *Quest*, July 3 2012
15. Hirschfield, 621
16. *Justice*, September 30 1899
17. *Justice*, November 4 1899
18. *Hobson, Lenin and anti-Imperialism*, BBC Radio 3, March 6 2011
19. Hobson, 189-197
20. *White Pride Worldwide* website, February 13 2012
21. Duignan and Gann, 59
22. Etherington, 73
23. Speech in Battersea Park, May 20 1900, Stop the War Committee
24. *Encyclopaedia Britannica*, 1911 edn
25. *Journal of Contemporary History*, 1980, 626
26. *The Sports Historian*, no. 15
27. Julius, 275
28. liberalhistory.org.uk
29. Allen Smith, 186
30. *Sheffield Independent*, May 25 1889

Notes

31. Evidence to the Chakrabarti Inquiry, June 1 2016
32. *Quest*, July 2 2012
33. Alderman, 123
34. Pick, 213
35. White, 74-76
36. 80-81
37. White, 84
38. Feldman, 266-267
39. Hirschfield, 621
40. *Quest*, July 12 2012
41. Times, May 11 1904
42. Fishman, 257
43. Fishman, 280-284
44. Fishman, 295
45. Endelman, chapters 3-5
46. Feldman, 119
47. *Walsall Pioneer*, March 26 1915
48. *Sunday Chronicle*, October 10 1915
49. Feldman, 267
50. Fishman, 306-307
51. *Sunday Chronicle*, October 10 1914
52. jewishmuseum.org.uk
53. *Moment*, June 16 2015
54. *Jewish Chronicle*, June 20 2016
56. *Jewish Chronicle*, June 20 2016
57. *Jewish Chronicle*, March 13 2017
58. Rosenberg, *The Immortals*, 1917
59. jewishmuseum.org.uk
60. *Jewish Chronicle*, March 13 2014
61. *International Socialism*, January 13 2017)
62. Jennifer Rosenberg, ThoughtCo, June 11 2018
63. UK Cabinet minutes, September 3 1917, Public Record Office
64. *Morning Post*, November 21 2018
65. *Times,* April 3 1919
66. *Jewish World*, January 28 1914

4. Between the Wars

1. Zangwill's Spitalfields app
2. Cohen, 107-108
3. Cleveland and Butler, 220
4. Klug, 199-210
5. Report of the Palm Commission, August 1920, 10
6. Johnson, 441
7. Wasserstein, 32
8. Watts, 190
9. Huneidi, 57
10. Quigley, 36
11. Renton, 16
12. Nicosia, 67
13. Monroe, 43
14. Schneer, 361
15. Marquand, 283
16. Morgan, 44-45
17. Cesarani, 141
18. International Socialism, January 3 2017
19. Taylor, 213-214
20. Morgan, MacDonald chapter
21. Socialist Review 2019
22. Mowat, 379-401
23. Beckett, 15-16
24. Benewick, 113
25. Thurlow, 114
26. Hodgson, 136
27. Benewick, 287-288
28. Benewick, 112
29. Benewick, 81
30. Benewick, 94
31. Dorril, 310
32. Benewick, 113
33. Skidelsky, 342
34. Hartley, 325
35. Mosley, 248
36. Durham, 43-45

259

37. Slate, April 14 2017
38. Atkinson, 182
39. Bristol Radical Pamphleteer, no 39, 2017
40. Pugh, 306
41. Times, April 15 1985
42. Hackney Gazette, December 30 2016
43. Weston, 2
44. Nigel Jones, 114
45. Weston, 3
46. Weston, 5
47. Donoughue and Jones, 225
48. Annual Register 1936, 91-94
49. Times, May 2 1940
50. Gottlieb, 324
51. Lineham, 112
52. Benewick, 211
53. Macklin, 14
54. TIME, April 18 1938
55. Jewish Chronicle, March 11 1966
56. Uglow, 371
57. Independent, June 9 1993
58. Independent, July 21 1994
59. Twitchell, 287
60. The Times Guide to the House of Commons 1945

5. George Orwell and the Fight against Fascism

1. *Forward*, August 2 2012
2. Mayne, 42-43
3. *The Adelphi*, Books Google
4. Stanley and Abraham, 26
5. *Guardian*, August 13 2002
6. *The American Interest*, November 17 2017
7. *Guardian*, August 13 2002
8. *Vanity Fair*, October 1996
9. *The American Interest*, November 17 2017
10. Hitchens, Introduction
11. *Forward*, August 2 2012
12. Orwell, *Contemporary Jewish Research Journal*, 1945
13. *Times*, August 23 2018
14. *Ibid.*
15. Kushner, Phd thesis, University of Sheffield
16. Orwell, *Contemporary Jewish Research Journal*, 1945
17. *Ibid.*
18. *Ibid.*
19. *Ibid.*
20. *Forward*, August 2 2012
21. *The Rubin Report*, October 29 2009
22. *The American Interest*, November 20 2017
23. Shatzkes, 5
24. *Daily Telegraph*, June 25 1947
25. *Times*, September 3 1942
26. London, 200
27. Kushner, 77
28. *Hansard*, December 17 1942
29. Cesarini, 577
30. London, 206
31. Gilbert, 109
32. *Hansard*, January 19 1943
33. Wassrstein, 117
34. Dudley Edwards, 375-376
35. *Daily Telegraph*, November 9 2002
36. Kushner, 139
37. Calder, 636
38. Pimlott, 289-290
39. Dalton, 739
40. Labour Party annual report 1945

6. Post-War Palpitations

1. Cesarani, 80-91
2. Khromeychuk, 119
3. Speech to Labour conference, Bournemouth, June 12 1946, General Public Statements, FO 371
4. Sachar, 296
5. Kramnick and Sheerman, 206-207
6. Wilson, 187
7. *International Socialist*, January 3 2017
8. Scammell, 252
9. Crossman and Foot, 31
10. *Tribune*, August 8 1947
11. Louis, 430
12. Hoffman, 48-52
13. *New Statesman*, May 23 2012
14. *Ibid*.
15. *Ibid*.
16. Morris, 77-78
17. Benny Morris, 602
18. Louis, 579
19. *Middle Eastern Studies*, Vol 31, issue 3, July 1995, 579
20. Israel Central Bureau of Statistics 2016
21. *Times*, August 23 2018
22. *Daily Telegraph*, December 7 2001
23. *Jewish Chronicle Online*, April 22 2009
24. *Guardian*, April 13 2009
25. Crossman, 61
26. Crossman, 58-59
27. Keleman, 128, 132
28. *International Socialist*, January 3 2017
29. Wyatt, 167
30. *International Socialist*, January 3 2017
31. Edwards, 38-39
32. Edwards, 48
33. Barbaris, McHugh and Tydesley, 194
34. *International Socialist*, January 3 2017
35. Watkins, 114-115
36. *CapX*, April 6 2018
37. *Soundings* blog, Lawrence and Wishart, September 18 2018
38. *Jewish Chronicle*, March 3 2016
39. *Jewish Chronicle*, March 20 2014
40. Rich, 98
41. *Hansard*, October 18 1973
42. *Guardian*, September 9 1974

7. Oh! Jeremy Corbyn

1. Church Times, September 8 2015
2. Bower, 6
3. Piven, 10
4. Horowitz, 6
5. Horowitz, 7
6. Bower, 18-19
7. Bower, 20
8. Bower, 33
9. Bower, 26
10. *Morning Star*, March 29 2016
11. Bower, 66
12. *Guardian*, September 10 1996
13. *Sunday Times*, May 14
14. newsletter.co.uk
15. *Sunday Times*, May 21 2017
16. PoliticsHome.com, May 27 2017
17. *London Evening Standard*, January 23 1987
18. Bower, 82
19. *Jewish Chronicle*, March 20 2014
20. Keleman, 2

21. *20th Century British History*, Vol 1, January 2000, 23-41
22. MacBride, 191-193
23. Schiff and Ya'ari, 283-284
24. Rich, 143-145
25. Keleman, 188
26. Staetsky, 61
27. *New Statesman*, July 4 2017
28. Bower, 133-134
29. RighteousJews.org, January 2008
30. Bower
31. TheyWorkForYou.com
32. *Guardian*, September 15 2005
33. Source to author, October 2019
34. *New Statesman* blog, May 6 2005
35. BBC News, May 6 2005
36. BBC News, May 11 2005
37. Bower, 193
38. Bower, 154
39. Human Rights Watch hrw.org/news
40. *Daily Telegraph*, May 9 2011
41. *Guardian*, August 1 2018
42. *Times*, August 1 2018
43. Bower, 207
44. Bower, 156
45. Bower, 158
46. *Sunday Times*, April 30 2019
47. *Times*, April 30 2019
48. *Jewish Chronicle*, November 6 2015
49. BBC News, March 23 2018
50. *London Evening Standard*, March 24 2018
51. MailOnLine, August 2018
52. *Guardian*, August 24 2018
53. *Jewish Chronicle*, March 26 2018
54. *Sunday Times*, April 1 2016
55. *Huffpost*, April 1 2018
56. *Independent*, May 1 2019
57. Horowitz, 11
58. *Spectator*, May 8 2019
59. *Jewish Chronicle*, August 25 2019
60. *The Canary*, February 25 2019
61. *Jerusalem Report*, September 17 2018
62. *Daily Mail*, August 24 2019

8. Labour Pains

1. Hirsh, 42-46
2. *Daily Telegraph*, May 20 2017
3. *Guardian*, August 17 2018
4. *Jerusalem Post*, April 5 2016
5. Bower, 192
6. Hursh, 45
7. *Jewish Chronicle*, August 18 2016
8. *Jewish Chronicle*. January 2018 2016
9. BBC News, July 24 2018
10. *Daily Telegraph*, July 24 2018
11. *Left Futures* blog, May 2 2016
12. *Jewish Chronicle*, January 28 2016
13. *Guardian*, November 7 2014
14. *New Statesman*, October 28 2015
15. BBC News, December 7 2017
16. *Labour List*, September 16 2016
17. *Times*, October 13 2015
18. *Daily Telegraph*, November 8 2015
19. *BBC News* archive
20. Interview with author, September 2019
21. *Guardian*, March 28 2019
22. *Independent*, March 9 2015
23. *Guardian*, April 9 2015
24. *Independent*, April 26 2016
25. *Open Democracy*, May 3 2016
26. *Independent*, May 4 2016
27. *Guardian*, April 27 2010
28. BBC News, April 27 2016

Notes

29. *BBC News*, July 18 2016
30. *Rotherham Advertiser*, August 25 2017
31. *Bradford Telegraph and Argus*, August 25 2017
32. *Times*, April 4 2018
33. *London Review of Books*, May 4 2016
34. *Guardian*, April 28 2016
35. *Independent*, April 28 2016
36. *BBC News*, April 5, 2017
37. *Guardian*, May 21 2018
38. *Jews for Justice for Palestine*, September 5 2016
39. *Jewish Chronicle*, May 4 2016
40. *Independent*, May 28 2016
41. Gerber, 51
42. *Labour Against the Witch-Hunt* website, September 5 2016
43. *Guardian*, September 28 2016
44. *Independent*, May 28 2016
45. *Independent*, October 8 2016
46. *Morning Star*, October 8 2016
47. *Dundee Courier*, March 19 2017
48. *Jewish Chronicle*, September 17 2017
49. *Jewish Chronicle*, June 14 2017
50. *Morning Star*, September 26 2018
51. *Guardian*, February 27 2019
52. *Channel4*.com, 2007
53. *Liberty* website, March 16 2011
54. *Daily Telegraph*, April 16 2013
55. *Guardian*, April 29 2016
56. Bower, 269-270
57. Chakrabarti Inquiry report, Pears Institute, June 30 2016
58. *Independent News and Media*, June 30 2016
59. Pears Institute, June 30 2016
60. *Guardian*, June 30 2016
61. *Stoke Sentinel*, February 27 2019
62. *Huffpost*, April 25 2016
63. *BBC News*, June 30 2016
64. *London Evening Standard*, June 30 2016
65. *Jewish News*, June 30 2016
66. *Jewish Chronicle*, August 4 2016
67. *Jewish Chronicle*, June 23 2017
68. *Observer*, October 16 2016
69. *BBC News*, April 16 2018
70. Bower, 308
71. *Economist*, March 15 2019
72. *BBC News*, September 26 2017
73. *Jewish Chronicle*, December 26 2017
74. *Times*, November 6 2017
75. *Economist*, April 3 2018
76. *The Herald*, August 2 2018
77. *Times*, May 1 2019
78. *Independent*, March 26 2018
79. *BBC News*, March 26 2018
80. *Guardian*, August 24 2018
81. Bower, 232
82. Interview with author, September 2019
83. *Sky TV*, September 26 2016
84. *Times*, September 15 2016
85. *Guido Fawkes* blog, September 15 2016
86. Copied to author, September 2019
87. Unpublished report obtained by author, September 2019
88. *Jewish Chronicle*, August 1 2018
89. *Huffpost UK*, February 14 2019
90. Interview with author, September 2019
91. *TotalPolitics*, May 28 2012
92. *Jewish Telegraphic Agency*, April 18 2005
93. *GQ*, February 18 2019

94. *Sunday Times*, September 8 2019
95. *Jewish Chronicle*, September 15 2011
96. *Jewish Chronicle*, June 27 2016
97. *BBC News*, October 20 2014
98. *Daily Telegraph*, December 18 2014
99. *Guardian*, February 10 2017
100. *Daily Mirror*, November 5 2014
101. *Sunday Times*, April 1 2018
102. *Jewish Chronicle*, April 3 2018
103. *Daily Mirror*, April 17 2018
104. *Times*, February 9 2019
105. *Guardian*, February 10 2019
106. *Sunday Times*, September 8 2019
107. *GQ*, February 18 2019
108. *Jewish Chronicle*, September 6 2019
109. *Times*, October 14 2019
110. *Jewish News*, October 3 2019
111. *BBC News*, October 16 2019
112. *Liverpool Echo*, October 17 2019
113. *Times*, October 18 2019
114. *Sunday Times*, October 20 2019
115. *ITN*, October 17 2019

9. Post-Natal Blues

1. *Sunday Times Magazine*, September 8 2019
2. *BBC News*, February 18 2019
3. *Haaretz*, April 4 2018
4. *New York Times*, April 3 2018
5. *Reuters*, April 3 2018
6. *Jewish Chronicle*, April 24 2018
7. *Independent*, April 24 2018
8. *BBC News*, August 15 2018
9. *Guardian*, April 13 2018
10. *Guardian*, April 24 2018
11. *openDemocracy*, October 11 2017
12. *Times of Israel*, May 17 2018
13. *Independent*, July 22 2018
14. *Jewish Chronicle*, July 20 2018
15. *Guardian*, July 12 2018
16. *Der Spiegel*, April 21 2018
17. *Guardian*, July 26 2018
18. *Guardian*, July 26 2018
19. *Spectator*, May 11 2019
20. *Politicos*, August 3 2018
21. *CNN*, August 17 2018
22. *Guardian*, September 30 2018
23. *BBC News*, September 26 2018
24. *Sky News*, February 13 2019
25. *Daily Mirror*, July 21 2019
26. *Guardian*, June 19 2019
27. *Independent*, July 24 2014
28. *Labour List*, May 14 2019
29. *Labour List*, July 23 2019
30. *BBC News*, July 9 2019
31. *Guardian*, July 22 2019
32. *Jewish News*, July 22 2019
33. *PoliticsHome*, July 11 2019
34. *The Canary*, July 30 2019
35. *Morning Star*, July 16 2019
36. *Guardian*, July 21 2019
37. *Middle East Eye*, August 2 2019
38. *Jewish Chronicle*, August 25 2017
39. *Jewish Chronicle*, June 19 2018
40. *Labour Briefing*, April 27 2018
41. *Labour List*, October 26 2018
42. *Jewish News*, December 14 2017
43. *Morning Star*, September 29 2017
44. *Jewish Chronicle*, March 28 2018
45. *Jewish Chronicle*, June 27 2018
46. *Jewish News*, May 16 2019
47. *Jewish Chronicle*, December 24 2018
48. *Guardian*, April 3 2018
49. *The Tablet*, October 16 2017
50. *Morning Star*, August 7 2018

Notes

51. *Jewish News*, September 28 2018
52. *BBC News*, February 2 2019
53. *Financial Times*, April 28 2016
54. *Guardian*, March 20 2006
55. *Jewish Chronicle*, November 23 2017
56. *Birthwrong* website, 2015
57. *Jewish Chronicle*, January 31 2016
58. *Guardian*, April 3 2018
59. *Daily Telegraph*, February 5 2007
60. *Independent*, September 23 2007
61. *Daily Telegraph*, February 5 2007
62. *Independent*, September 23 2007
63. *Independent Jewish Voices*, February 2007
64. *BBC News*, February 27 2019
65. *Morning Star*, July 2 2019
66. *Press Gazette*, August 5 2019
67. *Guardian*, August 4 2019
68. *Jewish Chronicle*, August 5 2019
69. *BBC News*, August 13 2019
70. *Guardian*, June 10 2019
71. *Jewish Chronicle*, August 18 2015
72. *Labour List*, April 25 2018
73. Jewish Socialist Group, April 25 2016
74. *Guardian*, April 24 2016
75. Socialist Party, May 9 2018
76. *BBC News*, February 21 2019
77. *Morning Star*, July 16 2019
78. *Labour Briefing*, August 4 2019
79. *openDemocracy*, April 27 2016
80. *openDemocracy*, May 7 2016
81. *openDemocracy*, May 3 2016
82. *International Socialism*, January 2 2017
83. *Jewish Chronicle*, June 14 2017
84. *Guardian*, April 2 2018
85. *Huffpost UK*, April 17 2018
86. *Middle East Eye*, April 6 2018
87. *Camden New Journal*, May 10 2018
88. *Jewish Quarterly*, October 17 2018
89. *Morning Star*, September 3 2018
90. *openDemocracy*, September 2018
91. *Forward*, August 21 2018
92. *Haaretz*, August 9 2018
93. *Patreon*, September 5 2018
94. *CounterPunch*, August 14 2018
95. *Morning Star*, July 5 2019
96. *Middle East Eye*, February 20 2019
97. *Spectator*, May 8 2019
98. *Channel 4 FactCheck*, April 25 2018
99. *Evolve Politics*, March 29 2018
100. Staetsky, 3-5
101. Staetsky, 44
102. *Jewish Chronicle*, December 14 2017
103. *Jewish Chronicle*, September 12 2018
104. *ITN*, March 31 2016
105. *Times*, July 22 2019
106. *BBC News*, September 8 2019
107. *Sunday Times*, September 8 2019
108. *BBC News*, November 18 2015
109. *Times*, September 17 2019
110. *Guardian*, August 30 2018
111. *BBC News*, April 1 2018
112. *Wolverhampton Express and Star*, February 18 2016
113. *BBC News*, June 1 2012
114. *Guardian*, November 8 2017
115. *Wolverhampton Express and Star*, March 15 2016
116. *BBC News*, March 19 2019
117. *Daily Mail*, July 5 2019
118. *Daily Mail*, September 11 2019

119. *Times*, September 17 2017
120. *BBC News*, September 29 2019

10. The End?

1. *Jewish Chronicle*, October 30 2019
2. *Jewish Chronicle*, November 1 2019
3. *Jewish Chronicle*, November 8 2019
4. *Jewish Chronicle*, November 7 2019
5. Jewish Chronicle, October 28 2019
6. *Times*, November 1 2019
7. *Jewish Chronicle*, October 30 2019
8. *Ibid.*
9. *Jewish Chronicle*, October 31 2019
10. *Daily Mail*, February 8 2019
11. *Jewish Chronicle*, November 1
12. *Daily Mail*, November 1 2019
13. *Jewish Chronicle*, October 29 2019
14. *Morning Star*, October 27 2019
15. *Jewish Chronicle*, October 31 2019
16. *BBC, Andrew Marr Show*, November 3 2019
17. *Daily Mail*, November 4 2019
18. *Sunday Times*, September 22 2019
19. *Today, BBC Radio 4*, November 7 2019
20. *Jewish Chronicle*, November 14 2019
21. *Times*, November 7 2019
22. *BBC Radio 5 Live*, November 8 2019
23. *BBC News*, November 14 2019
24. *Daily Mail*, November 9 2019
25. *Daily Mail*, November 11 2019
26. *Jewish Chronicle*, November 12 2019
27. *Ibid.*
28. *BBC News*, November 29 2019
29. *Jewish Chronicle*, November 9 2019
30. *Jewish Chronicle*, November 11 2019
31. *Jewish Chronicle*, November 8
32. *Jewish Chronicle*, November 15 2019
33. *Jewish Chronicle*, November 15
34. *Jewish Chronicle*, November 15
35. *Times*, November 19 2019
36. *Daily Mail*, November 15 2019
37. *Daily Mail*, November 18 2019
38. *Jewish Chronicle*, November 22 2019
39. BBC News, Dec 9 2019
40. *Jewish News*, December 13 2019
41. *Jewish Chronicle*, November 21 2019
42. *Jewish Chronicle*, November 22 2019
43. *Huffpost*, November 25 2019
44. *BBC News*, November 22 2019
45. *BBC News*, November 26 2019
46. *BBC News*, November 27 2019
47. *Times*, November 17 2019
48. *BBC News*, November 27 2019
49. *BBC Radio 5 Live*, November 29 2019
50. *BBC Radio 5* Live, November 26
51. *BBC News*, December 3 2019
52. *Daily Mail*, December 4 2019
53. *Jewish Chronicle*, November 21 2019
54. Labour Party Press Office, December 1 2019
55. *The Tablet*, November 6 2019
56. *Liverpool Echo*, December 2 2019
57. *BBC News*, December 5 2019

Notes

58. *Sky News*, December 6 2019
60. *BBC News*, December 6 2019
61. *Mail on Sunday*, December 8 2019
62. *Sunday Times*, December 8
63. *The Andrew Marr Show, BBC*, December 8
64. *Jewish Chronicle*, December 9 2019
65. *Jewish Chronicle*, December 8 2019
66. *BBC Breakfast*, December 9 2019
67. *Jewish Chronicle*, December 10 2019
68. *Jewish Chronicle*, December 13 2019
69. *Jewish News*, December 13 2019
70. *Independent*, December 13 2019
71. *Guardian*, December 13 2019
72. *Jewish News*, December 13 2019
73. *Sky News*, November 17 2019
74. *BBC News*, December 13 2019

Afterword

1. *The Tower Magazine*, April 29 2016
2. *Ibid.*
3. Philo, Berry, Schlosberg, Lerman and Miller, viii
4. *Guardian*, August 21 2019
5. *Daily Mail*, November 17 2019
6. *Jewish Chronicle*, November 14 2019
7. *Jewish Chronicle*, December 9 2019
8. *Times*, November 8 2019
9. *Times*, November 29 2019
10. *Times*, November 19 2019
11. *Times*, December 4 2019
12. *Sunday Times*, December 15 2019
13. *Jewish Chronicle*, December 13 2019
14. *Jewish News*, December 13 2019

Bibliography

Adler, Jacob, *A Life on the Stage: A Memoir* (Knopf, New York, 1999)

Alderman, Geoffrey, *Modern British Jewry* (Clarendon, Oxford, 1992)

Atkinson, Diane, *Rise Up, Women! The Remarkable Lives of the Suffragettes* (Bloomsbury, London 2018)

Barberis, Peter; McHugh, John; Tyldesley, Mike, *Encyclopedia of British and Irish Political Organizations* (Continuum International Publishing Group, London 2005)

Beckett, Francis, *The Rebel Who Lost His Cause – The Tragedy of John Beckett MP* (Allison and Busby, London 1999)

Beckham, Morris, *The 43 Group* (Centerprise Publication, June 2000)

Benewick, Robert, *Political Violence and Public Order: A Study of British Fascism* (Allen Lane, London 1969)

Bernstein, Iver, *The New York Draft Riots* (Oxford University Press, 1991)

Bolchover, Richard, *British Jewry and the Holocaust* (Littman Library of Jewish Civilization, 2003)

Cesarani, David, *Justice Delayed: How Britain Became a Refuge for Nazi War Criminals* (Heinemann, 1992)

Calder, Angus, *The People's War: Britain 1939-1945* (Jonathan Cape, London 1979)

Caldicott, Rosemary, *Lady Blackshirts. The perils of Perception - Suffragettes who became Fascists* (Bristol Radical Pamphletteer #39, 2017)

Calhoun, Craig J., *Classic Sociology Theory* (Oxford: Wiley-Blackwell, Oxford 2002)

Claeys, Gregory, *Imperial Sceptics - British Critics of Empire 1850-1920* (Cambridge University Press, 2010)

Clark, Barry Stewart, *Political Economy – A Comparative Approach* (ABC-CLIO, 1998)

Cleveland, William L., and Bunton, Martin, *A History of the Modern Middle East* (Avalon Publishing, 2016)

Bibliography

Cohen, Michael J., *Britain's Moment in Palestine: Retrospect and Perspectives, 1917-1948* (Routledge, 2014)

Copsey, Nigel, Anti-Fascism in Britain (Routledge., 2016)

Crick, Bernard, *George Orwell, A Life* (Penguin Books, London 1980)

Crossman, Richard, *A Nation Reborn: The Israel of Weizmann, Bevin and Ben-Gurion* (Hamish Hamilton, 1960)

Crossman, Richard and Michael Foot, *A Palestine Munich?* (Gollancz, London 1946)

Dalton, Hugh, 1986a, The Second World War Diary of Hugh Dalton 1940-45 (Jonathan Cape)

Davies, A.J., *To Build A New Jerusalem: The British Labour Party from Keir Hardie to Tony Blair* (Abacus, 1996)

Donoughue, Bernard, and Jones, G.W., *Herbert Morrison: Portrait of a Politician* (Phoenix, 2001)

Edmunds, June, *The Left and Israel: Party-Policy Change and Internal Democracy* (Macmillan, 2000)

Dorril, R., *Blackshirt – Sir Oswald Mosley and British Fascism* (Penguin, London 2007)

Dudley Edwards, Ruth, *Victor Gollancz: A Biography* (Gollancz, London 1987)

Duignan, Peter, and Gann, Lewis H., *Burden of Empire: An Appraisal of Western Colonialism in Africa South of the Sahara* (Hoover Press, 2013)

Durham, Martin, *Women and Fascism* (Routledge, London 1998)

Edmunds, June, *The Left and Israel: Party-Policy Change and Internal Democracy* (Macmillan, London 2000)

Endelman, Todd M., *The Jews of Britain, 1656 to 2000* (University of California Press, Berkeley, Los Angeles and London 2002)

Etherington, Norman, Theories of Imperialism: War, Conquest and Capital (Routledge, 1984)

Feldman, David, *Englishmen and Jews - Social Relations and Political Culture, 1840-1914* (Yale University Press, 1994)

Ferguson, Rob, *Antisemitism: The Far Right, Zionism And The Left* (Bookmarks, 2019)

Fine, Robert, *Karl Marx and the Radical Critique of Anti-Semitism Archived* (Engage Journal 2, May 2006)

Fishman, William J., *Jewish Radicals: From Czarist Stetl to London Ghetto* (Pantheon Books, New York 1974)

Flannery, Edward H. Gottlieb, J.V., *Feminine Fascism: Women in Britain's Fascist Movement* (I.B.Tauris, London 2003)

Griffiths, Richard, *Fellow Travellers of the Right: British enthusiasts for Nazi Germany, 1933-39* (Oxford University Press, 1983)

Gerber, Jane (editor), *The Jews in the Caribbean* (The Littman Library of Jewish Civilization, 2014) Gilbert, Martin, *Auschwitz and the Allies* (Pimlico Press, 2001)

Gottlieb, J.V., *Feminine Fascism: Women in Britain's Fascist Movement* (I.B.Tauris, London 2003)

Granach, Alexander, *There Goes an Actor* (Trask, Doubleday, Doran, New York 1945)

Graur, Mina, *An Anarchist Rabbi: The Life and Teachings of Rudolf Rocker* (St. Martin's Press, New York 1997)

Greenblatt, Stephen J., *Marlowe, Marx, and Anti-Semitism* (Critical Inquiry, volume 5, No. 2, Winter, 1978)

Griffiths, Richard, *Fellow Travellers of the Right: British enthusiasts for Nazi Germany, 1933-39* (Oxford University Press, 1983)

Havardi, Jeremy, *Refuting the Anti-Israel Narrative: A Case for the Historical, Legal and Moral Legitimacy of the Jewish State* (McFarland, 2016)

Hampsher-Monk, Iain, *A History of Modern Political Thought* (Blackwell Publishing, 1992)

Hirsh, David, *Contemporary Left Antisemitism* (Routledge, 2017)

Hitchens, Christopher, *Why Orwell Matters* (Basic Books, London 2002)

Hobsbawm, Eric, *How to Change the World: Tales of Marx and Marxism* (Little, Brown, London 2011)

Hobson, John Atkinson, *The War In South Africa: Its Causes And Effects* (Macmillian, New York 1900)

Hodgson, Keith, *Fighting Fascism: the British Left and the Rise of Fascism, 1919-39* (Manchester University Press, 2010)

Hook, Sidney Hook, *From Hegel to Marx: Studies in the Intellectual Development of Karl Marx* (Columbia University Press, 1994)

Howard, Anthony, *Crossman: The Pursuit of Power* (Pimlico Press, 1991)

Huneidi, Sahar, *A Broken Trust: Sir Herbert Samuel, Zionism and the Palestinians* (I.B.Tauris, London 2001)

Hutcheson, John, *Leopold Maxse and the National Review, 1893-1914 - Right-wing politics in the Edwardian Era* (Garland, New York and London 1989)

Jacobs, Jack, *Jews and Leftist Politics: Judaism, Israel, Antisemitism, and Gender* (Cambridge University Press, 2017)

Johnson, Paul, *History of the Jews* (Orion, London 2013)

Jones, J. Mervyn, *British Nationality Law and Practice* (Clarendon Press, Oxford 1947)

Judd, Denis; and Surridge, Keith, *The Boer War – A History* (I.B. Tauris, London 2013)

Julius, Anthony Julius, *Trials of the Diaspora: A History of Anti-Semitism in England* (Oxford University Press, 2012)

Kelemen, Paul, *Looking the Other Way: The British Labour Party, Zionism and the Palestinians* in *Jews, Labour and the Left 1918-1948* (Ashgate, 2000)

Kellerman, Aharon, *Society and Settlement: Jewish Land of Israel in the Twentieth Century* (State University of New York Press, 1993)

Bibliography

Khromeychuk, Olesya, *Undetermined" Ukrainians: Post-War Narratives of the Waffen SS "Galicia" Division* (Peter Lang, 2013)

Kluger, Richard, *The Paper: The Life and Death of the New York Herald Tribune* (Alfred A. Knopf, New York 1986)

Kramnick, Isaac, and Barry Sheerman, Harold Laski: A Life On The Left (Hamish Hamilton, 1993) Martin, Kingsley, *Harold Laski, 1893-1950* (Gollancz, 1953)

Kushner, Tony, *Antisemitism in Britain: Continuity and the Absence of a Resurgence?* from *Antisemitism Before and Since the Holocaust: Altered Contexts and Recent Perspectives* (Palgrave Macmillan 2017); *The Persistence of Prejudice* (University of Southampton, 1989)

Lebrecht, Norman, *Genius and Anxiety: How Jews Changed the World* (Oneworld, 2019)

Levine, Norman, *Divergent Paths: The Hegelian Foundations of Marx's Method* (Lexington Books, 2006)

Lewis, Bernard, *Semites and Anti-Semites: An Inquiry into Conflict and Prejudice* (W.W. Norton & Company, 1999)

Linehan, T.P., *British Fascism, 1918-39: Parties, Ideology and Culture* (Manchester University Press, 2000)

Lipstadt, Deborah E., *Antisemitism: Here and Now* (Schocken Books, 2019)

London, Louise, 2000, *Whitehall and the Jews, 1933-1948: British Immigration Policy, Jewish Refugees and the Holocaust* (Cambridge University Press, 2000)

Lodge, David, *The Rhetoric of Hard Times*, in *Twentieth Century Interpretations of Hard Time - A Collection of Critical Essays* (Prentice-Hall, Englewood Cliffs, New Jersey 1969)

Louis, William Roger, *The British Empire in the Middle East, 1945–1951: Arab Nationalism, the United States, and Postwar Imperialism* (Oxford University Press, 1986

Macklin, G., *Very Deeply Dyed in Black*, (I.B. Tauris, London 2007)

Marcus, Steven, *Dickens, From Pickwick to Dombey* (Basic Books, New York 1965)

Marlow, James E., *Charles Dickens: The Uses of Time* (Associated University Presses, London, Ontario and New Jersey 1994)

Marx, Karl, *On the Jewish Question*, in German *Zur Judenfrage* (Deutsch-Franzosische Jahrbucher, 1843) *Capital Volume I: The Process of Production of Capital*, in German, *Das Kapital* (1867); Capital, Volume II: The Process of Circulation of Capital (prepared by Engels from notes left by Marx and published posthumously, 1885): *Capital, Volume III, The Process of Capitalist Production as a Whole* (prepared by Engels from notes left by Marx and published posthumously, 1894)

Marx, Karl, and Engels, Freidrich, *The Communist Manifesto*, originally, *The Manifesto of the Communist Party*, in German, *Manifest der Kommunistischen Partei* (Workers' Educational Association, London 1848)

Mayne, Richard, *The World of George Orwell* (Weidenfeld and Nicholson, London 1971)

McLellan, David, *Karl Marx: A Biography* (fourth edition) (Palgrave MacMillan, Hampshire 2006)

McPherson, Angela; and McPherson, Susan, *Mosley's Old Suffragette – A Biography of Norah Elam* (Routledge, London 2011)

Maccoby, Hyam, *Antisemitism and Modernity: Innovation and Continuity* (Routledge, 2006)

Mehring, Franz, *Karl Marx* (Covici, Friede, New York 1935)

Monroe, Elizabeth, *Britain's Moment in the Middle East 1914-1971* (Johns Hopkins University Press, 1981)

Morgan, Kenneth O., *Hardie, (James) Keir (1856–1915)*, in *Oxford Dictionary of National Biography* (Oxford University Press, 2011)

Morgan, Kevin, *MacDonald* in *20 British Prime Ministers of the 20th Century* (Haus Publishing, 2006) Morris, Benny, *1948: A History of the First Arab-Israeli War* (Yale University Press, 2008)

Mosley, Nicholas, *Beyond the Pale: Sir Oswald Mosley and Family, 1933–1980* (Secker & Warburg, 1983)

Mowat, C.L., *Britain between the Wars, 1918–1940* (University of Chicago Press, 1955)

Newsinger, John, *Orwell, Anti-Semitism and the Holocaust* in *The Cambridge Companion to George Orwell* (Cambridge University Press, 2007)

Nicolaievsky, Boris, and Maenchen-Helfen, Otto, *Karl Marx: Man and Fighter* (Pelican, Harmondsworth and New York, 1936 and 1976)

Nicosia, Francis R., *Zionism and Anti-Semitism in Nazi Germany* (Cambridge University Press, 2008)

Orwell, George, *Down and Out in Paris and London* (Victor Gollancz Ltd, London 1933); *Burmese Days* (Harper & Brothers, London 1934); *The Road to Wigan Pier* (Left Book Club edition, February 1937; 1937 Victor Gollancz Ltd edition, March 1937); *Animal Farm* (Secker and Warburg, 1945); *AntiSemitism in Britain* (Contemporary Jewish Record Journal, 1945); *Nineteen Eighty-Four* (Secker and Warburg, 1949); *Shooting an Elephant and Other Essays* (Secker and Warburg, 1950); *England Your England and Other Essays* (Secker and Warburg, 1953)

Penkower, Monty Noam, *Decision on Palestine Deferred: America, Britain and Wartime Diplomacy, 1939-1945* (Routledge, 2000)

Philo, Greg; Berry, Mike; Schlosberg, Justin; Lerman Antony; and Miller, David, *Bad News for Labour Antisemitism, the Party and Public Belief* (Pluto Press, London 2019)

Pimlott, Ben, *Hugh Dalton: A Life* (Jonathan Cape, 1985)

Prince, Rosa, *Comrade Corbyn – Updated Edition* (Biteback Publishing, 2016)

Pugh, Martin, *Hurrah for the Blackshirts!: Fascists and Fascism in Britain between the Wars* (Pimlico, London 2006)

Quigley, John, *The Statehood of Palestine: International Law in the Middle East Conflict* (Cambridge University Press, 2010)

Bibliography

Ray, Larry, *Marx and the Radical Critique of Difference* (Engage Journal 3, September 2006)

Renton, James, *Flawed Foundations: The Balfour Declaration and the Palestine Mandate in Britain, Palestine and Empire: The Mandate Years* (Routledge, 2016)

Rich, Dave, *The Left's Jewish Problem: Jeremy Corbyn, Israel and Anti-Semitism* (Biteback Publishing, 2016)

Rubinstein, William, *A History of the Jews in the English-speaking World* (Macmillan, London 1996)

Runes, Dagobert D. (translator), *A World Without Jews* (translation *of On the Jewish Question* (The Philosopher's Library, 1959)

Sachar, Howard, *A History of Israel: From the Rise of Zionism to Our Time* (Knopf, 1996)

Sacks, Jonathan, *The Politics of Hope* (Jonathan Cape, London 1997)

Samuel, Herbert, *Memoirs* (Cresset Press, 1945)

Seddon, Mark, and Beckett, Francis, *Jeremy Corbyn and the Strange Rebirth of Labour England* (Biteback Publishing, 2018)

Scammell, Michael, *Koestler: The Indispensable Intellectual* (Faber, 2009)

Schneer, Jonathan, *The Balfour Declaration: The Origins of the Arab-Israeli Conflict* (Random House, London 2010)

Schindler, Colin, *From Zionist to Corbynist: The Evolution of Britain's Labour Left* (Jewish Quarterly, issue 63(2), 2016)

Seymour, Richard, *Corbyn: The Strange Rebirth of Radical Politics* (Verso Books, 2017)

Shatzkes, Pamela, *Holocaust and Rescue: Impotent or Indifferent? Anglo-Jewry 1938-1945* (Palgrave, 2002)

Skidelsky, Robert, *Oswald Mosley* (Macmillan, London 1981)

Smith, Warren Allen, *Who's Who in Hell, A Handbook and International Directory for Humanists, Freethinkers, Naturalists, Rationalists, and Non-Theists* (Barricade Books, New York 2000)

Sokolow, Nahum, *History of Zionism 1600-1918, Volume II* (Longmans Green & Co., 1919)

Staetsky, Daniel L., *Antisemitism in Contemporary Great Britain: A Study of Attitudes Towards Jews and Israel* (Institute for Jewish Policy Research, September 2017)

Stansky, Peter; and Abrahams, William, *Orwell, The Transformation* (Paladin, 1984)

Stansky, Peter (ed), *The Left and War: The British Labour Party and World War 1* (Oxford University Press, 1969)

Storrs, Ronald, *Lawrence of Arabia: Zionism and Palestine* (Penguin Books, 1943)

Taylor, A.J. P., *English History: 1914–1945* (Oxford History of England series, Clarendon Press, 1965) Taylor, D.J., *Orwell: The Life* (Henry Holt and Company, 2004)

Terwey, Susanne, *British Discourses on "the Jew" and "the Nation" 1899-1919* in *The Making of Antisemitism as a Political Movement. Political History as Cultural History, 1879-1914* (Quest, Issues in Contemporary Jewish History, Journal of Fondazione CDEC, number 3, July 2012)

Thurlow, Richard, *Fascism in Britain: From Oswald Mosley's Blackshirts to the National Front* (Tauris, London 2006)

Trilling, David, *Bloody Nasty People: the Rise of Britain's Far Right* (Verso, 2012)

Twitchell, Neville, *The Politics of the Rope* (Arena Books, Bury St Edmunds 2012)

Uglow, Jennifer S., *Phillips, Marion* in *The International Dictionary of Women's Biography* (Continuum, New York 1985)

Unger, Roberto Mangabeira, *Free Trade Reimagined: The World Division of Labor and the Method of Economics* (Princeton University Press, 2007)

Ward, Paul, *Red Flag and Union Jack. Englishness - Patriotism and the British Left 1881-1924* (Boydell Press, Rochester 1998)

Wasserstein, Bernard, *Britain and the Jews of Europe 1939-1943* (Leicester University Press, 1999); *Israel and Palestine: Why They Fight and Can They Stop?* (Profile Books, 2008)

Watkins, David, *Seventeen Years in Obscurity: Memoirs from the Back Benches* (Book Guild, 1996)

Watts, Tim, *The Balfour Declaration* in *The Encyclopedia of the Arab-Israeli Conflict: A Political, Social, and Military History* (ABC-CLIO, 2008)

Weizmann, Chaim, *Trial and Error, The Autobiography of Chaim Weizmann* (Jewish Publication Society of America, 1949); *The Letters and Papers of Chaim Weizmann: August 1898 – July 1933* (Transaction Publishers, 1983)

Weston, Reg, *1936 – Fascists and Police Routed – The Battle of Cable Street* (libcom.org/files/ 1936, 1998)

Wheeler, Michael, *English Fiction of the Victorian Period 1830-1890* (Longman, New York 1994)

Wheen, Francis, *Karl Marx* (Fourth Estate, London 2001)

White, Arnold Henry, *The Modern Jew* (W. Heinemann, London 1899); *Efficiency and Empire* (Harvester Press, London 1973);

Williams, Raymond, *Culture and Society, 1780-1950* (Columbia University Press, 1983) Wilson, Harold, *The Chariot of Israel: Britain, America and the State of Israel* (Weidenfeld and Nicolson, 1981)

Wistrich, Robert S., *From Ambivalence to Betrayal: The Left, the Jews and Israel* (University of Nebraska Press; Vidal Sassoon International Center for the Study of Antisemitism, 2012)

Wyatt, Woodrow, *Into The Dangerous World* (Weidenfeld and Nicolson, London 1952)

Newspapers, Websites and Periodicals

Alternative, The, website
American Interest, The, website
Arbeiter-Zeitung
Birthwrong website
Bradford Telegraph and Argus
Bristol Radical Pamphleteer
Camden New Journal
Canary, The
CapX
CNN
Contemporary Jewish Record Journal
CounterPunch
Daily Express
Daily Mail
Daily Mirror
Daily Sketch
Daily Telegraph
Der Sozialdemokrat
Der Spiegel
Deutsch-Franzosische Jarbucher
Die Deutsche Ideologie
Dundee Courier
Engage Journal
Evolve Politics
Financial Times
Forward
George Orwell Studies Journal
Guardian, The
Guido Fawkes website
GQHaaretz
Hackney Gazette
Herald, The
Huffpost UK
Independent, The
Independent Jewish Voices
Independent News and Media
International Socialist
Jerusalem Report

Jewish Chronicle
jewish.museum.org
Jewish News
Jewish Quarterly
Jewish Telegraphic Agency
Jewish World, The
Journal of Contemporary History
Journal of the History of Ideas
Justice
Labour Against the Witch-Hunts website
Labour Briefing
Labour List
Left Futures
liberalhistory.org.uk
Liberty website
Liverpool Echo
London Evening News
London Evening Standard
London Review of Books
Manchester Guardian
Manchester Sunday Chronicle
M.I.A Encyclopaedia online
Middle East Eye
Middle Eastern Studies
Moment
Morning Post
Morning Star
Nation, The,
National Review
Neue Rheinischer Zeitung
New Leader
New Statesman
New York Daily Tribune
New York Times
Open Democracy blog
Philosopher's Magazine, The
PoliticsHome.com
Press Association
Quest – Issues in Contemporary History
Quora

Bibliography

Reuters
RighteousJews.org
Rotherham Advertiser
Salford Star
Saturday Review
Sheffield Independent
Slate
Socialist Review
Soundings blog, Lawrence and Wishart
Soviet Jewish Affairs Journal
Spectator, The
Sports Historian, The
Stoke Sentinel
Sun, The
Sunday Chronicle
Sunday Magazine
Sunday Telegraph
Sunday Times,
Tablet, The
TheyWorkForYou.com
ThoughtCo, history and culture, website
TIME
Times, The
Times Literary Supplement
Tribune
Twentieth Century British History
Vanity Fair
Walsall Pioneer
Western Socialist, The
Westminster Gazette
Worker's Friend, The
Zangwill's Spitalfields app

Index

Abbott, Diane, politician, 133, 138, 147, 156, 231
Alderman, Geoffrey, academic, 147
Aliens Act 1904, 67
Allen, Heidi, politician, 194
Allen, Jim, playwright, 132
Allen, Mary Sophia, Suffragette and Fascist, 78
anarchism/anarchist, 37, 55, 57, 59
Anti-Defamation League, 126
anti-Semite riots, 1947, 112-116
Arbeter Fraint, Jewish anarchist group, 37, 57, 58
Ashby, Margaret Corbett, liberal campaigner, 96
Attlee, Clement, 76, 84, 104-106, 109, 120, 187, 193, 254
Austin, Ian, politician, 218, 219, 228, 234
Avineri, Shlomo, commentator, 15

Bakunin, Mikhail, revolutionary aristocrat, 36, 37
Baldwin, Stanley, politician, 72

Balfour, Arthur, politician, 44, 57, 63, 64, 67, 68, 124
Balfour Declaration 1917, 63-65, 67, 69, 70
Bashir, Martin, BBC religious editor, 236, 237
Bauer, Bruno, early socialist, 14, 17, 18
Beckett, John Warburton, politician, 76, 77
Ben-Gurion, David, statesman, 116, 117
Bennett, Molly, vox pop interviewee, 248
Berger, Luciana, politician, 146, 170, 174, 175, 177, 183, 185, 187-192, 194, 219, 224, 226, 230, 239, 240, 246
Bevan, Aneurin, 75, 89, 111, 121, 193
Bevin, Ernest, 10, 110, 111, 120, 125
Bibby, Kayla, activist, 185-187
Blackshirts, 11, 76, 79, 80, 82, 91, 98, 114, 130
Board of Deputies of British Jews, 61, 77, 79, 80, 84, 118, 124, 146, 163, 164, 167, 170, 173, 184, 195, 198,

Index

200, 207, 209, 213, 214, 223, 226, 227, 230, 239
Boers/Second Boer War, 41, 43, 47, 48, 51-53, 65, 71, 143
Bower, Tom, biographer, 128, 140, 142, 143, 165
Bracken, Brendan, information minister, 93
Brecht, Bertold, playwright, 256
British Brothers League, anti-immigrant group, 40
British Mandate for Palestine, 69, 70, 73, 85, 111, 116
British Union of Fascists (BUF), 75-79, 81-83, 118, 224
Burns, John, politician, 10, 41, 51, 52
Buruma, Ian, historian, 29, 30

Cable Street, Battle of, 79-81
capitalism, 13, 21, 25, 30, 36, 43, 47, 51, 52, 54, 71, 74, 104, 129, 130, 146, 150, 152, 253, 254 Carey of Clifton, Lord, former Archbishop of Canterbury, 146
Carpenter, Edward, socialist poet, 52, 53
Castro, Fidel, 127, 128, 136
Chakrabarti Inquiry, 53, 165-168, 171, 173, 177, 197
Chakrabarti, Shami, human rights campaigner, 164-168
Chomsky, Noam, scholar, 163, 213, 215
Children of the Ghetto, 38, 39
Churchill, Winston S., 61, 68, 69, 91-94, 104-107, 109, 242
civil war, 116, 117
Clarke, Lord Tony, former Labour chairman, 123
Cocks, Lady Valerie, pro-Israel peer, 124
Cohen, Ben, editor, 249
Collins, Philip, speechwriter, 224

communism/communist, 13, 79-82, 89, 90, 102, 107, 111, 114, 118, 119, 121, 126, 127, 137, 146, 208
Communist Manifesto, The, 13, 21, 43
Communist Workers' Educational Union, 37
Conditions of the Working Class in England, The, 21
Cooper, Duff, information minister, 92-94
Corbyn, Jeremy, 9-11, 79, 123, 126, 160, 163-177, 184, 185, 188, 189, 191-203, 206-233, 235-256 *passim*
Cowley, Jason, editor, 255, 256
Crick, Bernard, biographer, 97
Crossman, Richard, politician, 111, 119, 120
Cuba, 126, 127, 128, 135, 136, 146, 219

Dalton, Hugh, politician, 111, 121
Daniel Deronda, 31
Das Kapital, 13. 21, 22, 25, 28
de Pass, Frank Alexander, VC winner, 62
Deir Yassin Remembered (DYR), 137
Der Judenstaat, Zionist text, 66
Dickens, Charles, 32-36
Disraeli, Benjamin, 31, 41, 67
Doherty, Rosa, reporter, 251, 252
Donoughue, Lord Bernard, No 10 advisor, 124
Down and Out in Paris and London, 87, 88

Edict of Expulsion, 28
Eisen, Paul, anti-Zionist, 136, 137, 222
Elan, Norah, Suffragette and Fascist, 77, 78
Ellman, Dame Louise, 9, 11, 170, 174, 175, 177, 183, 185-187, 194-196, 239, 240, 244

Engels, Friedrich, 5, 13, 18, 20, 21, 23-25, 36
Equality and Human Rights Commission (EHRC), 205, 240
Extinction Rebellion, 234
Ezra, Michael, writer, 18, 19

Facebook, 144, 146, 156, 158-161, 176, 177, 184, 185, 188, 190, 196, 197, 218, 230, 241-243, 252
Fagin, Dickensian character, 33-36, 117
Farage, Nigel, politician, 233, 234
feudalism, 13
Fine, Robert, sociologist, 17
Finkelstein, Daniel, peer and columnist, 170
Finkelstein, Norman, academic, 159, 212, 215
Fischman, Dennis, writer, 15
Foges, Clare, columnist, 194
Foot, Michael, politician, 89, 111, 254
Formby, Jennie, Labour Party general secretary, 168, 186, 195, 200, 203-205, 215, 219, 244
Frederick the Great, 18, 28
Freedland, Jonathan, writer, 227

Gable, Gerry, anti-Fascist, 119
Gaitskill, Hugh, politician, 121
Galloway, George, politician, 131, 139, 158, 159, 210
Goebbels, Josef, 10
Goldberg, Emma, 250, 251
Golinkin, Lev, writer, 214
Gollancz, Victor, publisher, 87, 88, 106
Gould, Tommy, VC winner, 118
Granach, Alexander, actor, 32
Greeley, Horace, newspaper baron, 21
Greenstein, Tony, activist, 133, 136

Haden Guest, Leslie, politician, 83
Haganah, Jewish paramilitary force, 112
Hamas, 132, 140, 141, 146, 150, 151, 158, 171, 181, 220
Hamm, Jeffrey, Fascist, 117
Hampsher-Monk, Ian, political scientist, 16
Hardie, Keir, 10, 41, 42, 52, 54, 55, 70, 122
Hard Times, 36
Harman, Harriet, politician, 220
Harpin, Lee, journalist, 224
Hassassian, Manuel, Palestinian representative, 144, 145
Healy, Gerry, WRP activist, 131, 132
Heffer, Eric, politician, 124
Hertz, Chief Rabbi, 59
Herzl, Theodor, journalist, 66
Hezbollah, 132, 136, 140, 141, 146, 150, 151, 155, 171, 219
Hier, Rabbi Marvin, 242
Hitchens, Christopher, writer, 89
Hitler, Adolf, 20, 70, 74, 78-80, 87, 89, 91, 93, 96, 98-100, 106, 114, 130, 132, 137, 160, 165, 202, 218, 241-243
Hobson, J.A., writer, 41, 44, 50, 143, 144, 170, 254
Hodge, Dame Margaret, 147, 200, 207, 220, 225, 241, 248
Holocaust, 10, 25, 59, 65, 95, 105, 107, 109, 110, 115, 117, 121, 122, 126, 129, 133, 134, 137, 141, 143, 144, 146, 147, 151, 153, 155, 159, 161, 163, 165, 170, 172,, 189, 197-199, 202, 203, 210, 212, 215, 218, 228, 229, 233, 234, 236, 241, 243, 244
Holocaust Memorial Day, 141, 143, 162, 163, 170
Homage to Catalonia, 86

Index

Hore-Belisha, Leslie, war minister, 93
Horowitz, Irving, writer, 127, 146
Human Rights Watch, 141
Hyndman, H.M., writer, 41, 43, 44, 52, 56

Independent Labour Party (ILP), 42, 50, 54, 66, 76
Irgun, Jewish paramilitary force, 112
Irish Republican Army (IRA), 132, 133, 151, 152, 219, 243, 246
Irving, Henry, actor, 28, 31, 32
Isenberg, Amira, blogger, 15

Jacobson, Howard, writer, 150
Jahjah, Dyab Abu, extremist, 139, 140
Janner, Barnett, politician, 84
Jew of Malta, The, 30
Jew of Venice, The, 30
Jewish Labour Movement (JLM), 162, 169, 176, 182, 184, 195, 206, 207, 223, 224, 240, 241
Jewish Leadership Council, 198
Jewish Voice for Labour (JVL), 163, 171, 174, 205-207
Johnson, Alan, researcher, 150, 151
Jones, Arthur Creech, colonial secretary, 116
Joyce, William, traitor, 75, 93, 95
Judah, Ben, historian, 103

Karl Marx and Frederick Engels: Selected Correspondence, 1846-1895, 18
Kahn-Harris, Keith, blogger, 151, 152, 166
Kamm, Oliver, writer, 158
Katz, Mike, JLM chair, 223
Kautsky, Karl, philosopher and journalist, 23-25

Keleman, Paul, academic, 136
Keren, Yuval, rabbi, 225
Kilfoyle, Peter, politician, 158
King David Hotel bombing, 112
King, Oona, politician, 138, 139
Knight, Ted, Trotskyist, 131, 136
Kuenssberg, Laura, BBC political editor, 237
Kushner, Tony, academic, 95, 96

Labour Committee on Palestine, 135
Labour Middle East Council, 136
Labour Movement Campaign on Palestine, 133, 134
Labour Party, 40-42, 54, 62, 63, 66, 68, 70-74, 77, 81-83, 85, 99, 105, 111, 122-129, 136, 139, 141, 146, 148, 153, 155-173, 176-187, 190-196, 198-200, 202, 206-217, 219, 220, 224, 226- 233, 235-238, 240, 242-245, 250-255
Labour Memorandum on the Issues of the War 1917, 63
Labour Representation Committee, 155-173, 176-187
Lansman, Jon, Momentum co-founder, 156, 157, 160-162, 169, 200, 203, 207, 228
Lawrence, Susan, politician, 84, 85
Lenin, V.I., 50
Lever, Walter, riot witness, 113
Levitas, Max, riot witness, 114
Lewis, Clive, politician, 203
Lipman, Maureen, comic actress, 237
Lloyd George, David, 61, 62, 64, 68, 70, 72
Loach, Ken, film director, 132

MacBride, Sean, Nobel Peace Prize winner, 135

Maccoby, Hyam, writer, 15
MacDonald, Ramsay, 70-73, 83, 85
Magee, Patrick, Brighton bomber, 132
Mann, John, politician, 160, 166, 217, 218, 223, 256
Marx, Eleanor, 28, 43
Marx, Herschel, aka Heinrich, 12
Marx, Karl, 10, 12-28, 32-34, 36, 37, 42, 43, 50, 153
Maxse, James Leopold, editor and bigot, 58
Mayhew, Christopher, politician, 125
McCluskey, Len, union leader, 169, 206
McDonnell, John, politician, 25, 26, 159, 197, 198, 205, 207, 244, 255, 256
McGeever, Brendan, academic, 122
McKay, Margaret, politician, 121
Meadowcroft, Michael, politician, 54, 55
Mear One, artist, 144, 170, 189
Mehring, Franz, writer, 16
Merchant of Venice, The, 28-32
Merron, Gillian, 256
Meyer, Hajo, Auschwitz survivor, 141, 170
Militant Tendency, 130, 157, 158, 174, 179
Milne, Seamus, communications director, 141, 165, 228
Mirvis, Ephraim, Chief Rabbi, 166, 167, 237, 238
Momentum, 9, 156-158, 160, 162, 166, 174, 176, 177, 183-185, 189, 192, 197, 201, 206, 219, 226, 228, 239
Monroe, Elizabeth, historian, 70
Moran, Tommy, Fascist, 82-83
Morris, William, artist, 38
Morrison, Herbert, politician, 104, 105, 107, 121

Mosley, Diana, 118
Mosley, Lady Cynthia, 77
Mosley, Oswald, 11, 72-82, 91-93, 98, 107, 114, 118, 119, 130
Murphy, Karie, gatekeeper, 228, 229

Nation of Islam, 126
National Front, 130
National Socialism Movement, 119
National Union of Tailors and Garment Workers, 128
Neil, Andrew, TV interviewer, 237, 238
Neuberger, Julia, rabbi and writer, 122
Newsinger, John, editor, 72, 111, 120, 120, 212
New York Daily Tribune, 20, 21
Noonan, Robert, aka Tressell, 53

Oberman, Tracy-Ann, actor and politician, 244, 255
Oliver Twist, 34, 35, 117
On the Jewish Question, 13, 19, 26
Oppenheimer, Florence, aka Greenberg, nurse, food guru and heroine, 62
Orwell, George, 10, 72, 74, 77, 86-91, 95, 97-104, 106
Our Mutual Friend, 36

Palm Commission, 68
Paole Zion, Labour Party affiliate, 134
Peres, Shimon, statesman, 124
Pfeffer, Anshel, writer, 90
Phillips, Marion, politician, 83
Pickwick Papers, 34
Protocol of the Elders of Zion, forgery, 111, 141, 208

Radcliffe, Cyril, civil servant, 91, 92
Ray, Larry, scholar, 15, 17
Regev, Mark, ambassador, 141

Index

Rhodes, Cecil, imperialist, 53, 54
Rich, Ben, think tank head, 192, 193
Rich, Dave, writer, 43, 115, 122
Riley, Rachel, TV presenter, 209, 210
Rocker, Rudolf, editor and strike leader, 37, 57-59
Romain, Dr Jonathan, rabbi, 225
Rosenberg, Isaac, Nazi theorist, 70
Rosenberg, Isaac, war poet, 61
Rubin, Barry, writer, 102, 250
Runes, Dagobert D., philosopher and publisher, 19, 20
Rurup, Reinhard, historian, 30
Ryan, Joan, politician, 232, 233

Sabra and Shatila massacres, 135
Sacks, Lord Jonathan, former Chief Rabbi, 197
Salah, Raed, extremist, 140, 171, 222
Samuel, Herbert, Zionist leader, 60, 67, 69
Schindler, Colin, writer, 60
Seeley, Bob, Conservative MP, 25, 26
Segal, Marcus, WWI casualty, 61, 62
Shah, Naz, activist, 158-160, 177
Shatzkes, Pamela, writer, 104, 107
Shaw, George Bernard, 10
Shinwell, Emanuel 'Manny', politician, 67, 74, 83, 187
Shylock, Shakespearean character, 28, 30-32, 229
Silverman, Samuel, politician, 84, 105, 111
slave trade, 127, 128, 136
Smeeth, Ruth, politician, 166, 196, 224, 225, 235, 242, 248
Social Democrat Federation (SDF), 51, 52, 54, 66
Stanley, Oliver, politician, 105, 106, 108
Stopes, Marie, 11

Stop the War Coalition, 138, 139, 155, 158, 175
Strauss, George Russell, 84
Streeting, Wes, politician, 196
Sutcliffe, Gerry, politician, 9, 158

Taylor, D.J., historian, 87, 103
Terwey, Susanne, writer, 43
Tonge, Baroness Jenny, 192, 193
Trade Union Congress (TUC), 42, 54, 63, 121, 218
Trilling, David, writer, 113-115
Truman, President Harry S., 110

Ukranian Waffen SS Division, 109
Union Movement, 119
UN World Conference Against Racism, 137

Valman, Nadia, writer, 40
Versailles peace treaty, 64
Voluntary Service Overseas (VSO), 126, 127

Walker, Jackie, Momentum vice-chair, 160-164, 177, 198, 207, 223
Ware, John, TV journalist, 226
Watkins, David, politician, 121
Watson, Tom, politician, 158, 191, 205, 227, 228
Weizmann, Chaim, Zionist leader, 64, 67, 68, 116
Wess, Woolf, aka William, anarchist, 37, 38
Wheen, Francis, writer, 17
White, Arnold, rabble-rouser, 40
Williamson, Chris, politician, 164, 184, 185, 223, 226, 229
Wistrich, Robert, writer, 15
Witkop, Milly, Jewish anarchist, 37

Wolfron, Rhea, NEC member, 148
Worker's Friend, The, Yiddish newspaper, 37
Workers' Revolutionary Party (WRP), 131, 132
World Socialist Party of the U.S., 19
Wyatt, Woodrow, politician, 120

Young Hegelians, movement, 36

Zangwill, Israel, novelist, 38, 39, 57
Zionism, 10, 60, 63, 66, 70, 72, 84, 108, 111, 112, 119, 120, 122-125, 134, 137, 140, 145, 145, 148, 158, 160, 165, 170, 171, 175, 181, 199, 202, 208
Zur Judenfrage, see *On the Jewish Question*
Zyl, Marie van der, Board of Deputies President, 195, 207, 239

Also available from Amberley Publishing

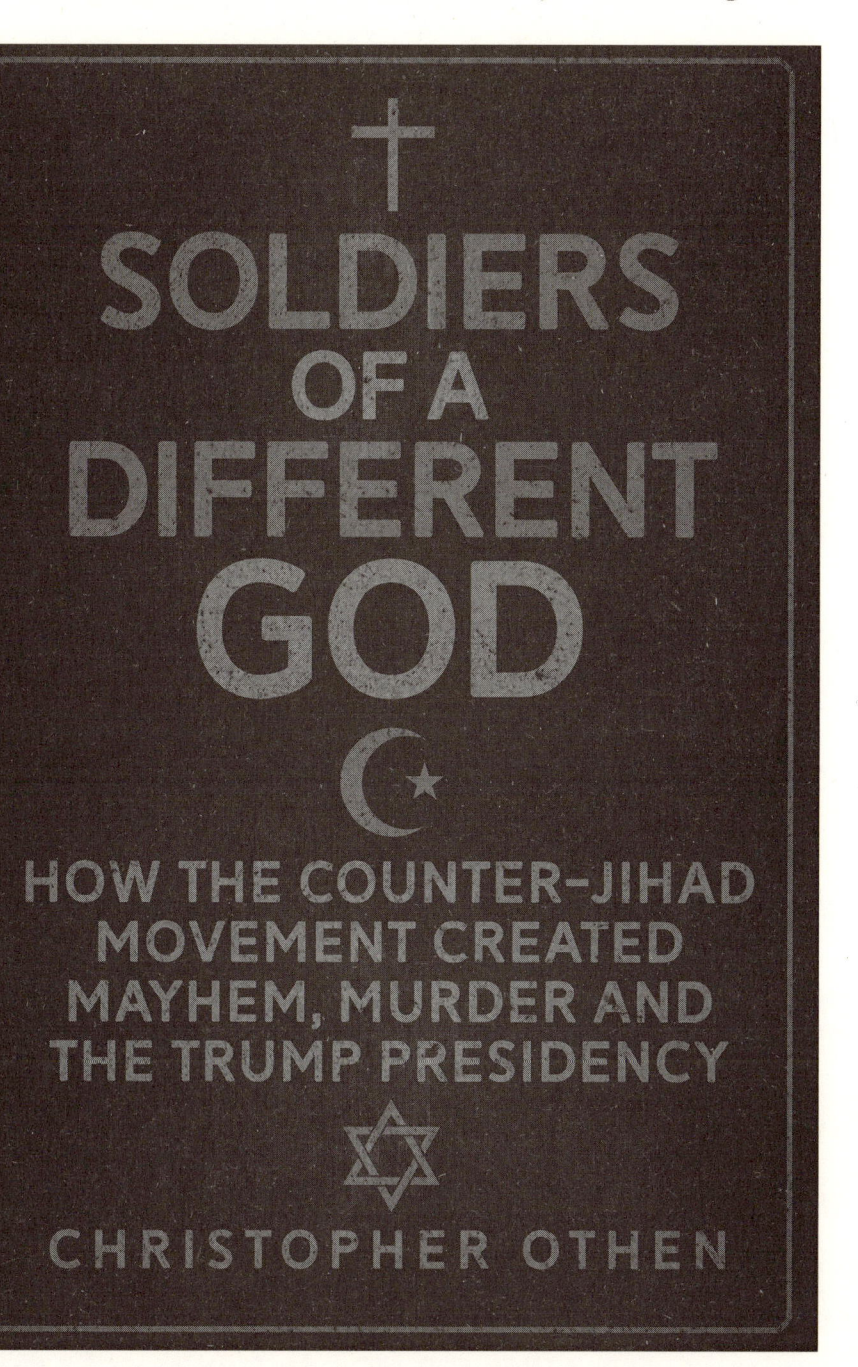

SOLDIERS OF A DIFFERENT GOD

HOW THE COUNTER-JIHAD MOVEMENT CREATED MAYHEM, MURDER AND THE TRUMP PRESIDENCY

CHRISTOPHER OTHEN

Available from all good bookshops or to order direct
Please call **01453-847-800**
www.amberley-books.com

Also available from Amberley Publishing

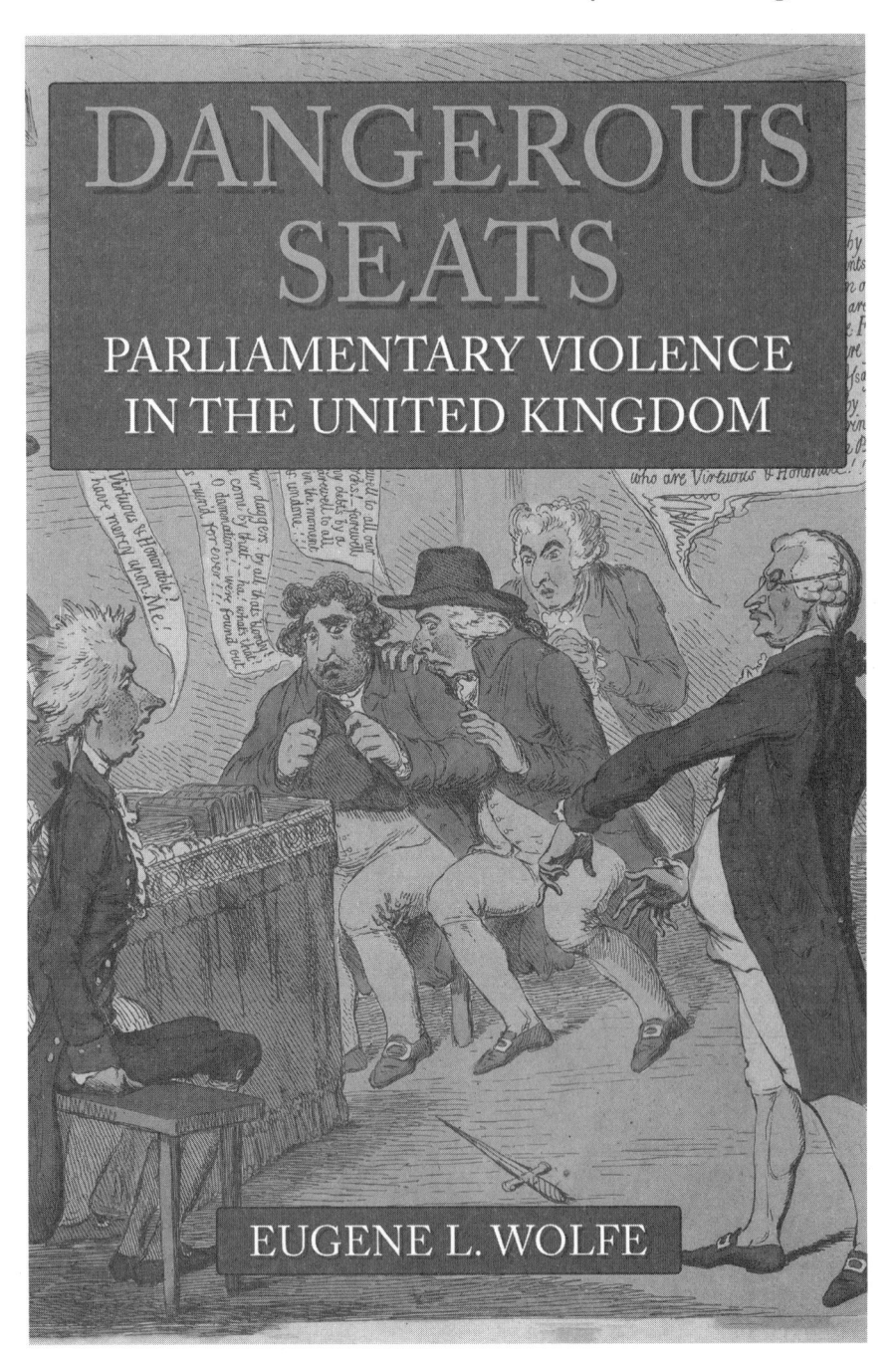

DANGEROUS SEATS
PARLIAMENTARY VIOLENCE IN THE UNITED KINGDOM

EUGENE L. WOLFE

Available from all good bookshops or to order direct
Please call **01453-847-800**
www.amberley-books.com

Also available from Amberley Publishing

"A brilliant, authoritative, and colourful insight into the hope and despair that is the world's youngest country. Unique in modern history, this untold story of South Sudan's birth carries lessons not just for Africa but for the rest of the world."

Jon Snow

A ROPE FROM THE SKY

THE MAKING AND UNMAKING OF THE WORLD'S NEWEST STATE

ZACH VERTIN

Available from all good bookshops or to order direct
Please call 01453-847-800
www.amberley-books.com